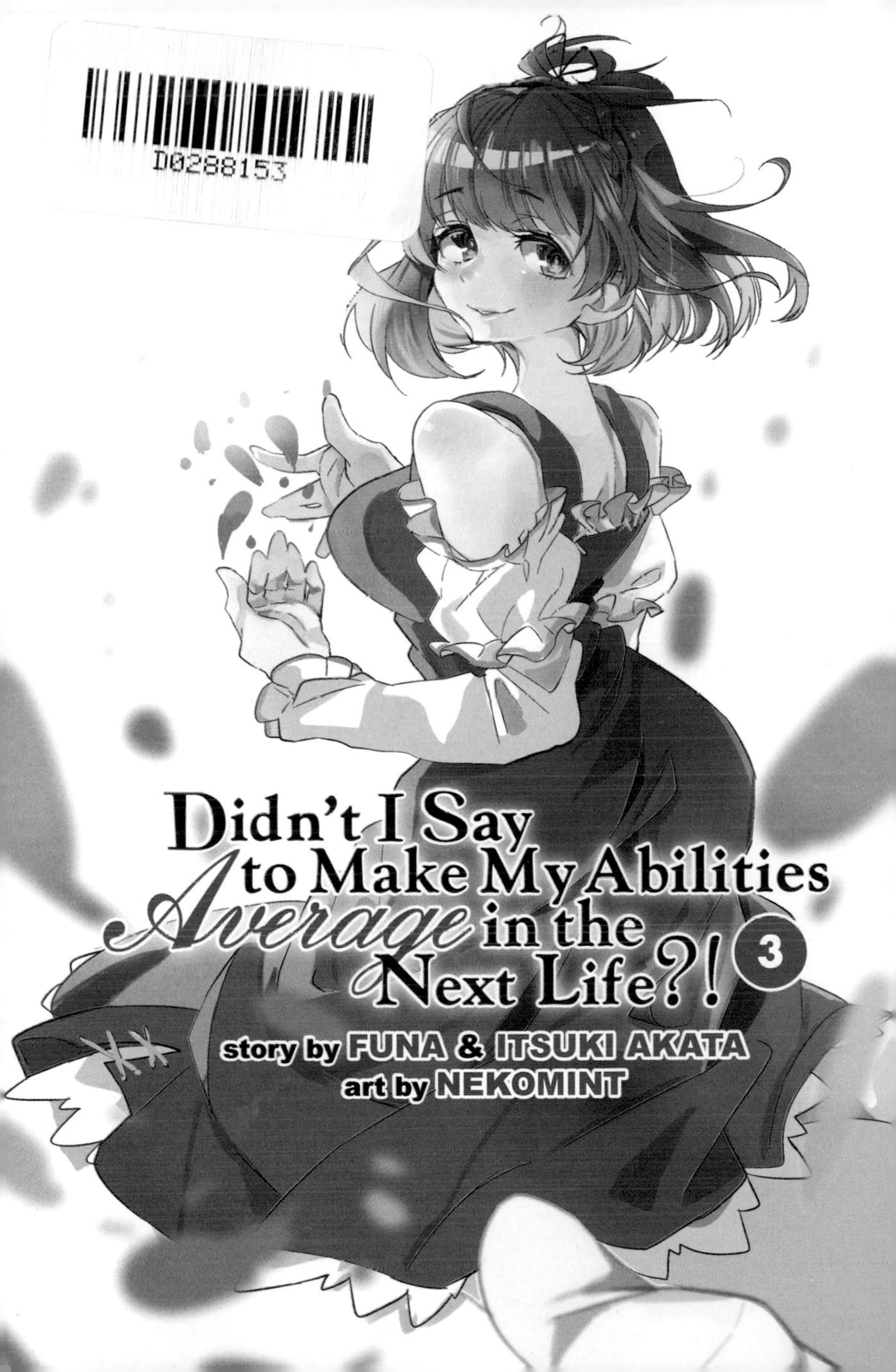

Didn't I Say to Make My Abilities *Average* in the Next Life?! 3

story by FUNA & ITSUKI AKATA

art by NEKOMINT

Didn't I Say to Make My Abilities Average in the Next Life?! 3

Contents

Character Introductions

Mile (Adele)

The current incarnation of a Japanese girl named Kurihara Misato, who was reborn into a fantasy world. She prayed to have "average" abilities in her new life, but instead was granted fantastic powers. During her time at Eckland Academy she was "Adele," but now at the Hunters' Prep School, she goes by "Mile."

Reina

A fifteen-year-old mage. Goes by the title "the Crimson Reina" and specializes in attack magic. She and Mile become roommates at the Hunters' Prep School. Though she has a forceful personality, she worries a great deal for Mile.

Mavis

A seventeen-year-old swordswoman.
Comes from a long line of knights.
She aimed to become a knight herself,
but her family opposed her, so she
ran away from home and enrolled
at the Hunters' Prep School. She
became roommates with the other
three and is the leader of their group.

Pauline

A fourteen-year-old mage specializing
in healing magic. The daughter of a
merchant's mistress. She has a relaxing
presence that envelops others in
warm feelings. She has an incredibly
sweet disposition, and yet...?!

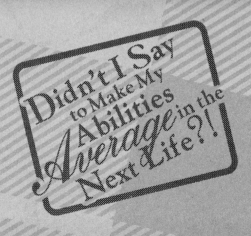

Didn't I Say
to Make My
Abilities
Average in the
Next Life?!

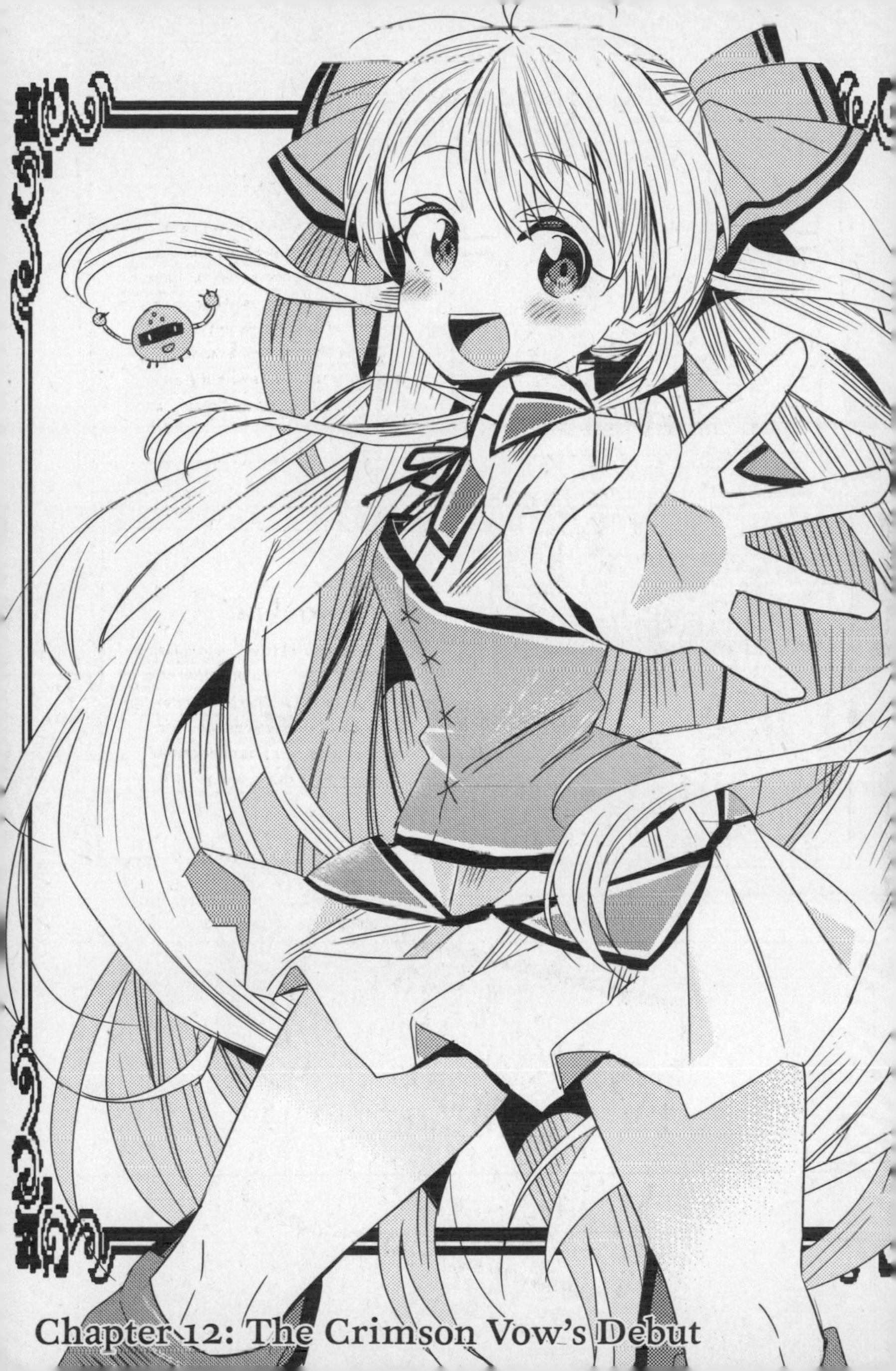

Chapter 12: The Crimson Vow's Debut

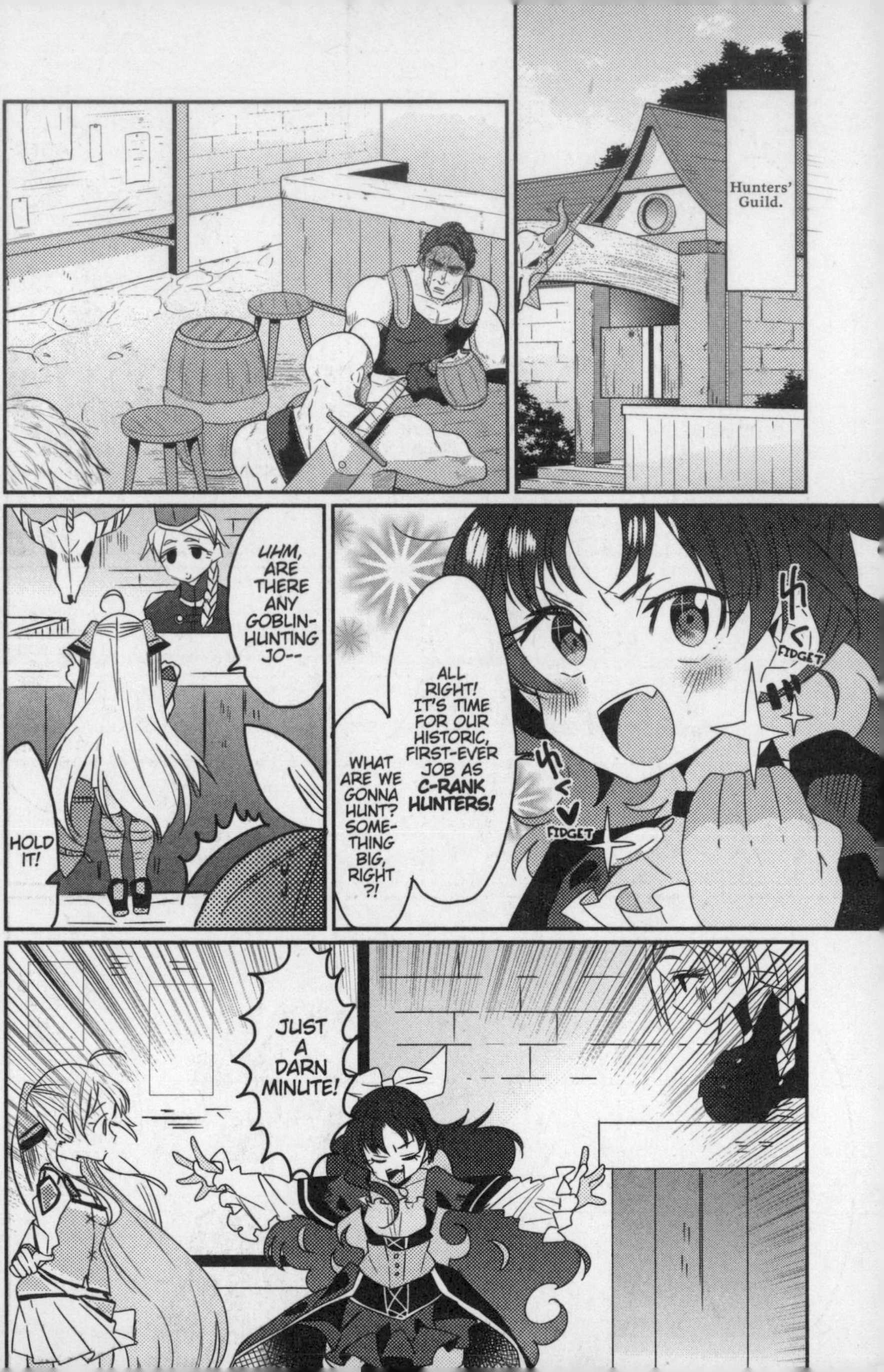
Hunters' Guild.
ALL RIGHT! IT'S TIME FOR OUR HISTORIC, FIRST-EVER JOB AS C-RANK HUNTERS!
WHAT ARE WE GONNA HUNT? SOMETHING BIG, RIGHT?!
FIDGET
FIDGET
UHM, ARE THERE ANY GOBLIN-HUNTING JO--
HOLD IT!
JUST A DARN MINUTE!

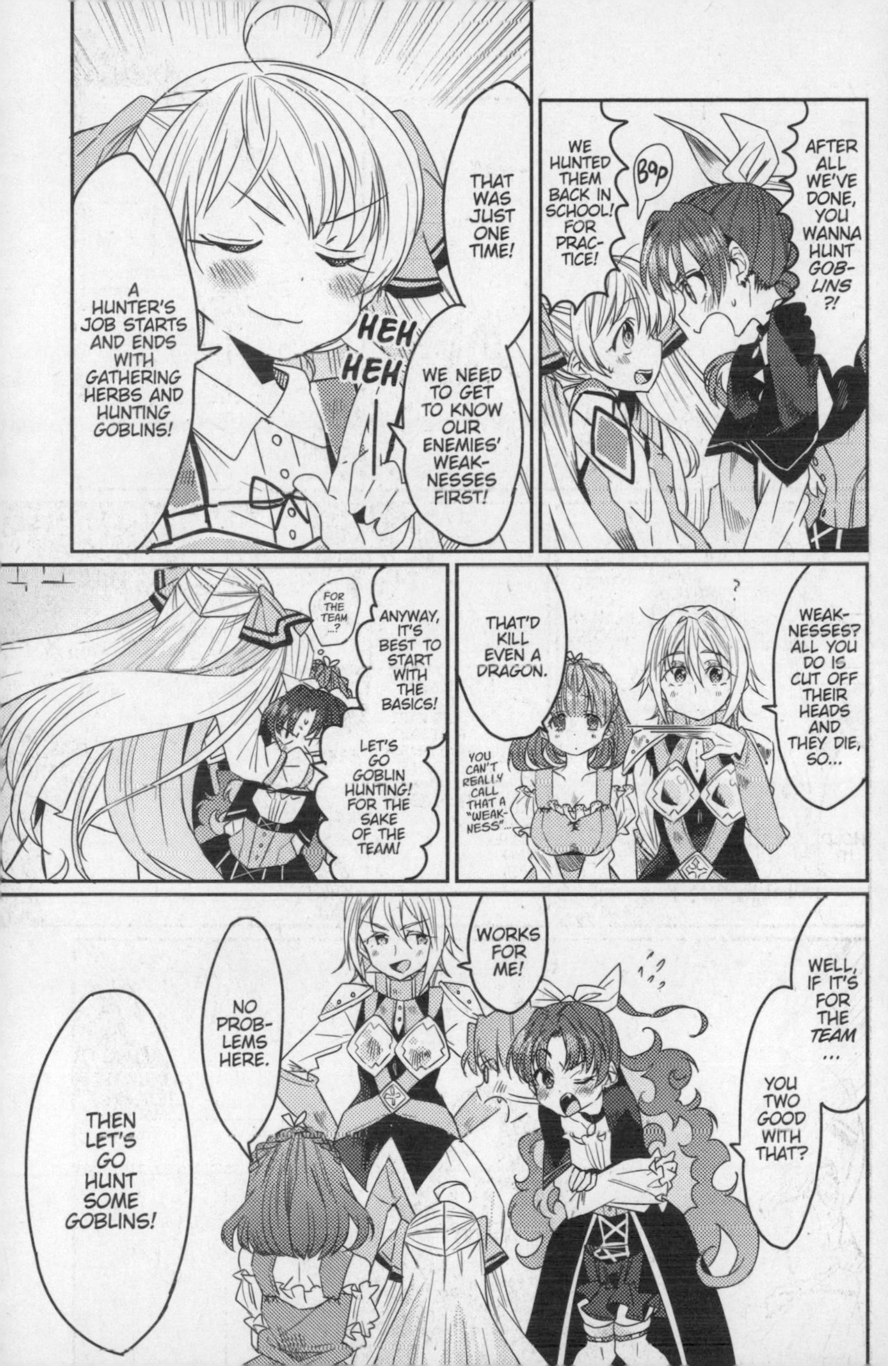
AFTER ALL WE'VE DONE, YOU WANNA HUNT GOBLINS?!
Bap
WE HUNTED THEM BACK IN SCHOOL! FOR PRACTICE!
THAT WAS JUST ONE TIME!
HEH HEH
WE NEED TO GET TO KNOW OUR ENEMIES' WEAKNESSES FIRST!
A HUNTER'S JOB STARTS AND ENDS WITH GATHERING HERBS AND HUNTING GOBLINS!
WEAKNESSES? ALL YOU DO IS CUT OFF THEIR HEADS AND THEY DIE, SO...
THAT'D KILL EVEN A DRAGON.
YOU CAN'T REALLY CALL THAT A "WEAKNESS"...
ANYWAY, IT'S BEST TO START WITH THE BASICS!
LET'S GO GOBLIN HUNTING! FOR THE SAKE OF THE TEAM!
FOR THE TEAM...?
WELL, IF IT'S FOR THE TEAM...
YOU TWO GOOD WITH THAT?
WORKS FOR ME!
NO PROBLEMS HERE.
THEN LET'S GO HUNT SOME GOBLINS!

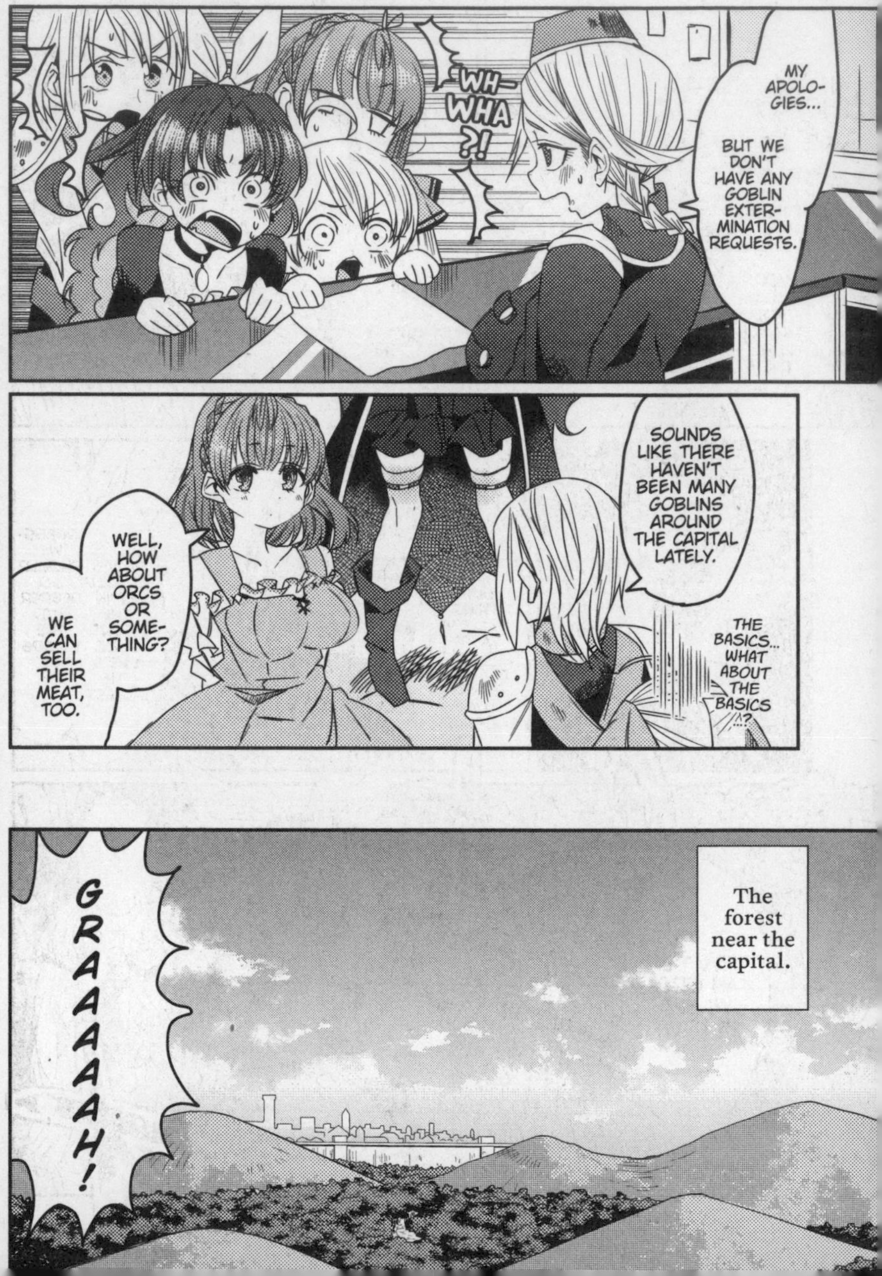
MY APOLOGIES...
BUT WE DON'T HAVE ANY GOBLIN EXTERMINATION REQUESTS.
WH-WHA?!
SOUNDS LIKE THERE HAVEN'T BEEN MANY GOBLINS AROUND THE CAPITAL LATELY.
THE BASICS... WHAT ABOUT THE BASICS...?
WELL, HOW ABOUT ORCS OR SOMETHING?
WE CAN SELL THEIR MEAT, TOO.
The forest near the capital.
GRAAAAAAH!

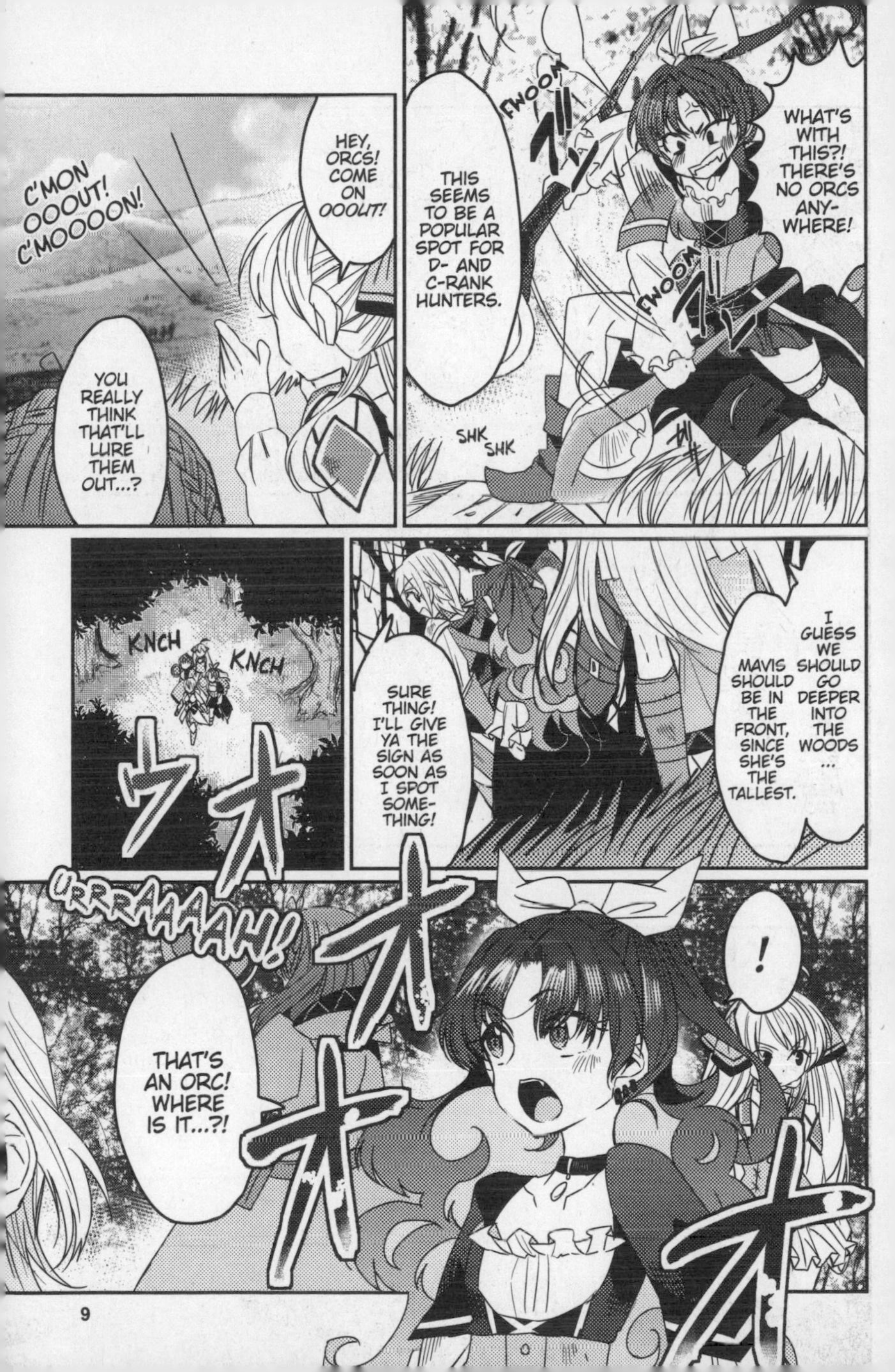
WHAT'S WITH THIS?! THERE'S NO ORCS ANYWHERE!
FWOOM
FWOOM
THIS SEEMS TO BE A POPULAR SPOT FOR D- AND C-RANK HUNTERS.
SHK SHK
HEY, ORCS! COME ON OOOUT!
C'MON OOOUT! C'MOOOON!
YOU REALLY THINK THAT'LL LURE THEM OUT...?
I GUESS WE SHOULD GO DEEPER INTO THE WOODS...
MAVIS SHOULD BE IN THE FRONT, SINCE SHE'S THE TALLEST.
SURE THING! I'LL GIVE YA THE SIGN AS SOON AS I SPOT SOMETHING!
KNCH KNCH
URRRAAAAAH!
!
THAT'S AN ORC! WHERE IS IT...?!

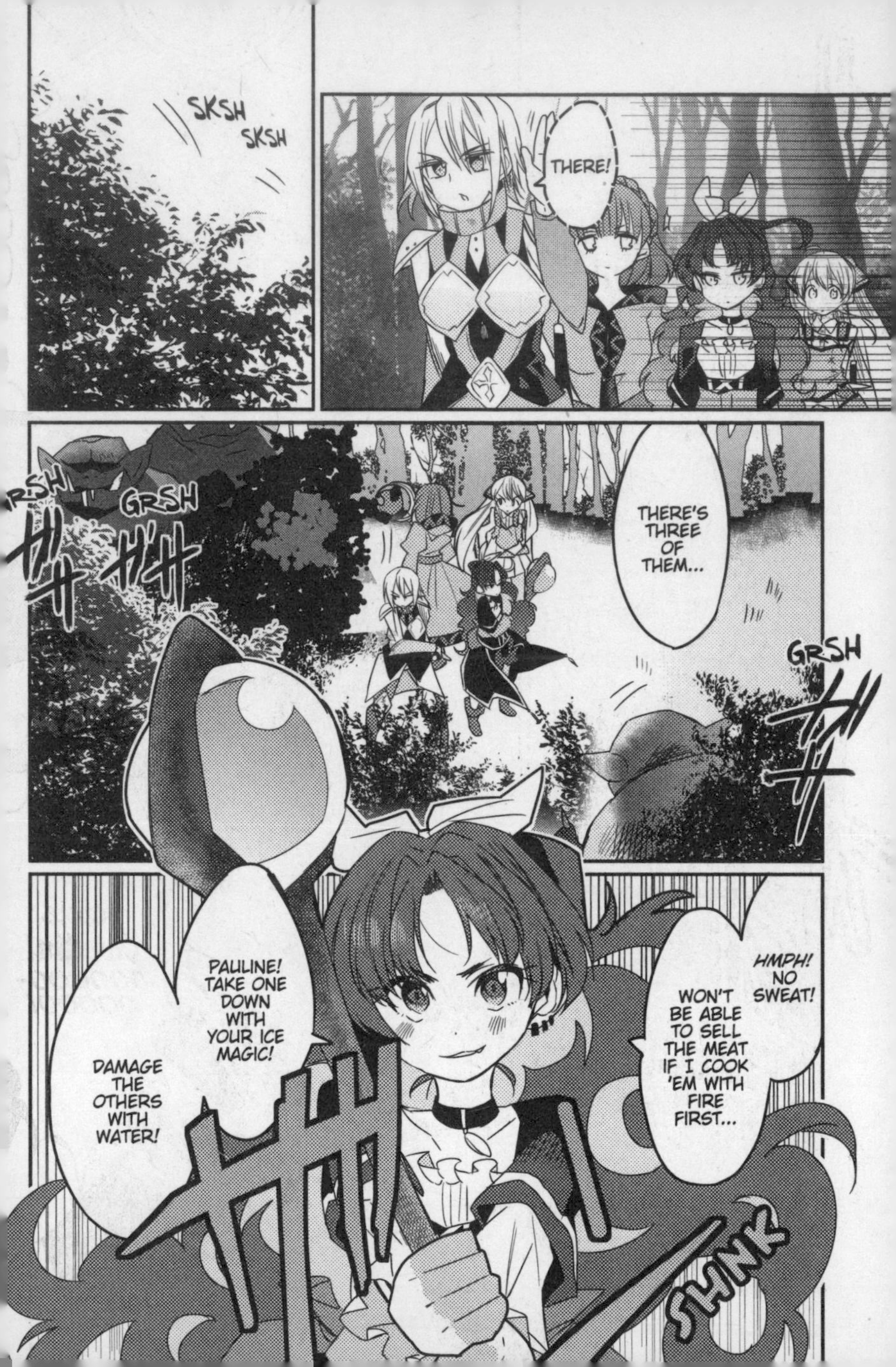
THERE!
SKSH
SKSH
THERE'S THREE OF THEM...
GRSH
GRSH
RSH
HMPH! NO SWEAT!
WON'T BE ABLE TO SELL THE MEAT IF I COOK 'EM WITH FIRE FIRST...
PAULINE! TAKE ONE DOWN WITH YOUR ICE MAGIC!
DAMAGE THE OTHERS WITH WATER!
SHNK

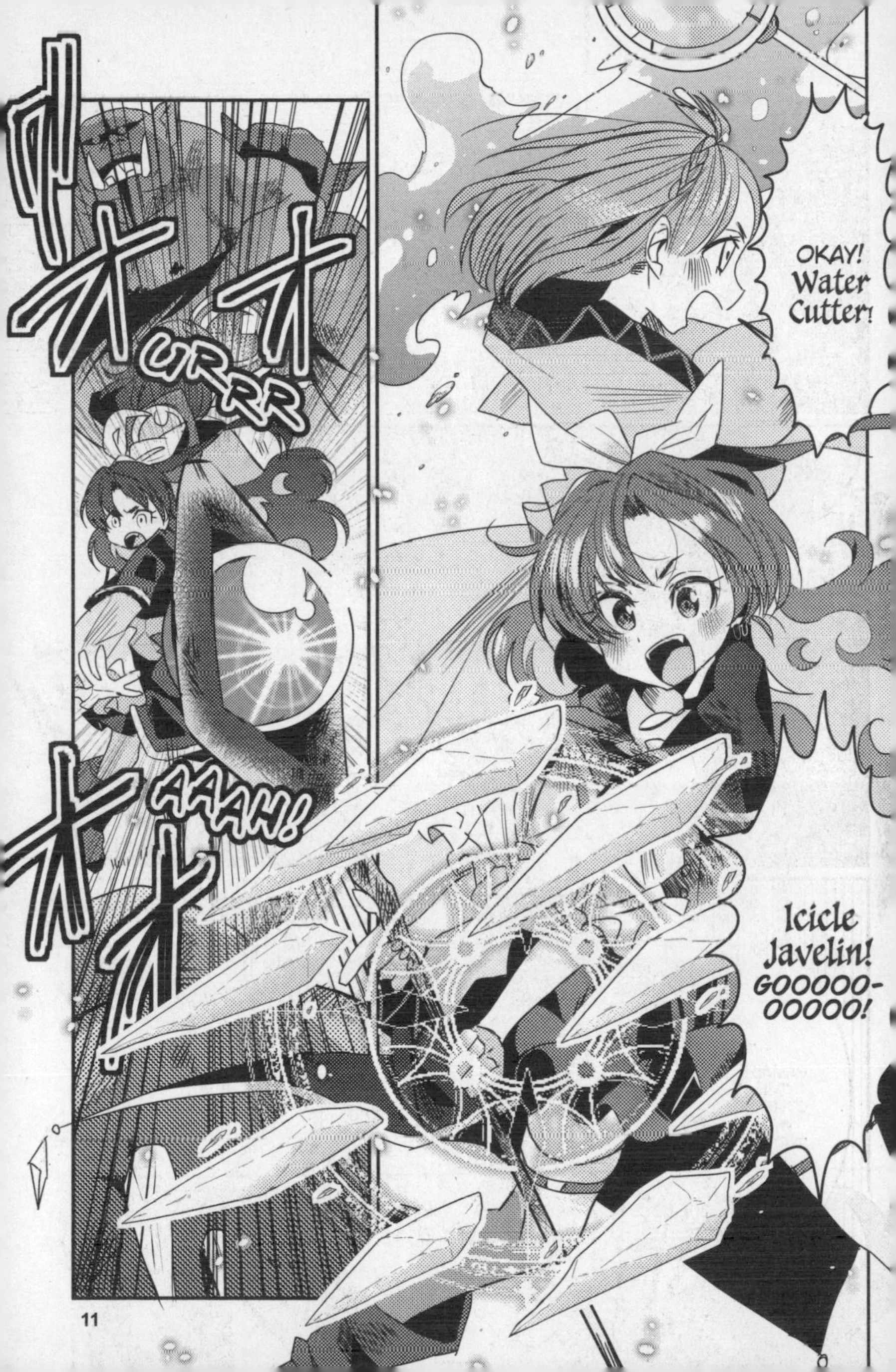
OKAY! Water Cutter!
Icicle Javelin! GOOOOOO-OOOOO!
URRR
AAAAH!

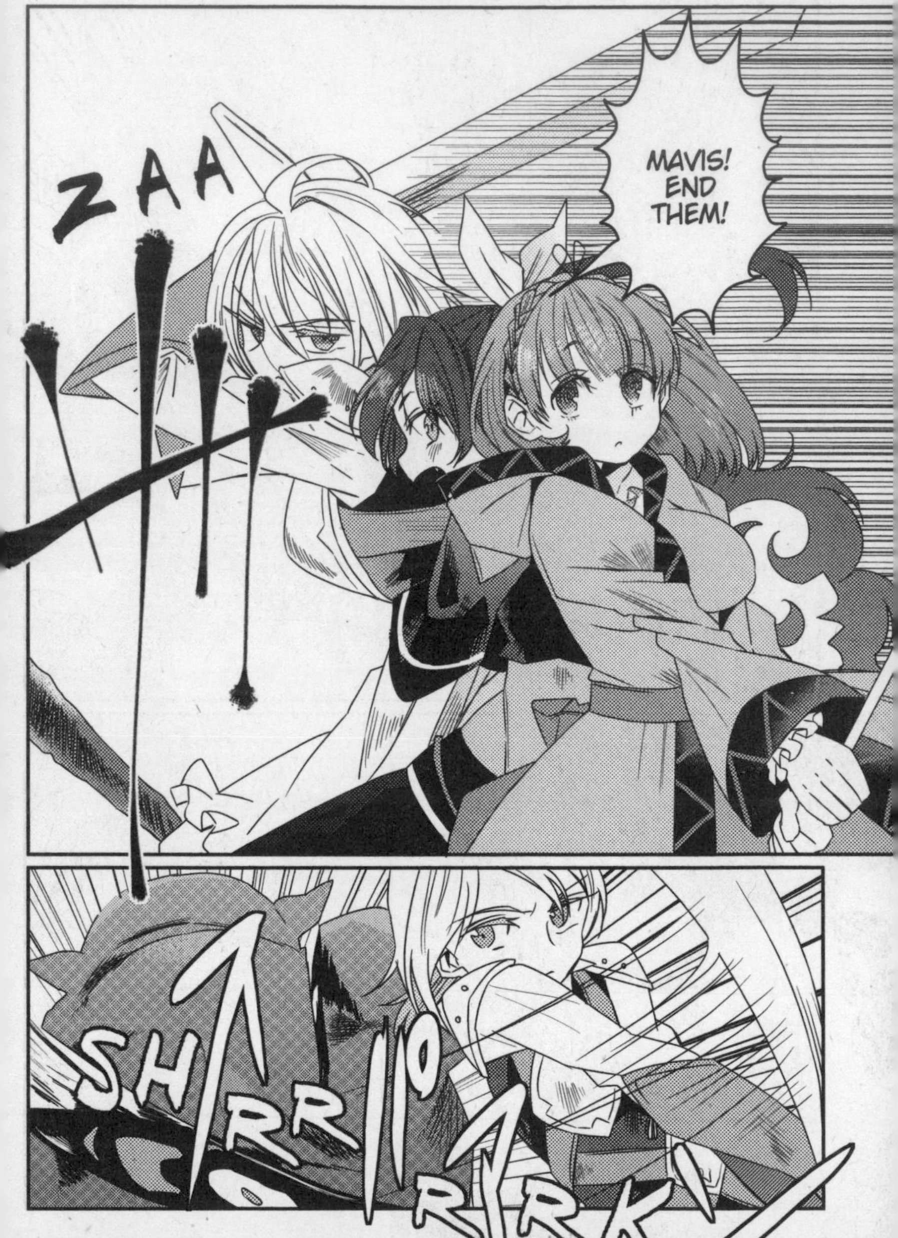
MAVIS! END THEM!
ZAA
SHRRIIIRRRRK

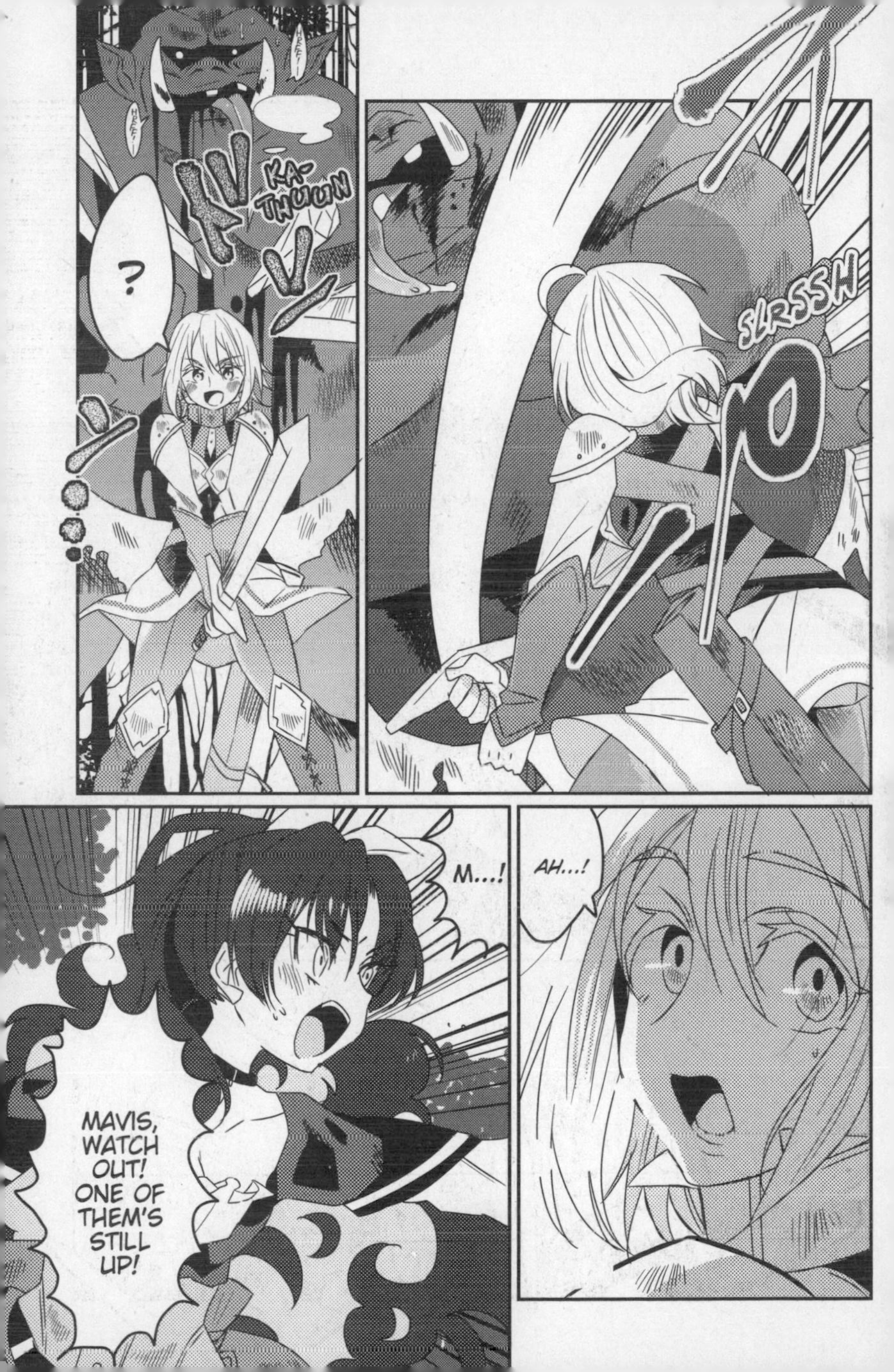
SLRSSH
HFEE!!
HFEE!!
KA-THUUN
?
AH...!
M...!
MAVIS, WATCH OUT! ONE OF THEM'S STILL UP!

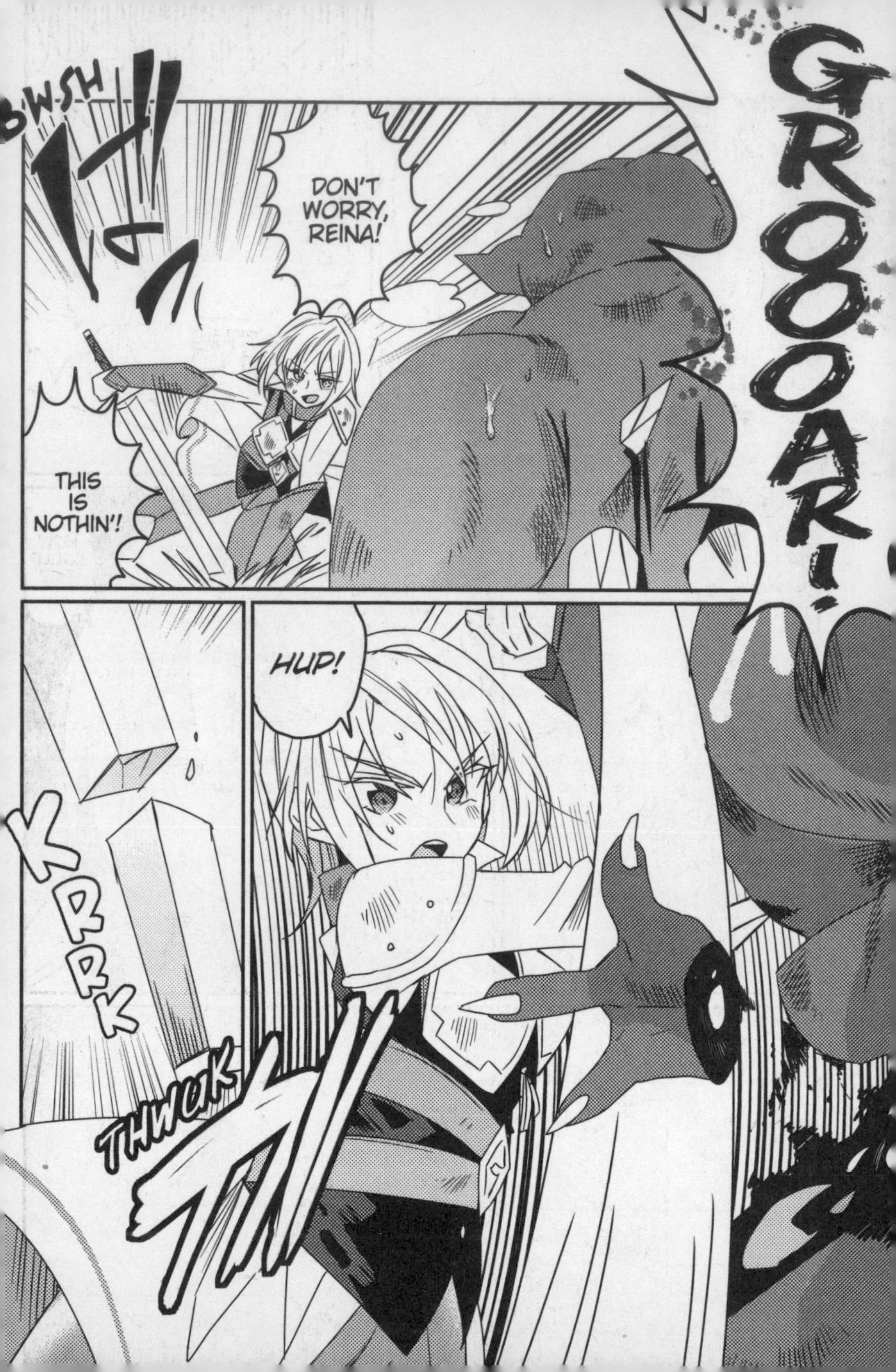
GROOOAR!
DON'T WORRY, REINA!
BWSH
THIS IS NOTHIN'!
HUP!
THWUK
KRRK

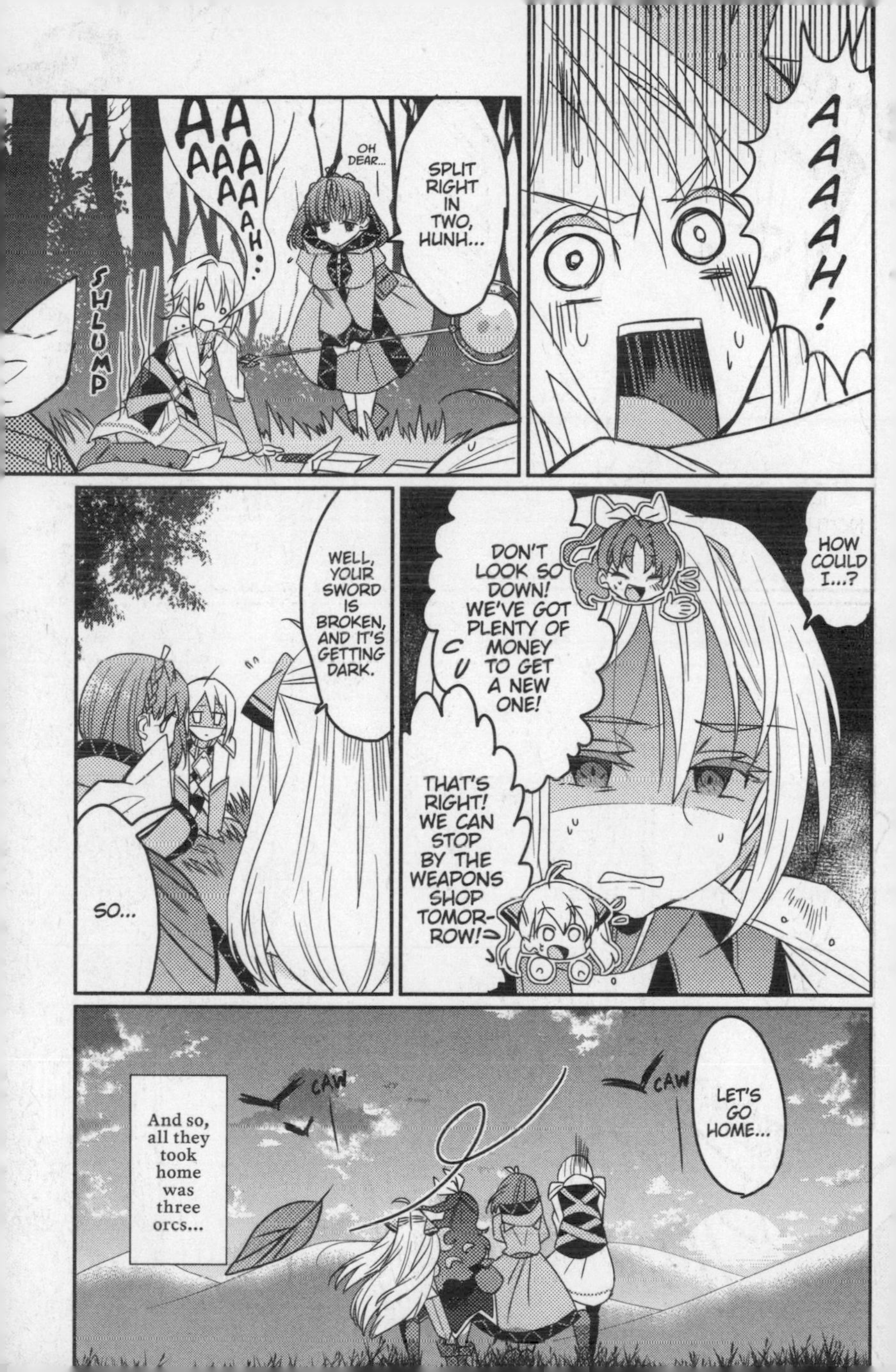
AAAAAH!
SPLIT RIGHT IN TWO, HUNH...
OH DEAR...
AAAAAAH...
SHLUMP
HOW COULD I...?
DON'T LOOK SO DOWN! WE'VE GOT PLENTY OF MONEY TO GET A NEW ONE!
THAT'S RIGHT! WE CAN STOP BY THE WEAPONS SHOP TOMORROW!
WELL, YOUR SWORD IS BROKEN, AND IT'S GETTING DARK.
SO...
LET'S GO HOME...
CAW
CAW
And so, all they took home was three orcs...

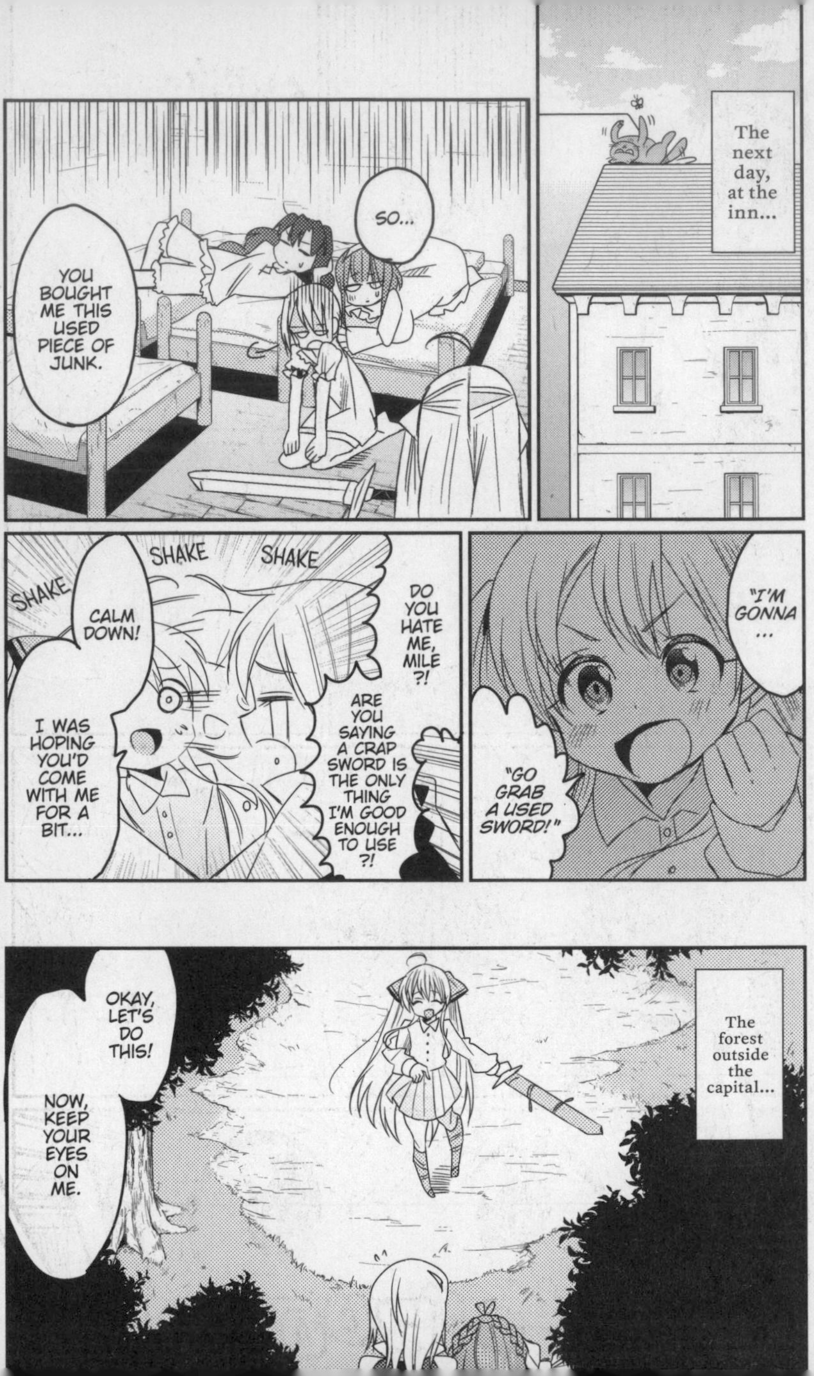
The next day, at the inn...
SO...
YOU BOUGHT ME THIS USED PIECE OF JUNK.
"I'M GONNA ...
"GO GRAB A USED SWORD!"
DO YOU HATE ME, MILE ?!
ARE YOU SAYING A CRAP SWORD IS THE ONLY THING I'M GOOD ENOUGH TO USE ?!
SHAKE
SHAKE
SHAKE
CALM DOWN!
I WAS HOPING YOU'D COME WITH ME FOR A BIT...
The forest outside the capital...
OKAY, LET'S DO THIS!
NOW, KEEP YOUR EYES ON ME.

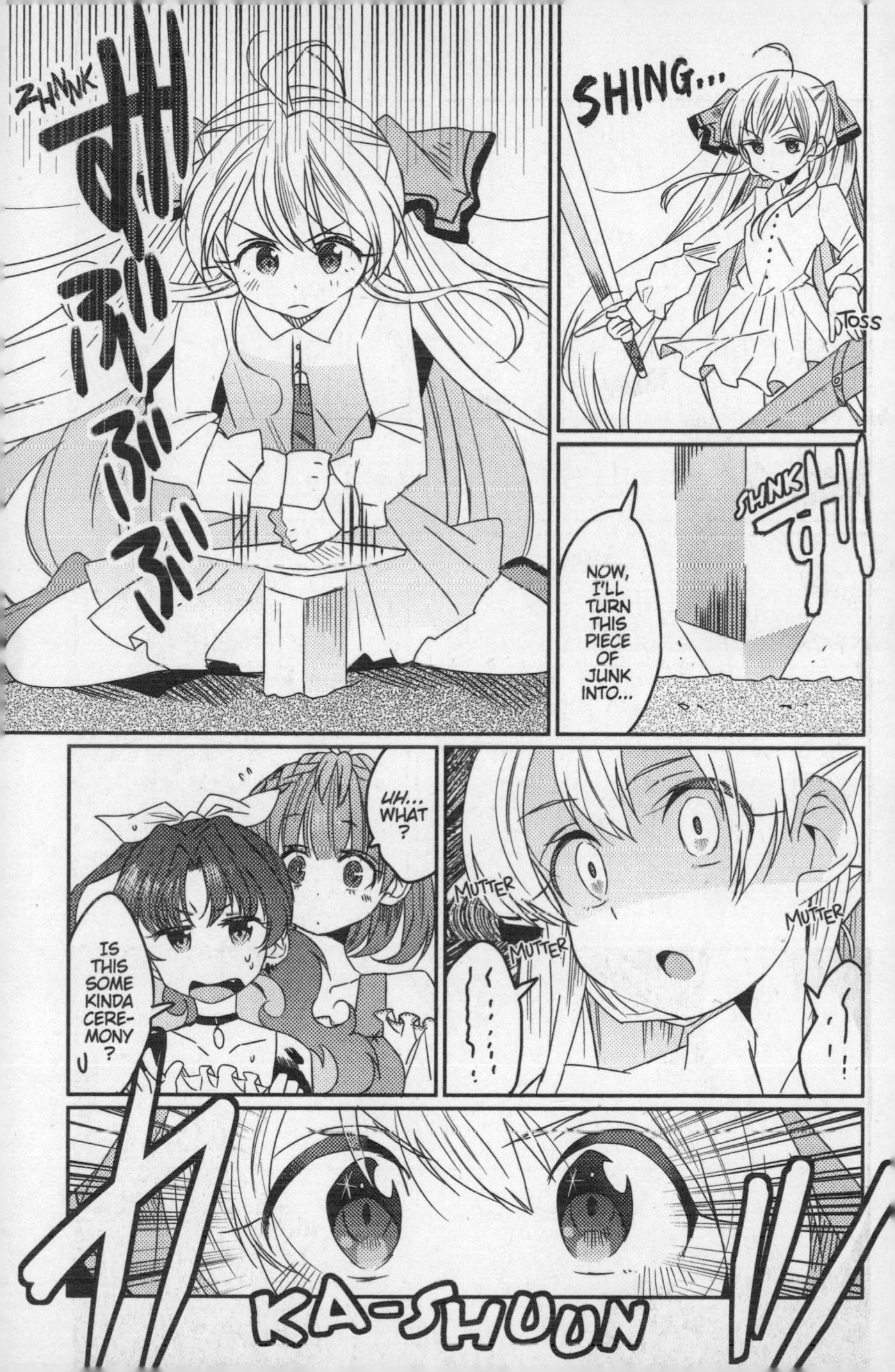
SHING...
TOSS
SHUNK
NOW, I'LL TURN THIS PIECE OF JUNK INTO...
ZHNNK
MUTTER
MUTTER
MUTTER
UH... WHAT?
IS THIS SOME KINDA CERE-MONY?
KA-SHUUN

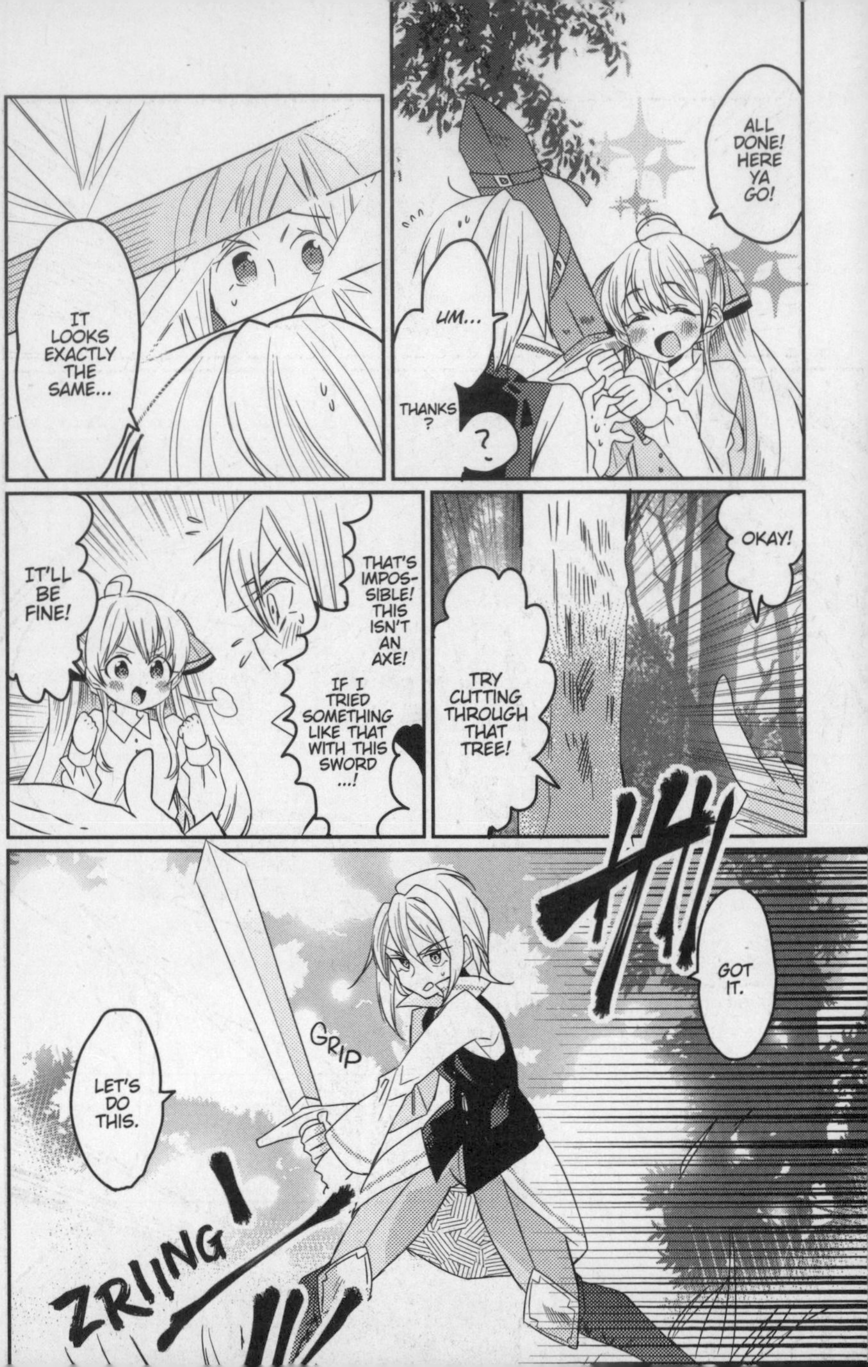
ALL DONE! HERE YA GO!
UM...
THANKS?
IT LOOKS EXACTLY THE SAME...
OKAY!
TRY CUTTING THROUGH THAT TREE!
THAT'S IMPOSSIBLE! THIS ISN'T AN AXE!
IF I TRIED SOMETHING LIKE THAT WITH THIS SWORD ...!
IT'LL BE FINE!
GOT IT.
GRIP
LET'S DO THIS.
ZRIING

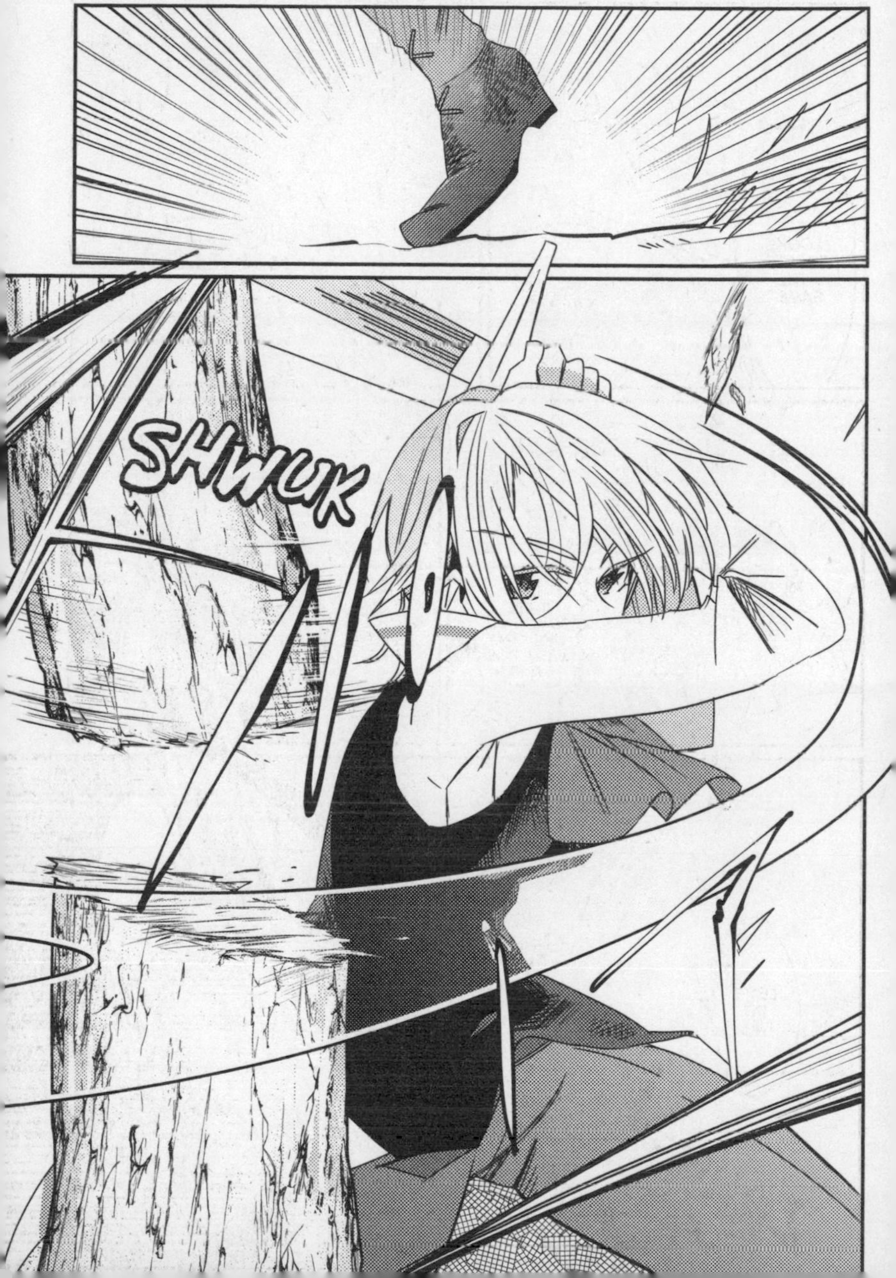
SHWUK

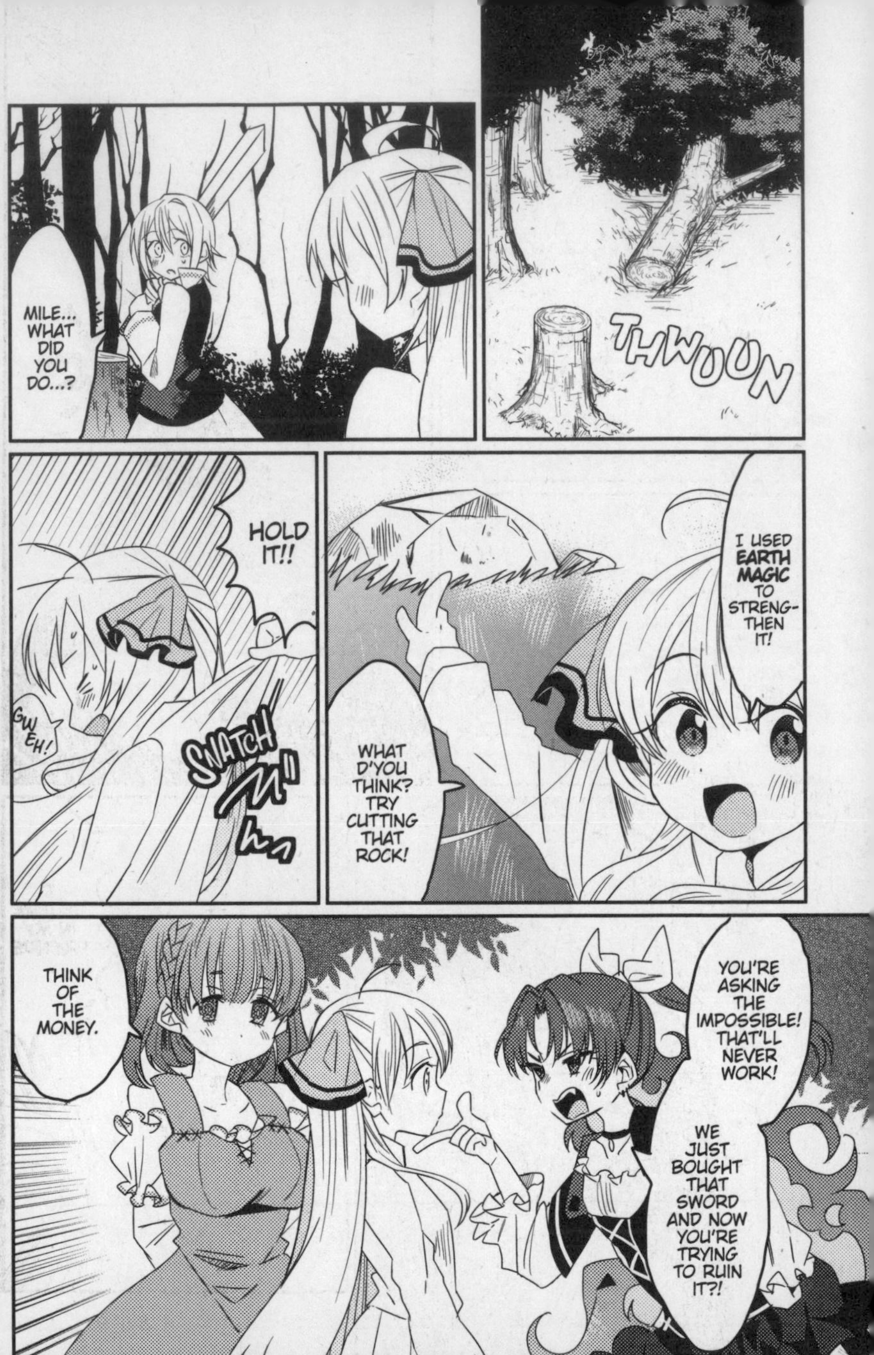
THWUUN
MILE... WHAT DID YOU DO...?
I USED **EARTH MAGIC** TO STRENG-THEN IT!
WHAT D'YOU THINK? TRY CUTTING THAT ROCK!
HOLD IT!!
SNATCH
GWEH!
YOU'RE ASKING THE IMPOSSIBLE! THAT'LL NEVER WORK!
WE JUST BOUGHT THAT SWORD AND NOW YOU'RE TRYING TO RUIN IT?!
THINK OF THE MONEY.

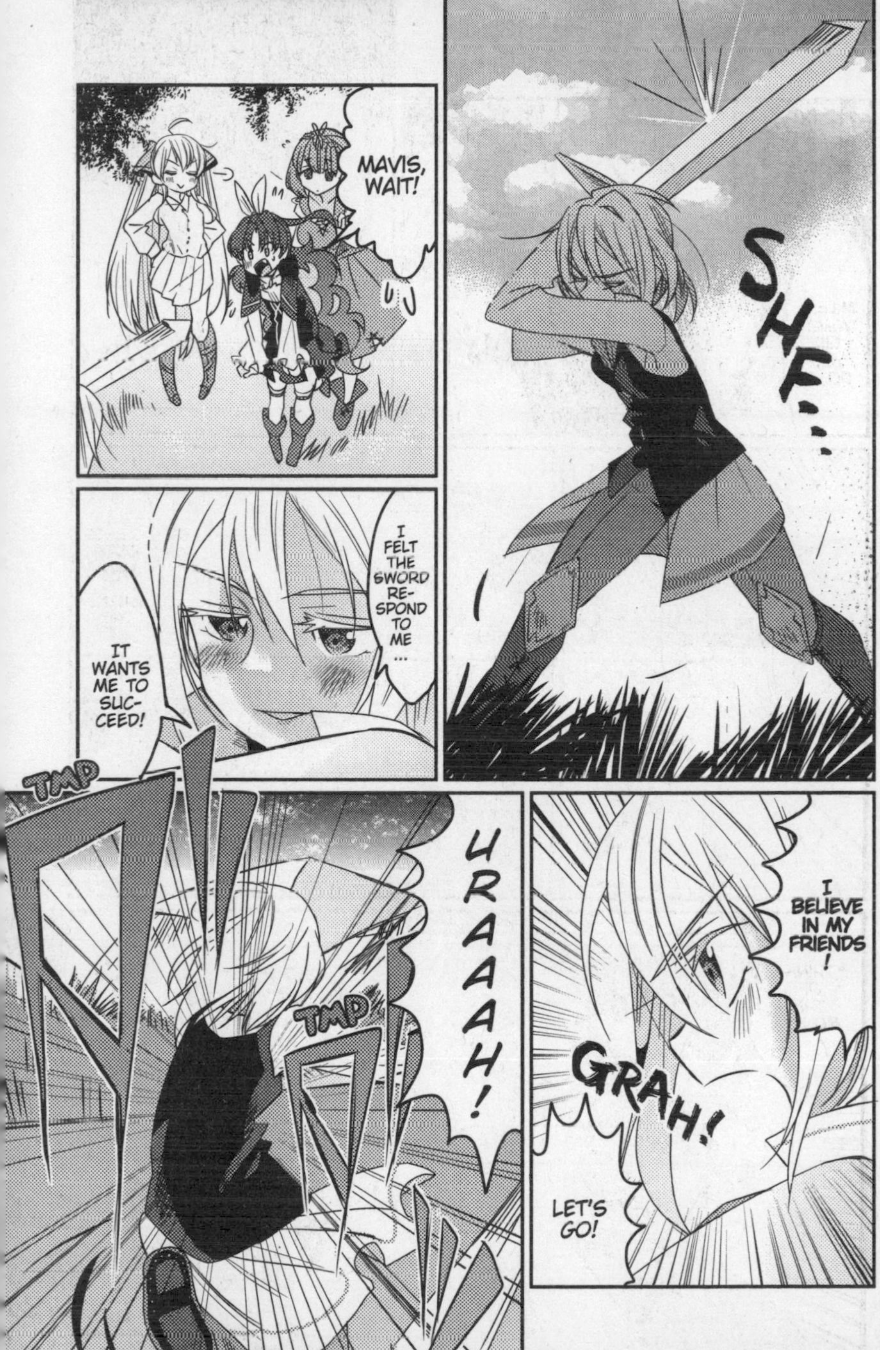
SHF...
MAVIS, WAIT!
I FELT THE SWORD RE-SPOND TO ME...
IT WANTS ME TO SUC-CEED!
I BELIEVE IN MY FRIENDS!
GRAH!
LET'S GO!
URAAAAH!
TMP
TMP

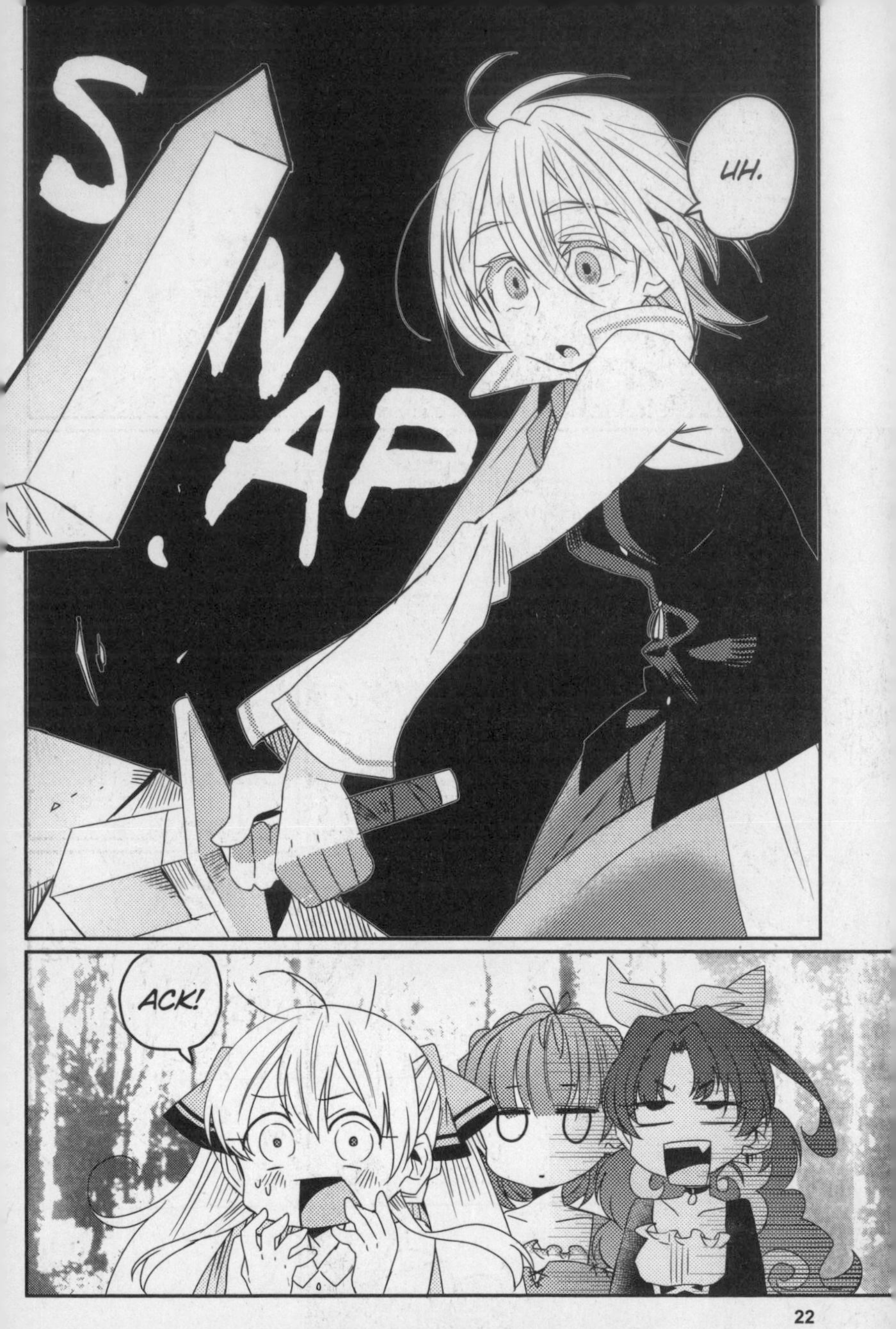
UH.
SNAP
ACK!

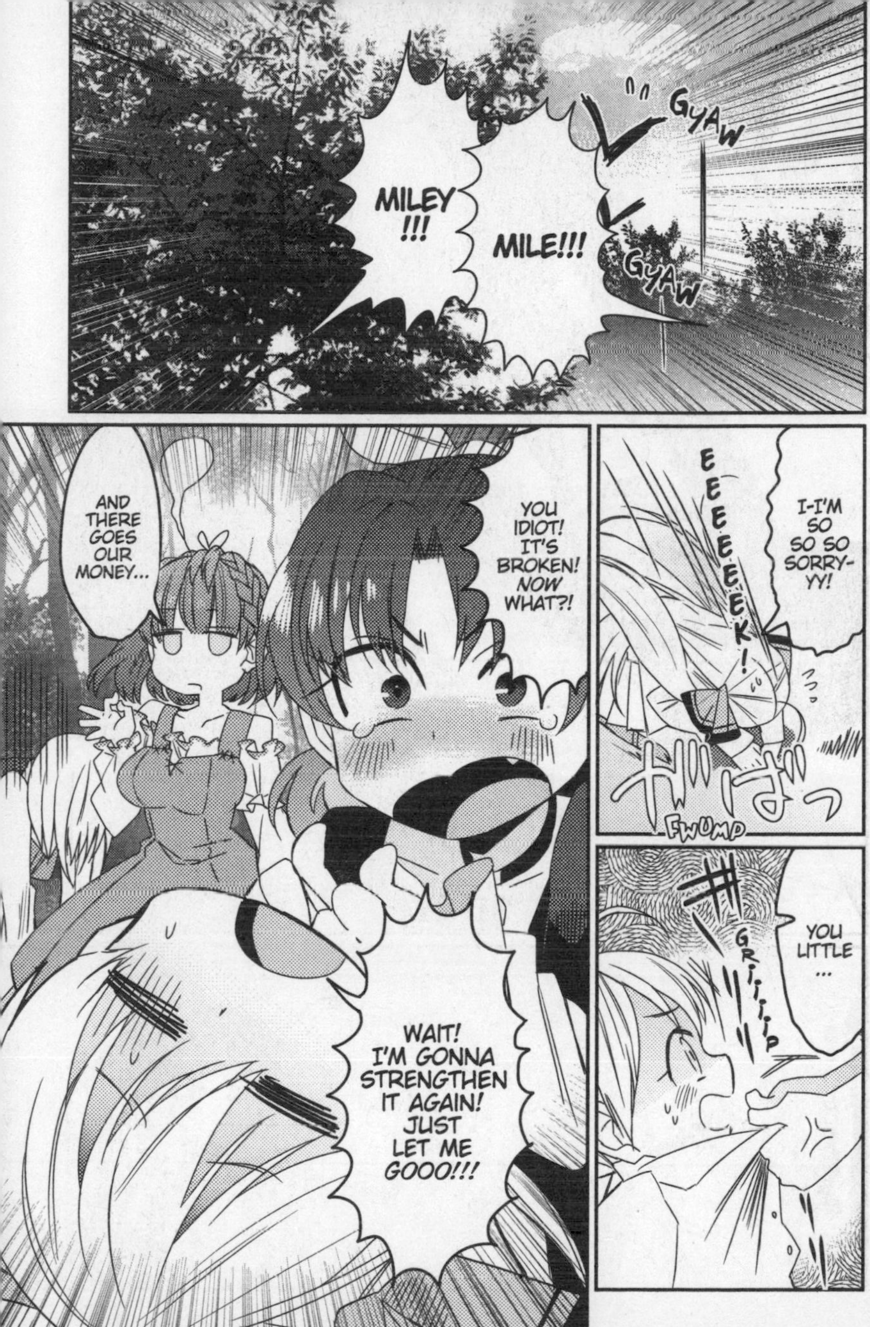
GYAW
GYAW
MILE!!!
MILEY !!!
I-I'M SO SO SO SORRY-YY!
EEEEEEEK!
FWUMP
YOU LITTLE ...
GRIIIIIP
YOU IDIOT! IT'S BROKEN! NOW WHAT?!
AND THERE GOES OUR MONEY...
WAIT! I'M GONNA STRENGTHEN IT AGAIN! JUST LET ME GOOO!!!

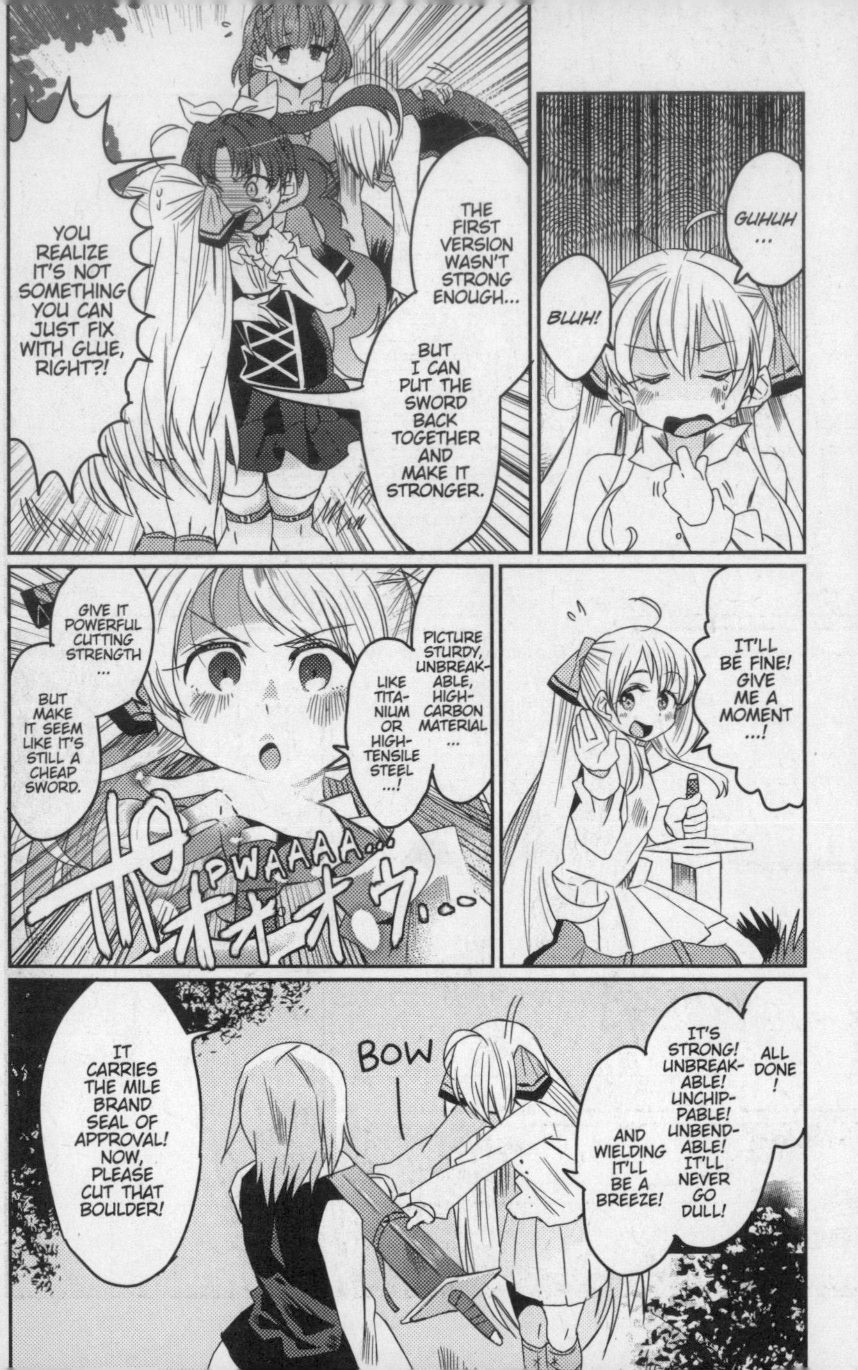
GUHUH...
BLUH!
THE FIRST VERSION WASN'T STRONG ENOUGH...
BUT I CAN PUT THE SWORD BACK TOGETHER AND MAKE IT STRONGER.
YOU REALIZE IT'S NOT SOMETHING YOU CAN JUST FIX WITH GLUE, RIGHT?!
IT'LL BE FINE! GIVE ME A MOMENT...!
PICTURE STURDY, UNBREAKABLE, HIGH-CARBON MATERIAL...
LIKE TITANIUM OR HIGH-TENSILE STEEL...!
GIVE IT POWERFUL CUTTING STRENGTH...
BUT MAKE IT SEEM LIKE IT'S STILL A CHEAP SWORD.
PWAAAA...
ALL DONE!
IT'S STRONG! UNBREAKABLE! UNCHIPPABLE! UNBENDABLE! IT'LL NEVER GO DULL!
AND WIELDING IT'LL BE A BREEZE!
BOW
IT CARRIES THE MILE BRAND SEAL OF APPROVAL! NOW, PLEASE CUT THAT BOULDER!

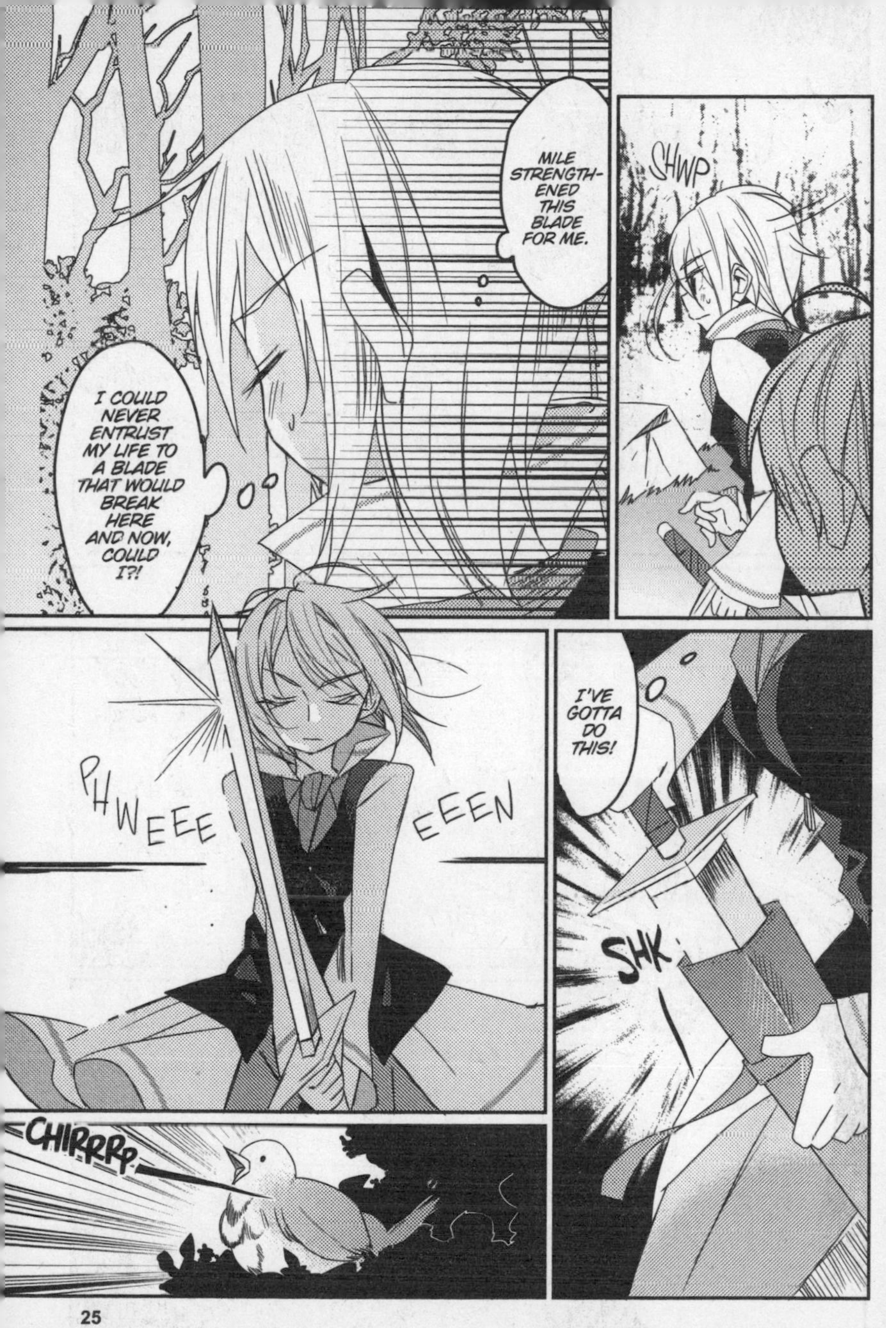
SHWP
MILE STRENGTHENED THIS BLADE FOR ME.
I COULD NEVER ENTRUST MY LIFE TO A BLADE THAT WOULD BREAK HERE AND NOW, COULD I?!
I'VE GOTTA DO THIS!
SHK
PHWEEE EEEN
CHIRRRP

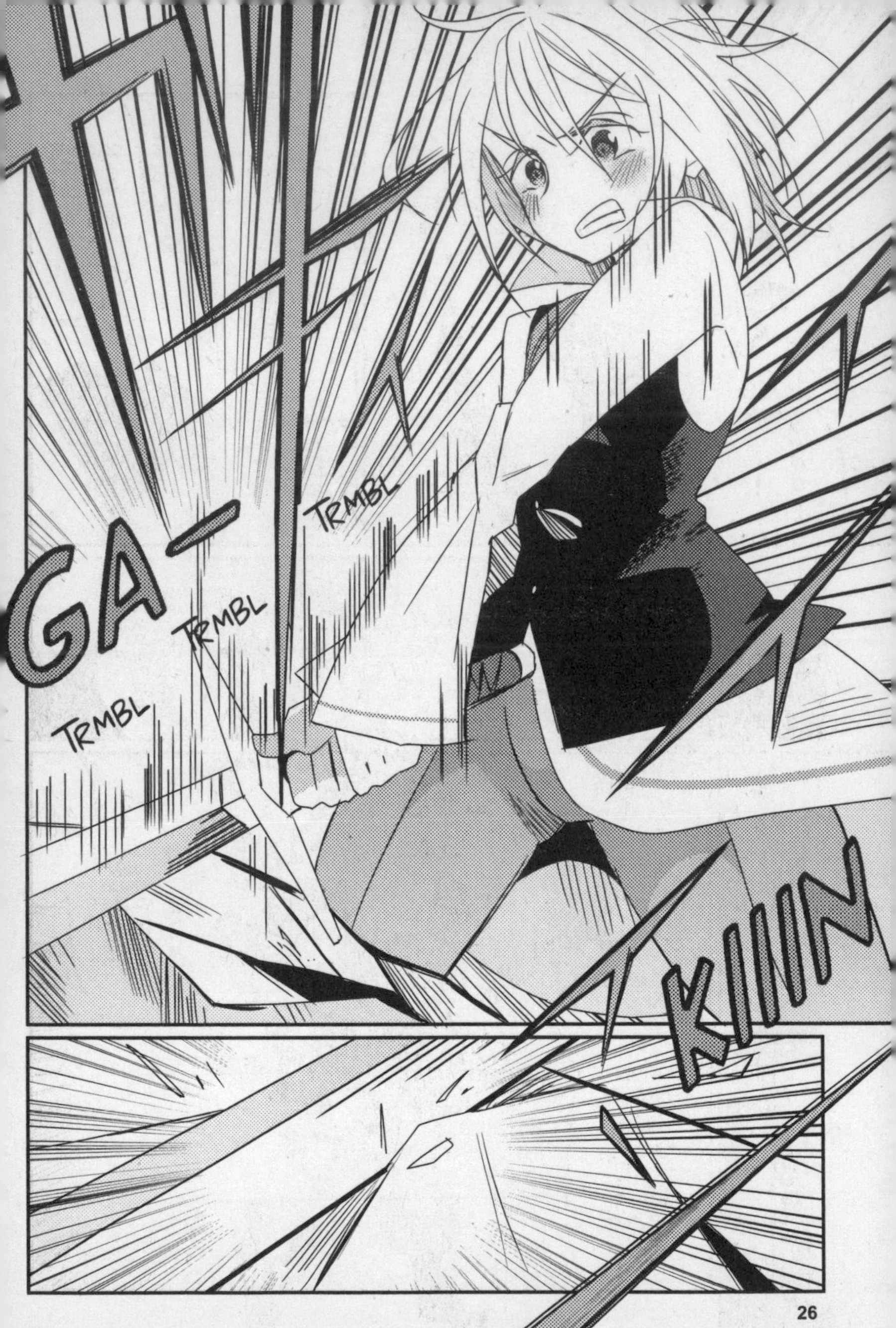
TRMBL
GA–
TRMBL
TRMBL
KIIIN

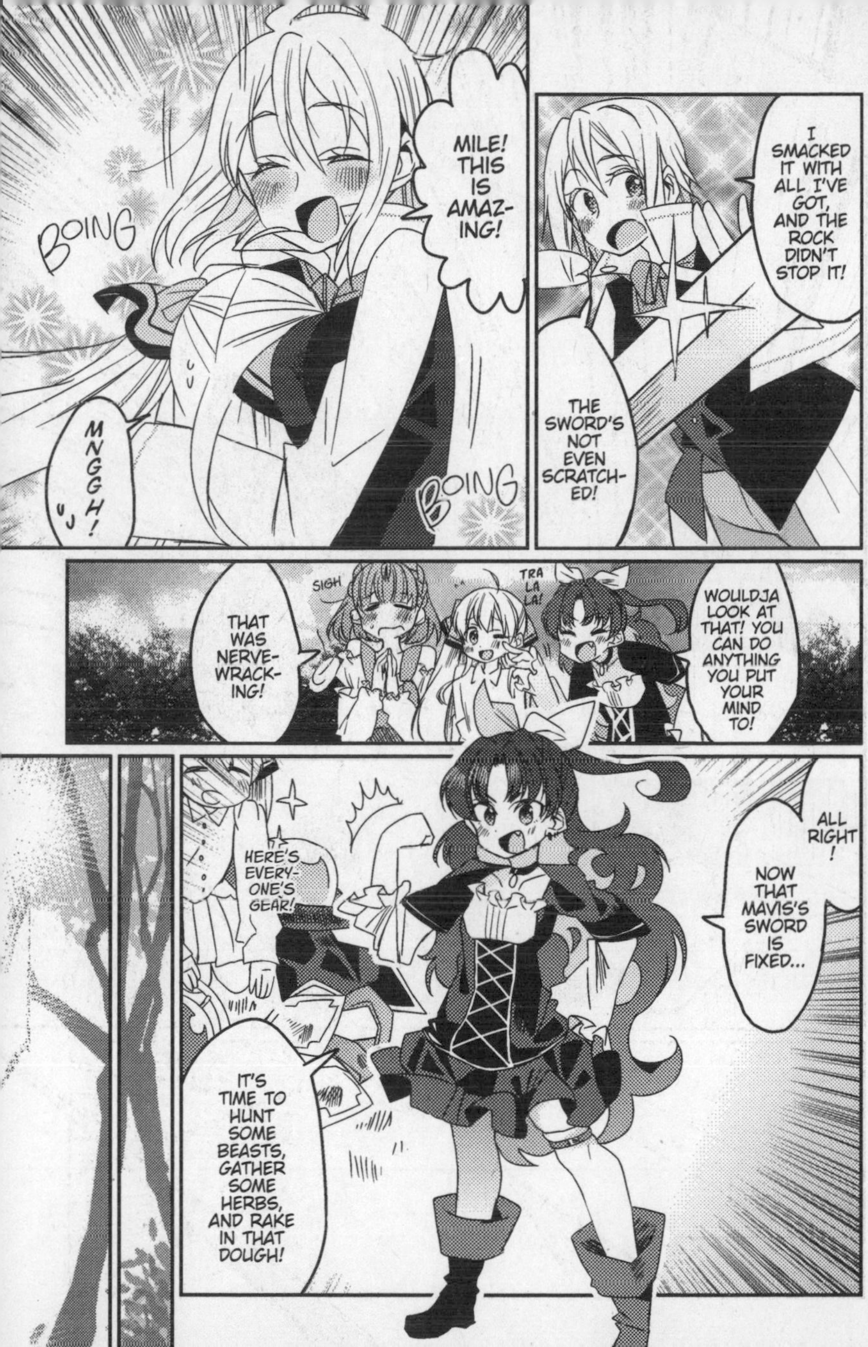
I SMACKED IT WITH ALL I'VE GOT, AND THE ROCK DIDN'T STOP IT!
THE SWORD'S NOT EVEN SCRATCHED!
MILE! THIS IS AMAZING!
BOING
MNGGH!
BOING
WOULDJA LOOK AT THAT! YOU CAN DO ANYTHING YOU PUT YOUR MIND TO!
TRA LA LA!
SIGH
THAT WAS NERVE-WRACKING!
ALL RIGHT!
NOW THAT MAVIS'S SWORD IS FIXED...
HERE'S EVERYONE'S GEAR!
IT'S TIME TO HUNT SOME BEASTS, GATHER SOME HERBS, AND RAKE IN THAT DOUGH!

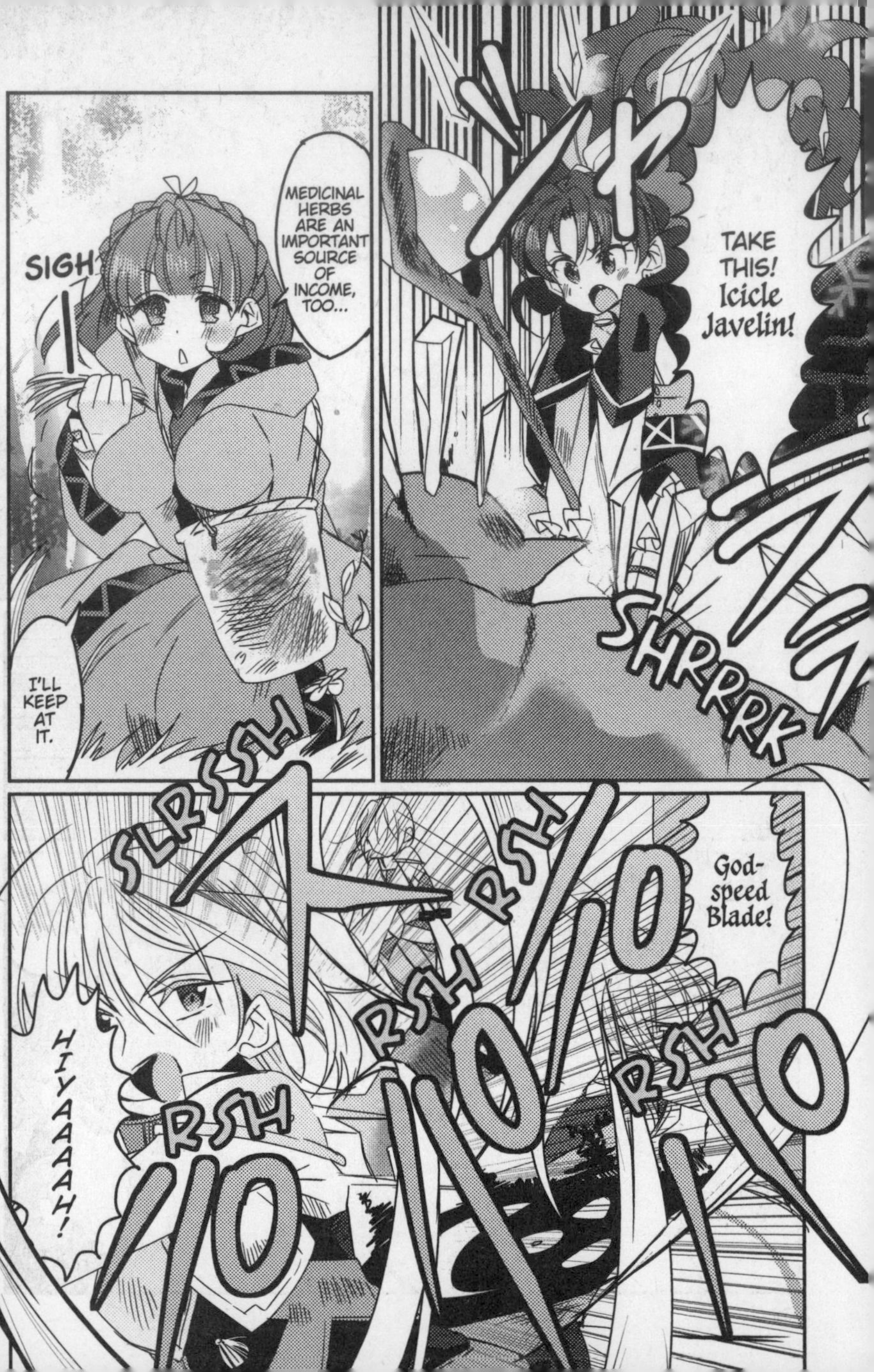
TAKE THIS! Icicle Javelin!
SHRRRK
MEDICINAL HERBS ARE AN IMPORTANT SOURCE OF INCOME, TOO...
SIGH
I'LL KEEP AT IT.
God-speed Blade!
SLRSSSH
RSH
RSH
RSH
RSH
HIYAAAAH!

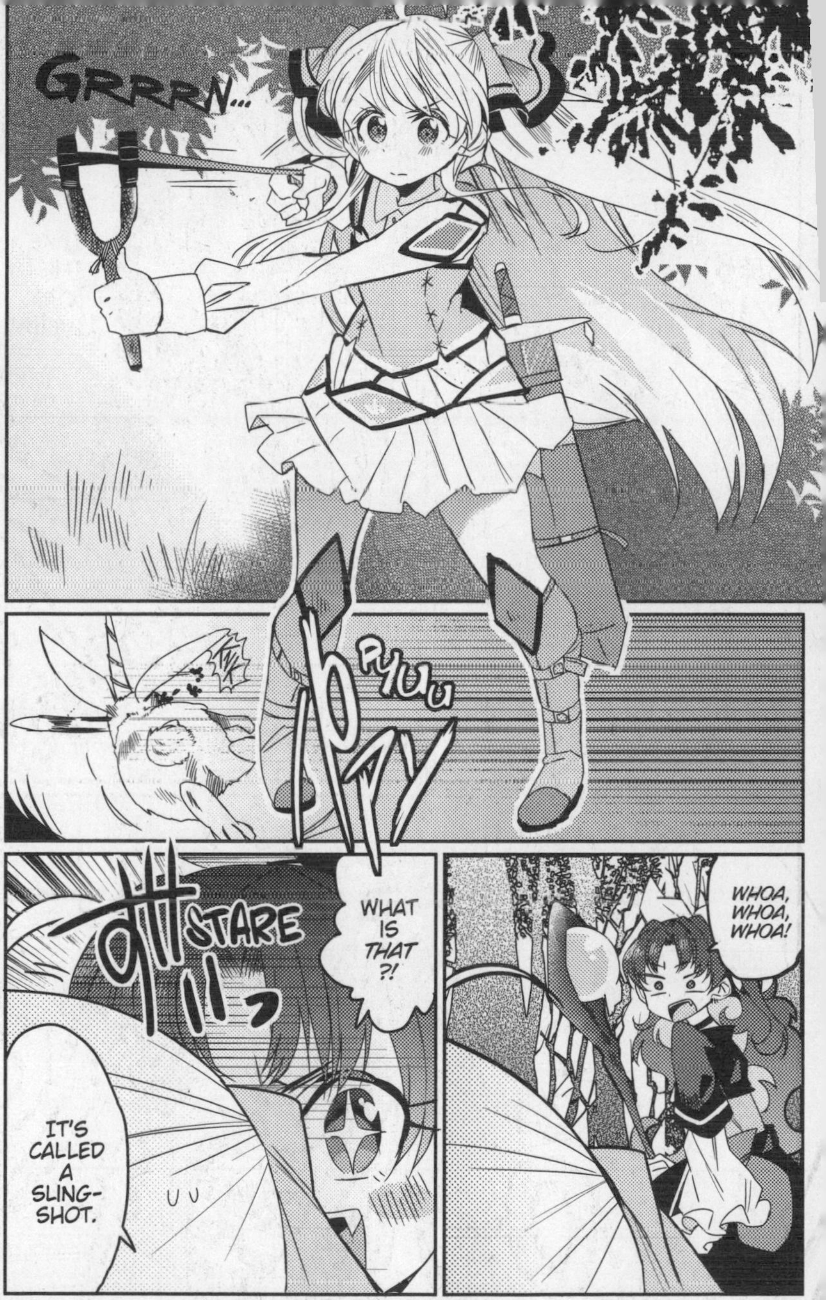
GRRRRN...
PYUUU
WHOA, WHOA, WHOA!
WHAT IS THAT?!
STARE
IT'S CALLED A SLING-SHOT.

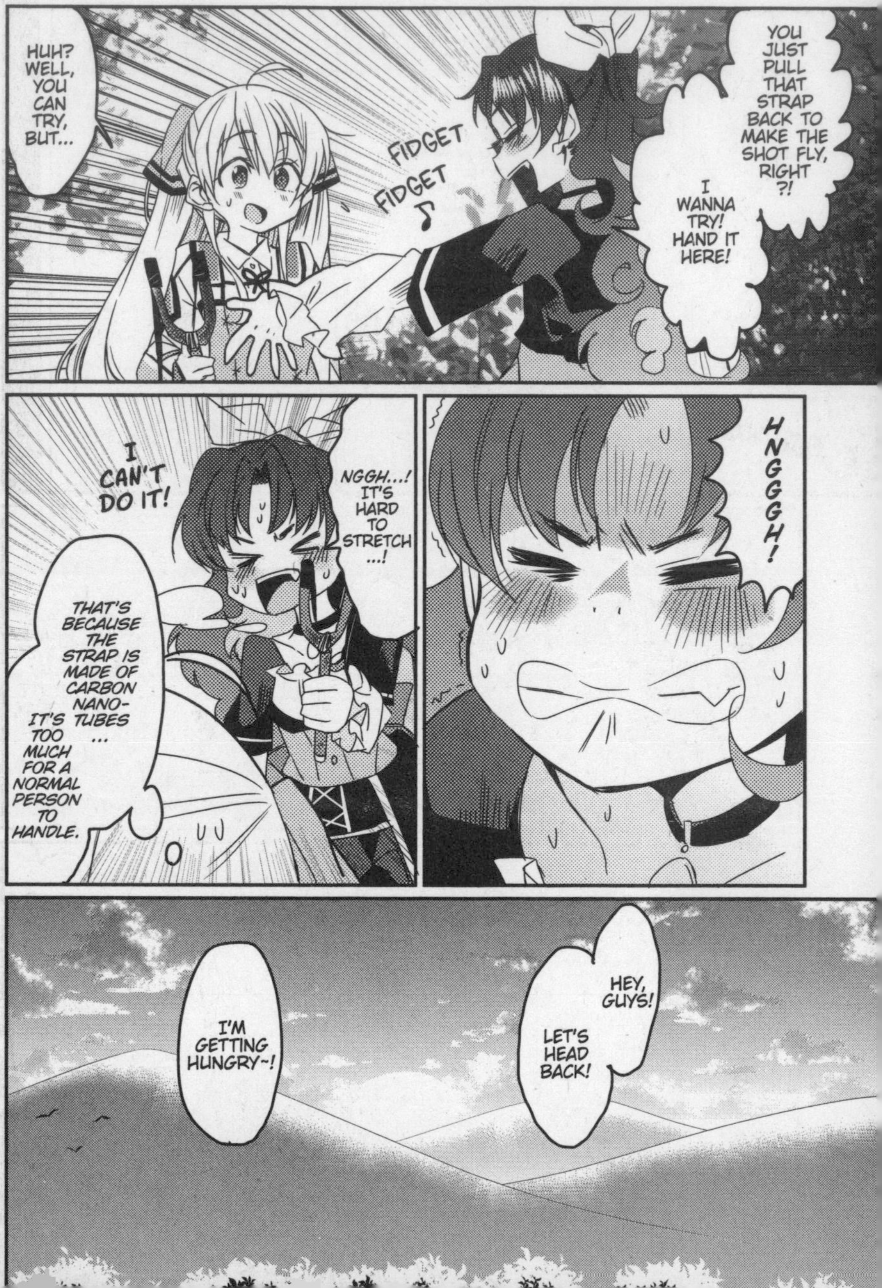
YOU JUST PULL THAT STRAP BACK TO MAKE THE SHOT FLY, RIGHT?!
I WANNA TRY! HAND IT HERE!
FIDGET FIDGET ♪
HUH? WELL, YOU CAN TRY, BUT...
HNGGGH!
NGGH...! IT'S HARD TO STRETCH...!
I CAN'T DO IT!
THAT'S BECAUSE THE STRAP IS MADE OF CARBON NANO-TUBES...
IT'S TOO MUCH FOR A NORMAL PERSON TO HANDLE.
HEY, GUYS!
LET'S HEAD BACK!
I'M GETTING HUNGRY~!

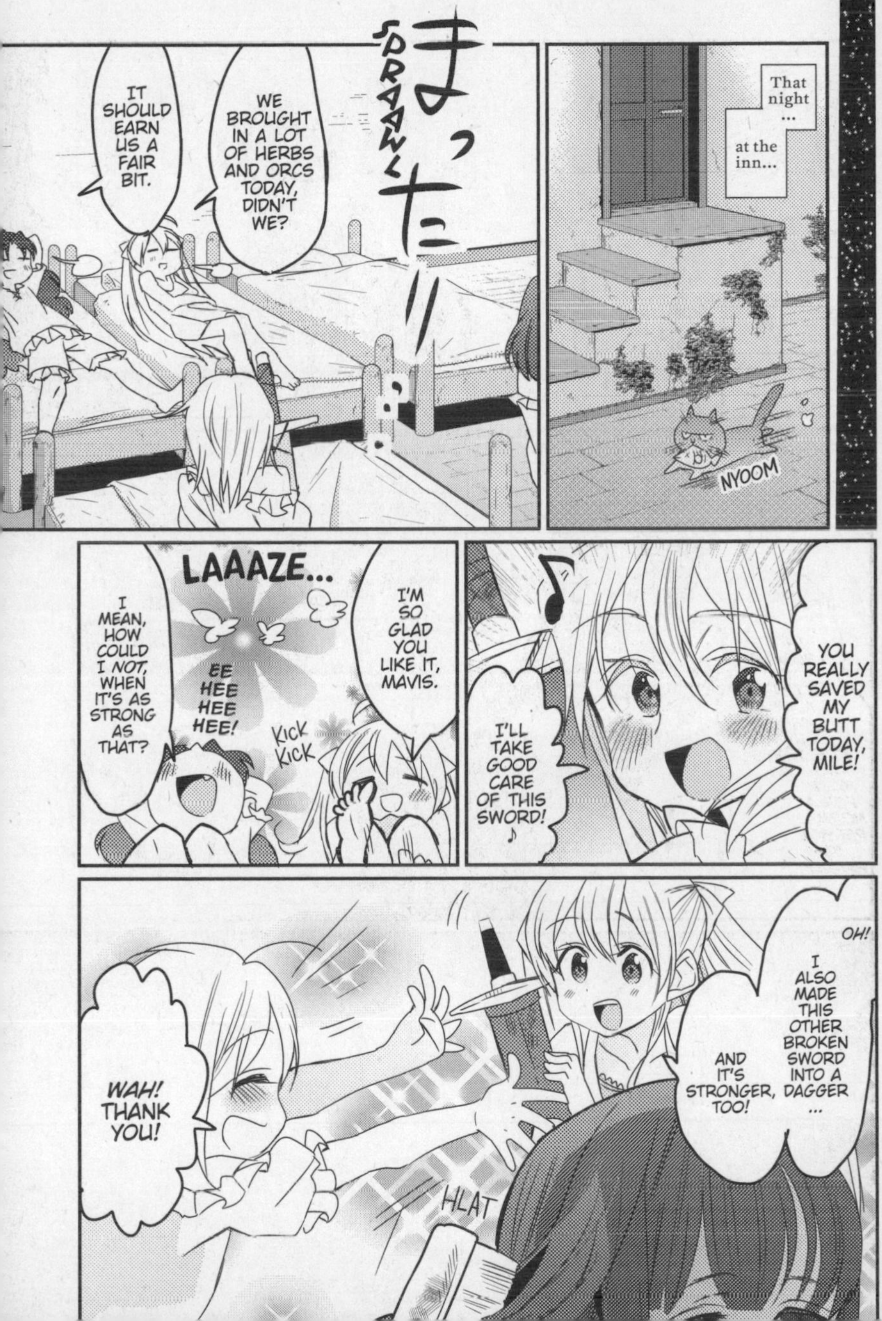
That night ... at the inn...
NYOOM
まったり
SPRAWL
WE BROUGHT IN A LOT OF HERBS AND ORCS TODAY, DIDN'T WE?
IT SHOULD EARN US A FAIR BIT.
YOU REALLY SAVED MY BUTT TODAY, MILE!
I'LL TAKE GOOD CARE OF THIS SWORD! ♪
I'M SO GLAD YOU LIKE IT, MAVIS.
KICK KICK
EE HEE HEE HEE!
LAAAZE...
I MEAN, HOW COULD I *NOT*, WHEN IT'S AS STRONG AS THAT?
OH!
I ALSO MADE THIS OTHER BROKEN SWORD INTO A DAGGER ...
AND IT'S STRONGER, TOO!
HLAT
WAH! THANK YOU!

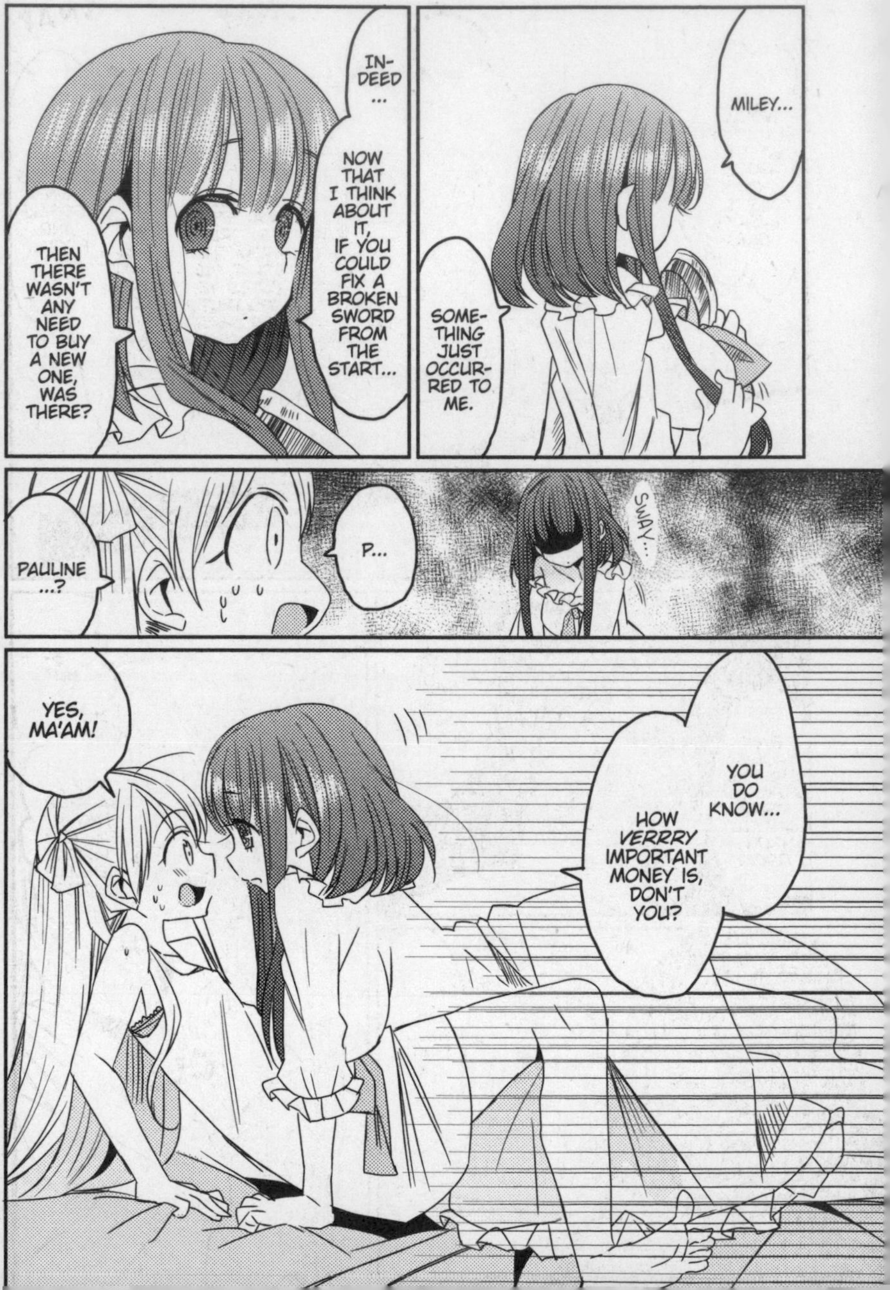
MILEY...
SOMETHING JUST OCCURRED TO ME.
IN-DEED...
NOW THAT I THINK ABOUT IT, IF YOU COULD FIX A BROKEN SWORD FROM THE START...
THEN THERE WASN'T ANY NEED TO BUY A NEW ONE, WAS THERE?
SWAY...
P...
PAULINE...?
YOU DO KNOW...
HOW VERRRY IMPORTANT MONEY IS, DON'T YOU?
YES, MA'AM!

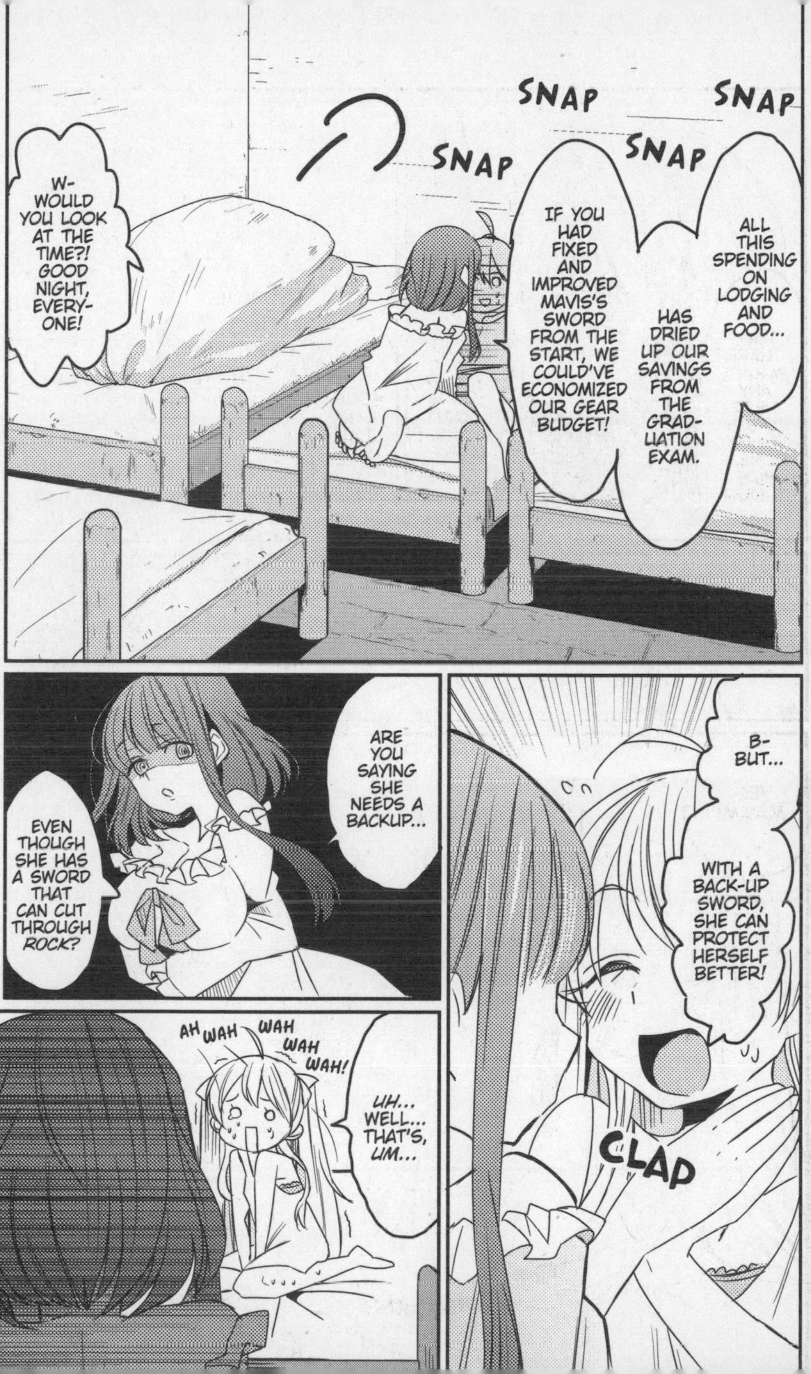
SNAP
SNAP
ALL THIS SPENDING ON LODGING AND FOOD...
HAS DRIED UP OUR SAVINGS FROM THE GRADUATION EXAM.
SNAP
IF YOU HAD FIXED AND IMPROVED MAVIS'S SWORD FROM THE START, WE COULD'VE ECONOMIZED OUR GEAR BUDGET!
SNAP
W-WOULD YOU LOOK AT THE TIME?! GOOD NIGHT, EVERYONE!
B-BUT...
WITH A BACK-UP SWORD, SHE CAN PROTECT HERSELF BETTER!
CLAP
ARE YOU SAYING SHE NEEDS A BACKUP...
EVEN THOUGH SHE HAS A SWORD THAT CAN CUT THROUGH *ROCK*?
AH WAH WAH WAH WAH!
UH... WELL... THAT'S, *UM...*

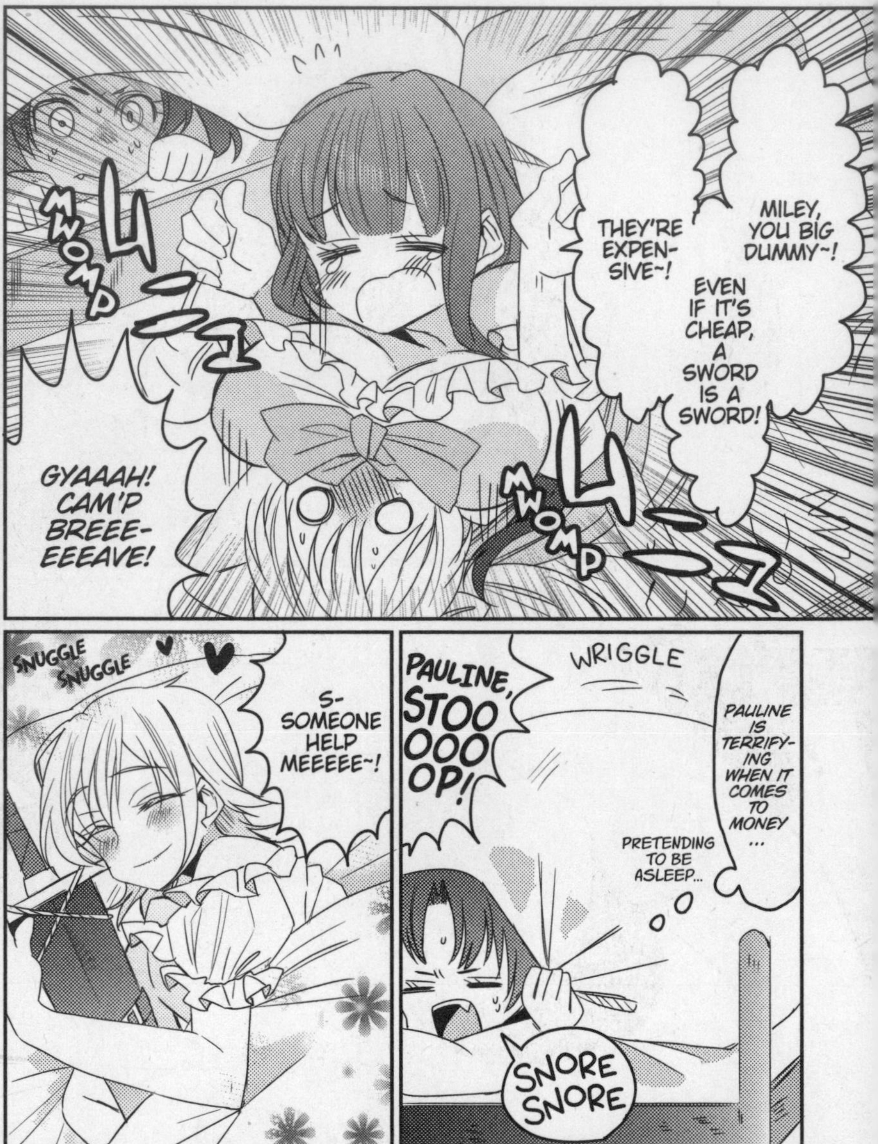
MILEY, YOU BIG DUMMY~!
EVEN IF IT'S CHEAP, A SWORD IS A SWORD!
THEY'RE EXPEN-SIVE~!
MWOMP
MWOMP
GYAAAH! CAM'P BREEE-EEEAVE!
WRIGGLE
PAULINE IS TERRIFY-ING WHEN IT COMES TO MONEY ...
PAULINE, STOOOOOOOP!
PRETENDING TO BE ASLEEP...
SNORE SNORE
SNUGGLE SNUGGLE
S-SOMEONE HELP MEEEEE~!

Chapter 13: Battle in the Rocky Mountains

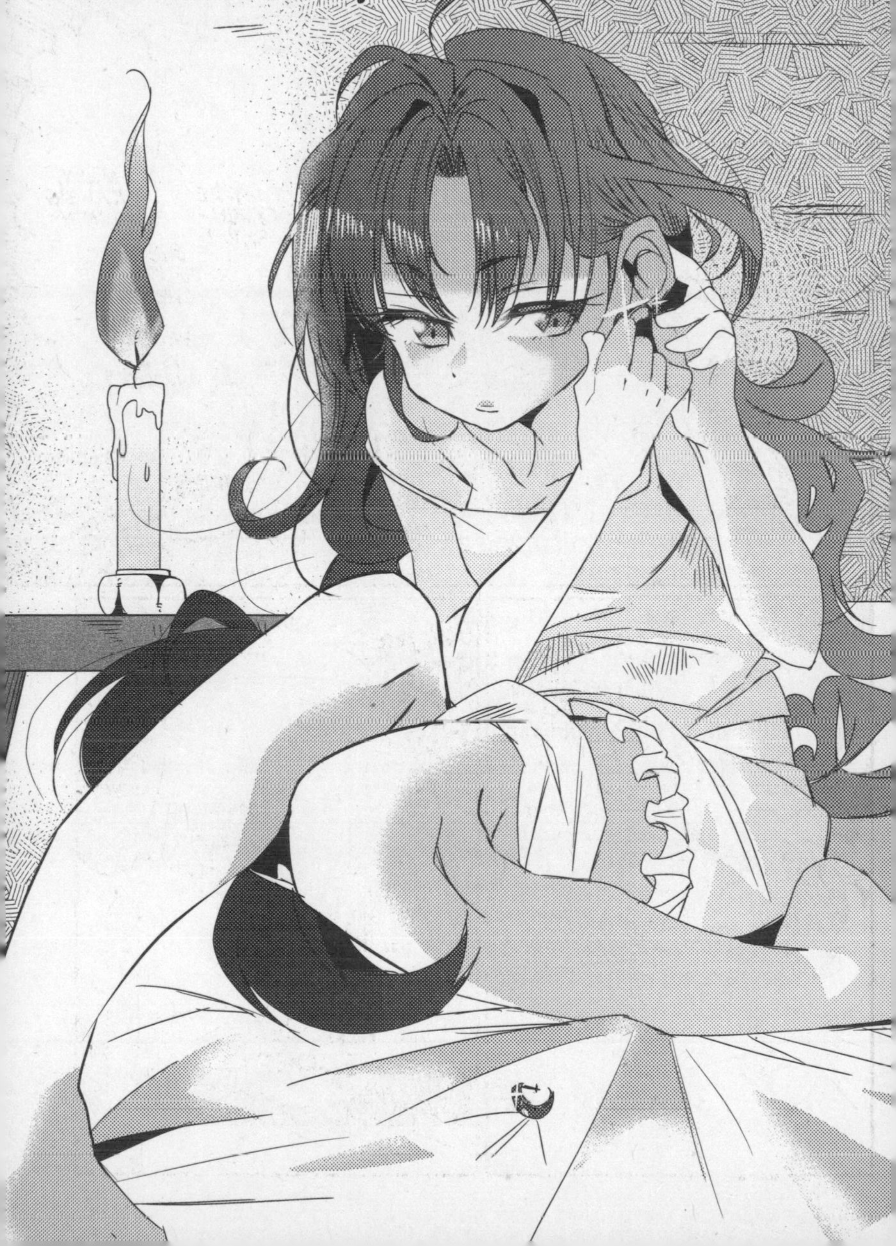

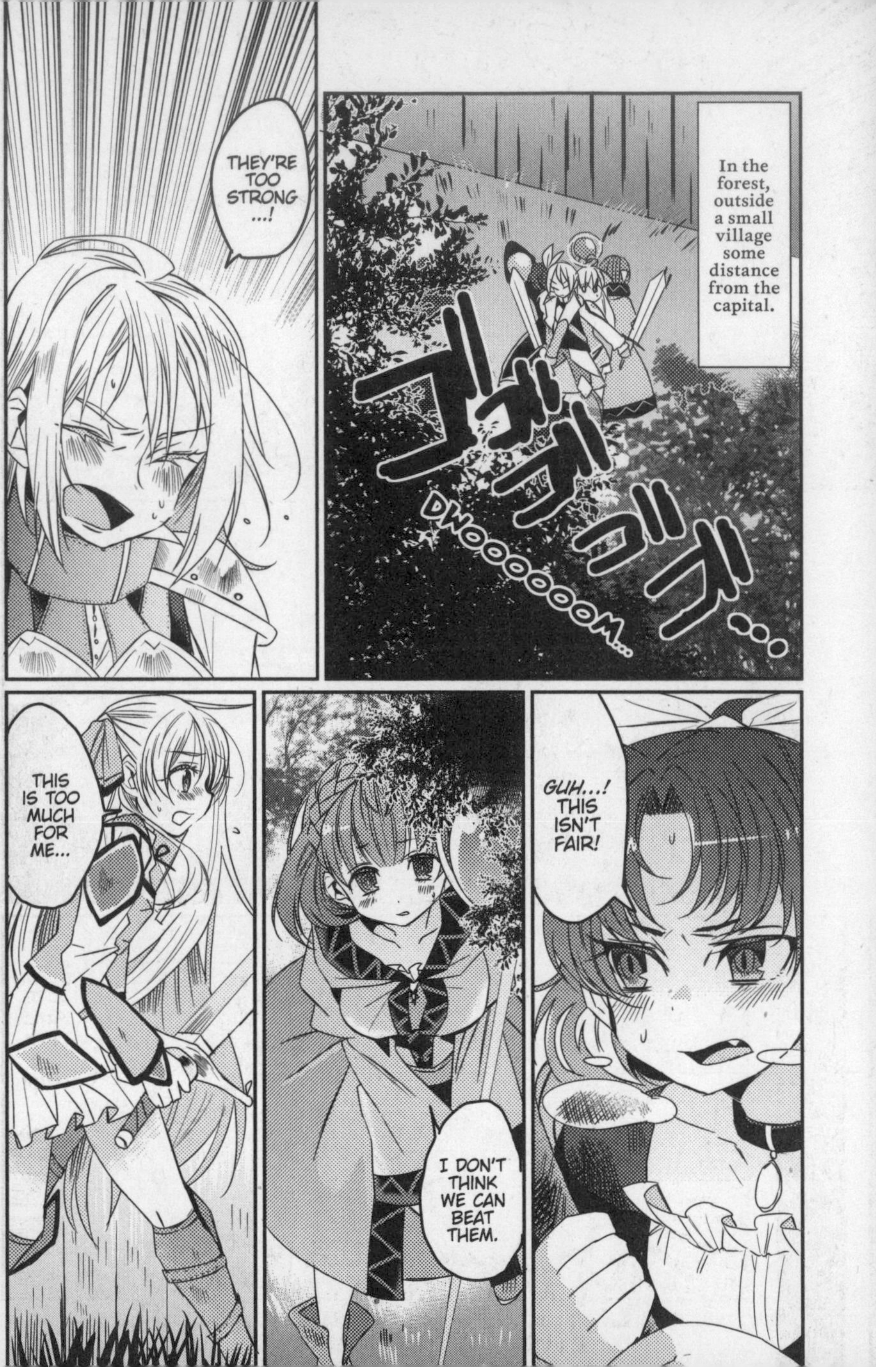

In the forest, outside a small village some distance from the capital.
DWOOOOOOOM...
THEY'RE TOO STRONG ...!
GUH...! THIS ISN'T FAIR!
I DON'T THINK WE CAN BEAT THEM.
THIS IS TOO MUCH FOR ME...

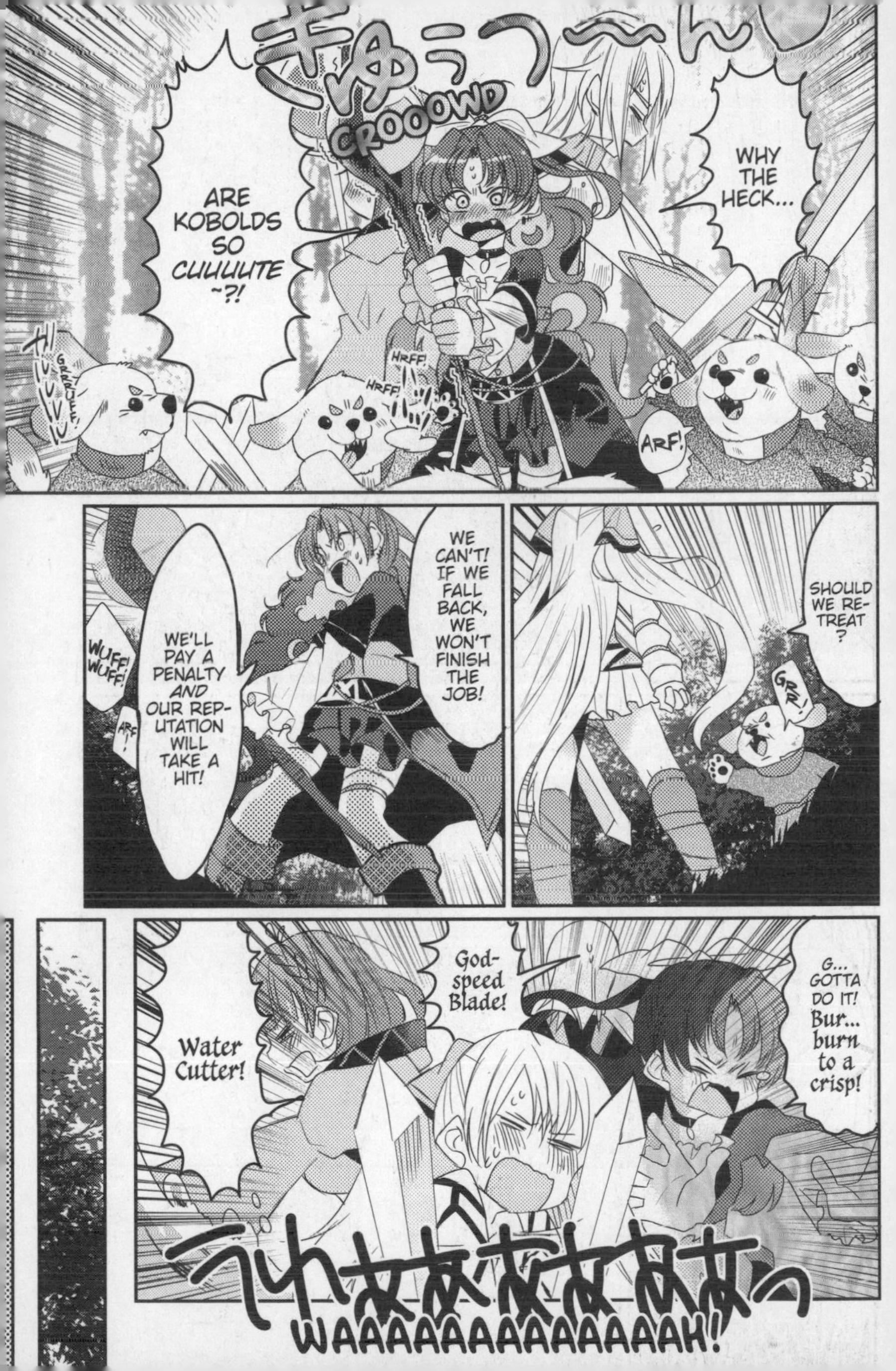
きゅうっ〜ん
CROOOWD
WHY THE HECK...
ARE KOBOLDS SO CUUUUTE ~?!
GRRRUFF
HRFF!
HRFF!
ARF!
SHOULD WE RE-TREAT?
GRR!
WE CAN'T! IF WE FALL BACK, WE WON'T FINISH THE JOB!
WE'LL PAY A PENALTY AND OUR REP-UTATION WILL TAKE A HIT!
WUFF! WUFF!
ARF!
G... GOTTA DO IT! Bur... burn to a crisp!
God-speed Blade!
Water Cutter!
うりゃああああああっ
WAAAAAAAAAAAAAAH!

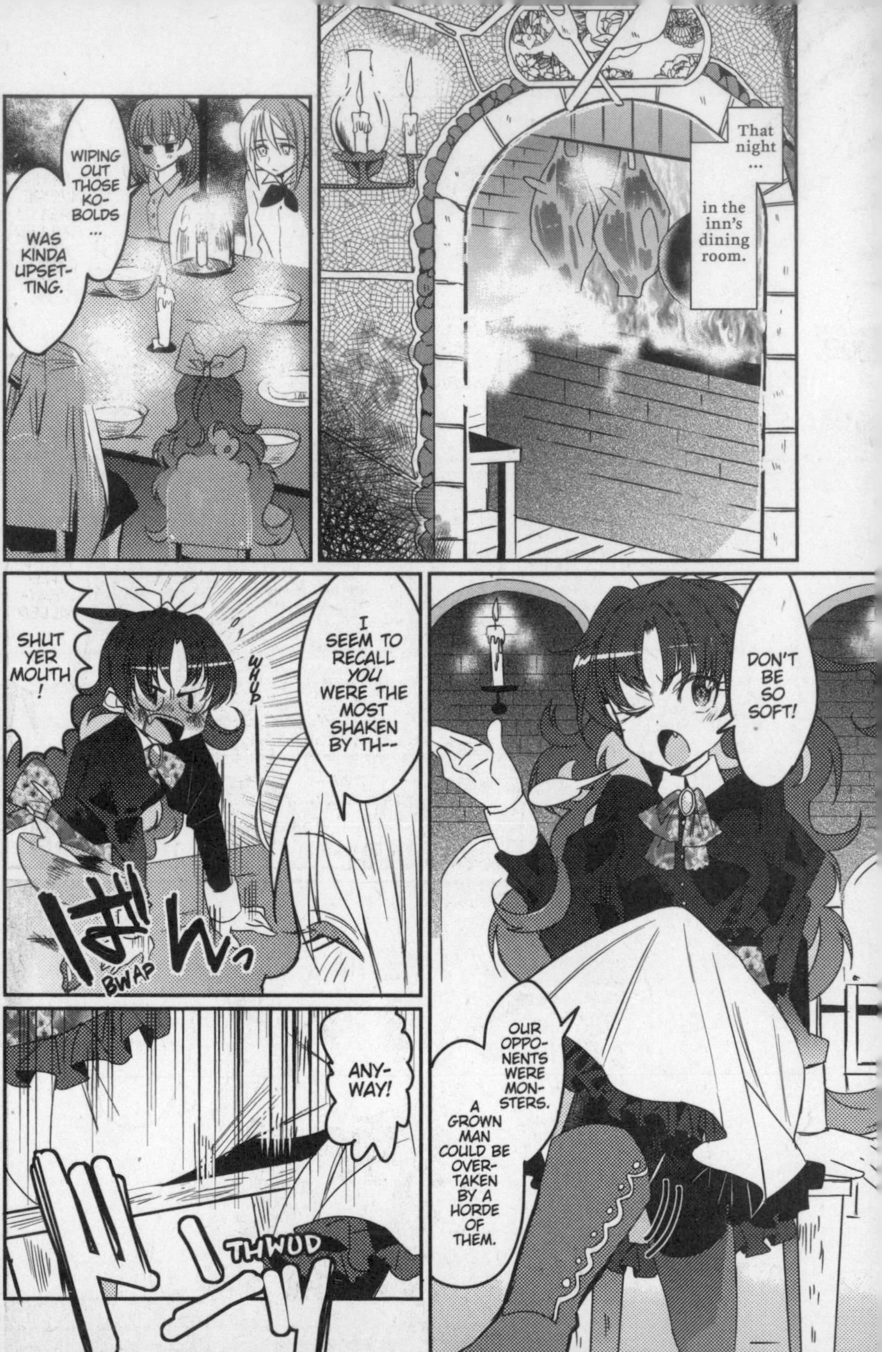
That night ...
in the inn's dining room.
WIPING OUT THOSE KO-BOLDS ...
WAS KINDA UPSET-TING.
DON'T BE SO SOFT!
OUR OPPO-NENTS WERE MON-STERS.
A GROWN MAN COULD BE OVER-TAKEN BY A HORDE OF THEM.
I SEEM TO RECALL YOU WERE THE MOST SHAKEN BY TH--
WHUP
SHUT YER MOUTH!
ばんっ
BWAP
ANY-WAY!
THWUD

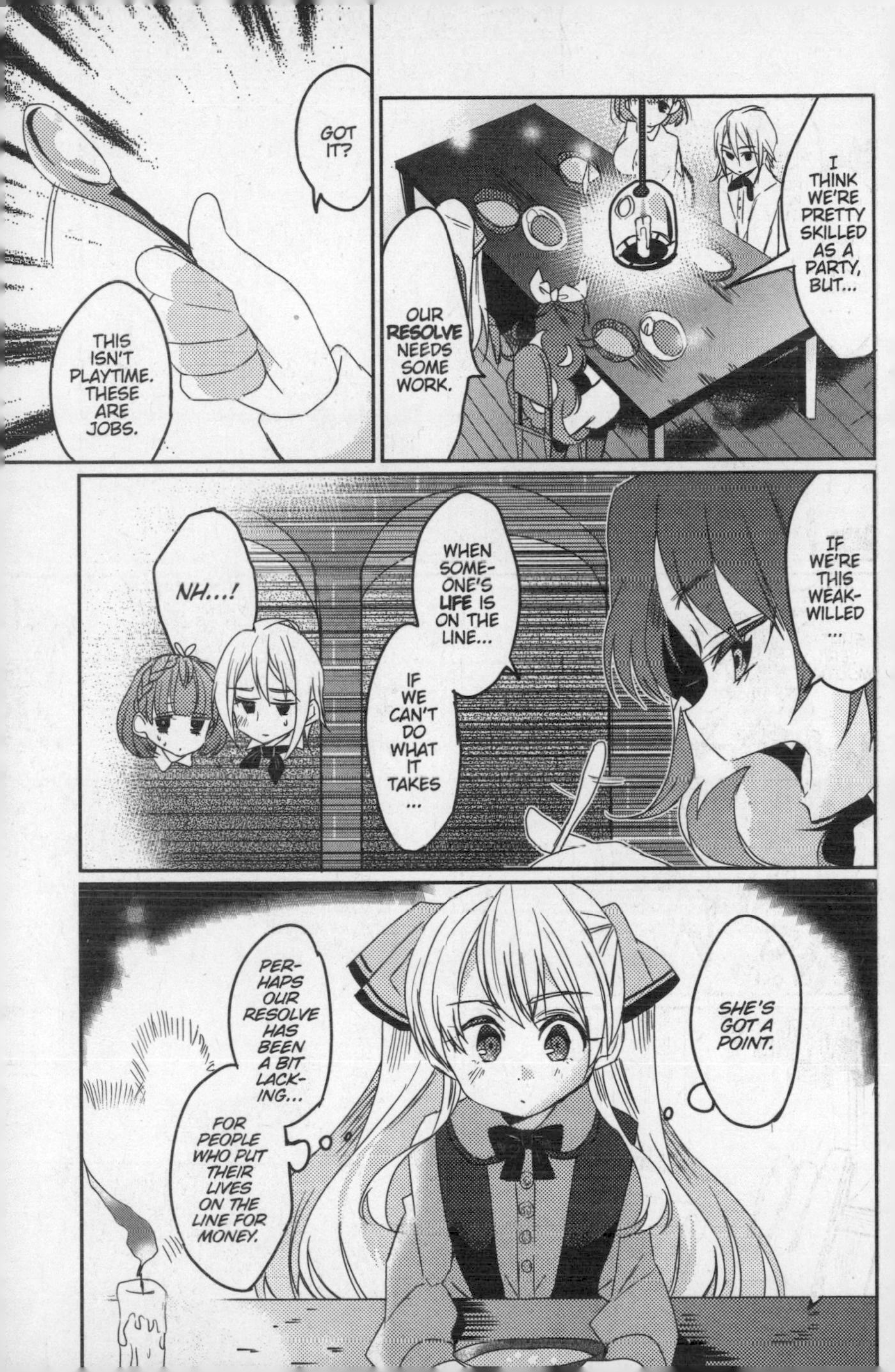
I THINK WE'RE PRETTY SKILLED AS A PARTY, BUT...
OUR RESOLVE NEEDS SOME WORK.
GOT IT?
THIS ISN'T PLAYTIME. THESE ARE JOBS.
IF WE'RE THIS WEAK-WILLED...
WHEN SOMEONE'S LIFE IS ON THE LINE...
IF WE CAN'T DO WHAT IT TAKES...
NH...!
SHE'S GOT A POINT.
PERHAPS OUR RESOLVE HAS BEEN A BIT LACKING...
FOR PEOPLE WHO PUT THEIR LIVES ON THE LINE FOR MONEY.

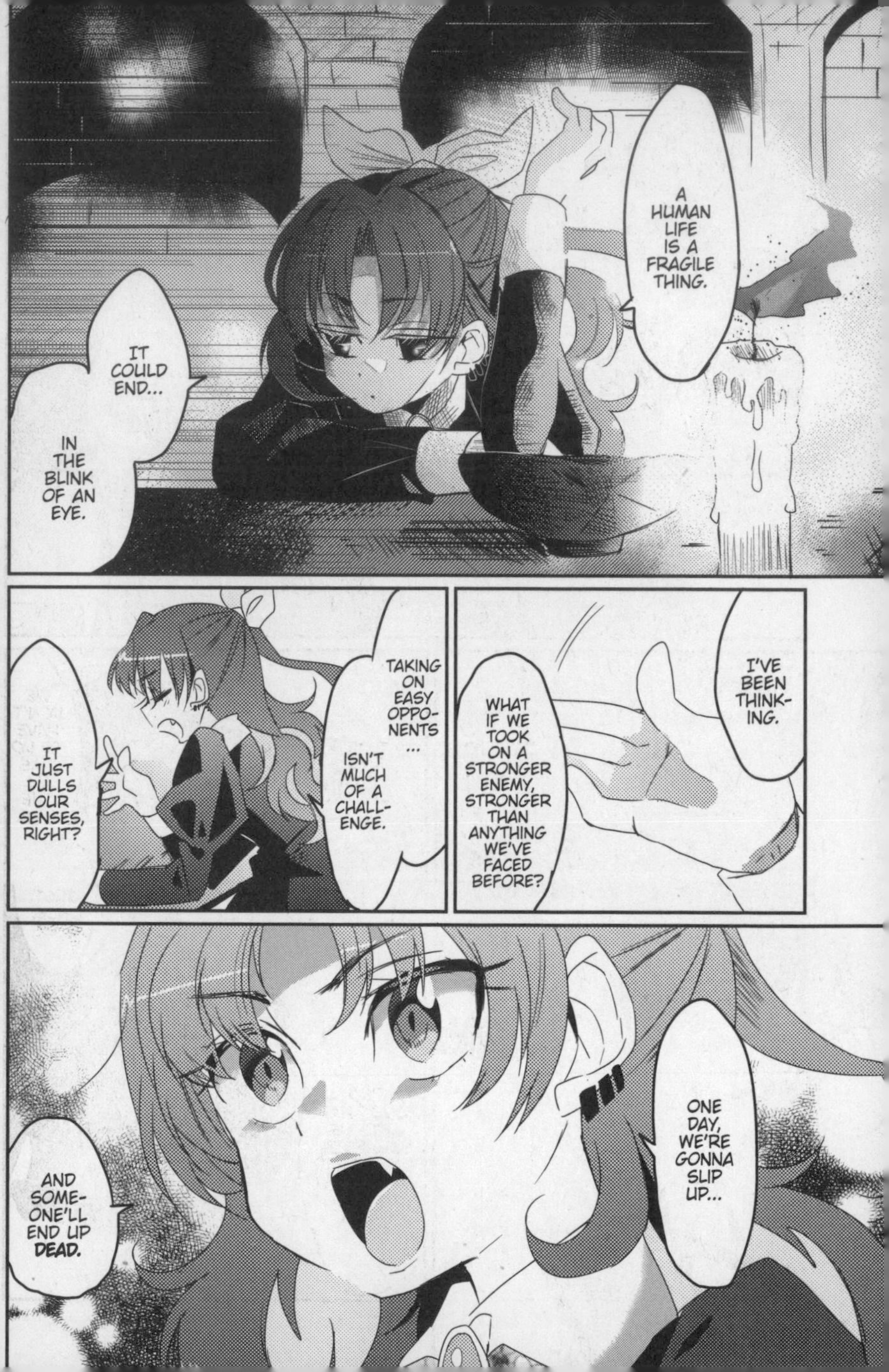
A HUMAN LIFE IS A FRAGILE THING.
IT COULD END...
IN THE BLINK OF AN EYE.
I'VE BEEN THINK-ING.
WHAT IF WE TOOK ON A STRONGER ENEMY, STRONGER THAN ANYTHING WE'VE FACED BEFORE?
TAKING ON EASY OPPO-NENTS ...
ISN'T MUCH OF A CHALL-ENGE.
IT JUST DULLS OUR SENSES, RIGHT?
ONE DAY, WE'RE GONNA SLIP UP...
AND SOME-ONE'LL END UP **DEAD.**

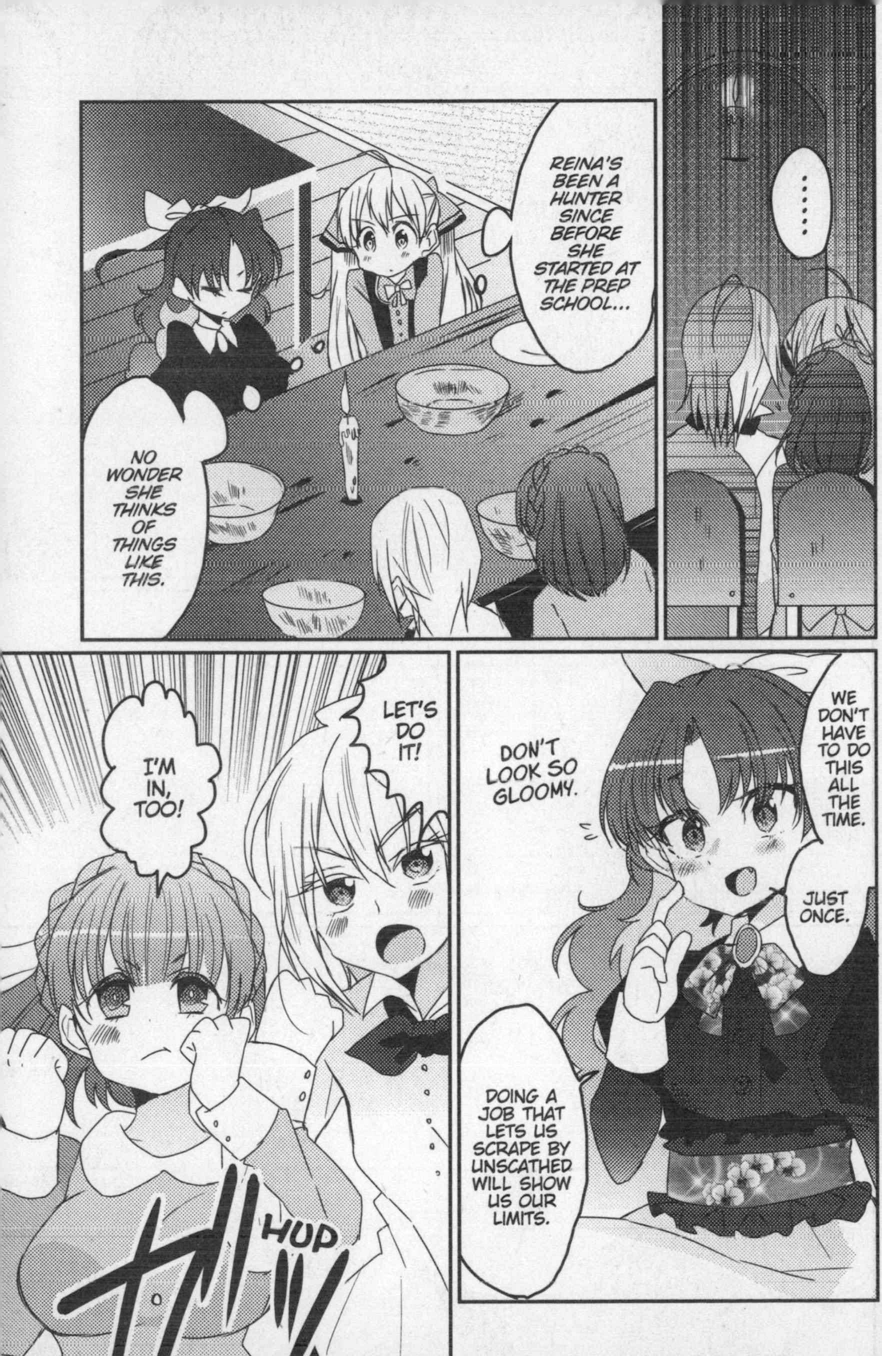
......
REINA'S BEEN A HUNTER SINCE BEFORE SHE STARTED AT THE PREP SCHOOL...
NO WONDER SHE THINKS OF THINGS LIKE THIS.
WE DON'T HAVE TO DO THIS ALL THE TIME.
JUST ONCE.
DON'T LOOK SO GLOOMY.
DOING A JOB THAT LETS US SCRAPE BY UNSCATHED WILL SHOW US OUR LIMITS.
LET'S DO IT!
I'M IN, TOO!
HUP

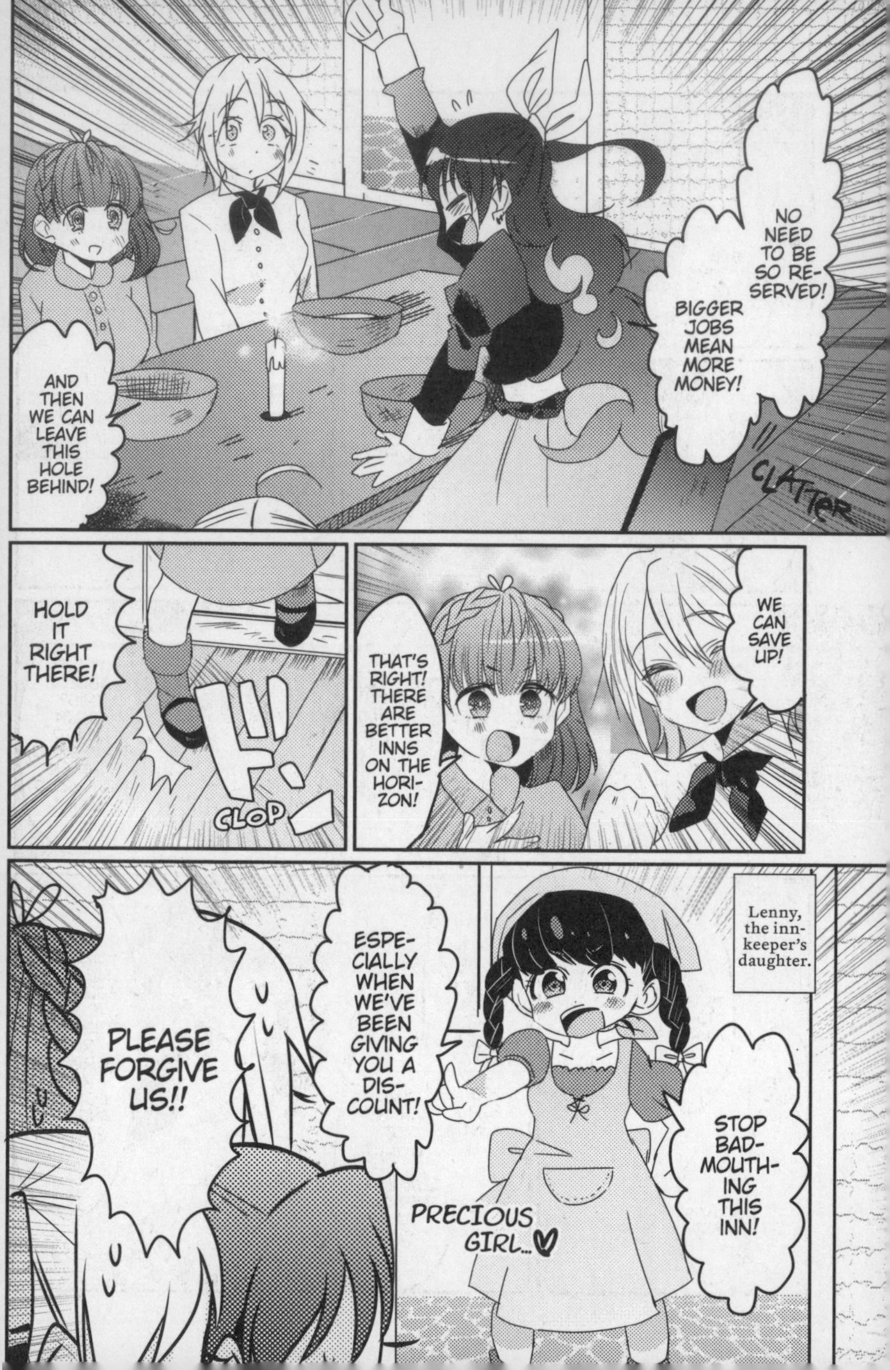
NO NEED TO BE SO RE-SERVED!
BIGGER JOBS MEAN MORE MONEY!
CLATTER
AND THEN WE CAN LEAVE THIS HOLE BEHIND!
WE CAN SAVE UP!
THAT'S RIGHT! THERE ARE BETTER INNS ON THE HORI-ZON!
HOLD IT RIGHT THERE!
CLOP
Lenny, the innkeeper's daughter.
STOP BAD-MOUTHING THIS INN!
ESPE-CIALLY WHEN WE'VE BEEN GIVING YOU A DIS-COUNT!
PRECIOUS GIRL...♥
PLEASE FORGIVE US!!

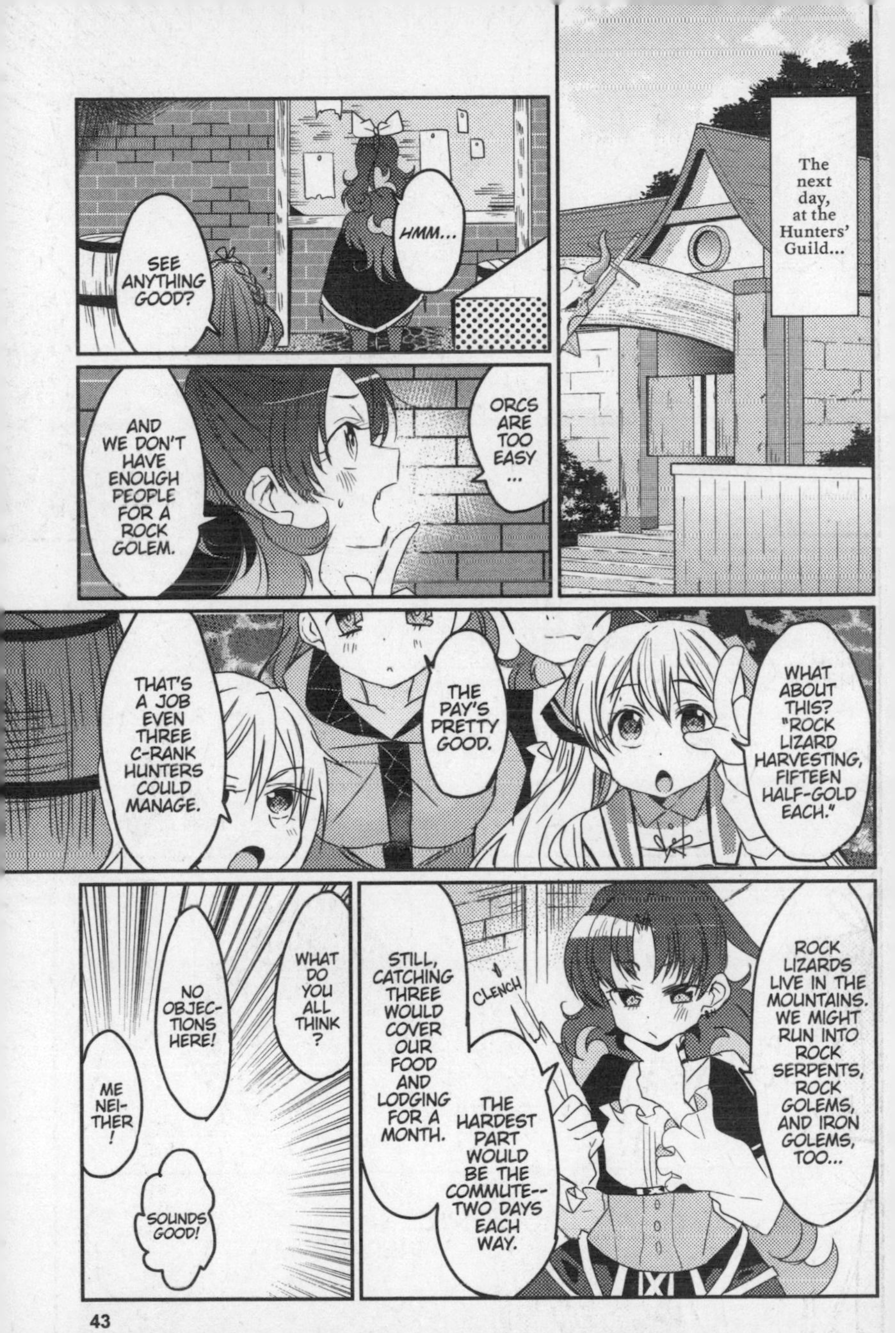
The next day, at the Hunters' Guild...
HMM...
SEE ANYTHING GOOD?
ORCS ARE TOO EASY...
AND WE DON'T HAVE ENOUGH PEOPLE FOR A ROCK GOLEM.
WHAT ABOUT THIS? "ROCK LIZARD HARVESTING, FIFTEEN HALF-GOLD EACH."
THE PAY'S PRETTY GOOD.
THAT'S A JOB EVEN THREE C-RANK HUNTERS COULD MANAGE.
ROCK LIZARDS LIVE IN THE MOUNTAINS. WE MIGHT RUN INTO ROCK SERPENTS, ROCK GOLEMS, AND IRON GOLEMS, TOO...
CLENCH
STILL, CATCHING THREE WOULD COVER OUR FOOD AND LODGING FOR A MONTH.
THE HARDEST PART WOULD BE THE COMMUTE--TWO DAYS EACH WAY.
WHAT DO YOU ALL THINK?
NO OBJECTIONS HERE!
ME NEITHER!
SOUNDS GOOD!

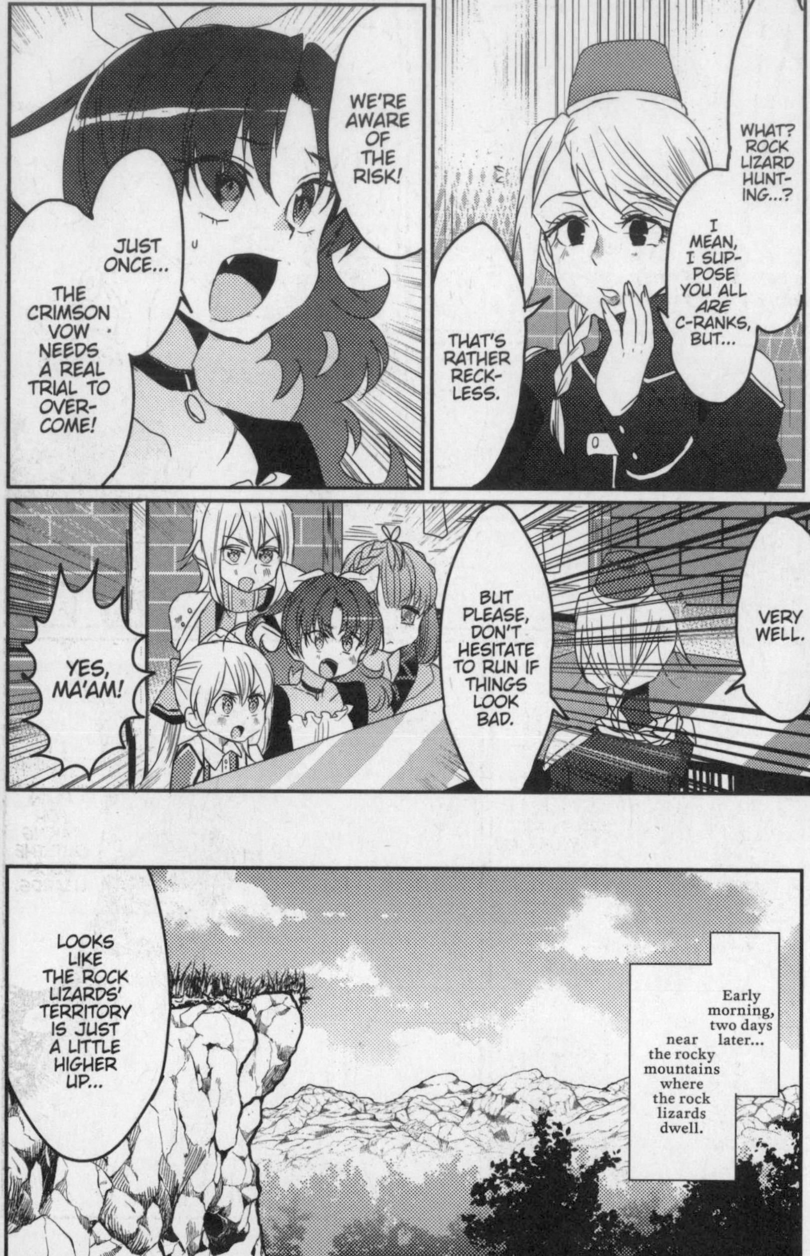
WHAT? ROCK LIZARD HUNTING...?
I MEAN, I SUPPOSE YOU ALL ARE C-RANKS, BUT...
THAT'S RATHER RECKLESS.
WE'RE AWARE OF THE RISK!
JUST ONCE... THE CRIMSON VOW NEEDS A REAL TRIAL TO OVERCOME!
VERY WELL.
BUT PLEASE, DON'T HESITATE TO RUN IF THINGS LOOK BAD.
YES, MA'AM!
Early morning, two days later... near the rocky mountains where the rock lizards dwell.
LOOKS LIKE THE ROCK LIZARDS' TERRITORY IS JUST A LITTLE HIGHER UP...

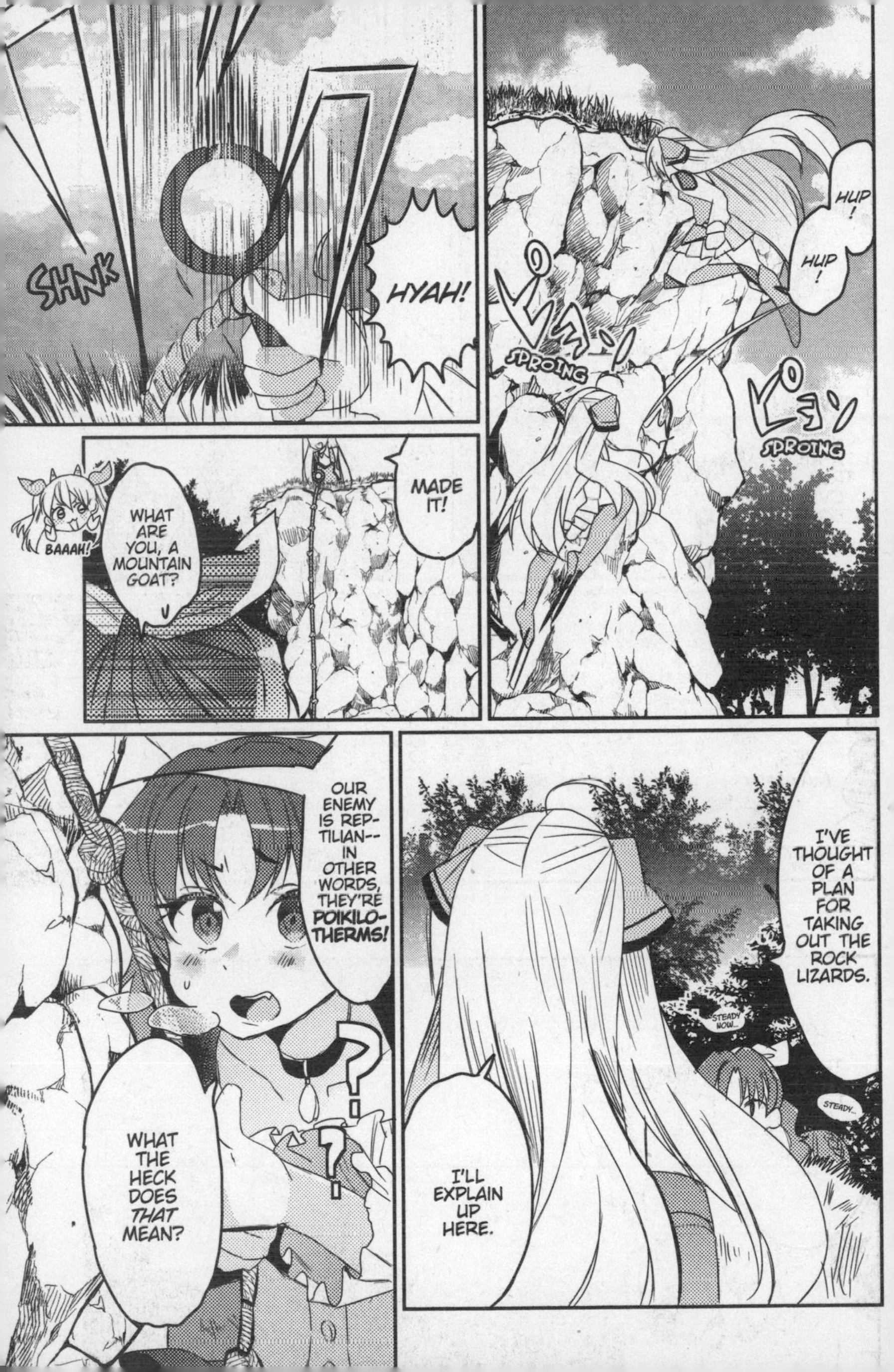

HUP!
HUP!
SPROING
SPROING
HYAH!
SHNK
MADE IT!
WHAT ARE YOU, A MOUNTAIN GOAT?
BAAAH!
I'VE THOUGHT OF A PLAN FOR TAKING OUT THE ROCK LIZARDS.
STEADY NOW...
STEADY...
I'LL EXPLAIN UP HERE.
OUR ENEMY IS REPTILIAN--IN OTHER WORDS, THEY'RE **POIKILOTHERMS!**
WHAT THE HECK DOES *THAT* MEAN?

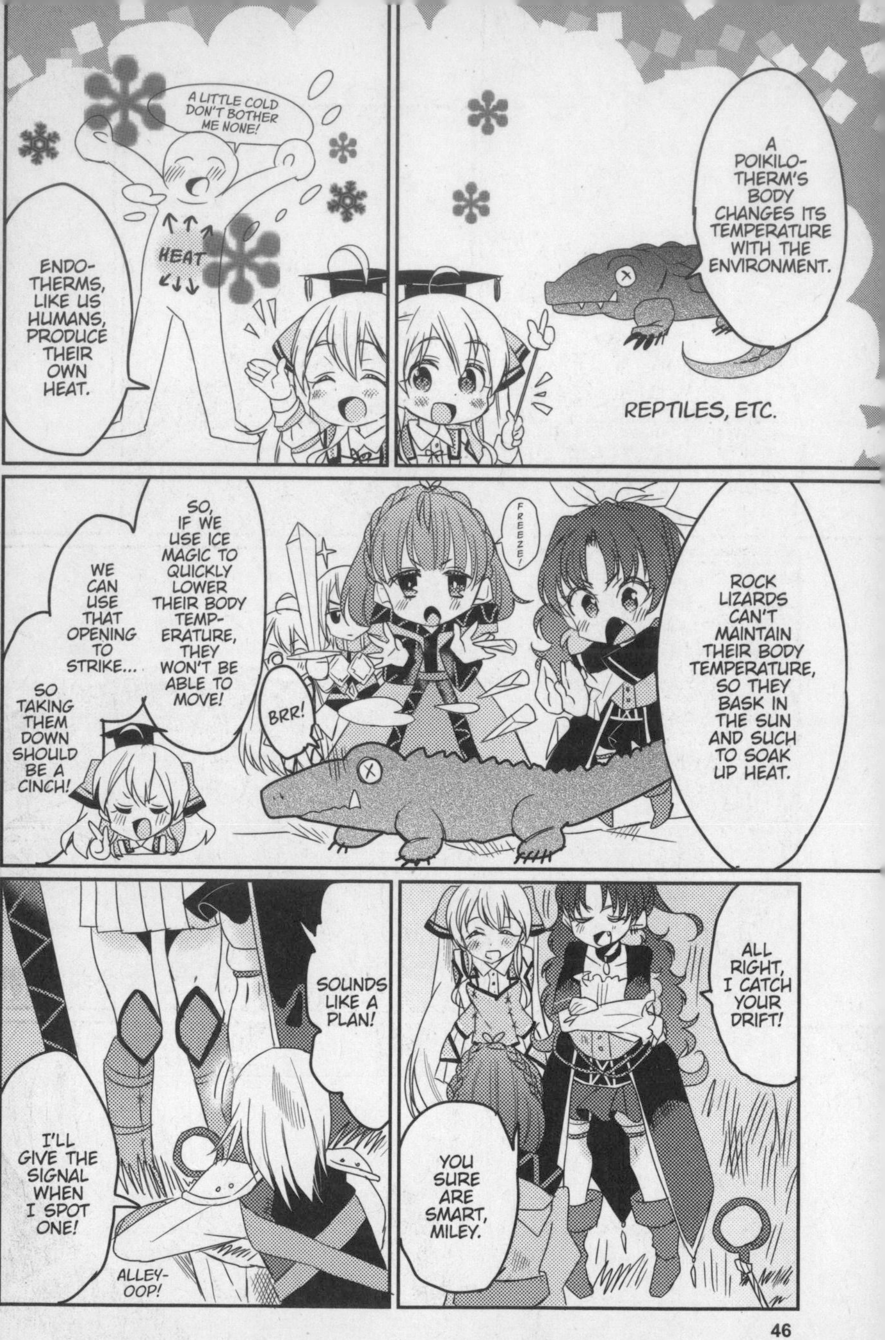
A POIKILO-THERM'S BODY CHANGES ITS TEMPERATURE WITH THE ENVIRONMENT.
REPTILES, ETC.
A LITTLE COLD DON'T BOTHER ME NONE!
HEAT
ENDO-THERMS, LIKE US HUMANS, PRODUCE THEIR OWN HEAT.
ROCK LIZARDS CAN'T MAINTAIN THEIR BODY TEMPERATURE, SO THEY BASK IN THE SUN AND SUCH TO SOAK UP HEAT.
FREEZE!
SO, IF WE USE ICE MAGIC TO QUICKLY LOWER THEIR BODY TEMP-ERATURE, THEY WON'T BE ABLE TO MOVE!
BRR!
WE CAN USE THAT OPENING TO STRIKE...
SO TAKING THEM DOWN SHOULD BE A CINCH!
ALL RIGHT, I CATCH YOUR DRIFT!
YOU SURE ARE SMART, MILEY.
SOUNDS LIKE A PLAN!
I'LL GIVE THE SIGNAL WHEN I SPOT ONE!
ALLEY-OOP!

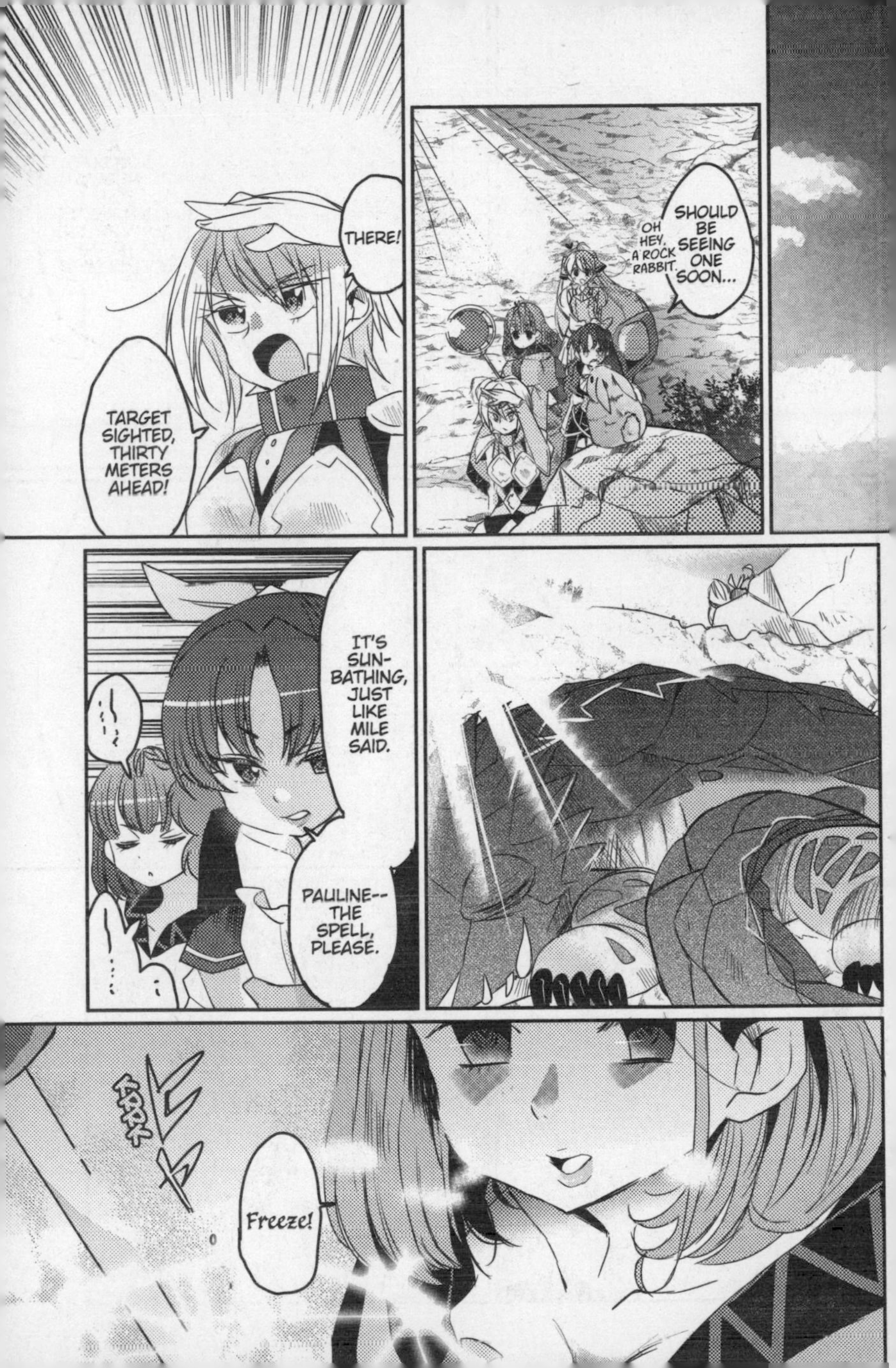
SHOULD BE SEEING ONE SOON...
OH HEY, A ROCK RABBIT.
THERE!
TARGET SIGHTED, THIRTY METERS AHEAD!
IT'S SUN-BATHING, JUST LIKE MILE SAID.
PAULINE--THE SPELL, PLEASE.
KRRK
Freeze!

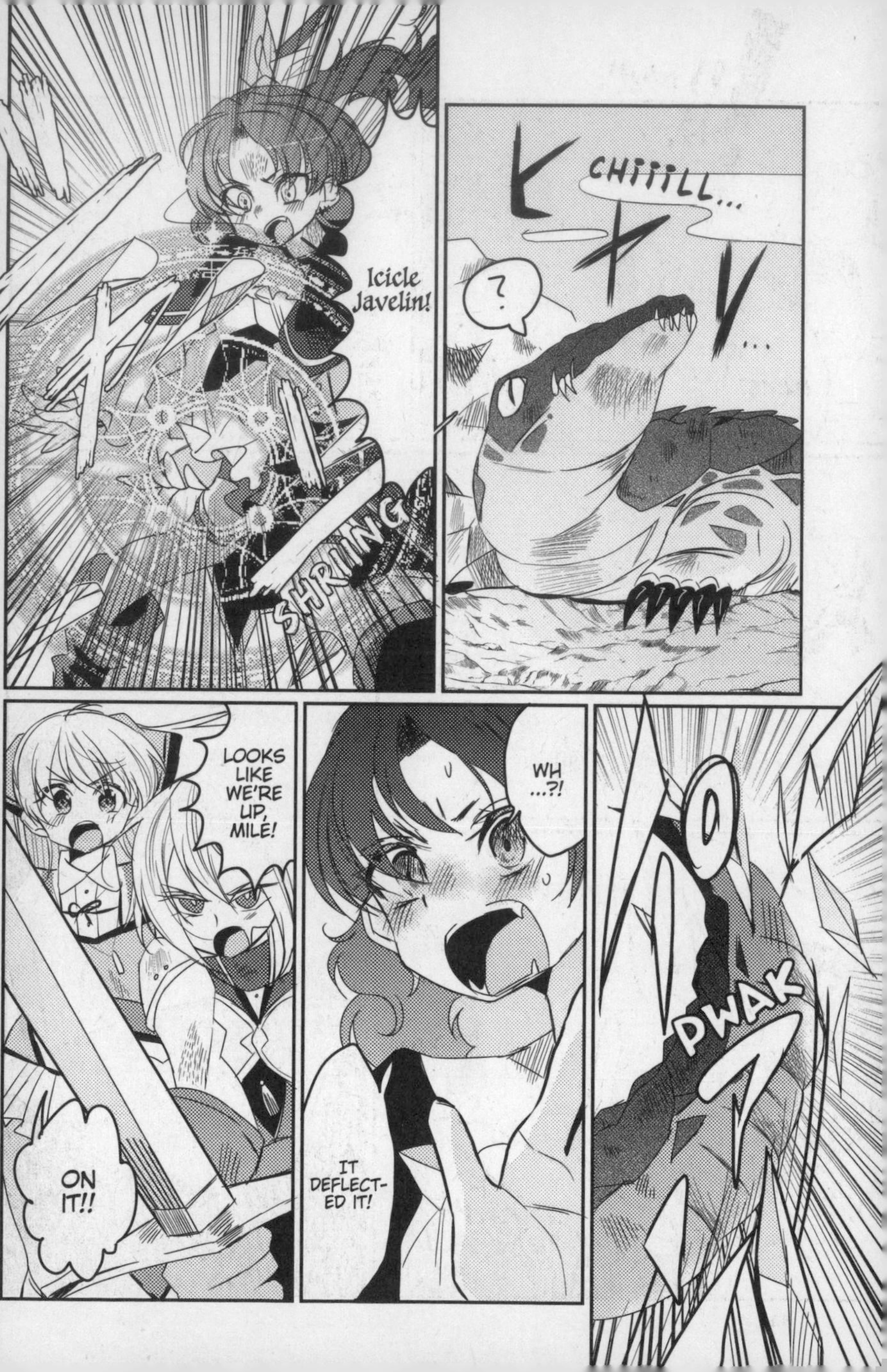
CHIIILL...
?
Icicle Javelin!
SHRING
PWAK
WH ...?!
IT DEFLECT-ED IT!
LOOKS LIKE WE'RE UP, MILE!
ON IT!!

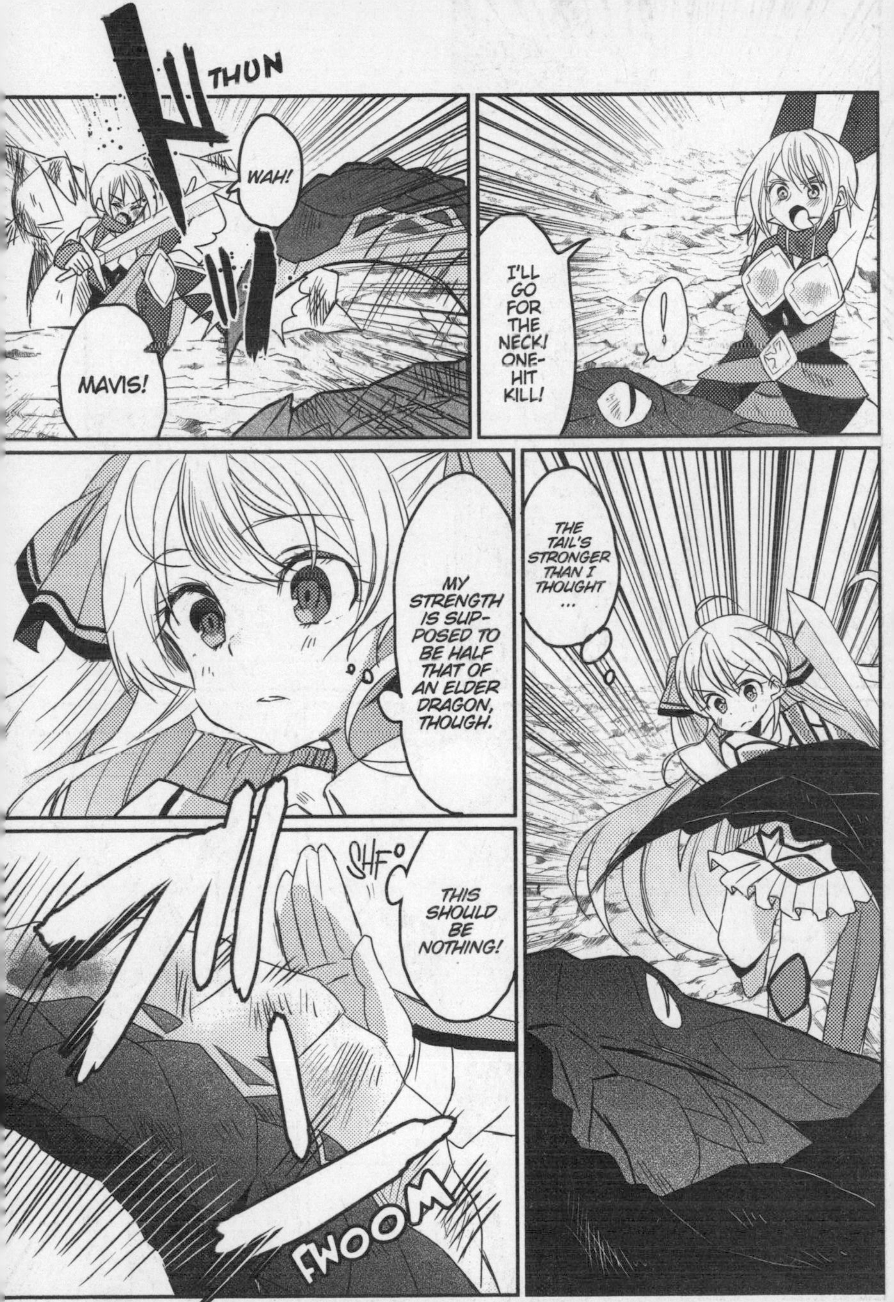

I'LL GO FOR THE NECK! ONE-HIT KILL!
!
THUN
WAH!
MAVIS!
THE TAIL'S STRONGER THAN I THOUGHT...
MY STRENGTH IS SUP-POSED TO BE HALF THAT OF AN ELDER DRAGON, THOUGH.
SHF
THIS SHOULD BE NOTHING!
FWOOM

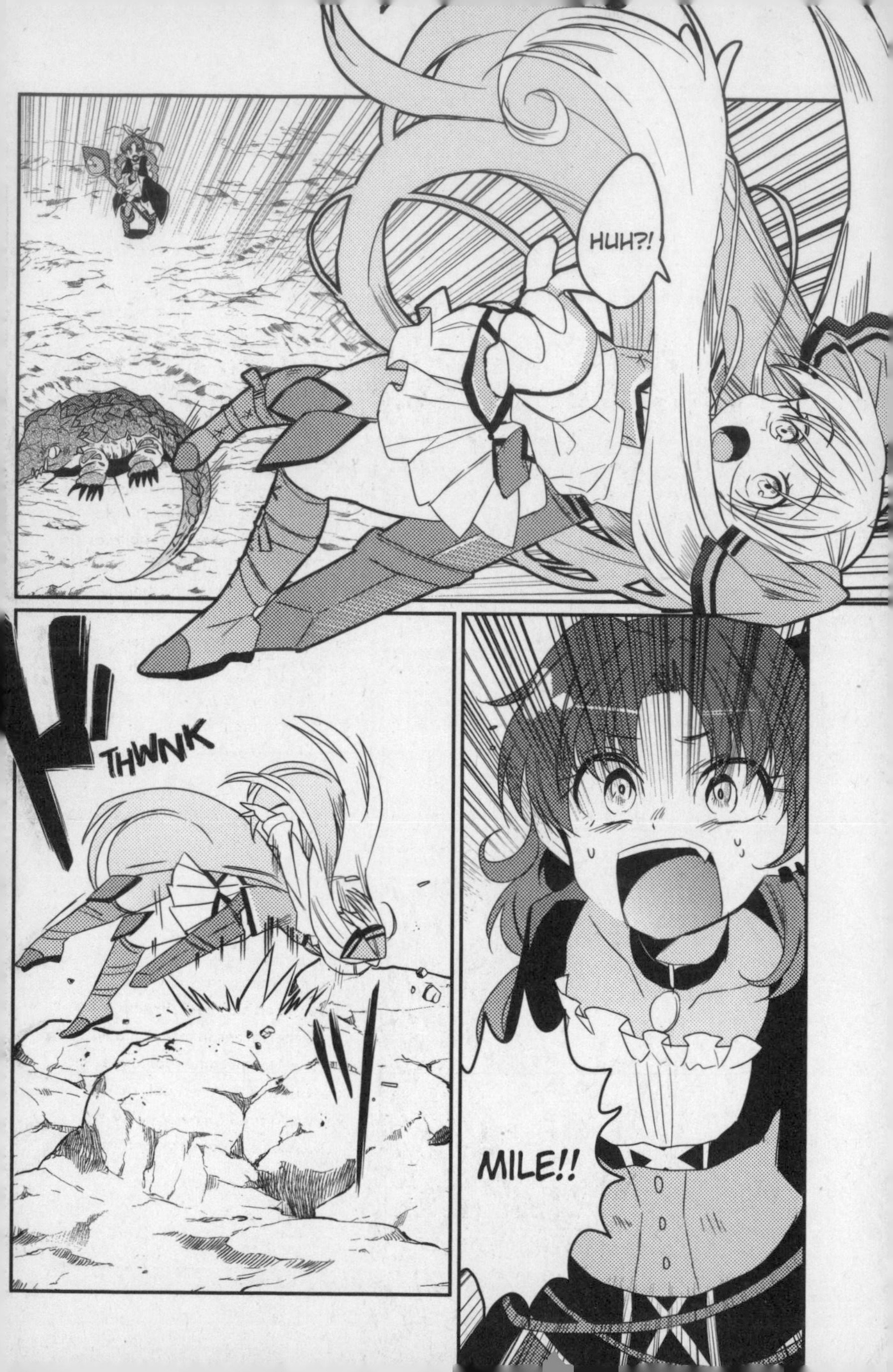
HUH?!
MILE!!
THWNK

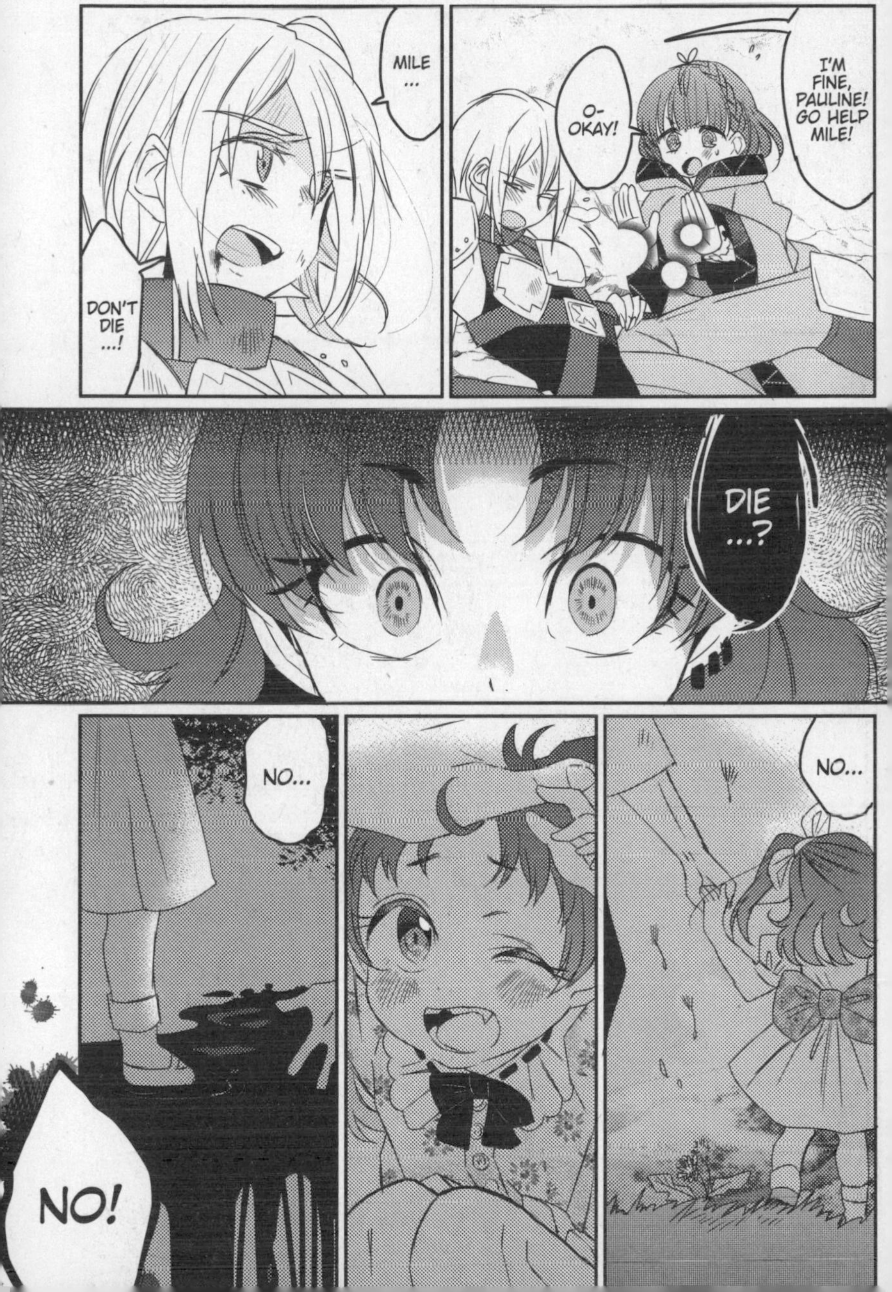
I'M FINE, PAULINE! GO HELP MILE!
O-OKAY!
MILE ...
DON'T DIE ...!
DIE ...?
NO...
NO...
NO!

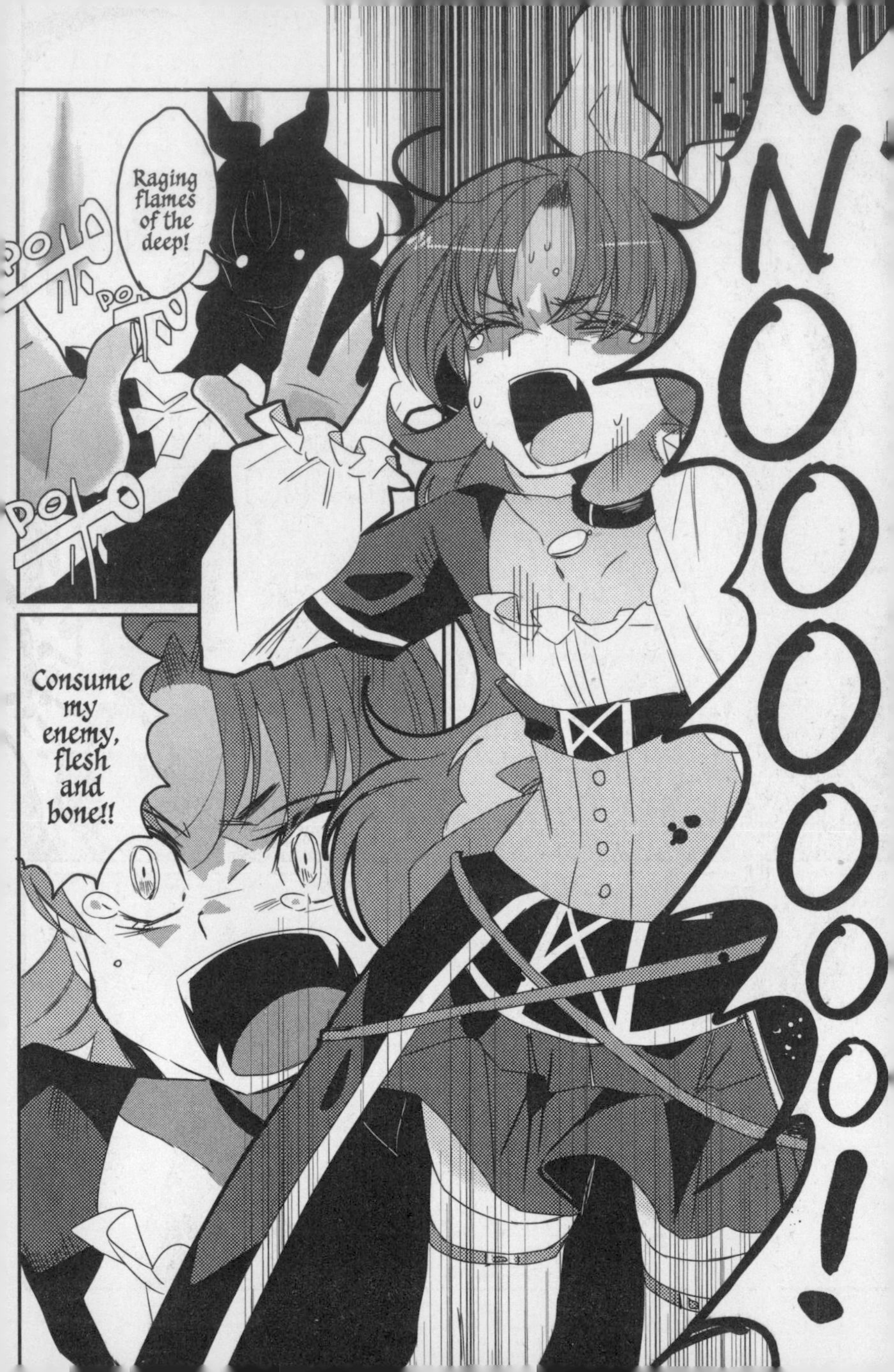
NNOOOOOO!
Raging flames of the deep!
Consume my enemy, flesh and bone!!

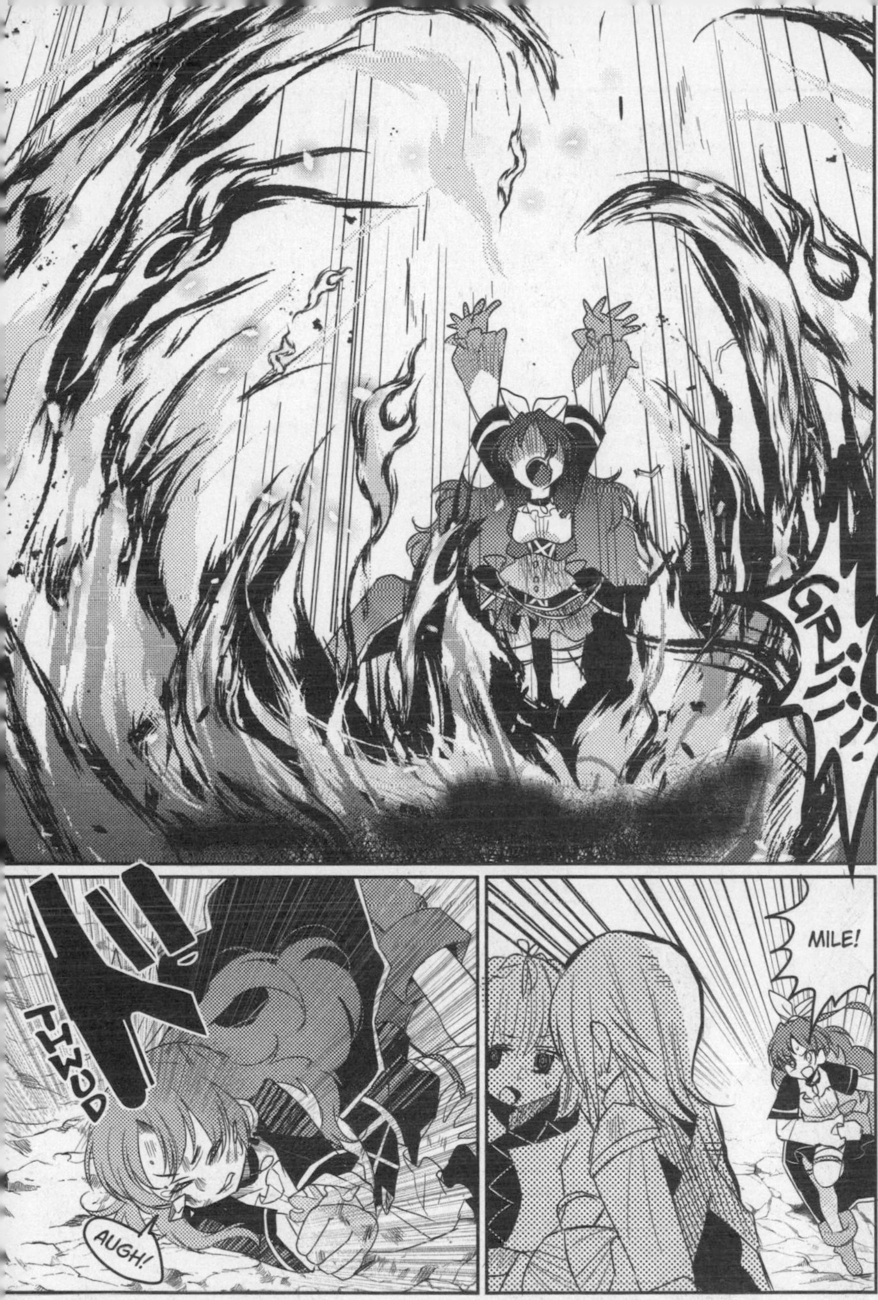
GRIIII!!
MILE!
THWUD
AUGH!

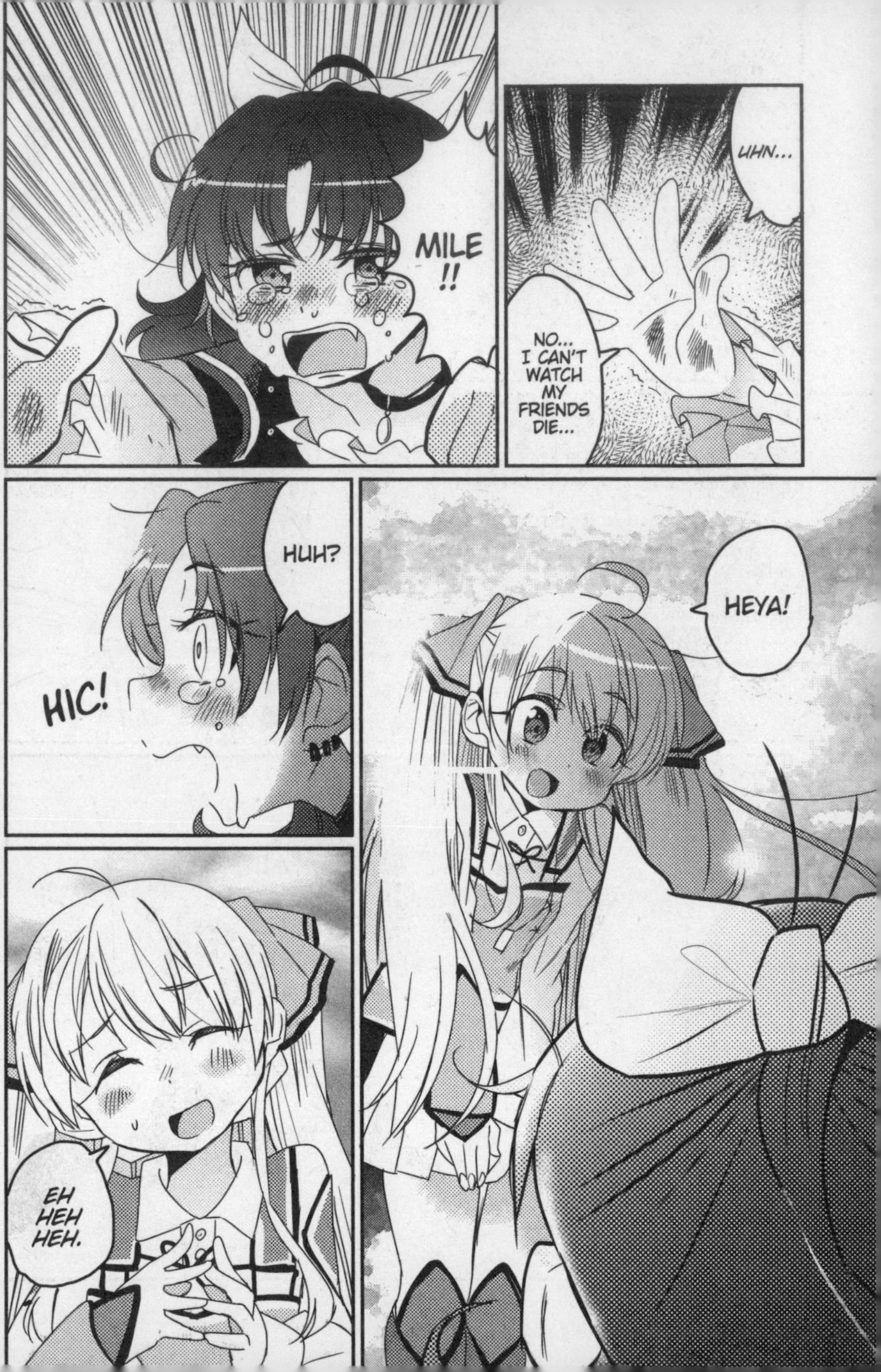
UHN...
NO... I CAN'T WATCH MY FRIENDS DIE...
MILE !!
HEYA!
HUH?
HIC!
EH HEH HEH.

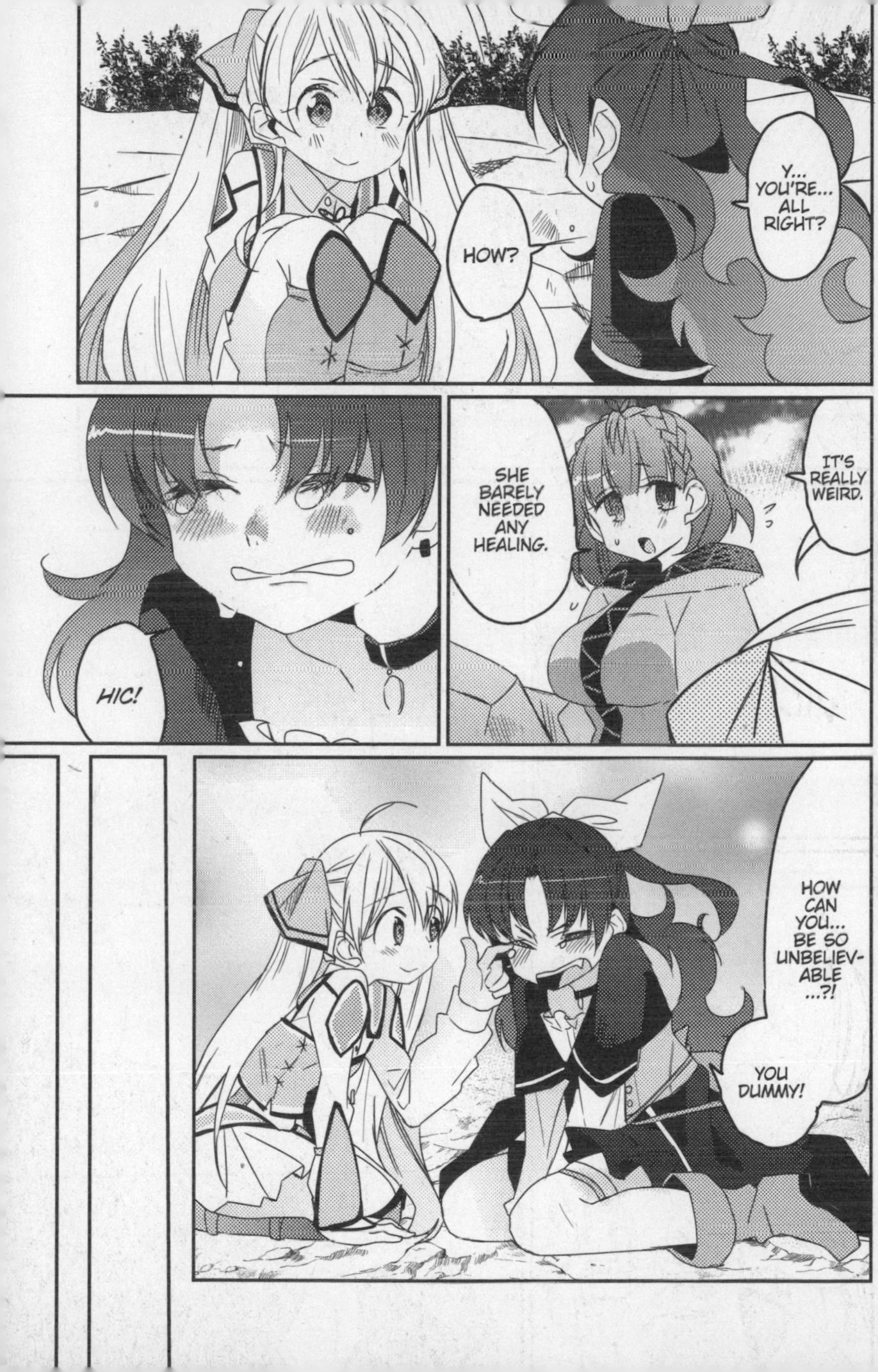
Y... YOU'RE... ALL RIGHT?
HOW?
IT'S REALLY WEIRD.
SHE BARELY NEEDED ANY HEALING.
HIC!
HOW CAN YOU... BE SO UNBELIEV-ABLE ...?!
YOU DUMMY!

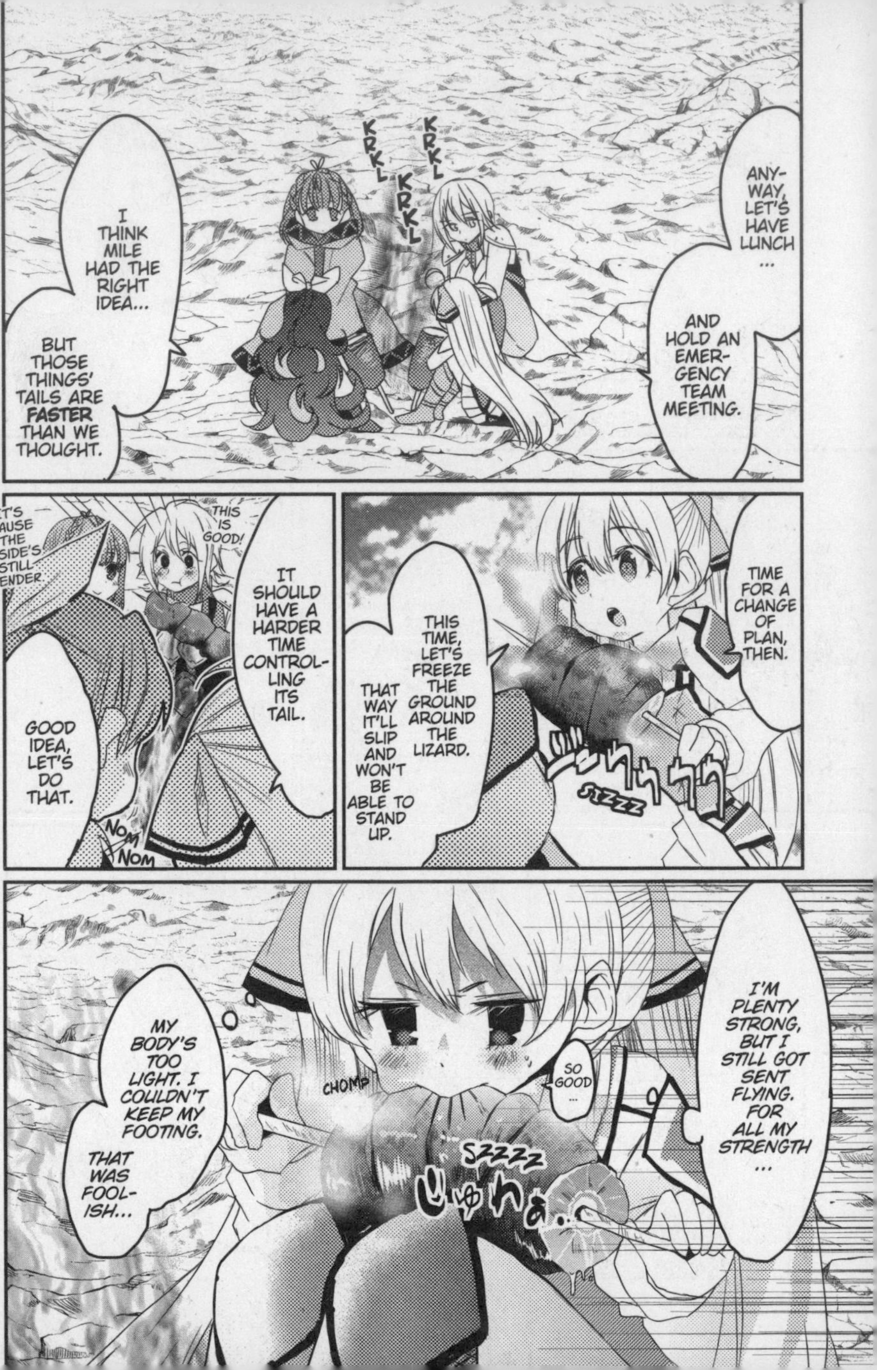
ANY-WAY, LET'S HAVE LUNCH...
AND HOLD AN EMERGENCY TEAM MEETING.
KRKL KRKL KRKL
I THINK MILE HAD THE RIGHT IDEA...
BUT THOSE THINGS' TAILS ARE **FASTER** THAN WE THOUGHT.
TIME FOR A CHANGE OF PLAN, THEN.
THIS TIME, LET'S FREEZE THE GROUND AROUND THE LIZARD.
THAT WAY IT'LL SLIP AND WON'T BE ABLE TO STAND UP.
SIZZZ
IT SHOULD HAVE A HARDER TIME CONTROLLING ITS TAIL.
THIS IS GOOD!
IT'S 'CAUSE THE INSIDE'S STILL TENDER.
GOOD IDEA, LET'S DO THAT.
NOM NOM
I'M PLENTY STRONG, BUT I STILL GOT SENT FLYING. FOR ALL MY STRENGTH...
SO GOOD...
MY BODY'S TOO LIGHT. I COULDN'T KEEP MY FOOTING.
THAT WAS FOOLISH...
CHOMP
SZZZZ

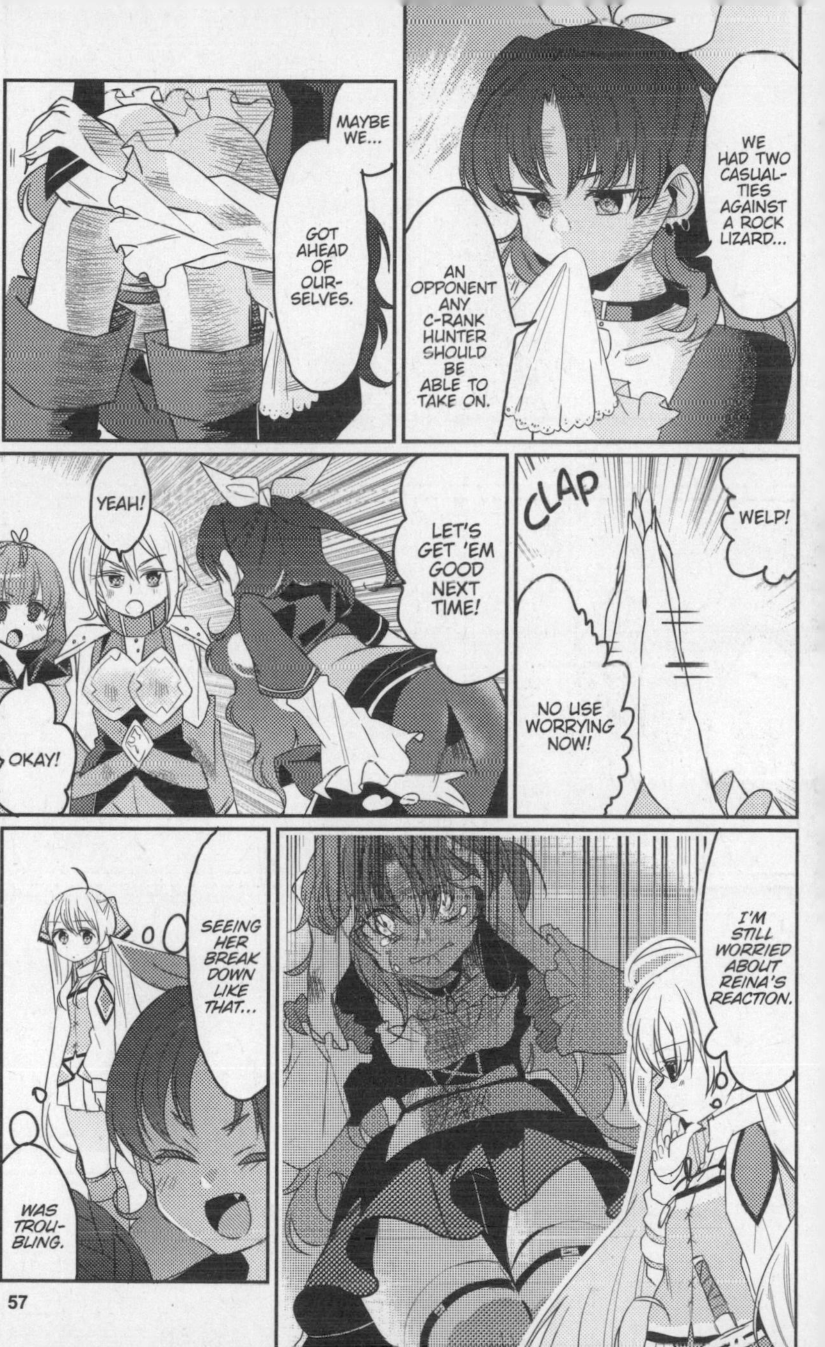

WE HAD TWO CASUALTIES AGAINST A ROCK LIZARD...
AN OPPONENT ANY C-RANK HUNTER SHOULD BE ABLE TO TAKE ON.
MAYBE WE...
GOT AHEAD OF OURSELVES.
WELP!
CLAP
NO USE WORRYING NOW!
LET'S GET 'EM GOOD NEXT TIME!
YEAH!
OKAY!
I'M STILL WORRIED ABOUT REINA'S REACTION.
SEEING HER BREAK DOWN LIKE THAT...
WAS TROUBLING.

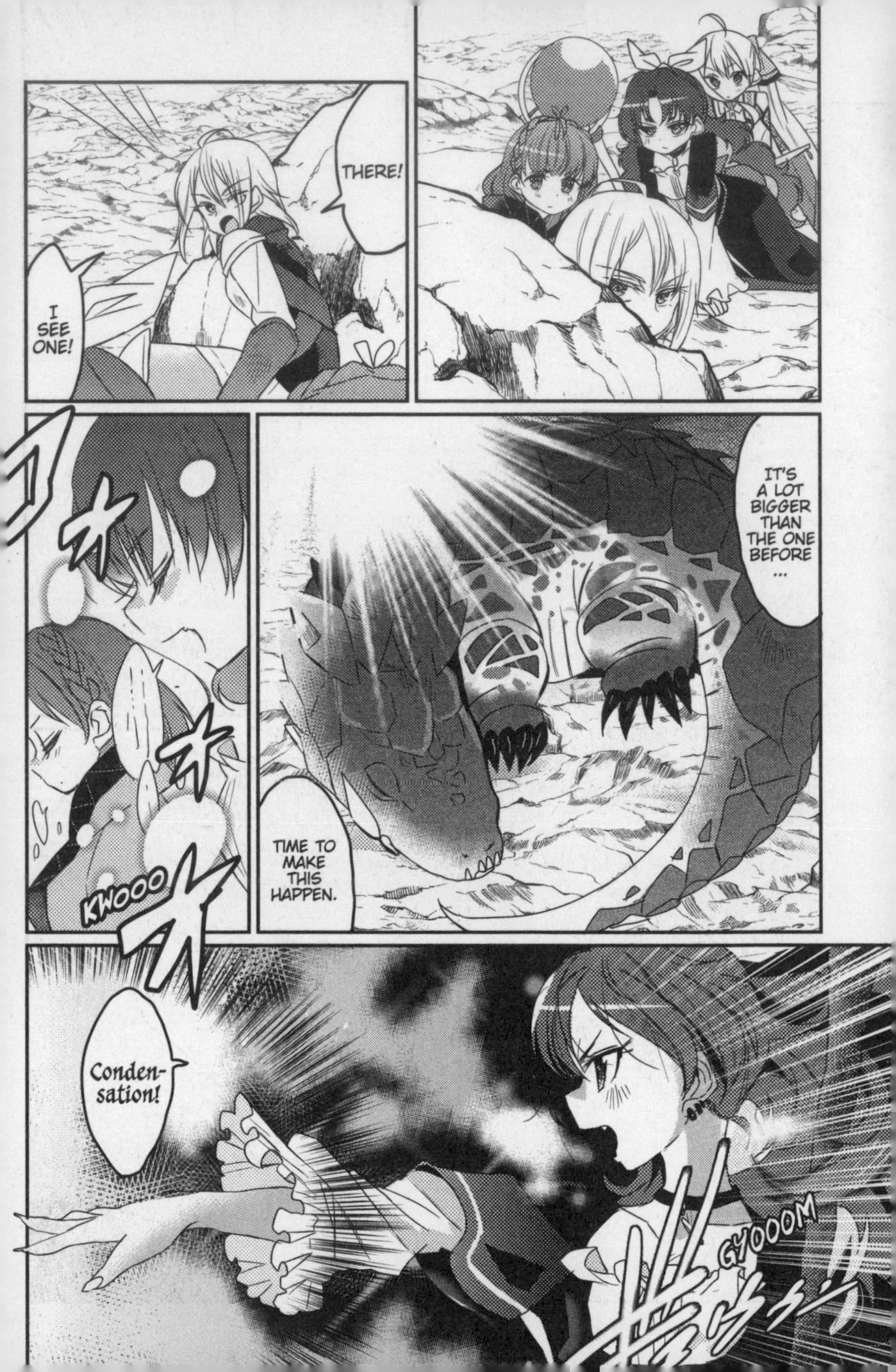
THERE!
I SEE ONE!
IT'S A LOT BIGGER THAN THE ONE BEFORE ...
TIME TO MAKE THIS HAPPEN.
KWOOO
Conden-sation!
GYOOOM

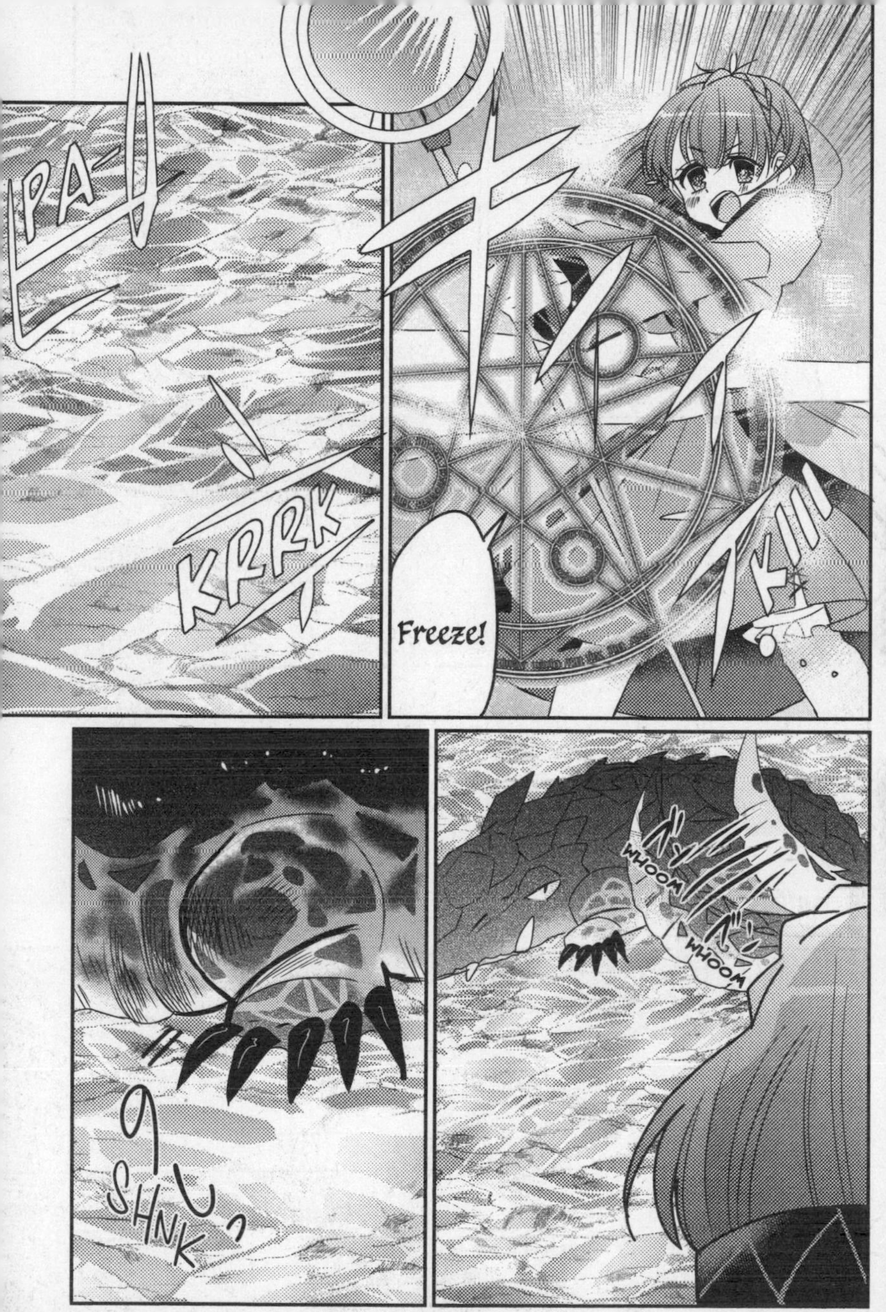
Freeze!
KIII
PA-
KRRK
WHOOM
WHOOM
SHNK

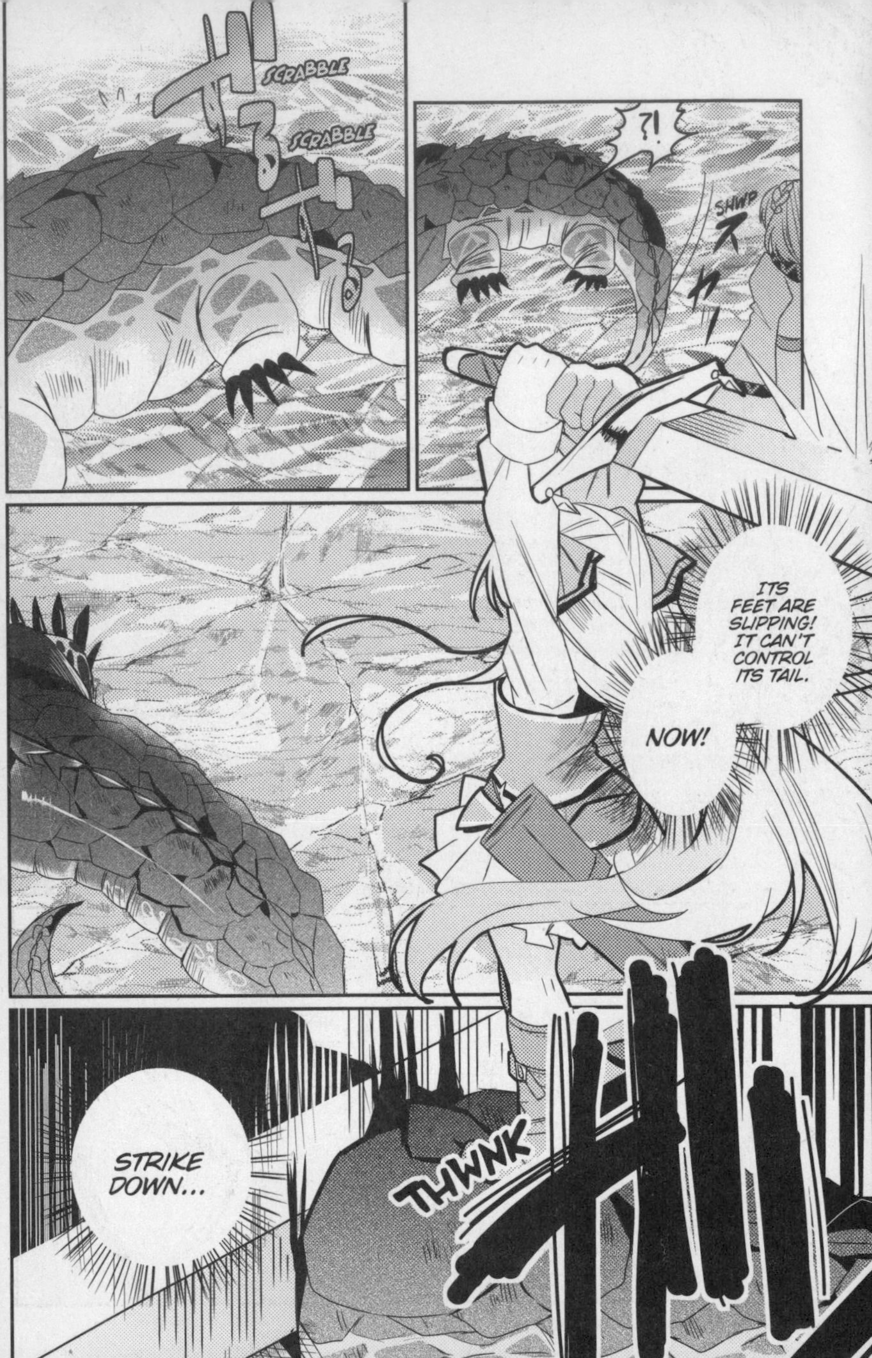
?!
SHWP
SCRABBLE
SCRABBLE
ITS FEET ARE SLIPPING! IT CAN'T CONTROL ITS TAIL.
NOW!
STRIKE DOWN...
THWNK

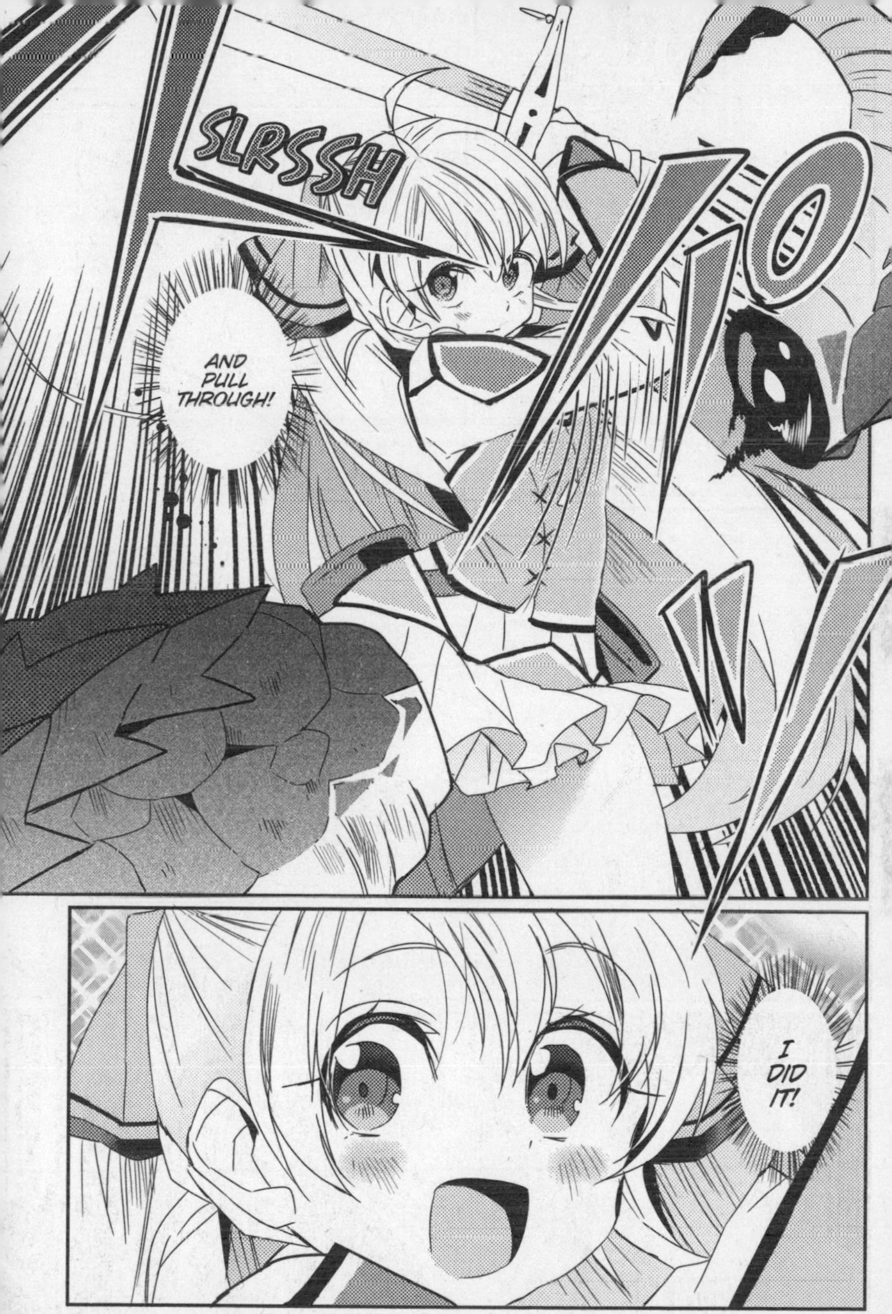
SLRSSH
AND PULL THROUGH!
I DID IT!

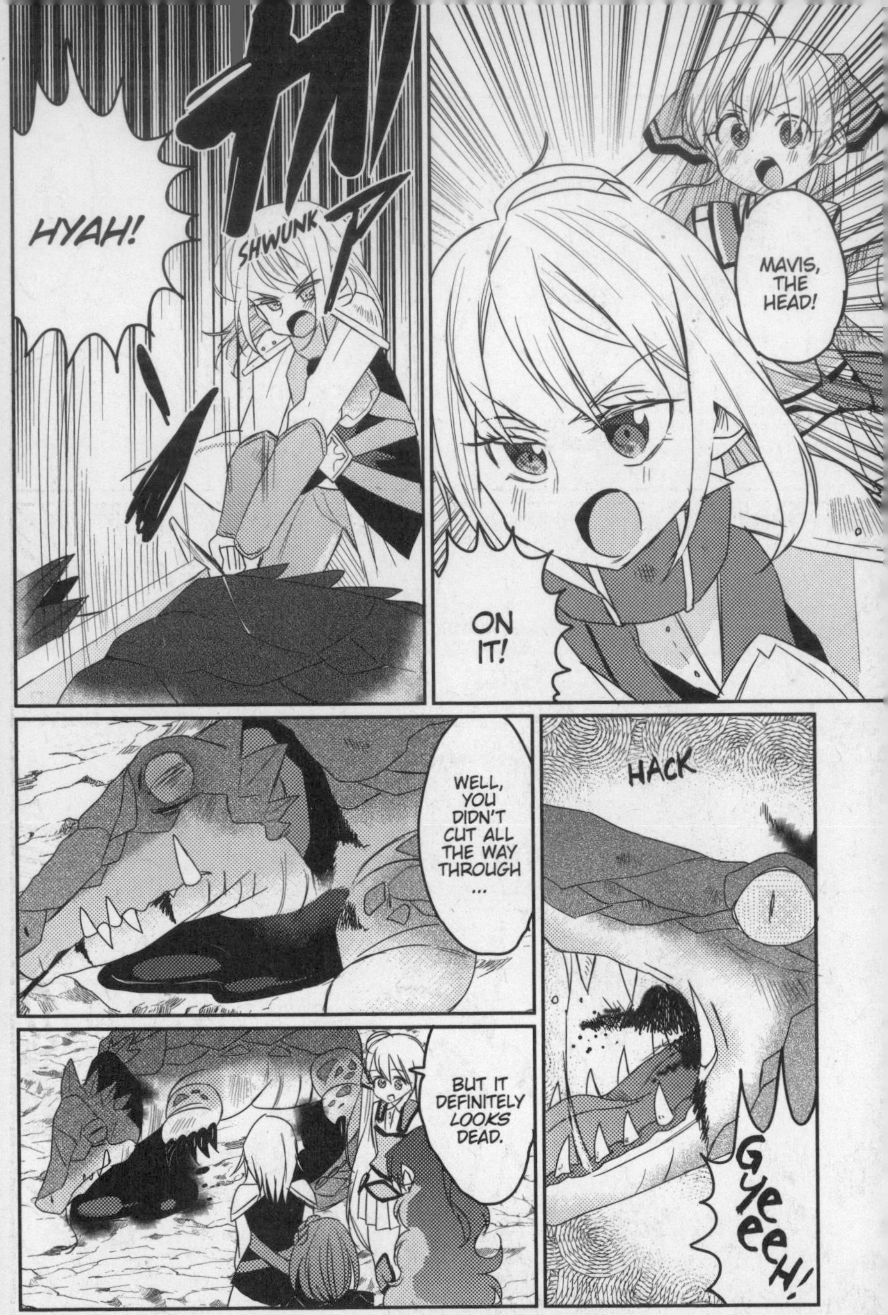
MAVIS, THE HEAD!
ON IT!
SHWUNK
HYAH!
HACK
GYEEEH!
WELL, YOU DIDN'T CUT ALL THE WAY THROUGH ...
BUT IT DEFINITELY LOOKS DEAD.

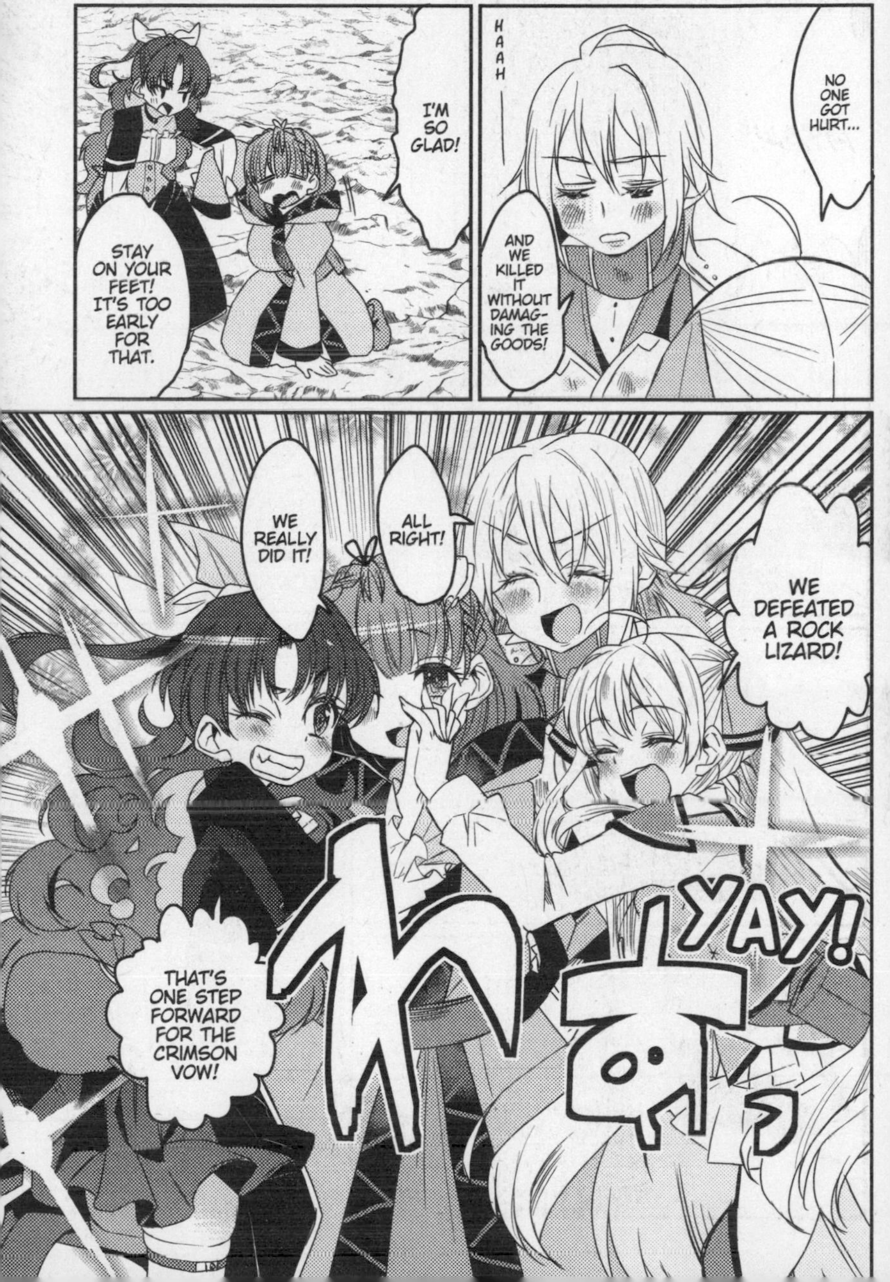
HAAH
NO ONE GOT HURT...
AND WE KILLED IT WITHOUT DAMAGING THE GOODS!
I'M SO GLAD!
STAY ON YOUR FEET! IT'S TOO EARLY FOR THAT.
WE DEFEATED A ROCK LIZARD!
ALL RIGHT!
WE REALLY DID IT!
YAY!
THAT'S ONE STEP FORWARD FOR THE CRIMSON VOW!

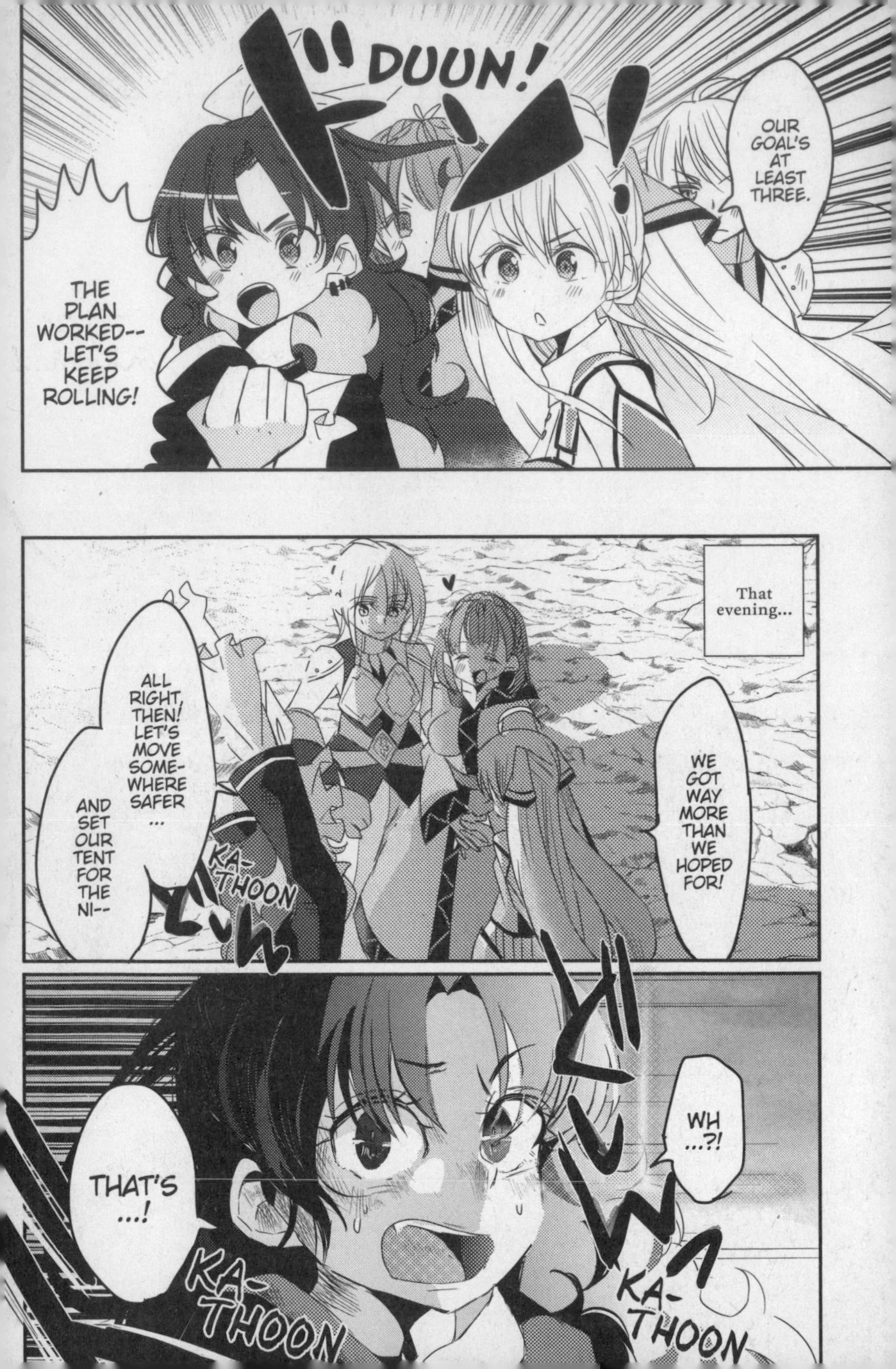
OUR GOAL'S AT LEAST THREE.
DUUN!
THE PLAN WORKED--LET'S KEEP ROLLING!
That evening...
WE GOT WAY MORE THAN WE HOPED FOR!
ALL RIGHT, THEN! LET'S MOVE SOME-WHERE SAFER ...
AND SET OUR TENT FOR THE NI--
KA-THOON
WH ...?!
KA-THOON
THAT'S ...!
KA-THOON

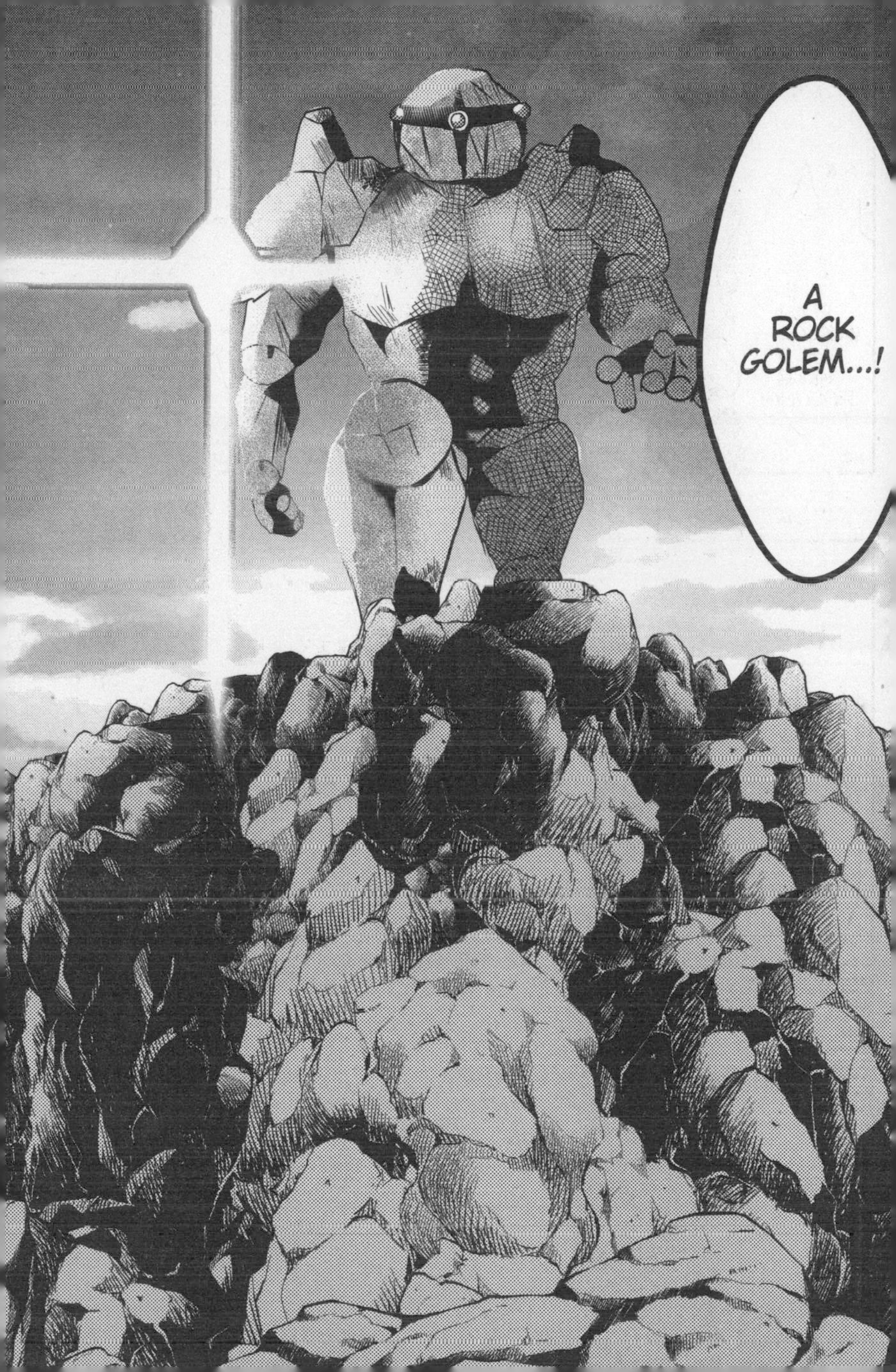
A ROCK GOLEM...!

Didn't I Say to Make My Abilities *Average* in the Next Life?!

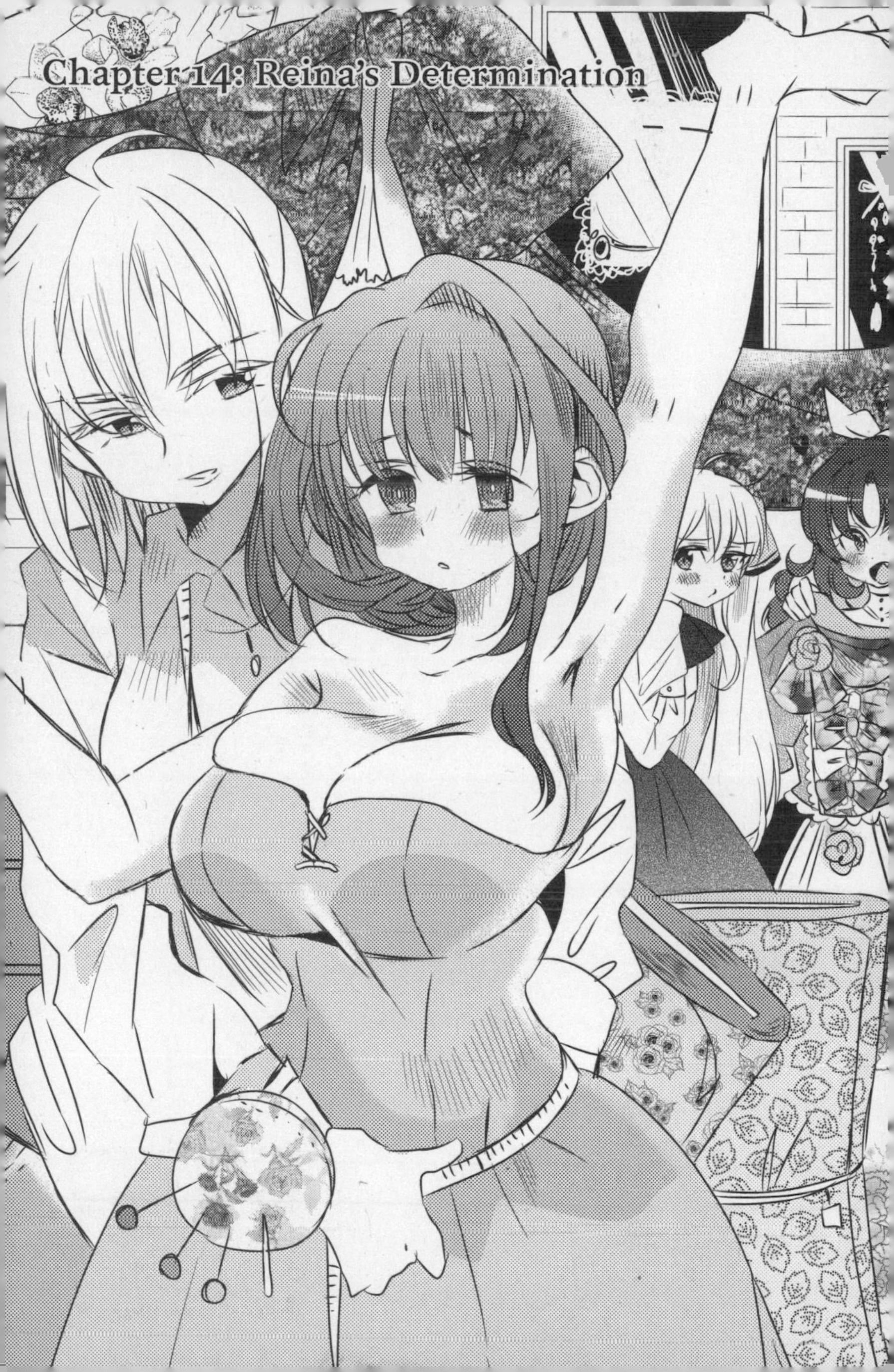
Chapter 14: Reina's Determination

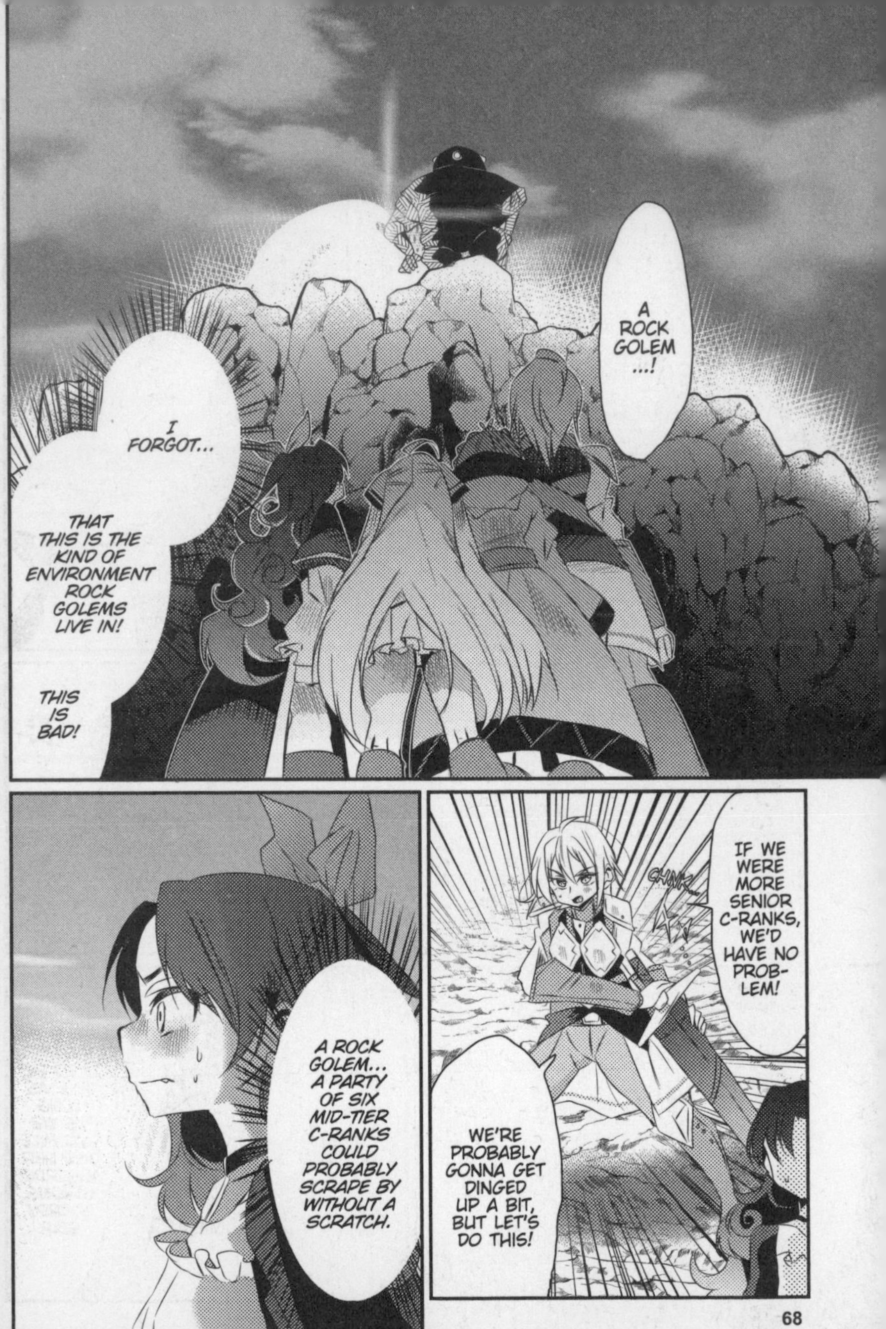
A ROCK GOLEM ...!
I FORGOT...
THAT THIS IS THE KIND OF ENVIRONMENT ROCK GOLEMS LIVE IN!
THIS IS BAD!
IF WE WERE MORE SENIOR C-RANKS, WE'D HAVE NO PROB-LEM!
CHINK...
WE'RE PROBABLY GONNA GET DINGED UP A BIT, BUT LET'S DO THIS!
A ROCK GOLEM... A PARTY OF SIX MID-TIER C-RANKS COULD PROBABLY SCRAPE BY WITHOUT A SCRATCH.

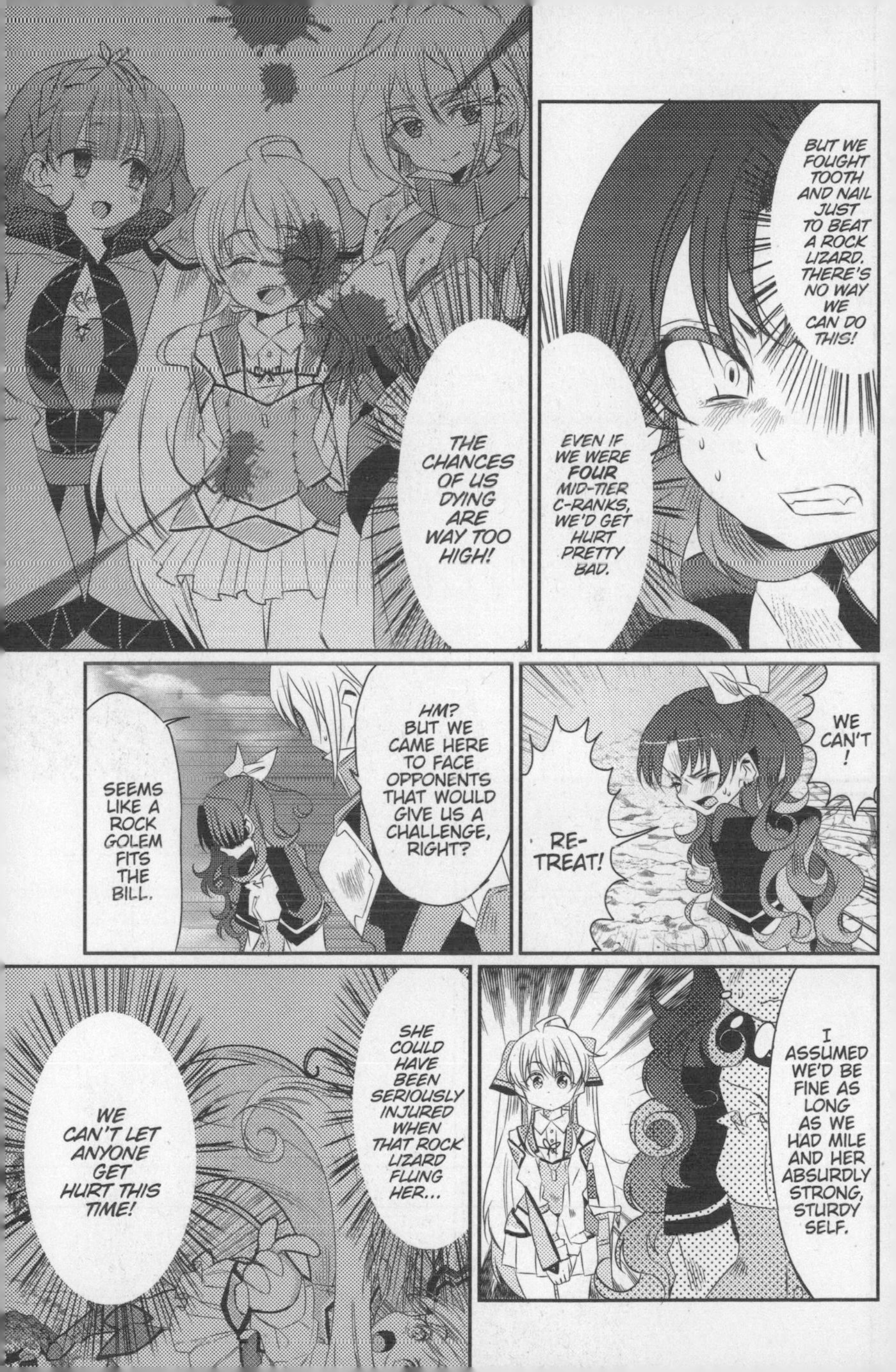
BUT WE FOUGHT TOOTH AND NAIL JUST TO BEAT A ROCK LIZARD. THERE'S NO WAY WE CAN DO THIS!
EVEN IF WE WERE FOUR MID-TIER C-RANKS, WE'D GET HURT PRETTY BAD.
THE CHANCES OF US DYING ARE WAY TOO HIGH!
WE CAN'T!
RE-TREAT!
HM? BUT WE CAME HERE TO FACE OPPONENTS THAT WOULD GIVE US A CHALLENGE, RIGHT?
SEEMS LIKE A ROCK GOLEM FITS THE BILL.
I ASSUMED WE'D BE FINE AS LONG AS WE HAD MILE AND HER ABSURDLY STRONG, STURDY SELF.
SHE COULD HAVE BEEN SERIOUSLY INJURED WHEN THAT ROCK LIZARD FLUNG HER...
WE CAN'T LET ANYONE GET HURT THIS TIME!

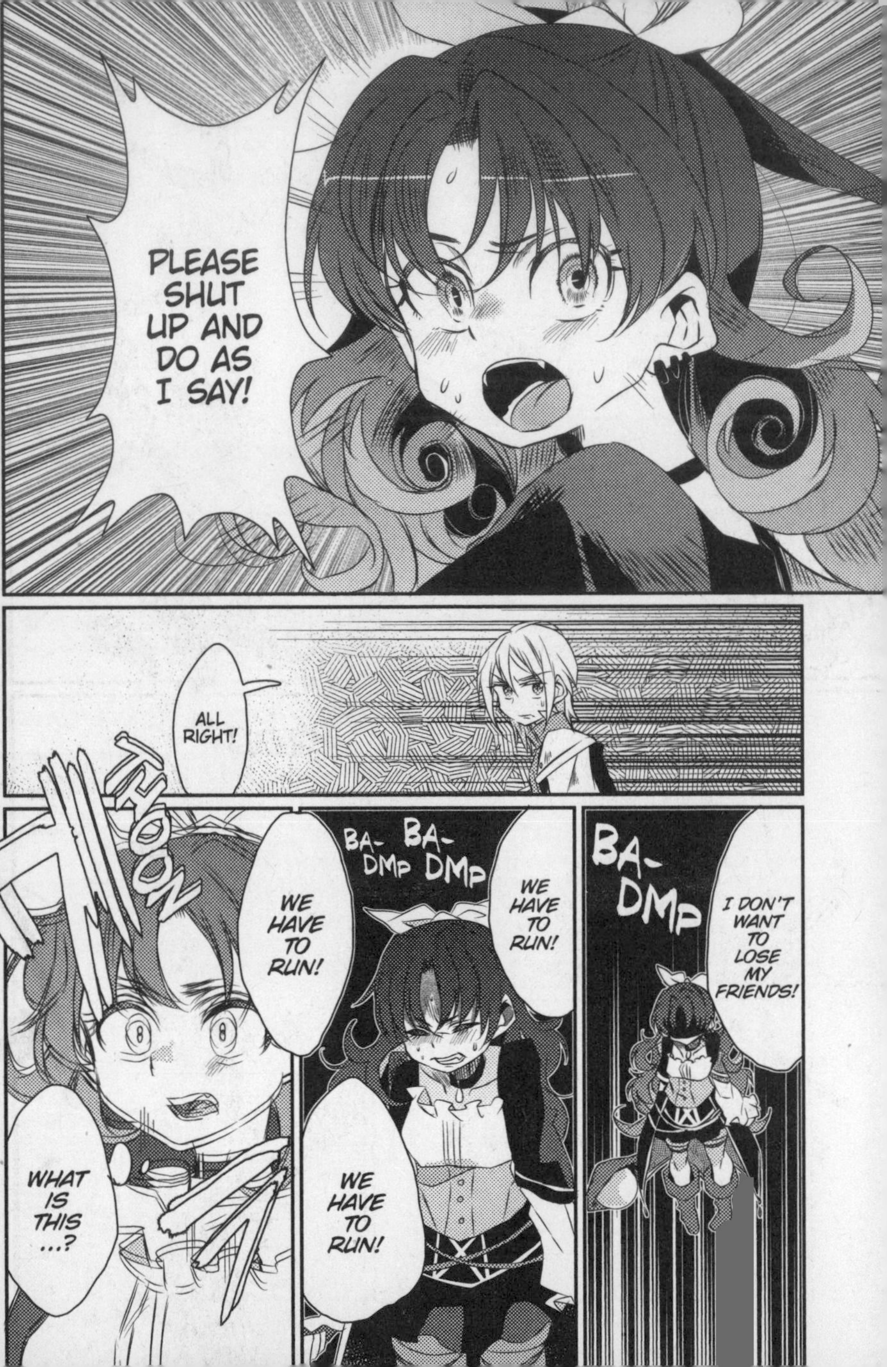
PLEASE SHUT UP AND DO AS I SAY!
ALL RIGHT!
BA-DMP
I DON'T WANT TO LOSE MY FRIENDS!
BA-DMP BA-DMP
WE HAVE TO RUN!
WE HAVE TO RUN!
WE HAVE TO RUN!
THOON
WHAT IS THIS ...?

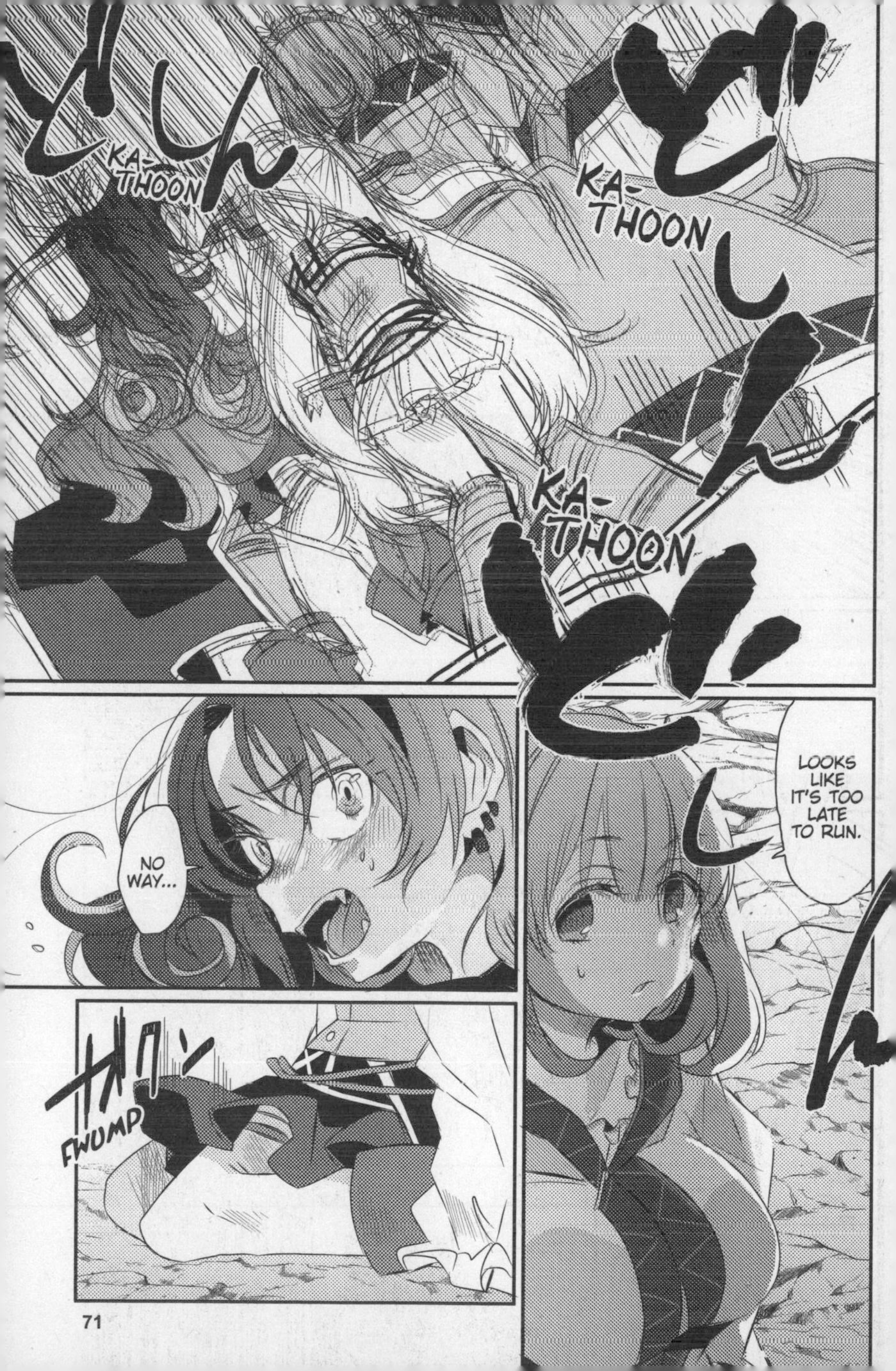
KA-THOON
KA-THOON
KA-THOON
LOOKS LIKE IT'S TOO LATE TO RUN.
NO WAY...
FWUMP

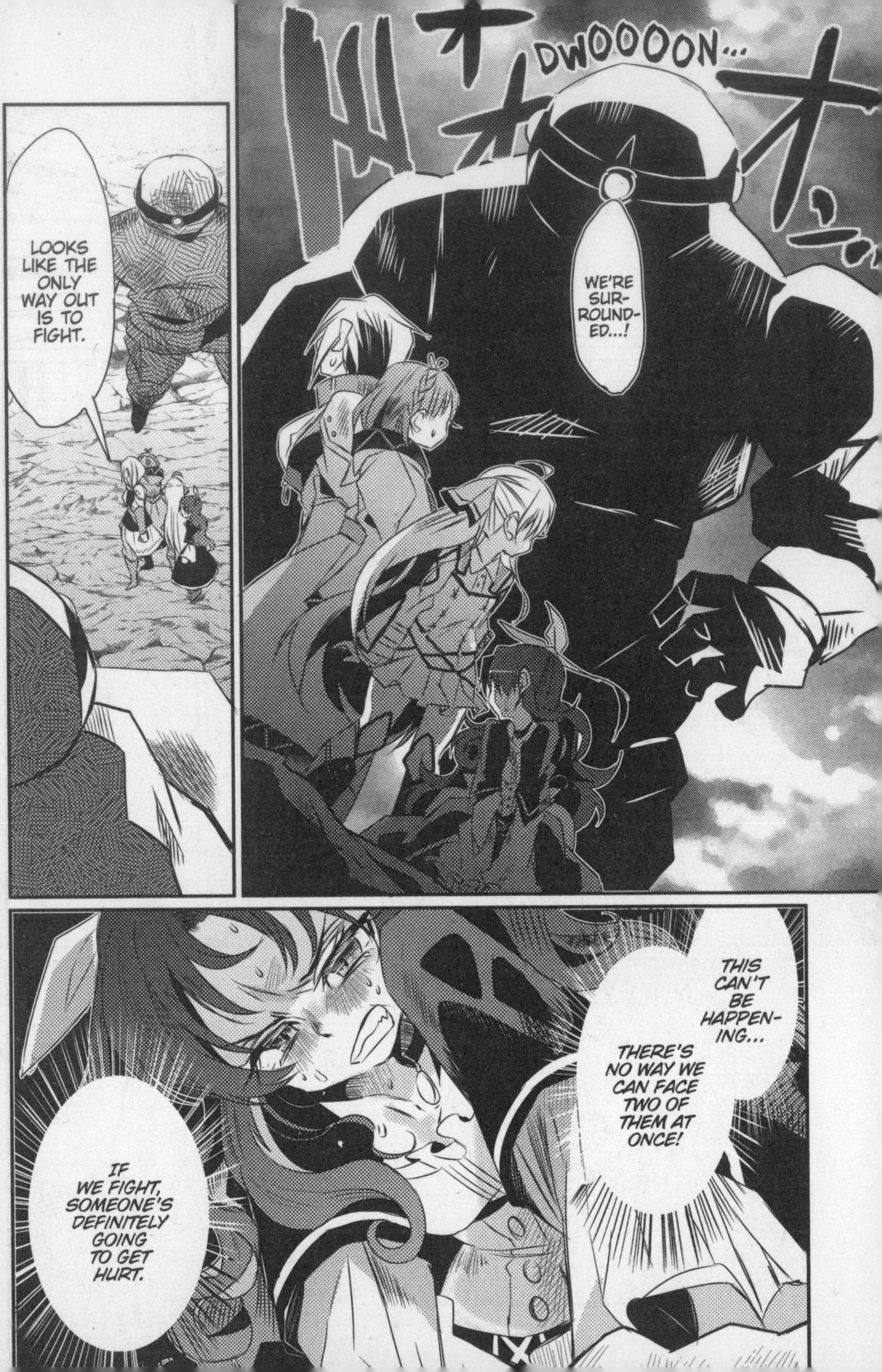
DWOOOON...
WE'RE SURROUNDED...!
LOOKS LIKE THE ONLY WAY OUT IS TO FIGHT.
THIS CAN'T BE HAPPENING...
THERE'S NO WAY WE CAN FACE TWO OF THEM AT ONCE!
IF WE FIGHT, SOMEONE'S DEFINITELY GOING TO GET HURT.

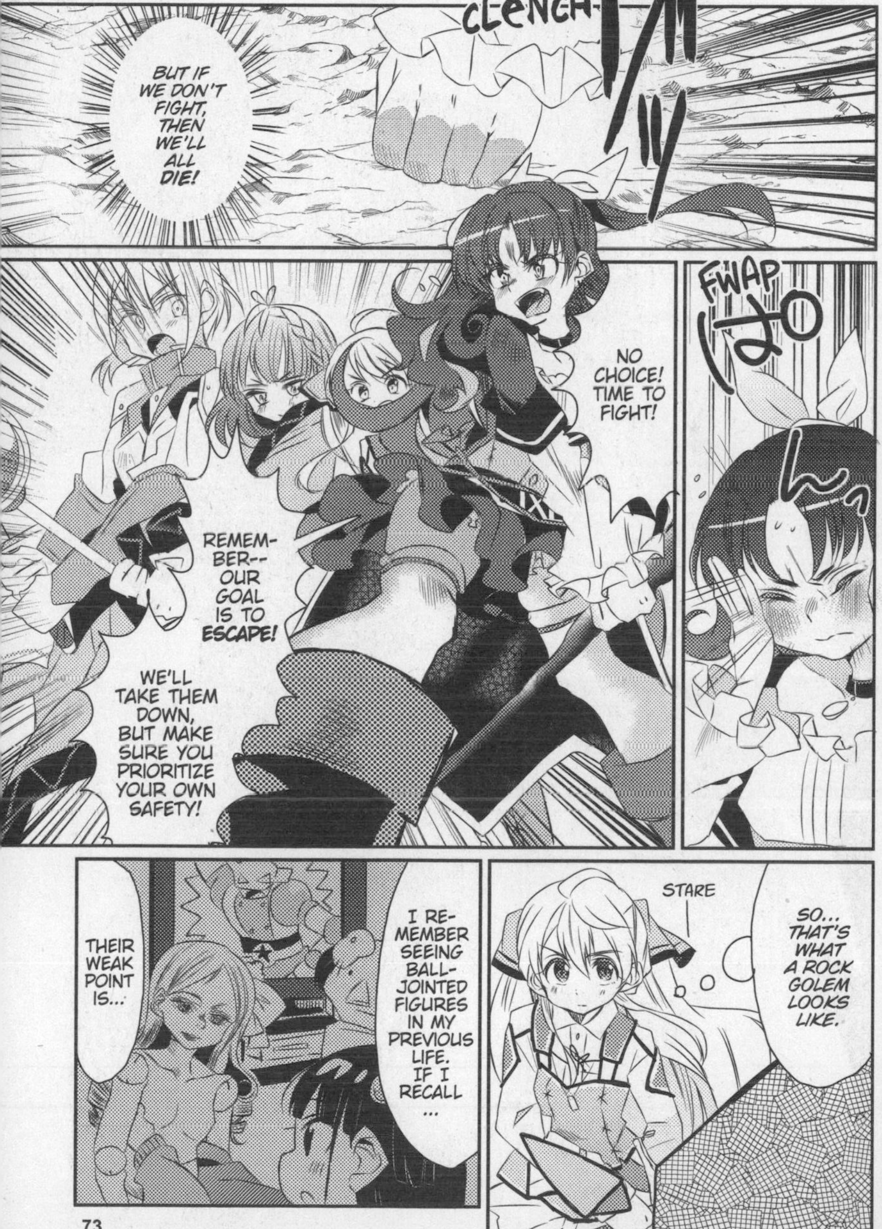
CLENCH
BUT IF WE DON'T FIGHT, THEN WE'LL ALL DIE!
FWAP
NO CHOICE! TIME TO FIGHT!
REMEMBER--OUR GOAL IS TO ESCAPE!
WE'LL TAKE THEM DOWN, BUT MAKE SURE YOU PRIORITIZE YOUR OWN SAFETY!
STARE
SO... THAT'S WHAT A ROCK GOLEM LOOKS LIKE.
I REMEMBER SEEING BALL-JOINTED FIGURES IN MY PREVIOUS LIFE. IF I RECALL...
THEIR WEAK POINT IS...

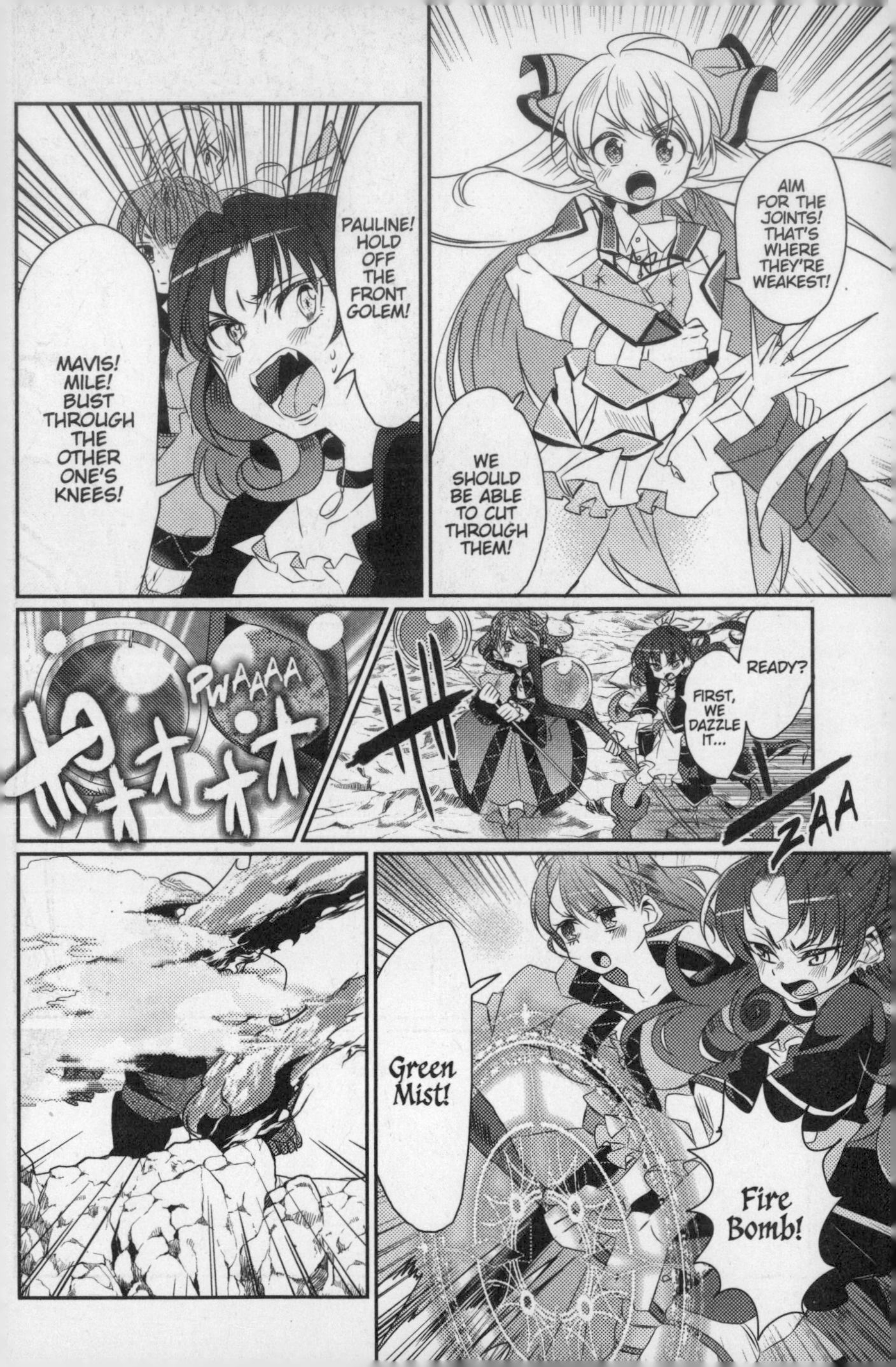
AIM FOR THE JOINTS! THAT'S WHERE THEY'RE WEAKEST!
WE SHOULD BE ABLE TO CUT THROUGH THEM!
PAULINE! HOLD OFF THE FRONT GOLEM!
MAVIS! MILE! BUST THROUGH THE OTHER ONE'S KNEES!
READY?
FIRST, WE DAZZLE IT...
PWAAAA
ZAA
Green Mist!
Fire Bomb!

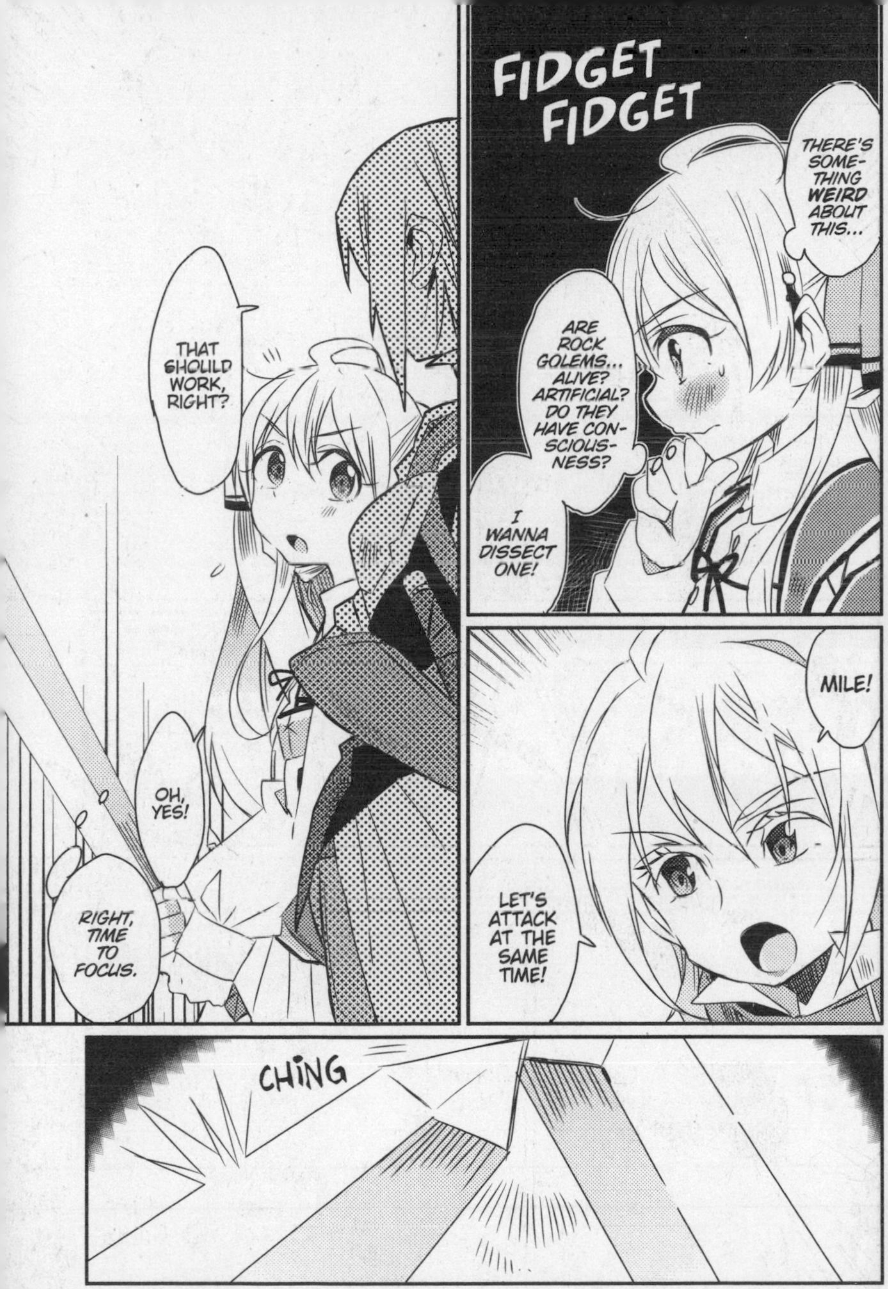
FIDGET FIDGET
THERE'S SOMETHING WEIRD ABOUT THIS...
ARE ROCK GOLEMS... ALIVE? ARTIFICIAL? DO THEY HAVE CONSCIOUSNESS?
I WANNA DISSECT ONE!
MILE!
LET'S ATTACK AT THE SAME TIME!
THAT SHOULD WORK, RIGHT?
OH, YES!
RIGHT, TIME TO FOCUS.
CHING

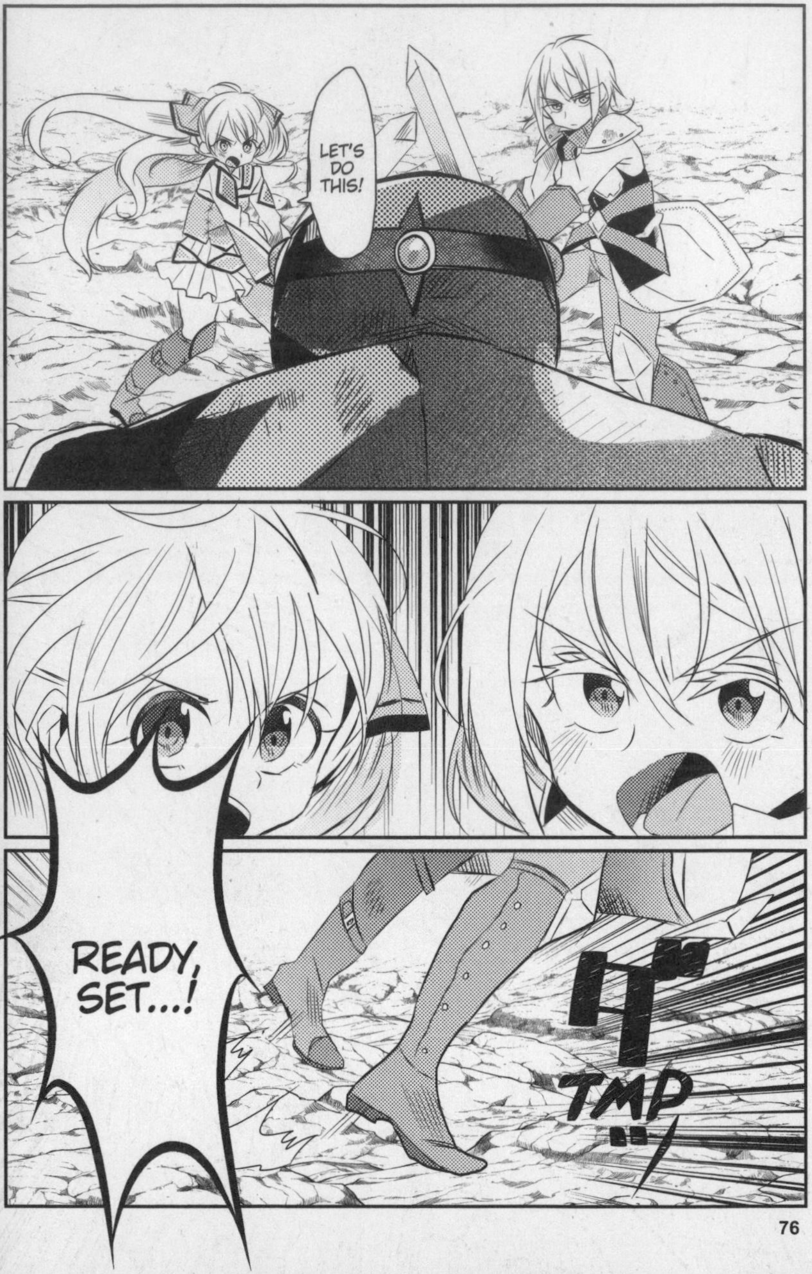
LET'S DO THIS!
TMP!!
READY, SET...!

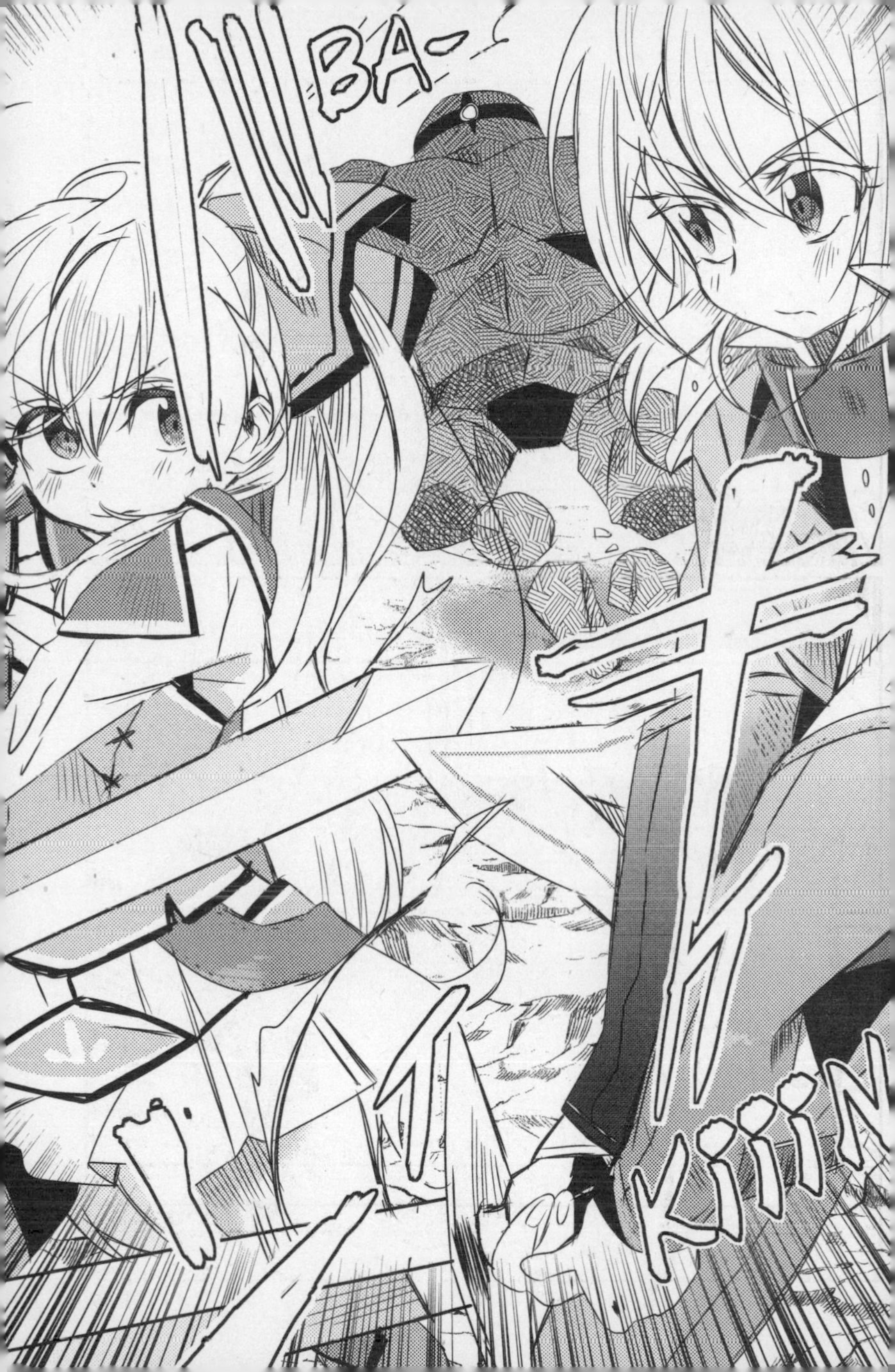
BA-
Kiiin

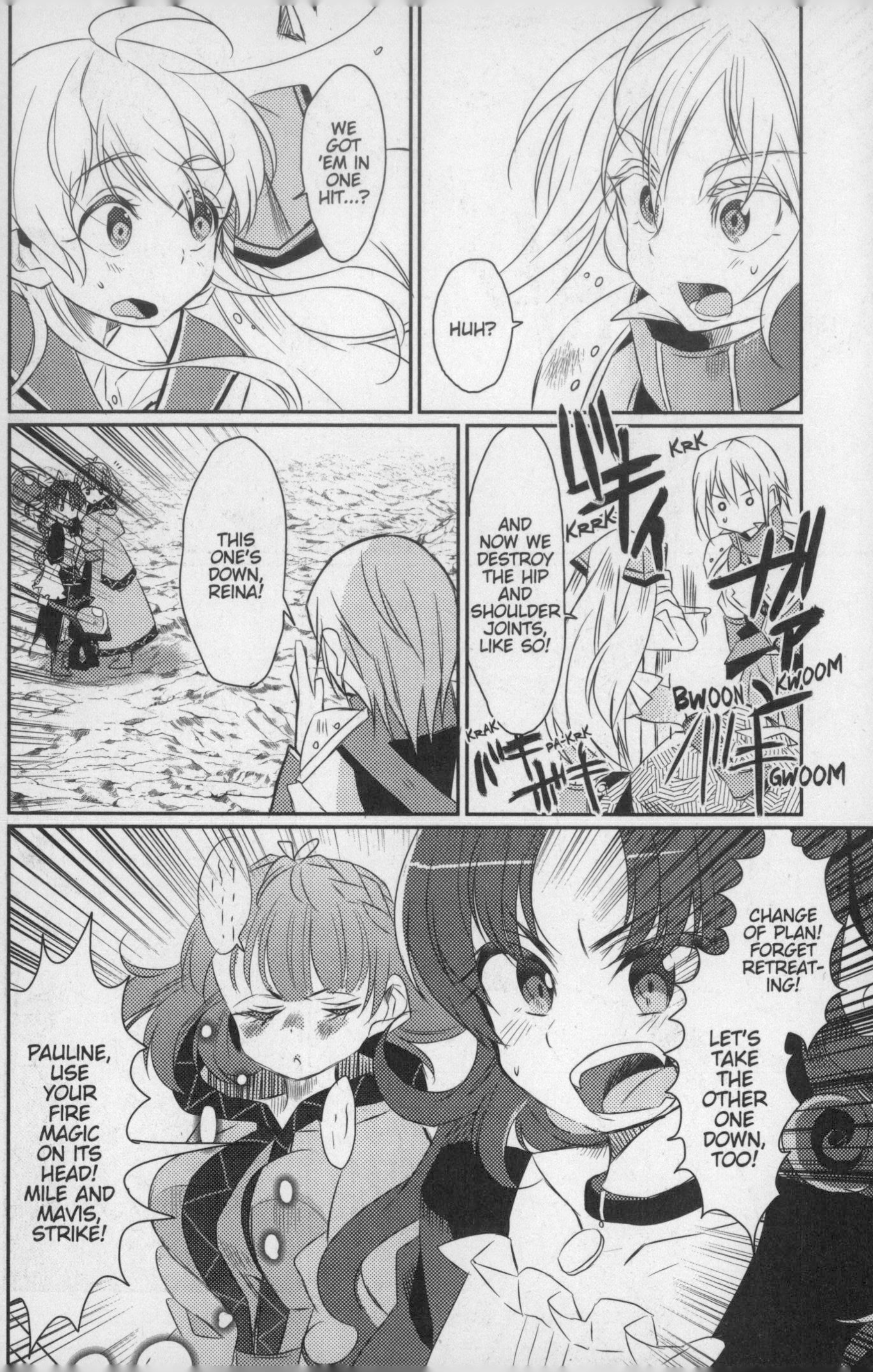
HUH?
WE GOT 'EM IN ONE HIT...?
KRK
KRRK
AND NOW WE DESTROY THE HIP AND SHOULDER JOINTS, LIKE SO!
KWOOM
BWOON
GWOOM
PA-KRK
KRAK
THIS ONE'S DOWN, REINA!
CHANGE OF PLAN! FORGET RETREAT-ING!
LET'S TAKE THE OTHER ONE DOWN, TOO!
PAULINE, USE YOUR FIRE MAGIC ON ITS HEAD! MILE AND MAVIS, STRIKE!

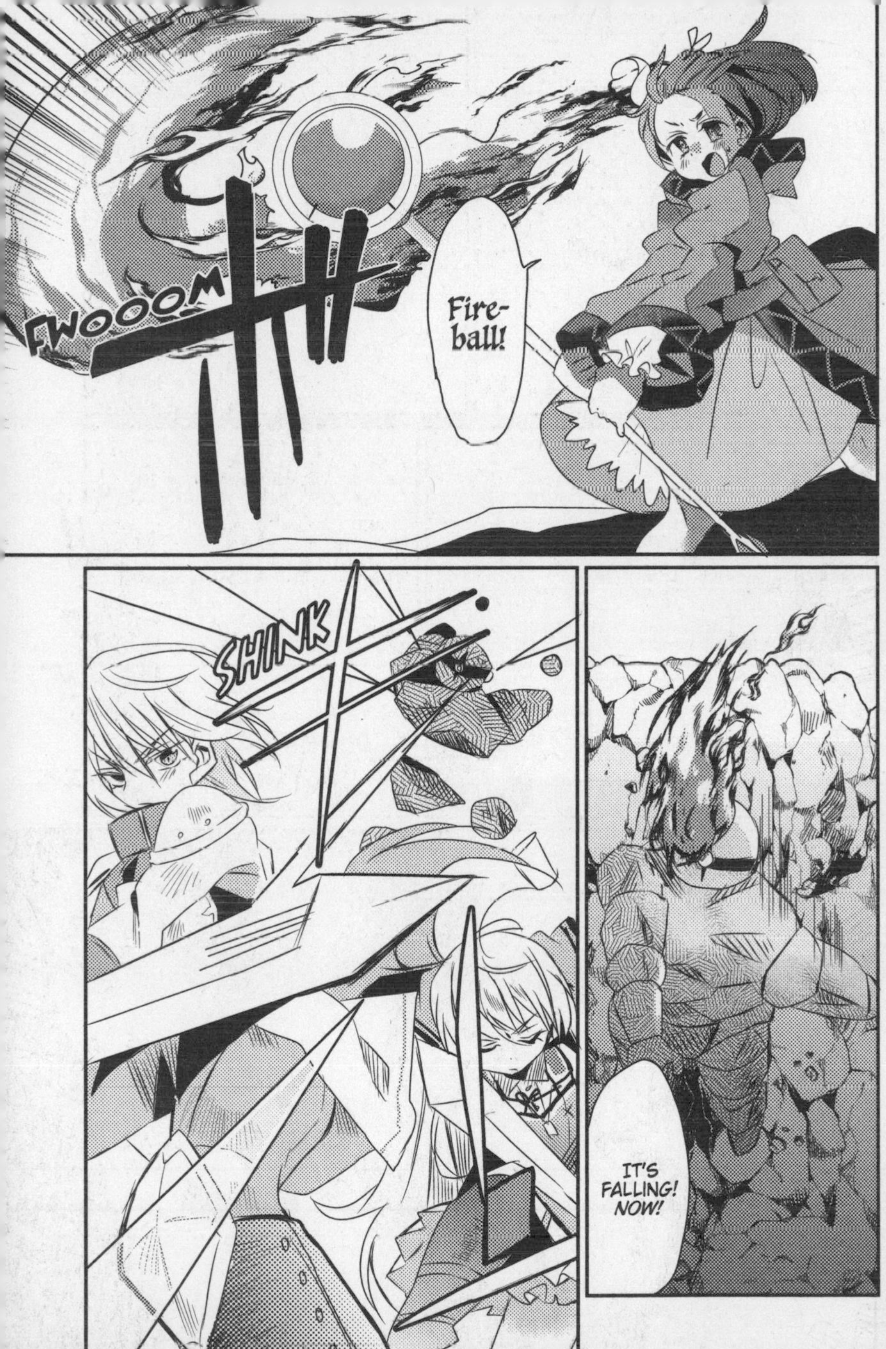
Fire-ball!
FWOOOM
IT'S FALLING! NOW!
SHINK

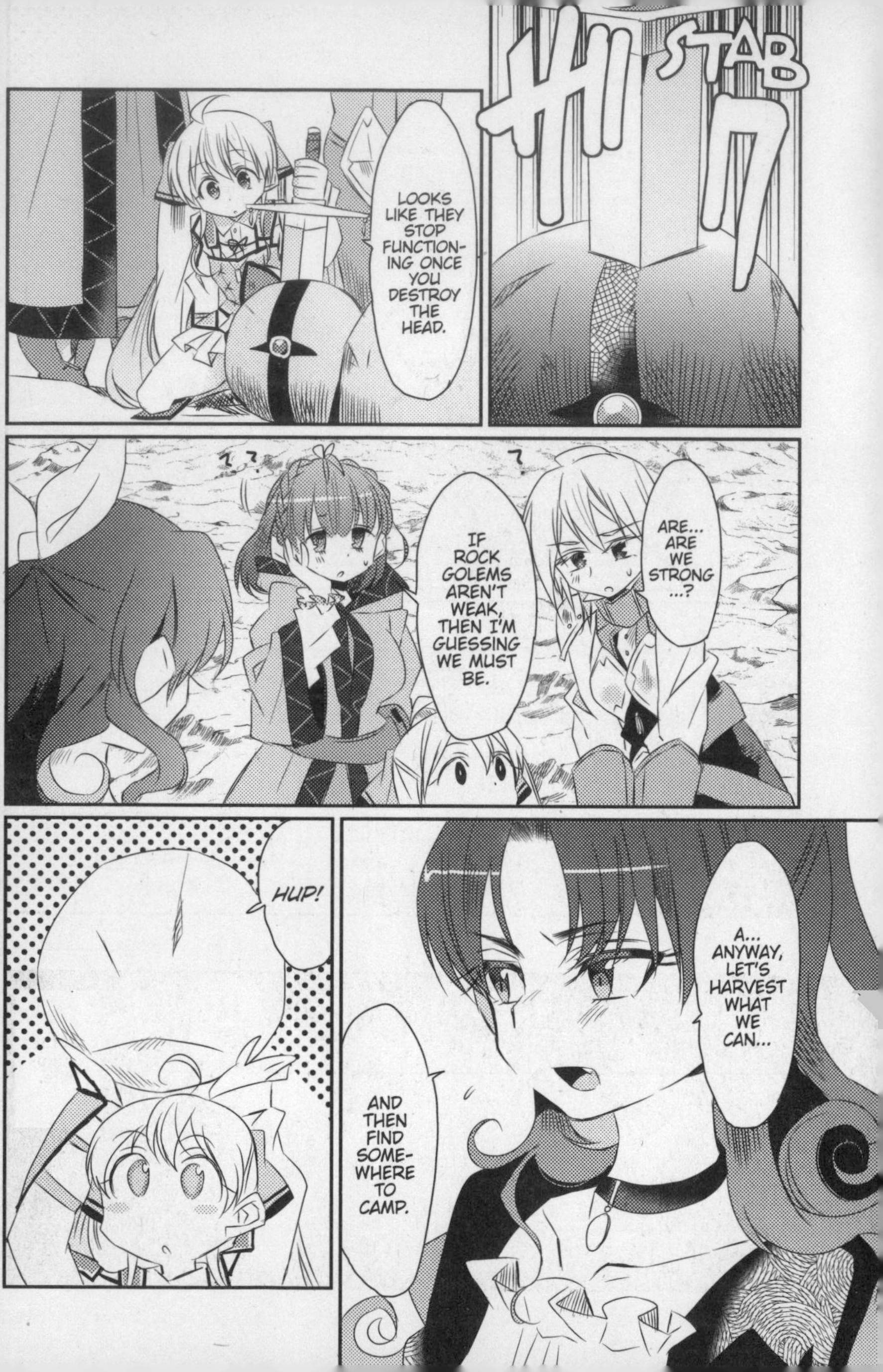
HIT
STAB
LOOKS LIKE THEY STOP FUNCTION-ING ONCE YOU DESTROY THE HEAD.
ARE... ARE WE STRONG ...?
IF ROCK GOLEMS AREN'T WEAK, THEN I'M GUESSING WE MUST BE.
A... ANYWAY, LET'S HARVEST WHAT WE CAN...
AND THEN FIND SOME-WHERE TO CAMP.
HUP!

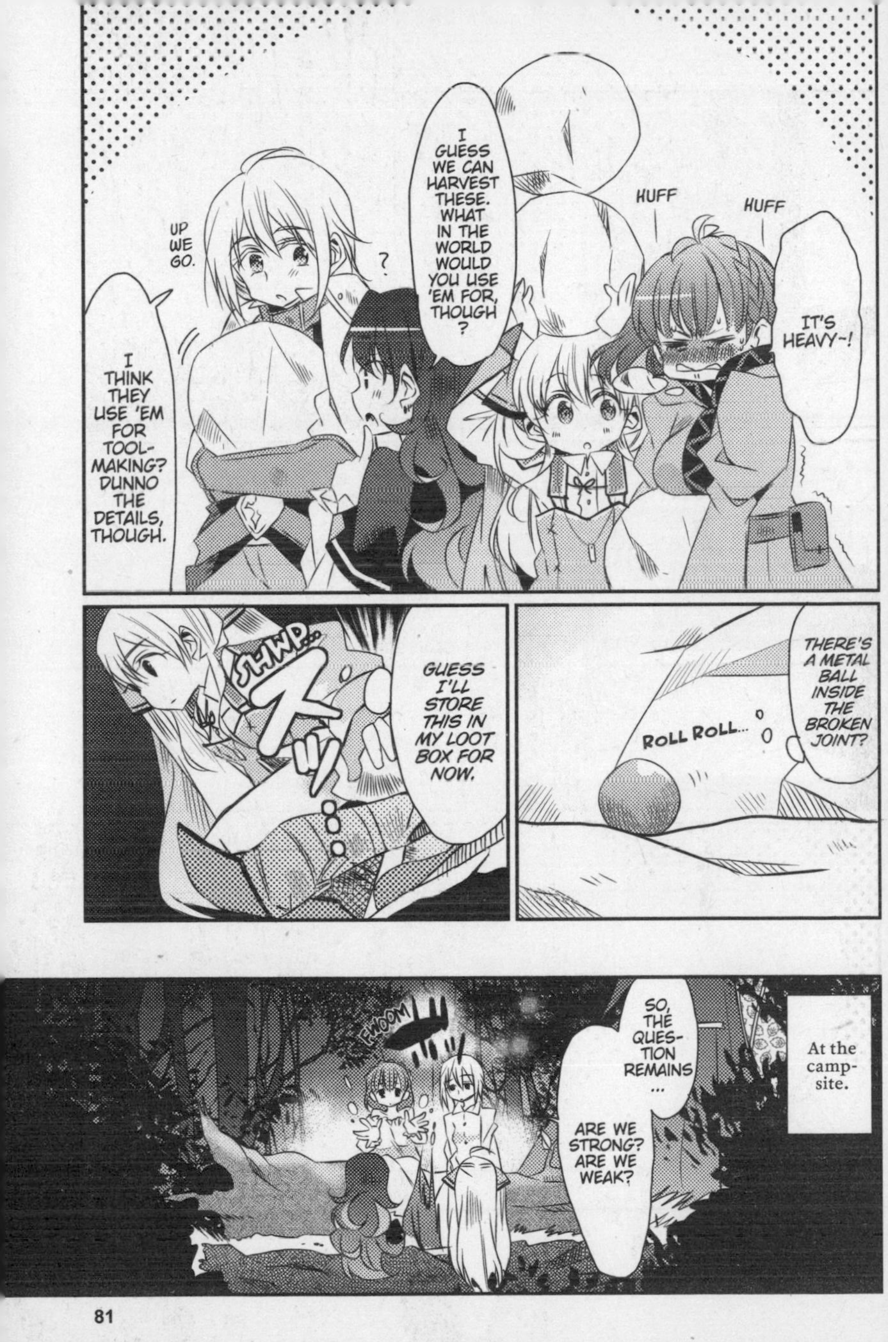
HUFF
HUFF
IT'S HEAVY~!
I GUESS WE CAN HARVEST THESE. WHAT IN THE WORLD WOULD YOU USE 'EM FOR, THOUGH?
?
UP WE GO.
I THINK THEY USE 'EM FOR TOOL-MAKING? DUNNO THE DETAILS, THOUGH.
THERE'S A METAL BALL INSIDE THE BROKEN JOINT?
ROLL ROLL...
GUESS I'LL STORE THIS IN MY LOOT BOX FOR NOW.
SHWP...
At the campsite.
SO, THE QUESTION REMAINS...
ARE WE STRONG? ARE WE WEAK?
FWOOM

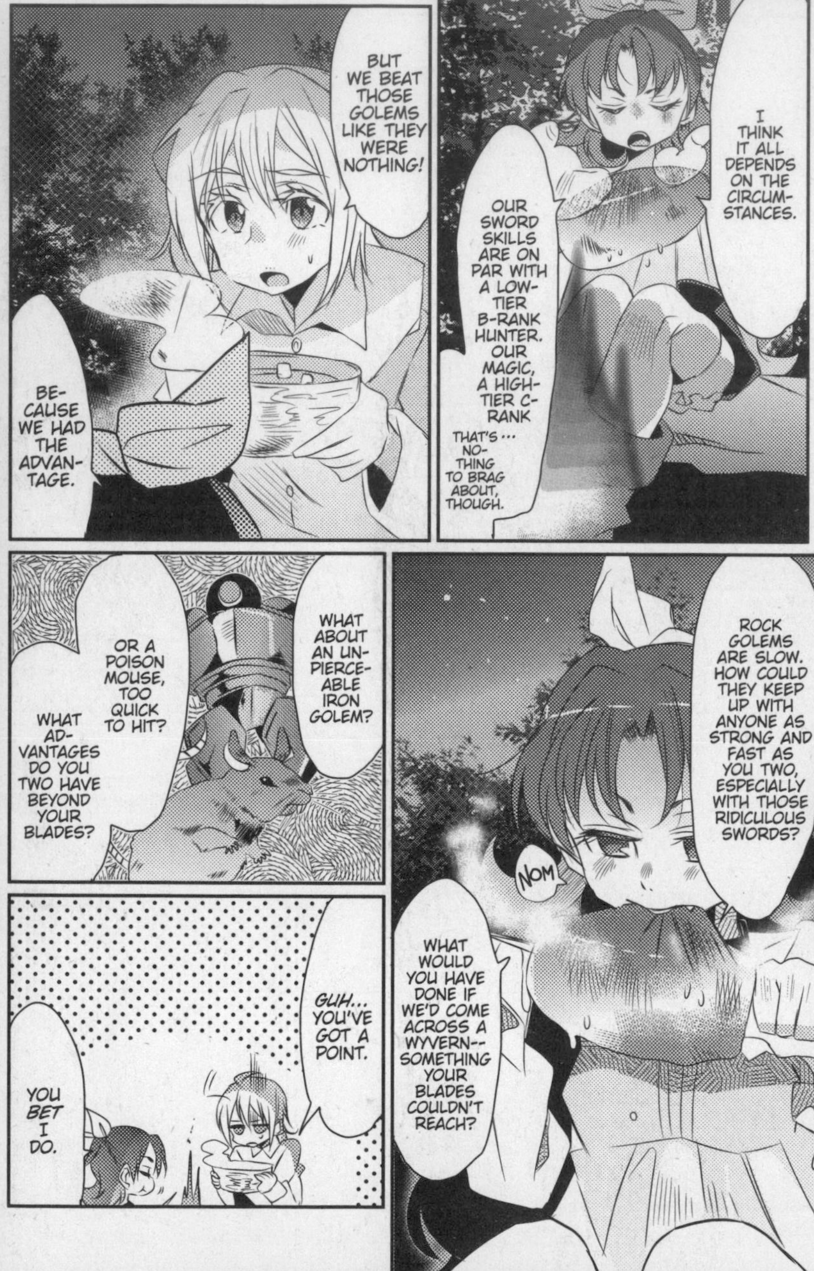
I THINK IT ALL DEPENDS ON THE CIRCUMSTANCES.
OUR SWORD SKILLS ARE ON PAR WITH A LOW-TIER B-RANK HUNTER. OUR MAGIC, A HIGH-TIER C-RANK
THAT'S... NOTHING TO BRAG ABOUT, THOUGH.
BUT WE BEAT THOSE GOLEMS LIKE THEY WERE NOTHING!
BECAUSE WE HAD THE ADVANTAGE.
ROCK GOLEMS ARE SLOW. HOW COULD THEY KEEP UP WITH ANYONE AS STRONG AND FAST AS YOU TWO, ESPECIALLY WITH THOSE RIDICULOUS SWORDS?
NOM
WHAT WOULD YOU HAVE DONE IF WE'D COME ACROSS A WYVERN--SOMETHING YOUR BLADES COULDN'T REACH?
WHAT ABOUT AN UNPIERCEABLE IRON GOLEM?
OR A POISON MOUSE, TOO QUICK TO HIT?
WHAT ADVANTAGES DO YOU TWO HAVE BEYOND YOUR BLADES?
GUH... YOU'VE GOT A POINT.
YOU BET I DO.

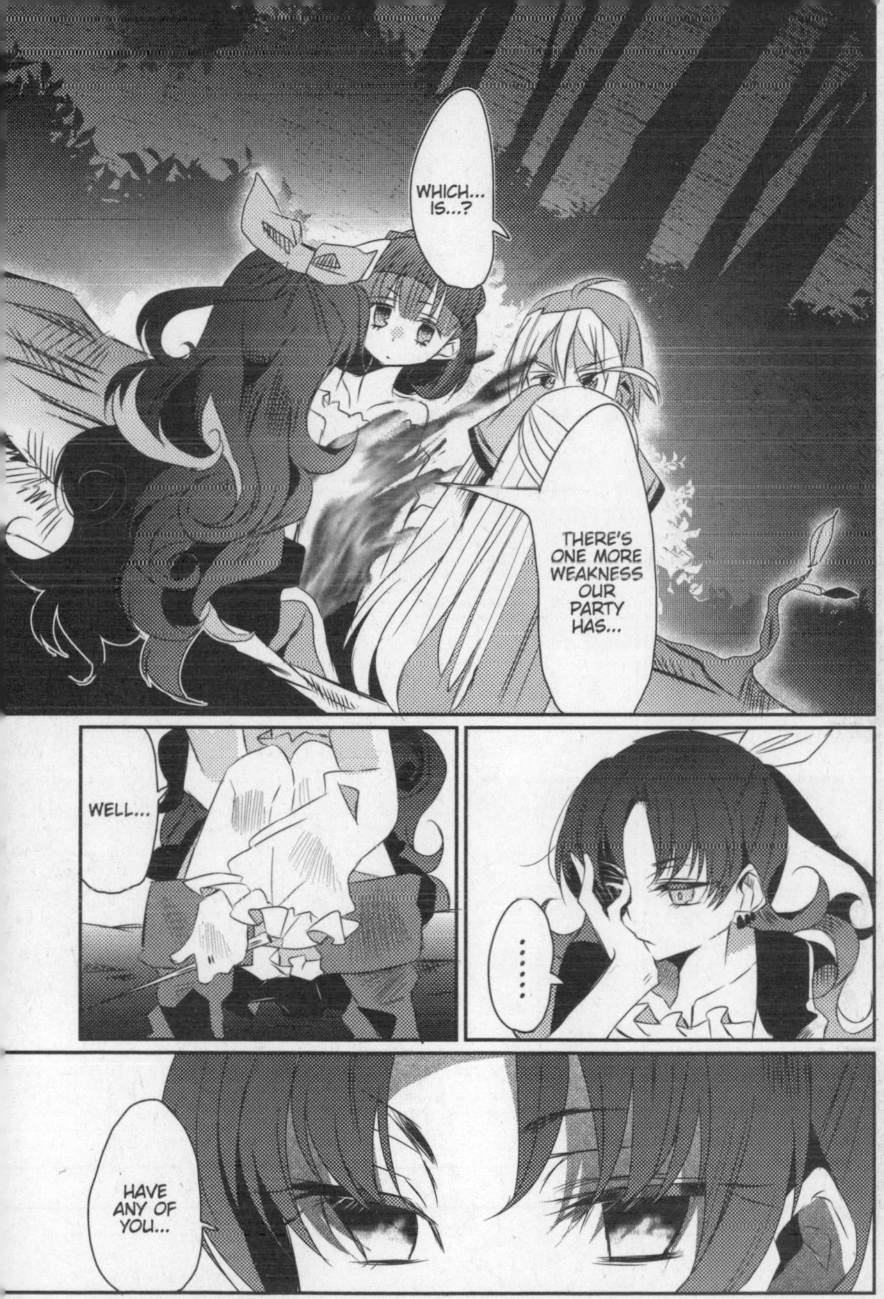
THERE'S ONE MORE WEAKNESS OUR PARTY HAS...
WHICH... IS...?
......
WELL...
HAVE ANY OF YOU...

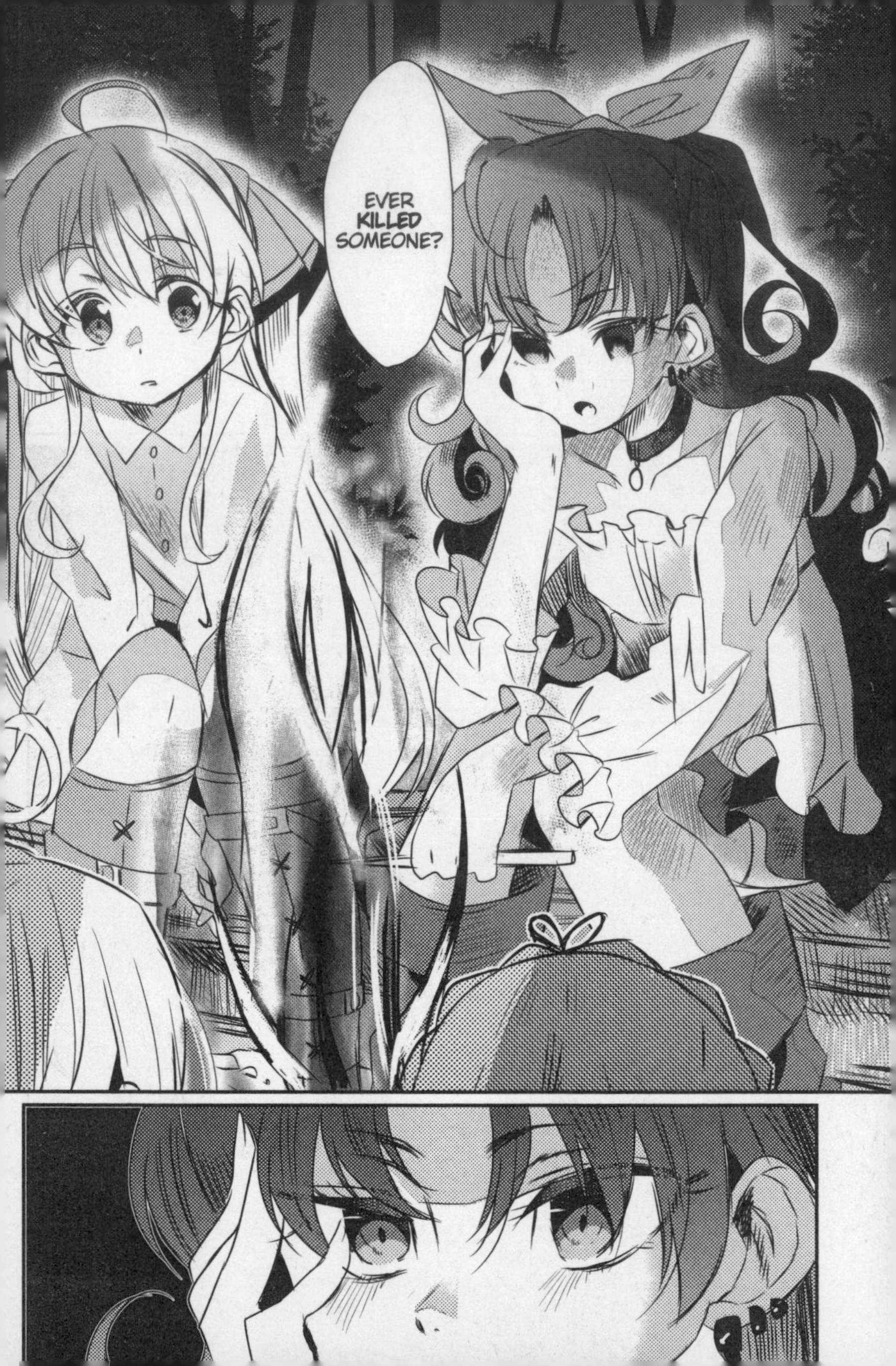
EVER KILLED SOMEONE?

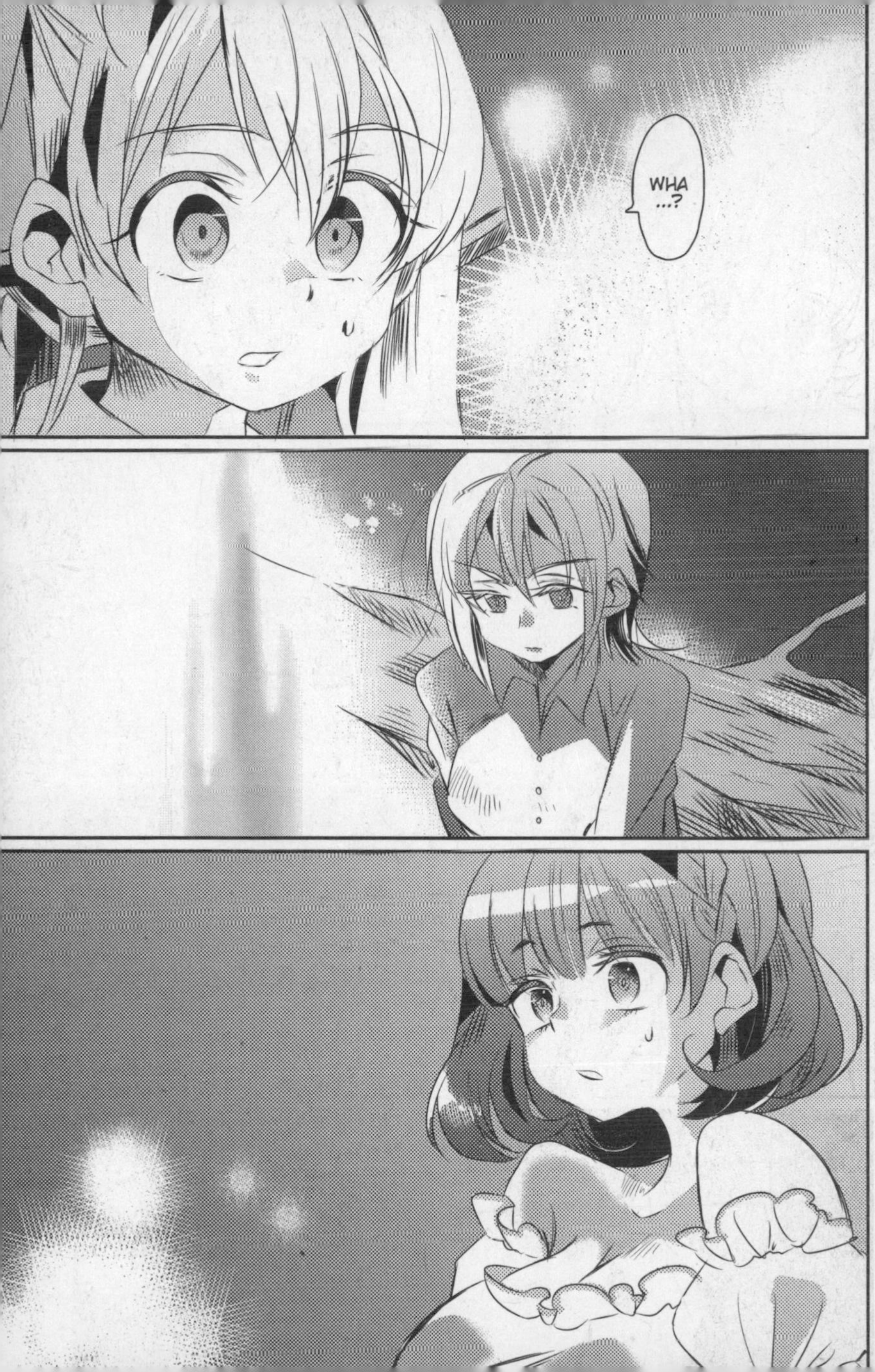
WHA ...?

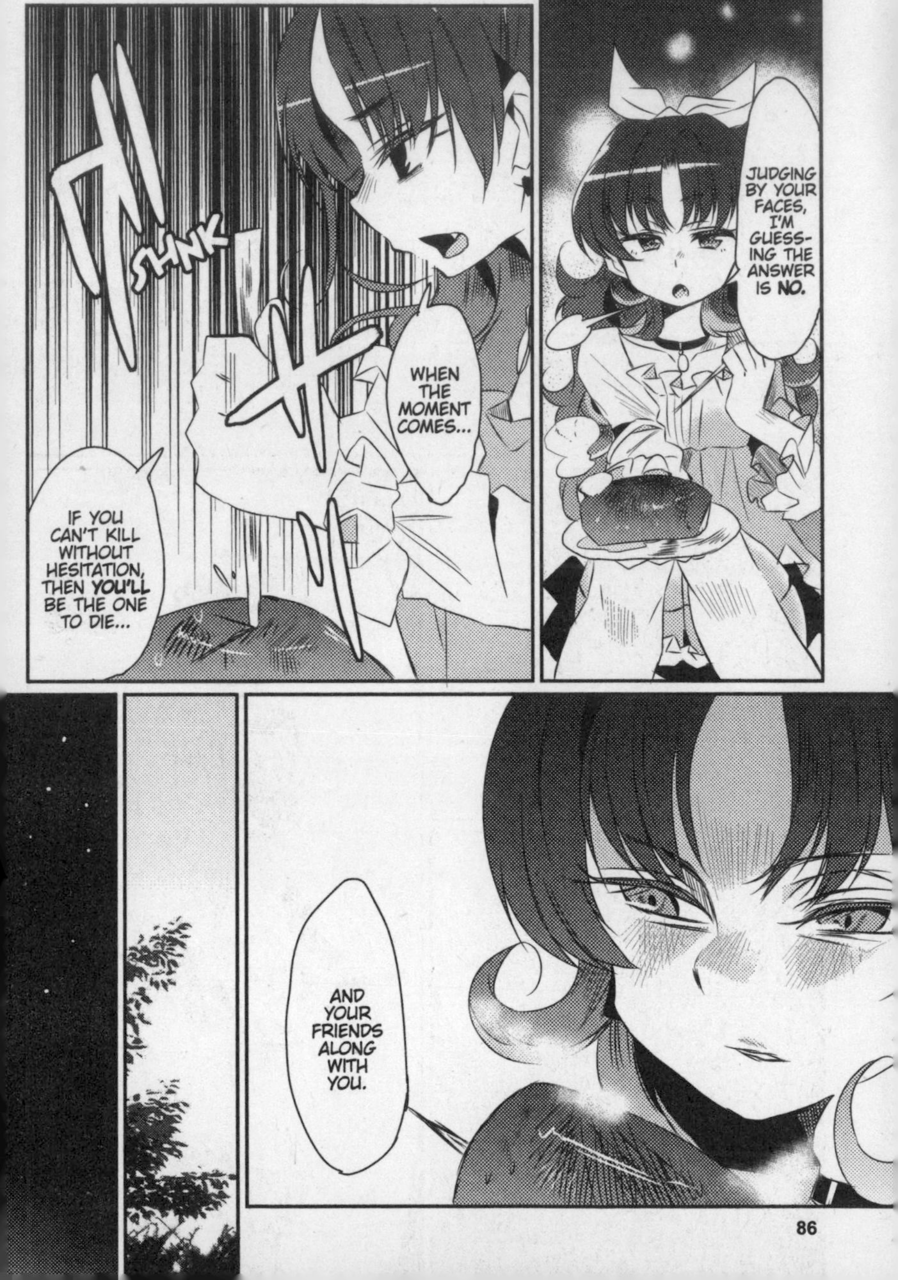
JUDGING BY YOUR FACES, I'M GUESSING THE ANSWER IS NO.
WHEN THE MOMENT COMES...
SHNK
IF YOU CAN'T KILL WITHOUT HESITATION, THEN YOU'LL BE THE ONE TO DIE...
AND YOUR FRIENDS ALONG WITH YOU.

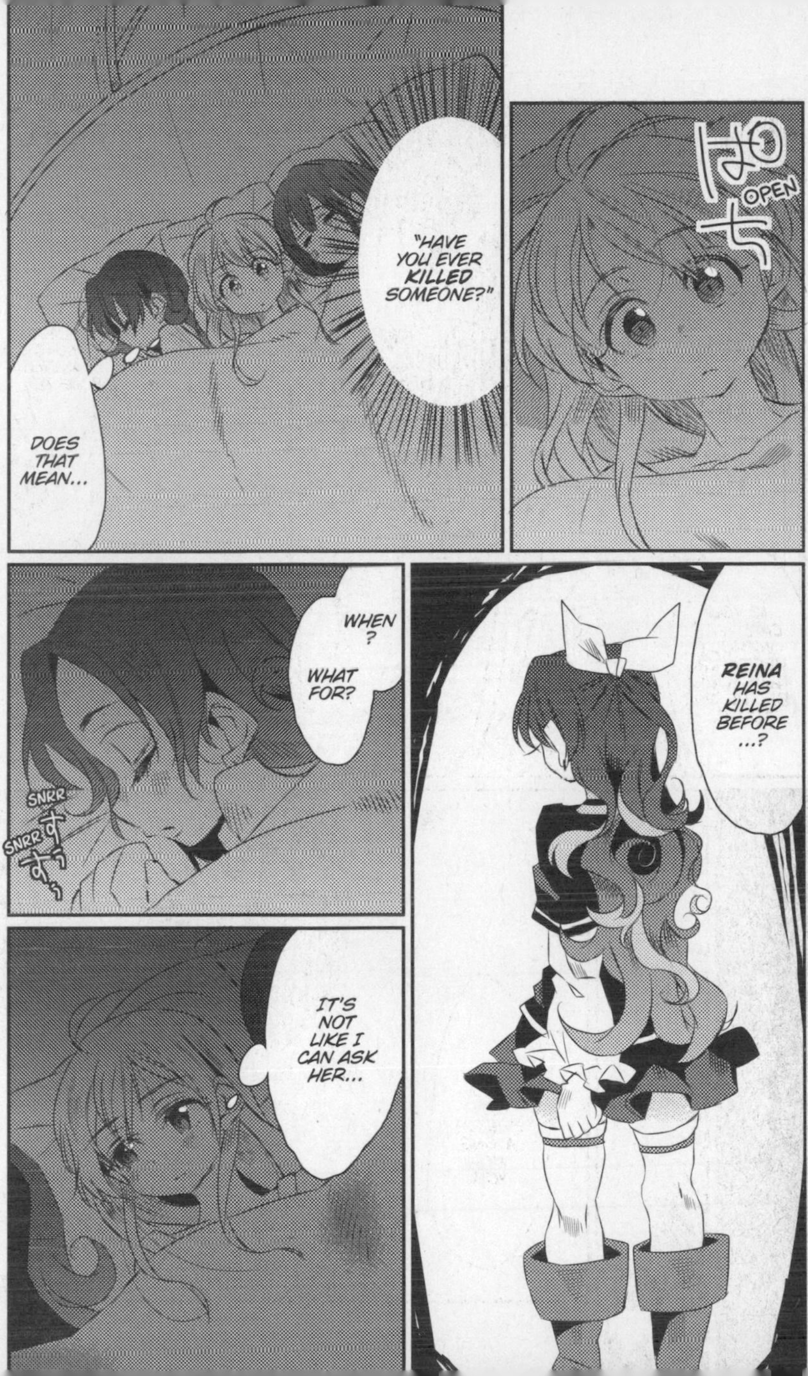
ぱち
OPEN
"HAVE YOU EVER KILLED SOMEONE?"
DOES THAT MEAN...
REINA HAS KILLED BEFORE ...?
WHEN? WHAT FOR?
SNRR SNRR
すぅ すぅ
IT'S NOT LIKE I CAN ASK HER...

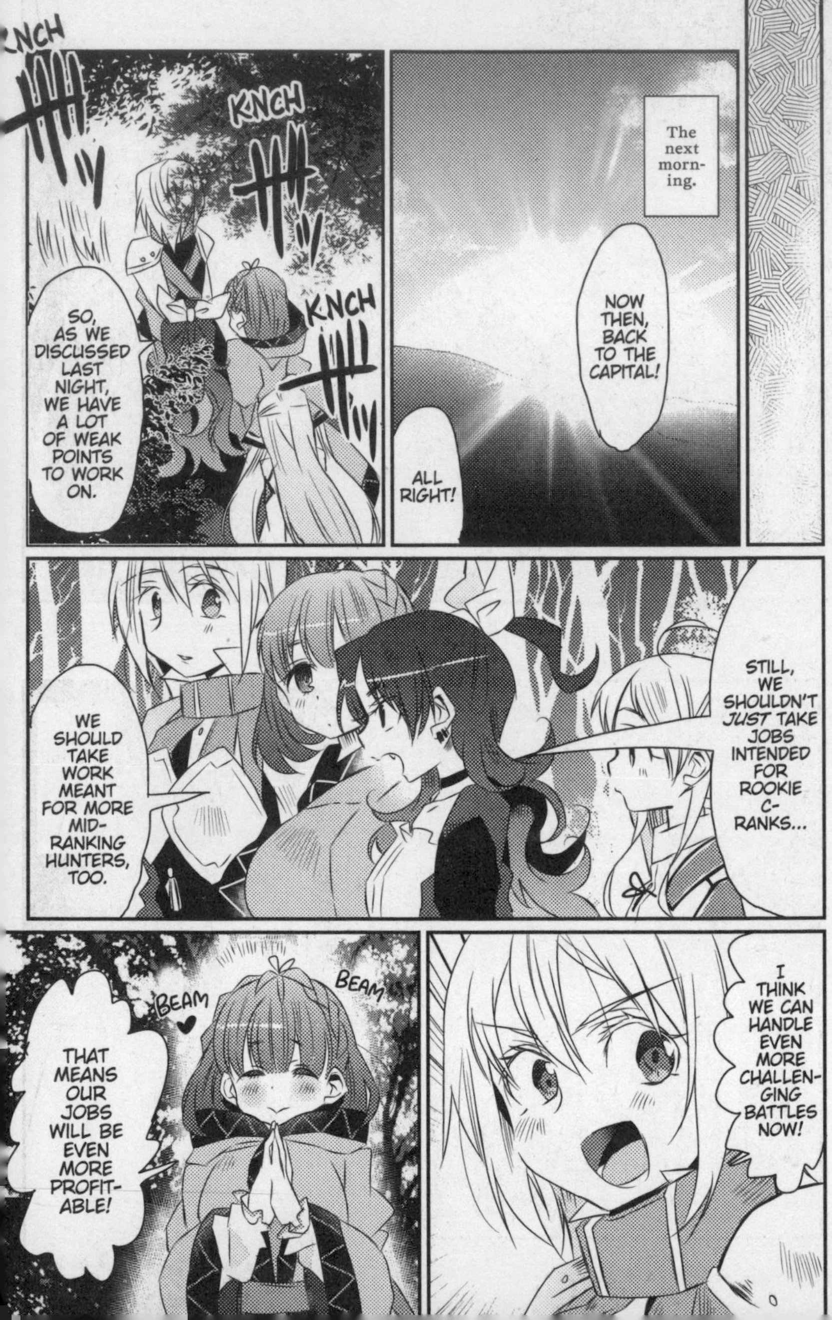
The next morning.
NOW THEN, BACK TO THE CAPITAL!
ALL RIGHT!
KNCH
KNCH
KNCH
SO, AS WE DISCUSSED LAST NIGHT, WE HAVE A LOT OF WEAK POINTS TO WORK ON.
STILL, WE SHOULDN'T *JUST* TAKE JOBS INTENDED FOR ROOKIE C-RANKS...
WE SHOULD TAKE WORK MEANT FOR MORE MID-RANKING HUNTERS, TOO.
I THINK WE CAN HANDLE EVEN MORE CHALLENGING BATTLES NOW!
BEAM
BEAM
THAT MEANS OUR JOBS WILL BE EVEN MORE PROFITABLE!

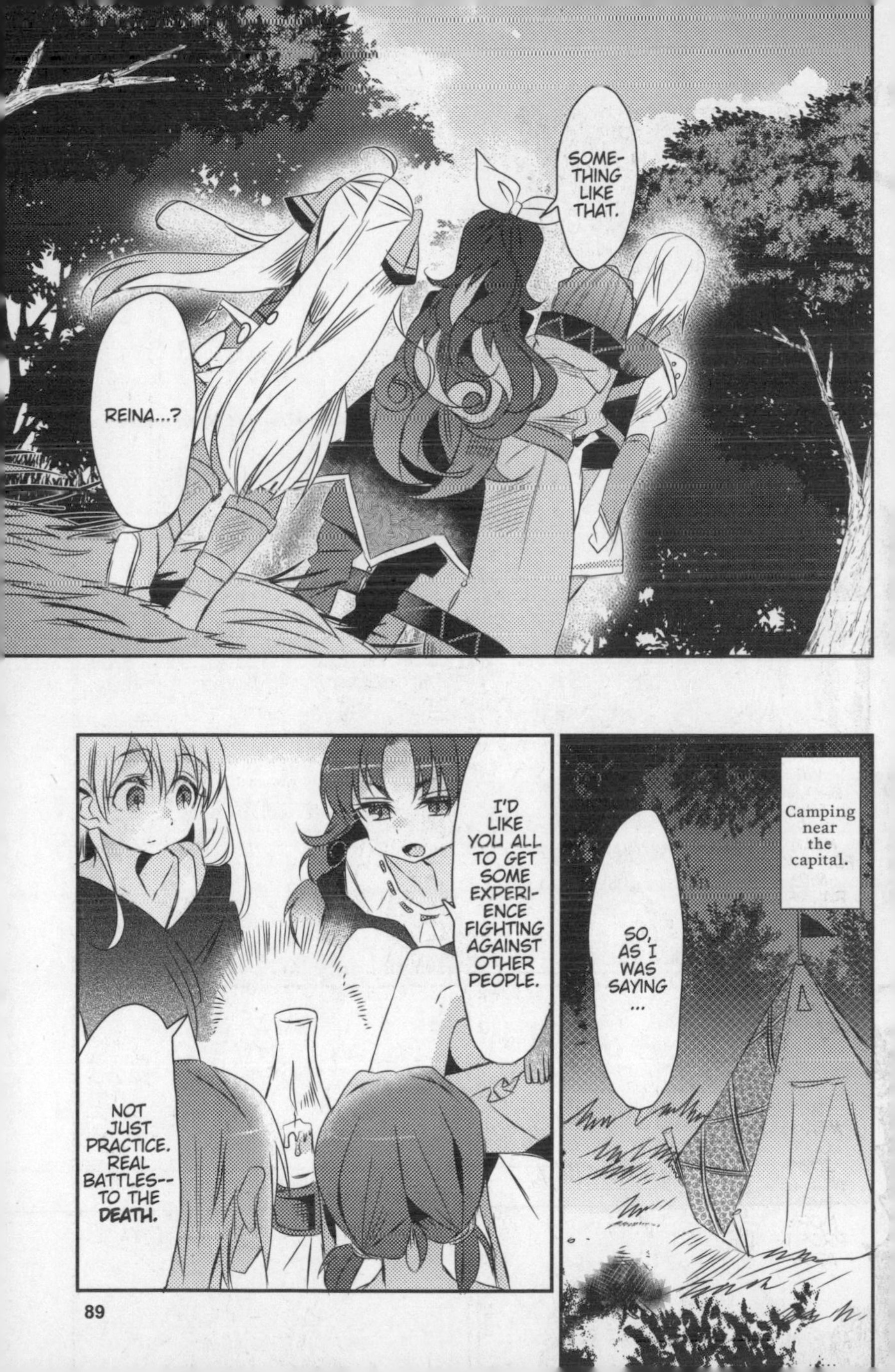
SOME-THING LIKE THAT.
REINA...?
Camping near the capital.
SO, AS I WAS SAYING...
I'D LIKE YOU ALL TO GET SOME EXPERI-ENCE FIGHTING AGAINST OTHER PEOPLE.
NOT JUST PRACTICE. REAL BATTLES--TO THE DEATH.

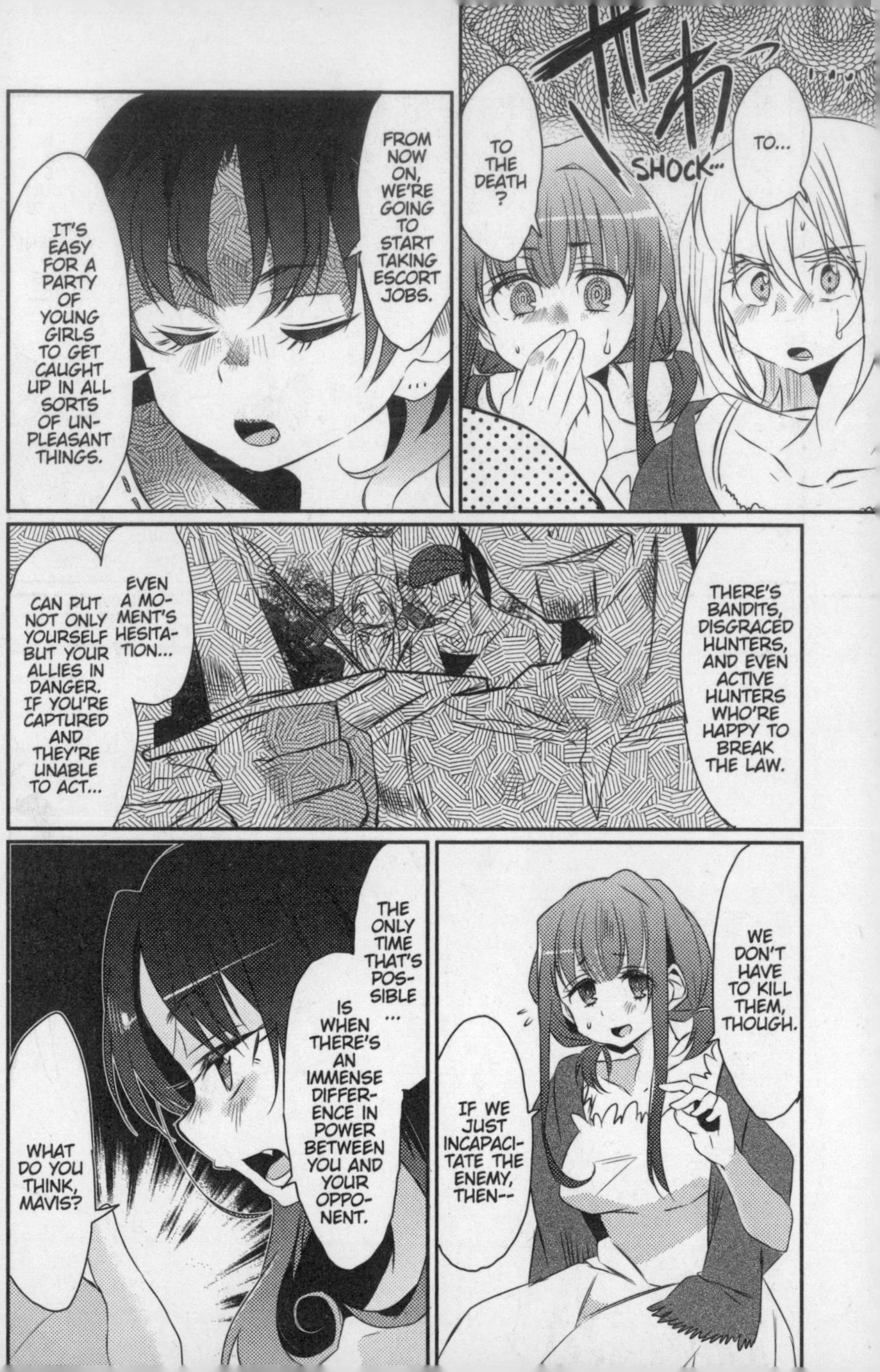
TO...
SHOCK...
TO THE DEATH?
FROM NOW ON, WE'RE GOING TO START TAKING ESCORT JOBS.
...
IT'S EASY FOR A PARTY OF YOUNG GIRLS TO GET CAUGHT UP IN ALL SORTS OF UNPLEASANT THINGS.
THERE'S BANDITS, DISGRACED HUNTERS, AND EVEN ACTIVE HUNTERS WHO'RE HAPPY TO BREAK THE LAW.
EVEN A MOMENT'S HESITATION...
CAN PUT NOT ONLY YOURSELF BUT YOUR ALLIES IN DANGER. IF YOU'RE CAPTURED AND THEY'RE UNABLE TO ACT...
WE DON'T HAVE TO KILL THEM, THOUGH.
IF WE JUST INCAPACITATE THE ENEMY, THEN--
THE ONLY TIME THAT'S POSSIBLE...
IS WHEN THERE'S AN IMMENSE DIFFERENCE IN POWER BETWEEN YOU AND YOUR OPPONENT.
WHAT DO YOU THINK, MAVIS?

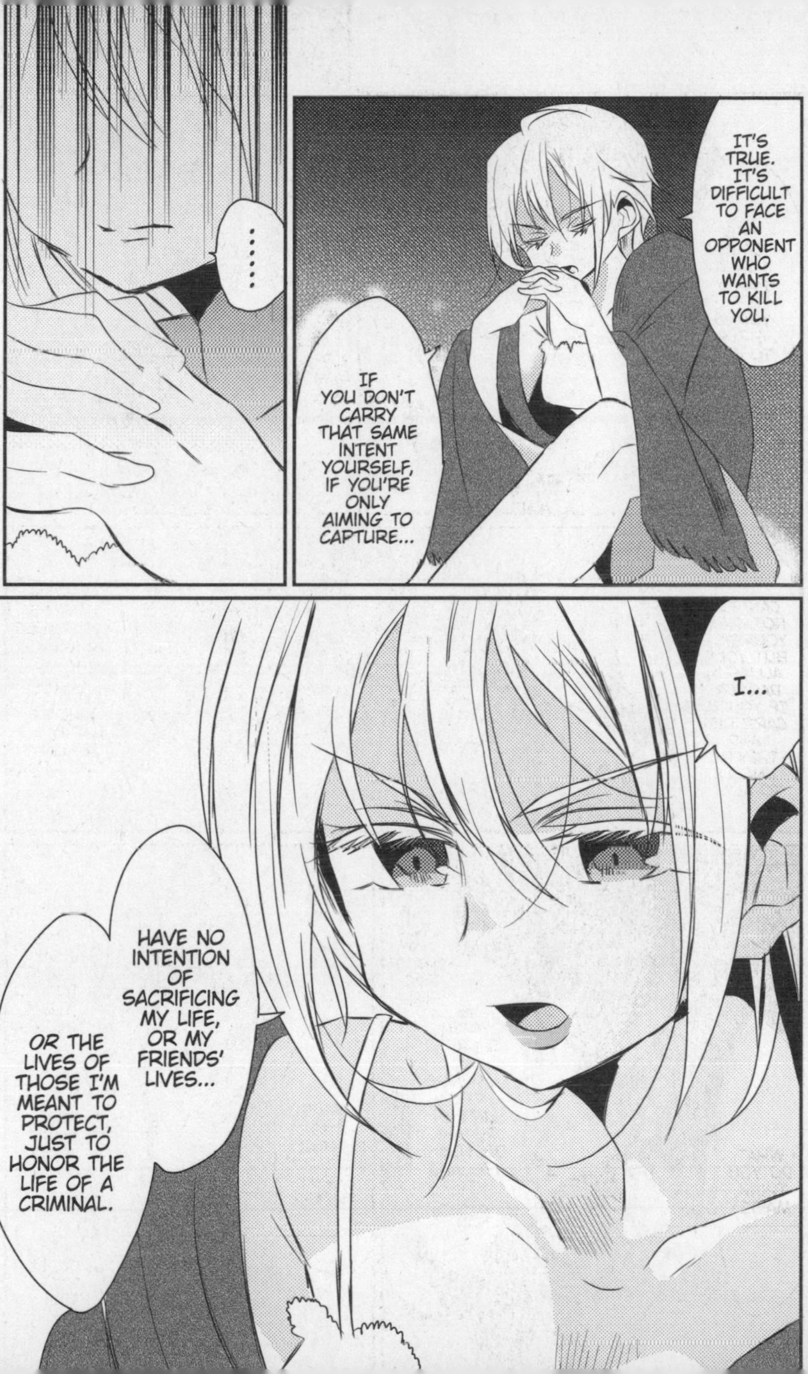

IT'S TRUE. IT'S DIFFICULT TO FACE AN OPPONENT WHO WANTS TO KILL YOU.
IF YOU DON'T CARRY THAT SAME INTENT YOURSELF, IF YOU'RE ONLY AIMING TO CAPTURE...
......
I...
HAVE NO INTENTION OF SACRIFICING MY LIFE, OR MY FRIENDS' LIVES...
OR THE LIVES OF THOSE I'M MEANT TO PROTECT, JUST TO HONOR THE LIFE OF A CRIMINAL.

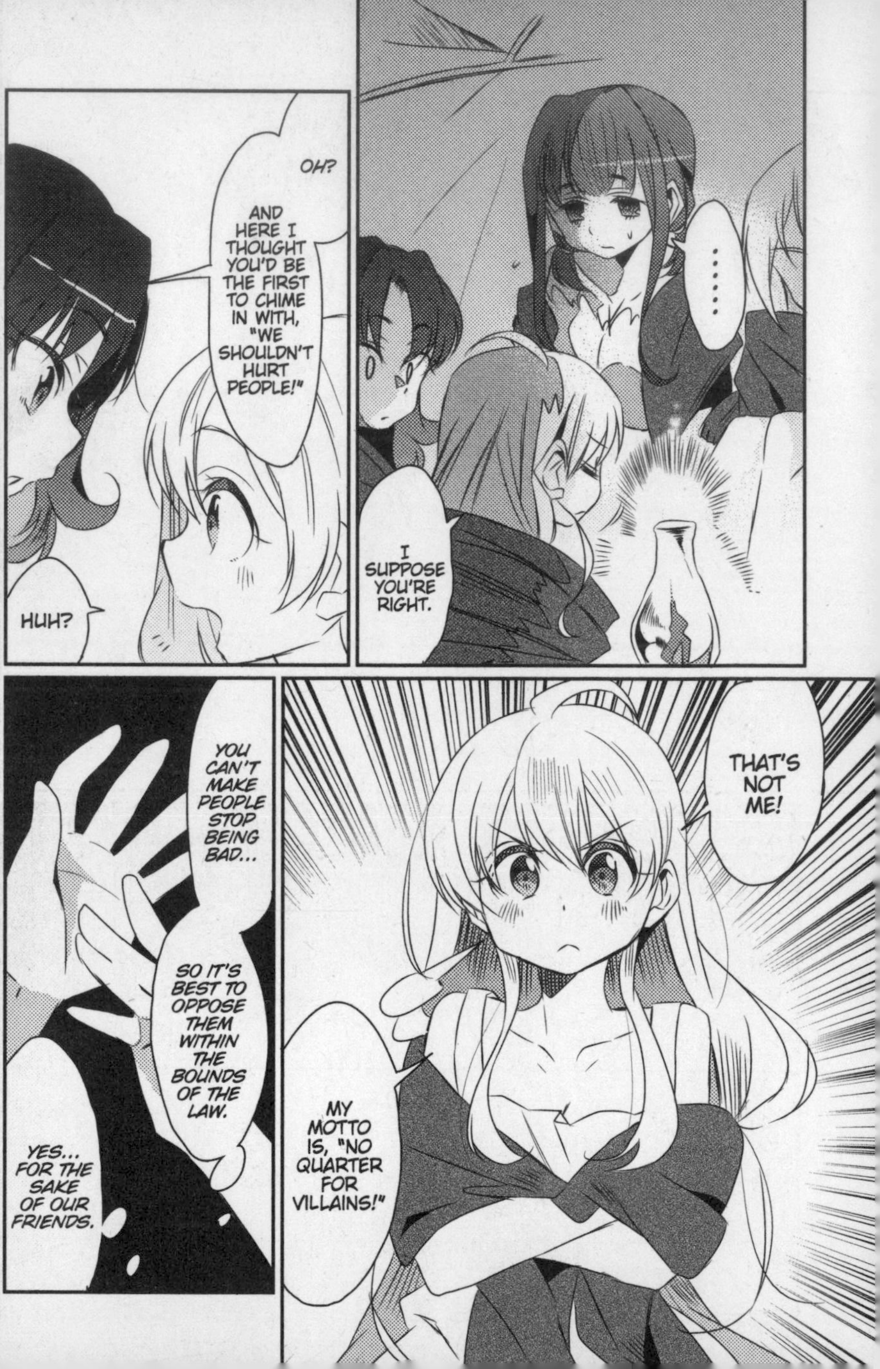
......
I SUPPOSE YOU'RE RIGHT.
OH?
AND HERE I THOUGHT YOU'D BE THE FIRST TO CHIME IN WITH, "WE SHOULDN'T HURT PEOPLE!"
HUH?
THAT'S NOT ME!
MY MOTTO IS, "NO QUARTER FOR VILLAINS!"
YOU CAN'T MAKE PEOPLE STOP BEING BAD...
SO IT'S BEST TO OPPOSE THEM WITHIN THE BOUNDS OF THE LAW.
YES... FOR THE SAKE OF OUR FRIENDS.

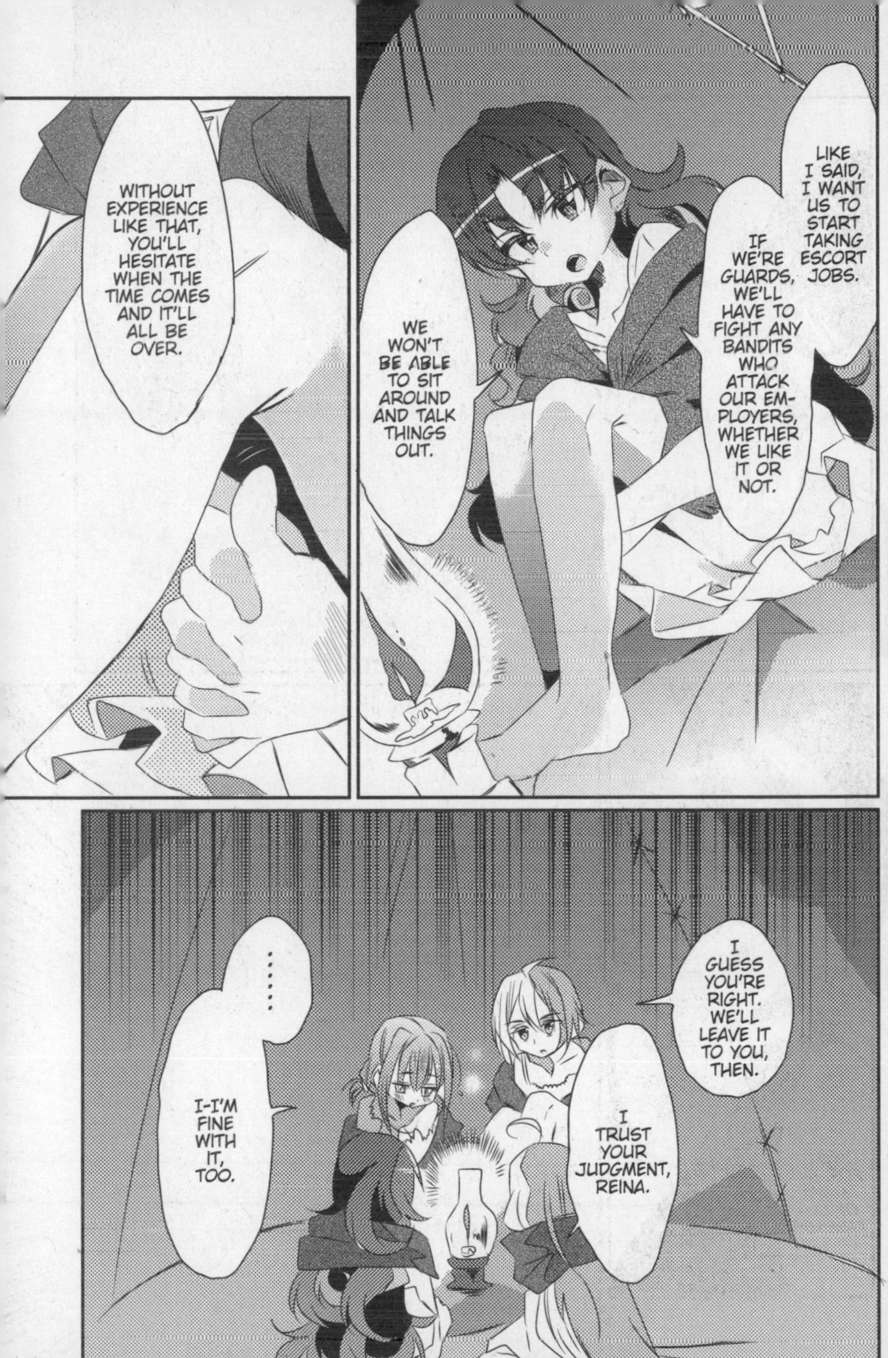
LIKE I SAID, I WANT US TO START TAKING ESCORT JOBS.
IF WE'RE GUARDS, WE'LL HAVE TO FIGHT ANY BANDITS WHO ATTACK OUR EM-PLOYERS, WHETHER WE LIKE IT OR NOT.
WE WON'T BE ABLE TO SIT AROUND AND TALK THINGS OUT.
WITHOUT EXPERIENCE LIKE THAT, YOU'LL HESITATE WHEN THE TIME COMES AND IT'LL ALL BE OVER.
I GUESS YOU'RE RIGHT. WE'LL LEAVE IT TO YOU, THEN.
I TRUST YOUR JUDGMENT, REINA.
......
I-I'M FINE WITH IT, TOO.

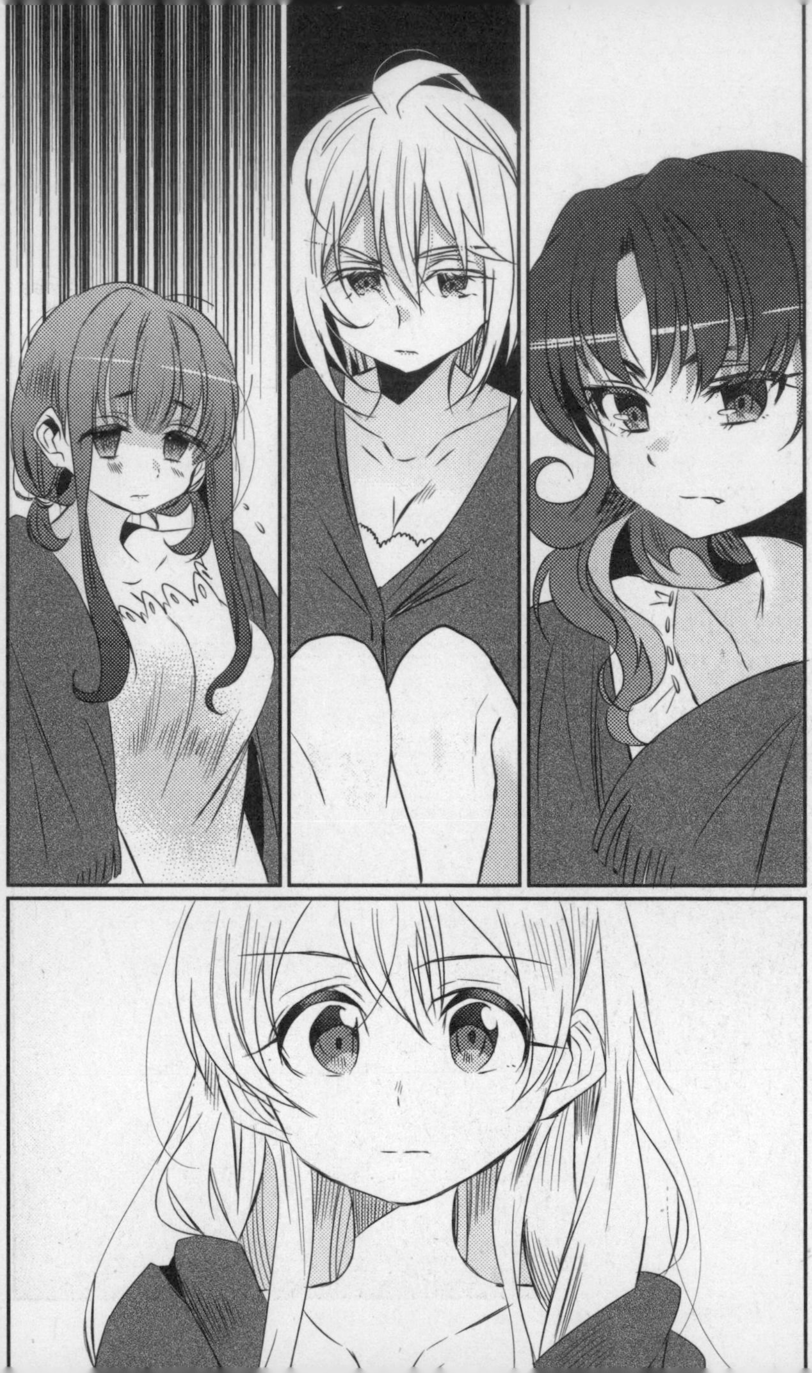

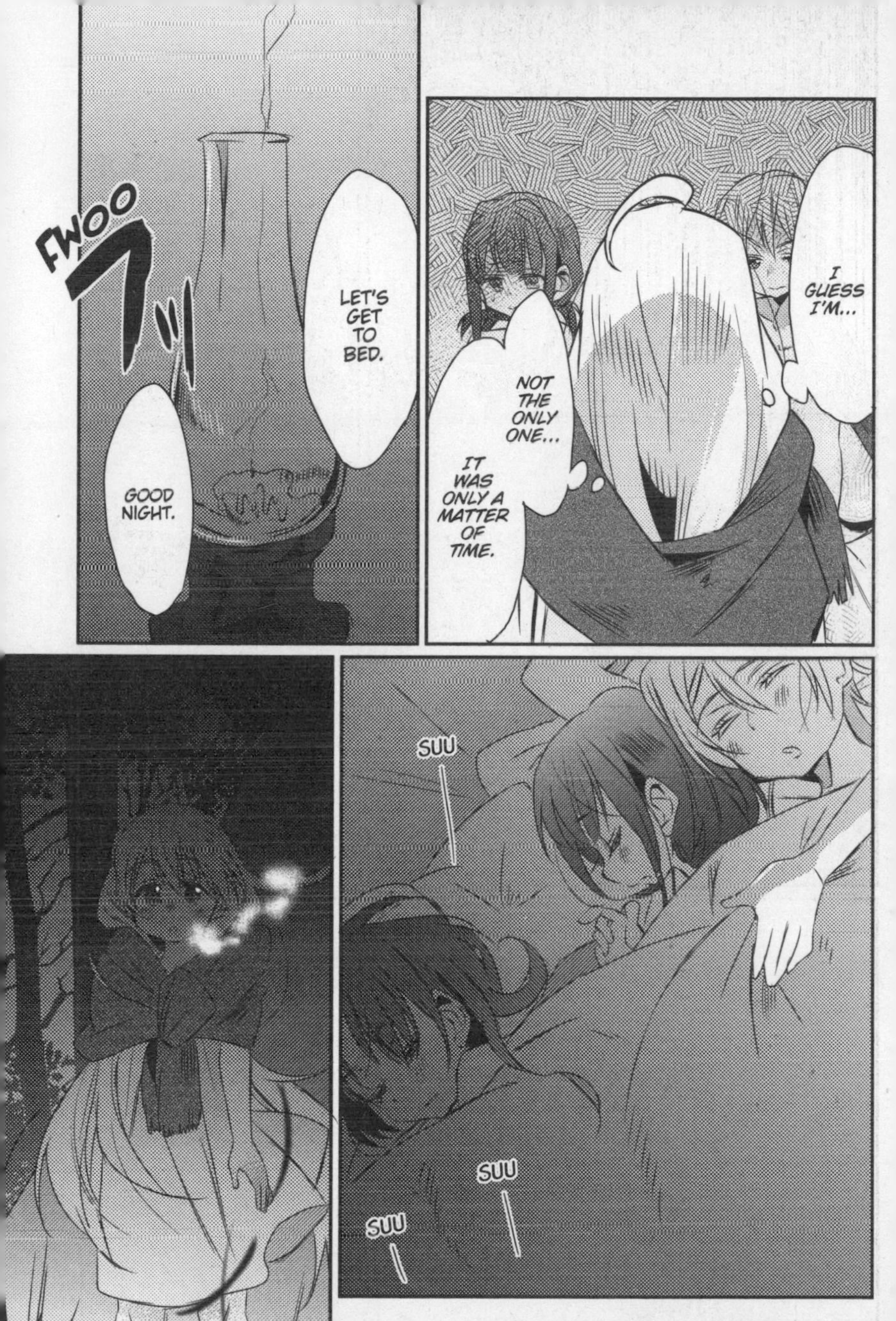
I GUESS I'M...
NOT THE ONLY ONE...
IT WAS ONLY A MATTER OF TIME.
LET'S GET TO BED.
FWOO
GOOD NIGHT.
SUU
SUU
SUU

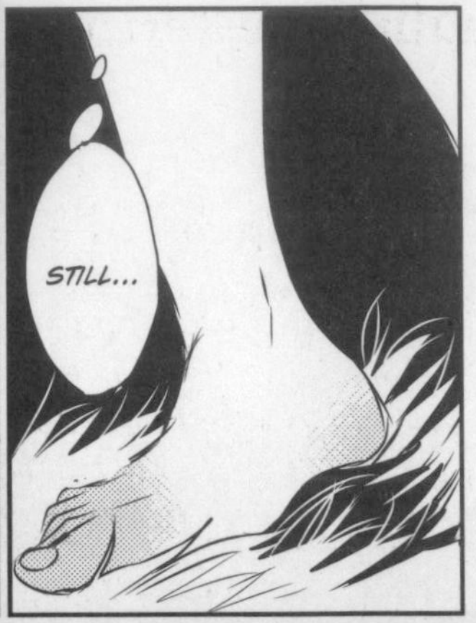
STILL...

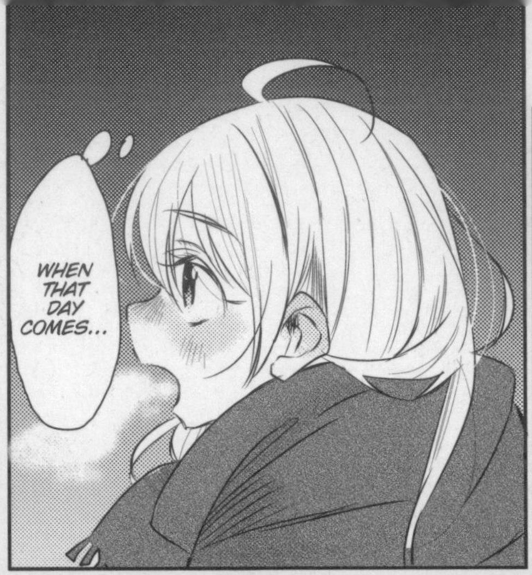
WHEN THAT DAY COMES...

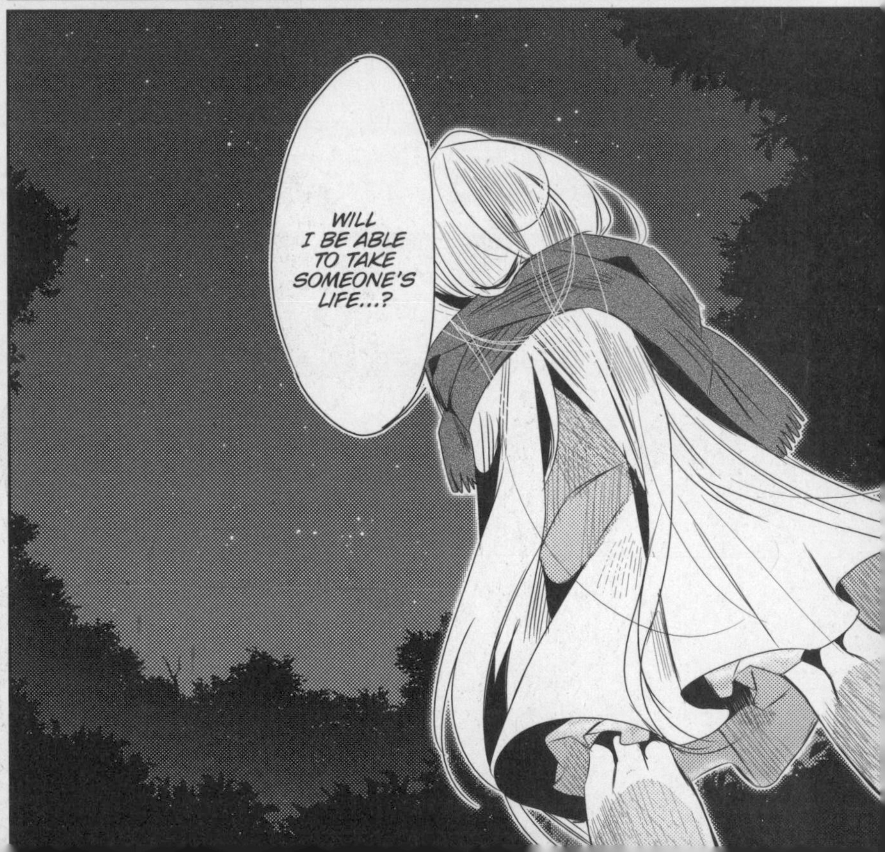
WILL I BE ABLE TO TAKE SOMEONE'S LIFE...?

Chapter 15: Pauline the Terrible

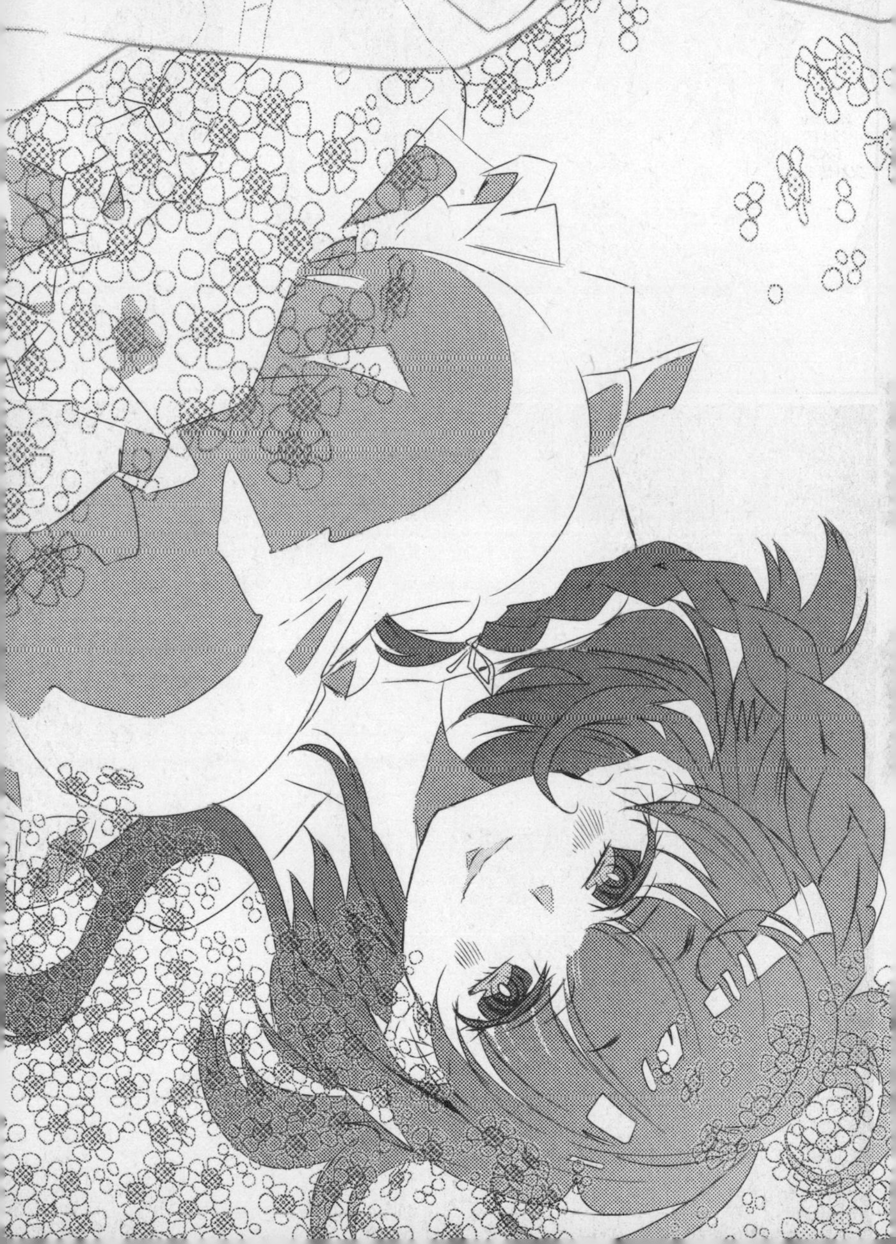

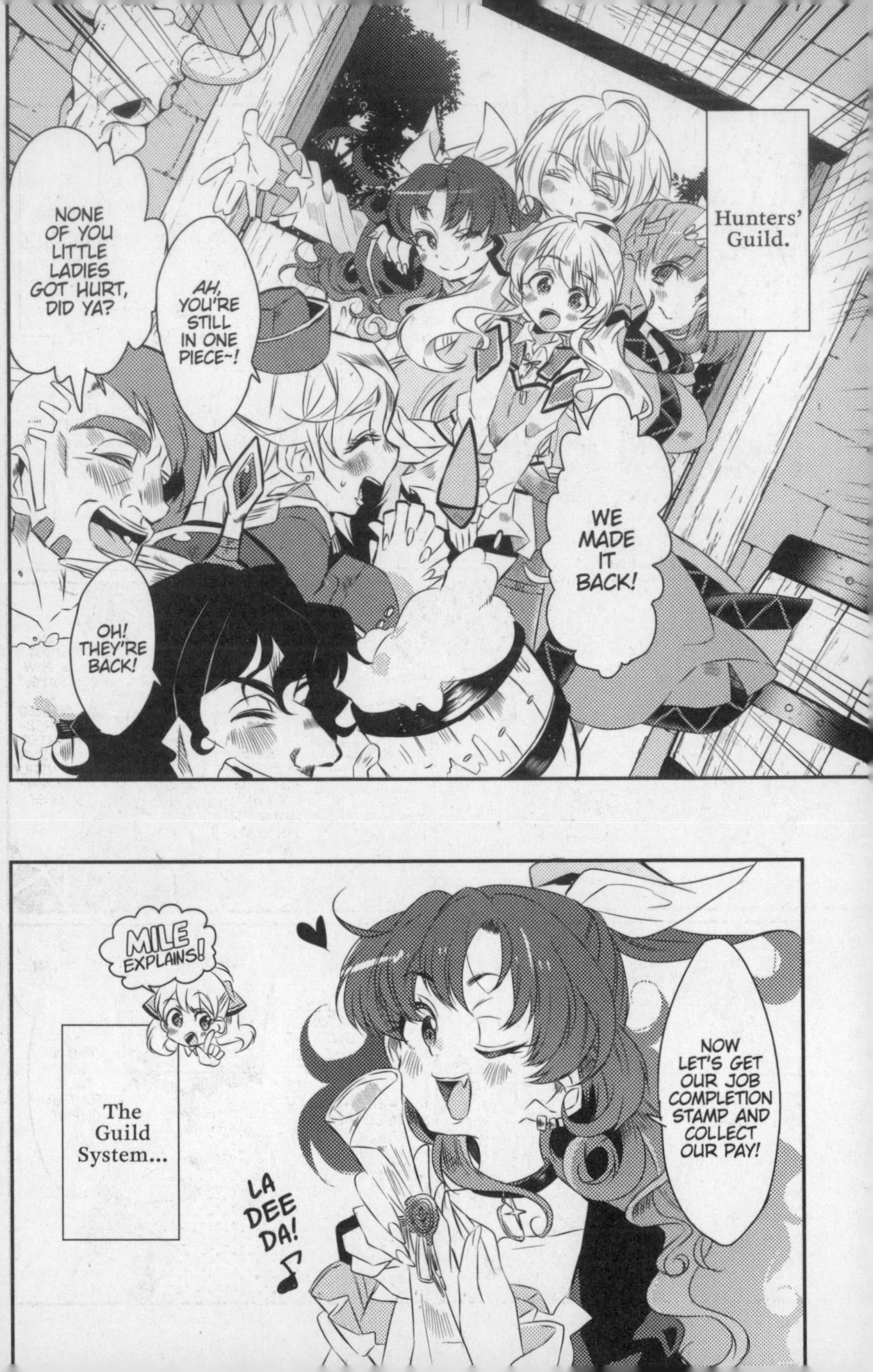
Hunters' Guild.
WE MADE IT BACK!
AH, YOU'RE STILL IN ONE PIECE~!
NONE OF YOU LITTLE LADIES GOT HURT, DID YA?
OH! THEY'RE BACK!
NOW LET'S GET OUR JOB COMPLETION STAMP AND COLLECT OUR PAY!
LA DEE DA!
The Guild System...
MILE EXPLAINS!

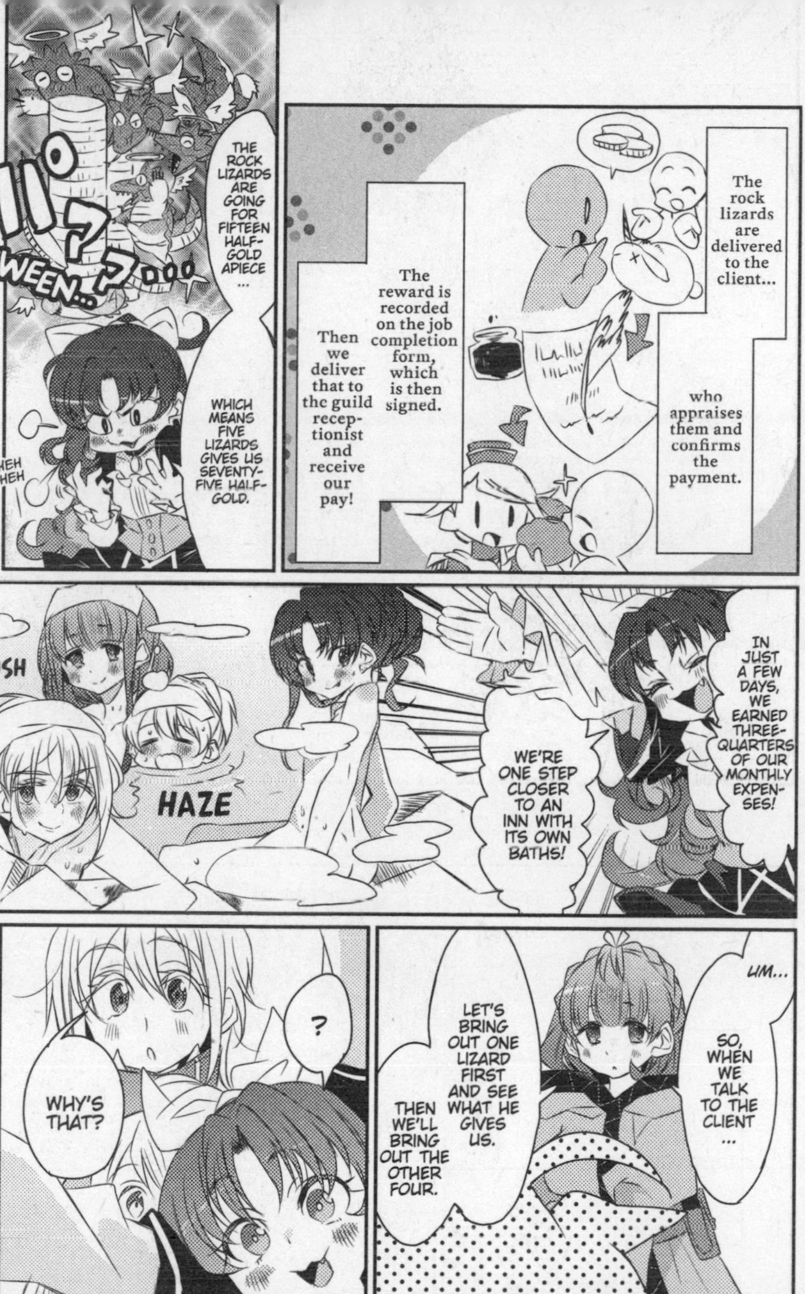
The rock lizards are delivered to the client...
who appraises them and confirms the payment.
The reward is recorded on the job completion form, which is then signed.
Then we deliver that to the guild receptionist and receive our pay!
THE ROCK LIZARDS ARE GOING FOR FIFTEEN HALF-GOLD APIECE...
SHWEEN...?
WHICH MEANS FIVE LIZARDS GIVES US SEVENTY-FIVE HALF-GOLD.
HEH HEH
IN JUST A FEW DAYS, WE EARNED THREE-QUARTERS OF OUR MONTHLY EXPENSES!
WE'RE ONE STEP CLOSER TO AN INN WITH ITS OWN BATHS!
HAZE
BLUSH
UM...
SO, WHEN WE TALK TO THE CLIENT...
LET'S BRING OUT ONE LIZARD FIRST AND SEE WHAT HE GIVES US.
THEN WE'LL BRING OUT THE OTHER FOUR.
?
WHY'S THAT?

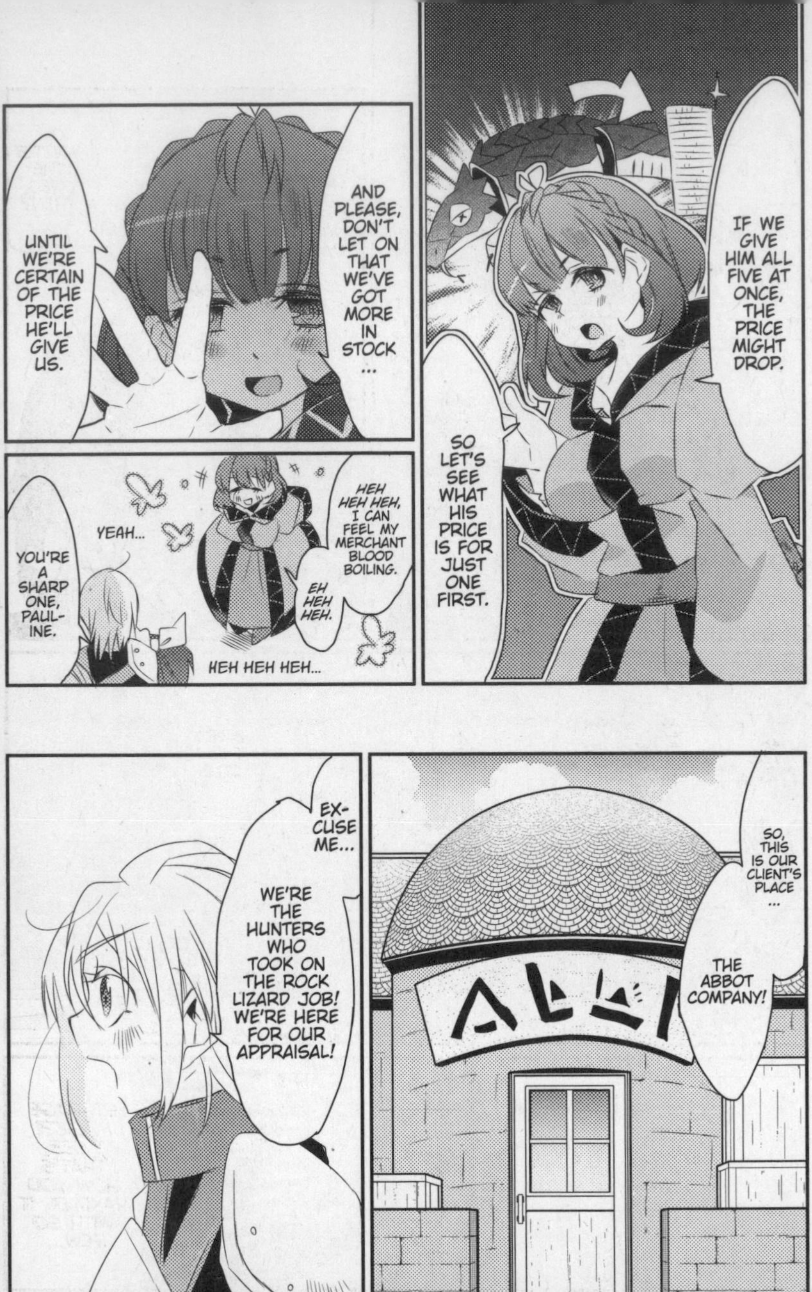
IF WE GIVE HIM ALL FIVE AT ONCE, THE PRICE MIGHT DROP.
SO LET'S SEE WHAT HIS PRICE IS FOR JUST ONE FIRST.
AND PLEASE, DON'T LET ON THAT WE'VE GOT MORE IN STOCK ...
UNTIL WE'RE CERTAIN OF THE PRICE HE'LL GIVE US.
HEH HEH HEH, I CAN FEEL MY MERCHANT BLOOD BOILING.
EH HEH HEH.
YEAH...
YOU'RE A SHARP ONE, PAUL-INE.
HEH HEH HEH...
SO, THIS IS OUR CLIENT'S PLACE ...
THE ABBOT COMPANY!
EX-CUSE ME...
WE'RE THE HUNTERS WHO TOOK ON THE ROCK LIZARD JOB! WE'RE HERE FOR OUR APPRAISAL!

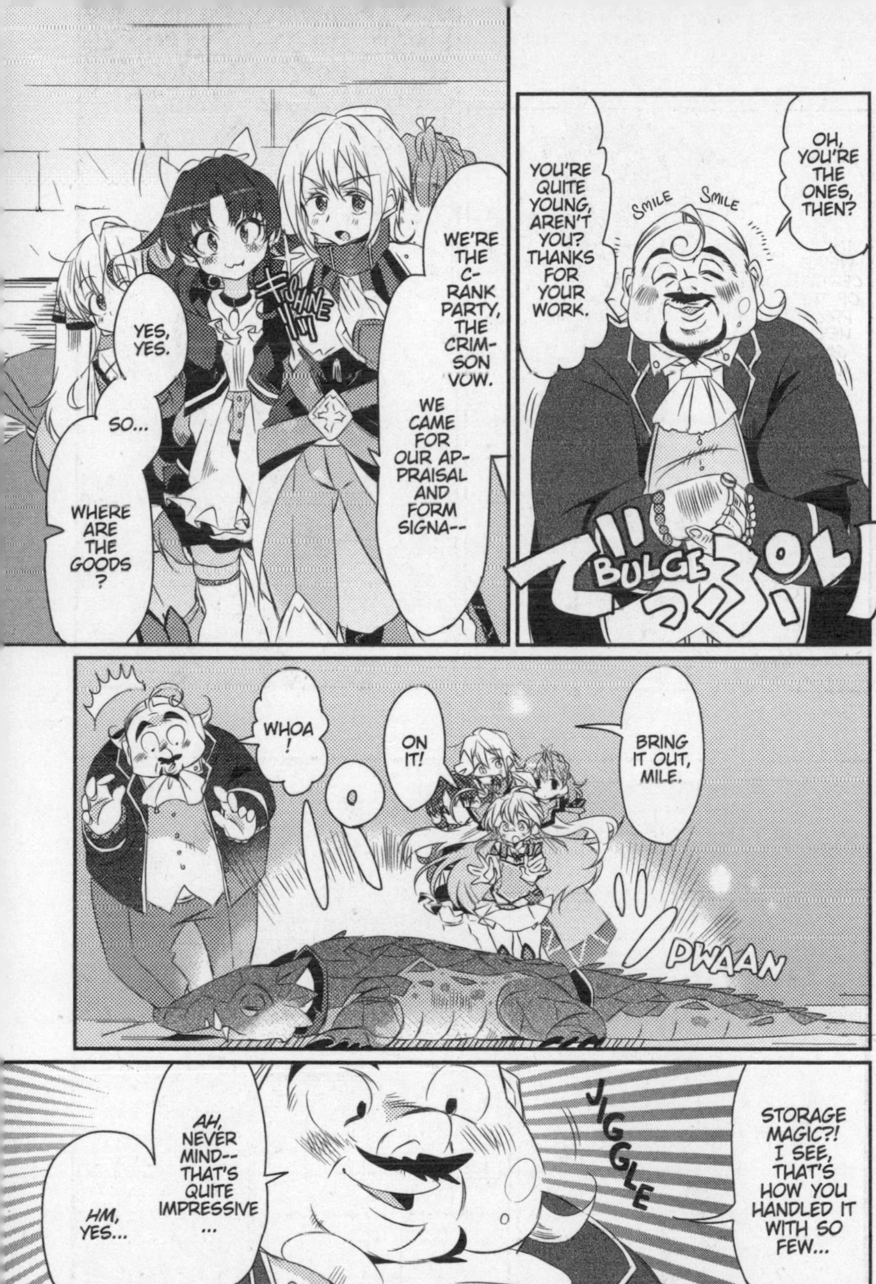
OH, YOU'RE THE ONES, THEN?
SMILE SMILE
YOU'RE QUITE YOUNG, AREN'T YOU? THANKS FOR YOUR WORK.
BULGE
WE'RE THE C-RANK PARTY, THE CRIMSON VOW.
WE CAME FOR OUR APPRAISAL AND FORM SIGNA--
SHINE
YES, YES.
SO...
WHERE ARE THE GOODS?
BRING IT OUT, MILE.
ON IT!
WHOA!
PWAAN
STORAGE MAGIC?! I SEE, THAT'S HOW YOU HANDLED IT WITH SO FEW...
JIGGLE
AH, NEVER MIND--THAT'S QUITE IMPRESSIVE...
HM, YES...

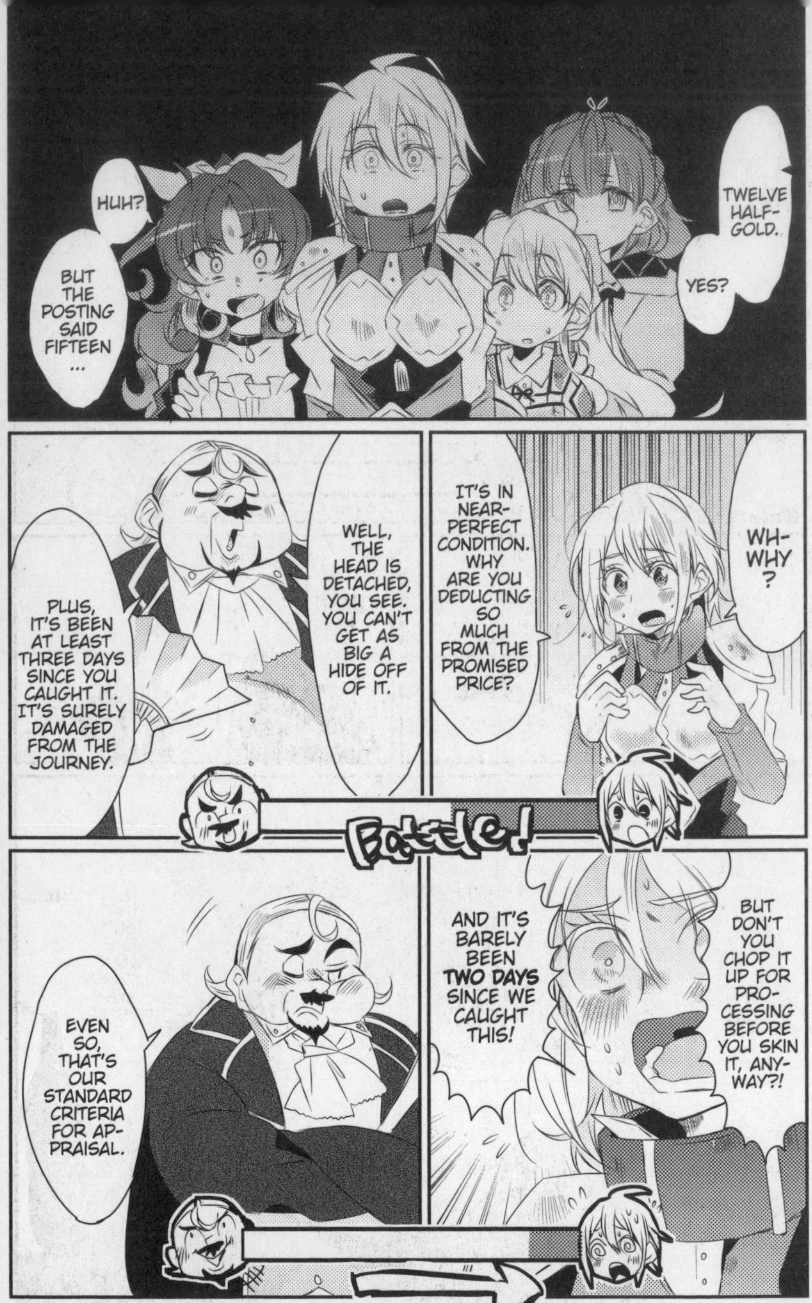
TWELVE HALF-GOLD.
YES?
HUH?
BUT THE POSTING SAID FIFTEEN...
WH-WHY?
IT'S IN NEAR-PERFECT CONDITION. WHY ARE YOU DEDUCTING SO MUCH FROM THE PROMISED PRICE?
WELL, THE HEAD IS DETACHED, YOU SEE. YOU CAN'T GET AS BIG A HIDE OFF OF IT.
PLUS, IT'S BEEN AT LEAST THREE DAYS SINCE YOU CAUGHT IT. IT'S SURELY DAMAGED FROM THE JOURNEY.
Battle!
BUT DON'T YOU CHOP IT UP FOR PROCESSING BEFORE YOU SKIN IT, ANYWAY?!
AND IT'S BARELY BEEN TWO DAYS SINCE WE CAUGHT THIS!
EVEN SO, THAT'S OUR STANDARD CRITERIA FOR APPRAISAL.

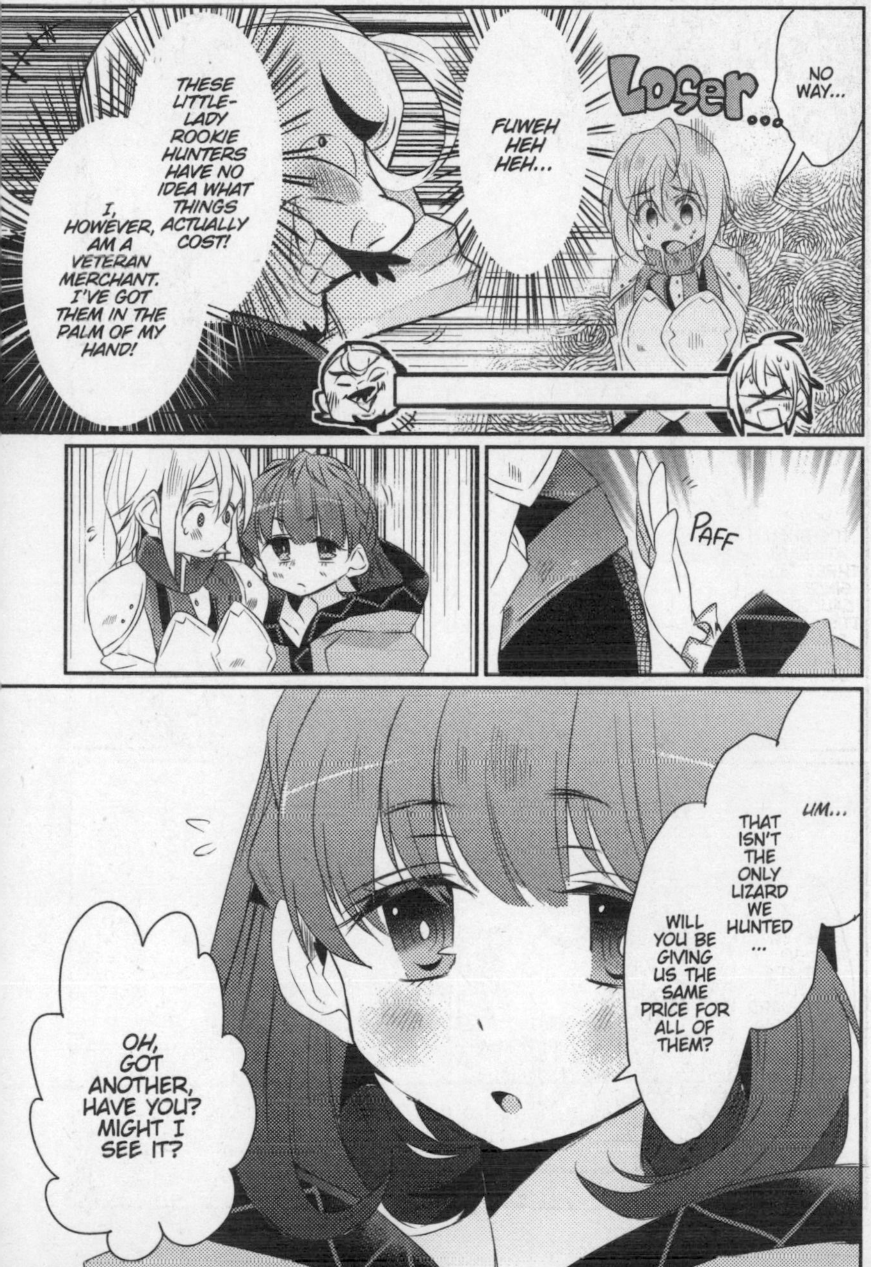
NO WAY...
LOSER...
FUWEH HEH HEH...
THESE LITTLE-LADY ROOKIE HUNTERS HAVE NO IDEA WHAT THINGS ACTUALLY COST!
I, HOWEVER, AM A VETERAN MERCHANT. I'VE GOT THEM IN THE PALM OF MY HAND!
PAFF
UM...
THAT ISN'T THE ONLY LIZARD WE HUNTED ...
WILL YOU BE GIVING US THE SAME PRICE FOR ALL OF THEM?
OH, GOT ANOTHER, HAVE YOU? MIGHT I SEE IT?

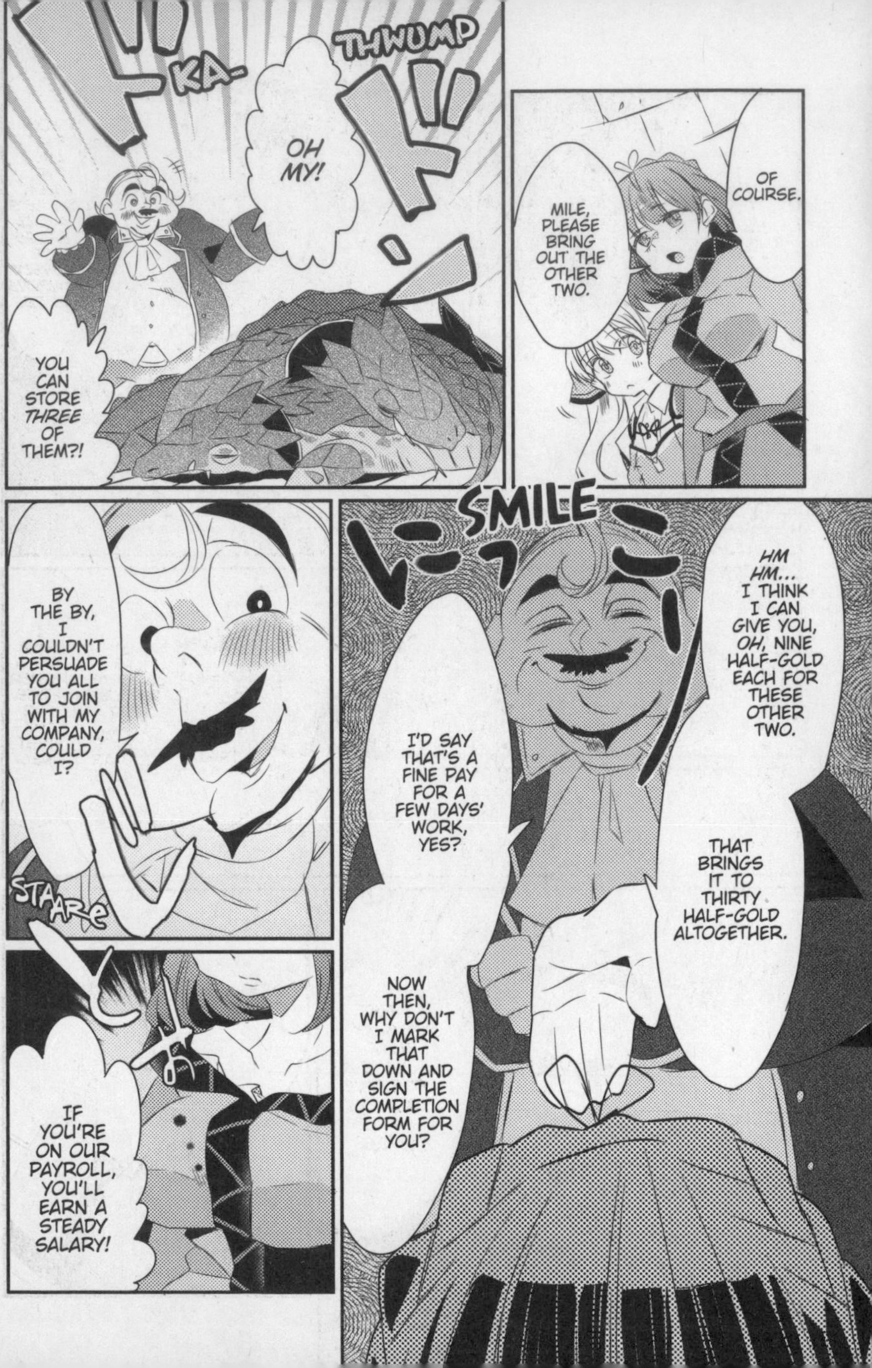
MILE, PLEASE BRING OUT THE OTHER TWO.
OF COURSE.
KA-
THWUMP
OH MY!
YOU CAN STORE *THREE* OF THEM?!
SMILE
HM HM... I THINK I CAN GIVE YOU, *OH*, NINE HALF-GOLD EACH FOR THESE OTHER TWO.
THAT BRINGS IT TO THIRTY HALF-GOLD ALTOGETHER.
I'D SAY THAT'S A FINE PAY FOR A FEW DAYS' WORK, YES?
NOW THEN, WHY DON'T I MARK THAT DOWN AND SIGN THE COMPLETION FORM FOR YOU?
BY THE BY, I COULDN'T PERSUADE YOU ALL TO JOIN WITH MY COMPANY, COULD I?
STAARE
IF YOU'RE ON OUR PAYROLL, YOU'LL EARN A STEADY SALARY!

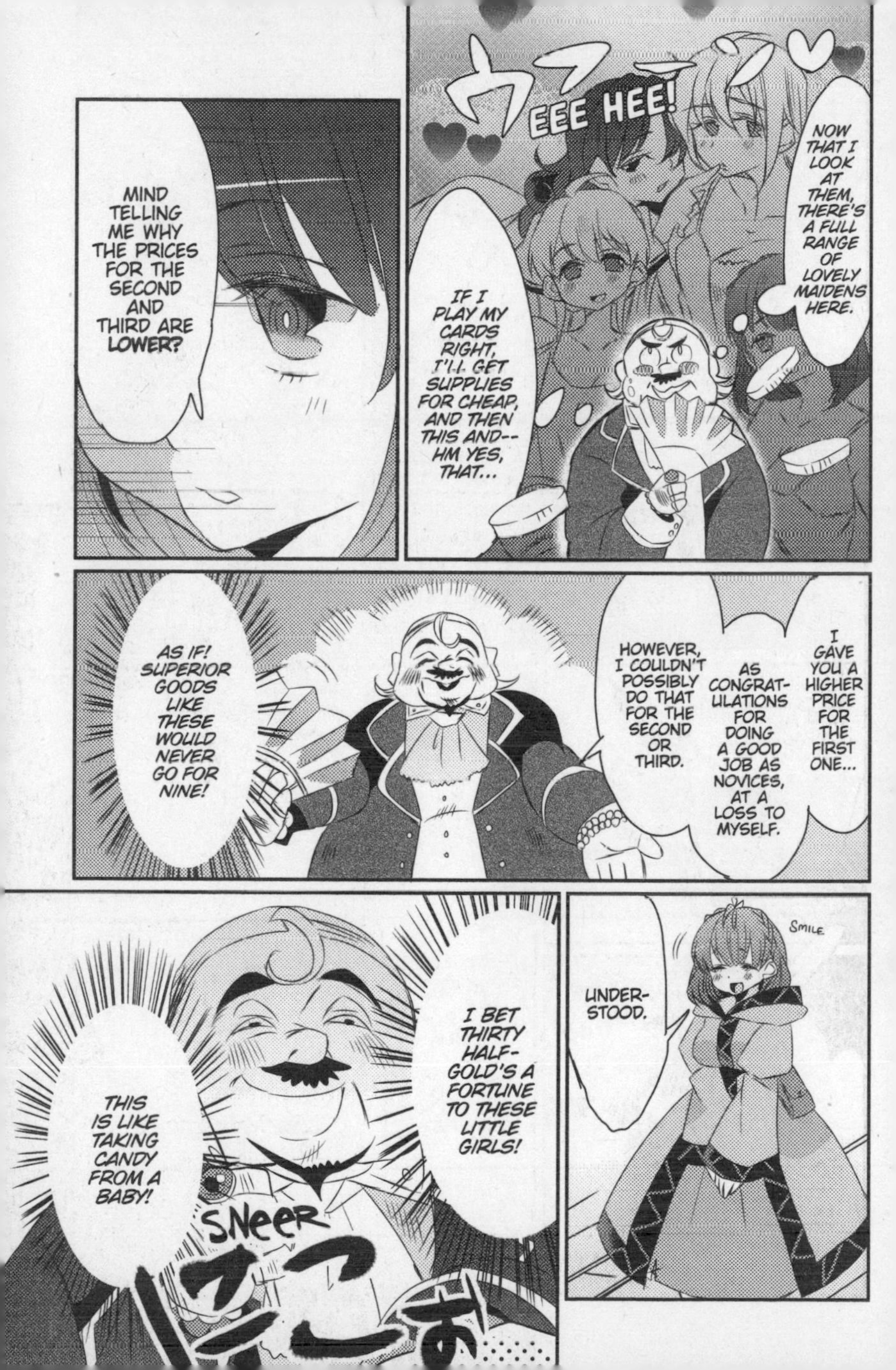
EEE HEE!
NOW THAT I LOOK AT THEM, THERE'S A FULL RANGE OF LOVELY MAIDENS HERE.
IF I PLAY MY CARDS RIGHT, I'LL GET SUPPLIES FOR CHEAP, AND THEN THIS AND-- HM YES, THAT...
MIND TELLING ME WHY THE PRICES FOR THE SECOND AND THIRD ARE LOWER?
I GAVE YOU A HIGHER PRICE FOR THE FIRST ONE...
AS CONGRAT-ULATIONS FOR DOING A GOOD JOB AS NOVICES, AT A LOSS TO MYSELF.
HOWEVER, I COULDN'T POSSIBLY DO THAT FOR THE SECOND OR THIRD.
AS IF! SUPERIOR GOODS LIKE THESE WOULD NEVER GO FOR NINE!
SMILE
UNDER-STOOD.
I BET THIRTY HALF-GOLD'S A FORTUNE TO THESE LITTLE GIRLS!
THIS IS LIKE TAKING CANDY FROM A BABY!
SNEER

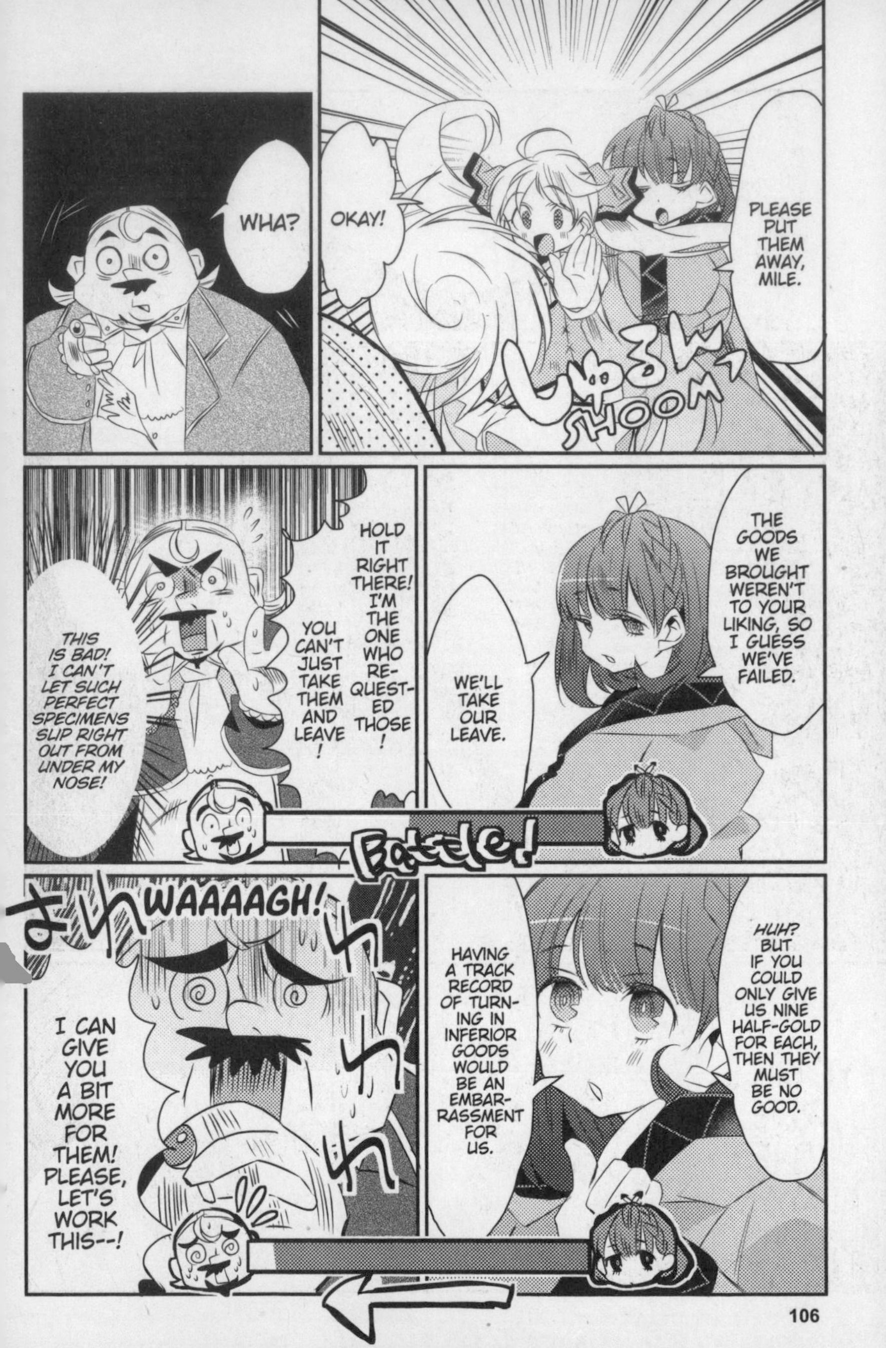
PLEASE PUT THEM AWAY, MILE.
OKAY!
しゅるん SHOOM
WHA?
THE GOODS WE BROUGHT WEREN'T TO YOUR LIKING, SO I GUESS WE'VE FAILED.
WE'LL TAKE OUR LEAVE.
HOLD IT RIGHT THERE! I'M THE ONE WHO RE-QUEST-ED THOSE!
YOU CAN'T JUST TAKE THEM AND LEAVE!
THIS IS BAD! I CAN'T LET SUCH PERFECT SPECIMENS SLIP RIGHT OUT FROM UNDER MY NOSE!
Battle!
HUH? BUT IF YOU COULD ONLY GIVE US NINE HALF-GOLD FOR EACH, THEN THEY MUST BE NO GOOD.
HAVING A TRACK RECORD OF TURN-ING IN INFERIOR GOODS WOULD BE AN EMBAR-RASSMENT FOR US.
はわ WAAAAGH!
I CAN GIVE YOU A BIT MORE FOR THEM! PLEASE, LET'S WORK THIS--!

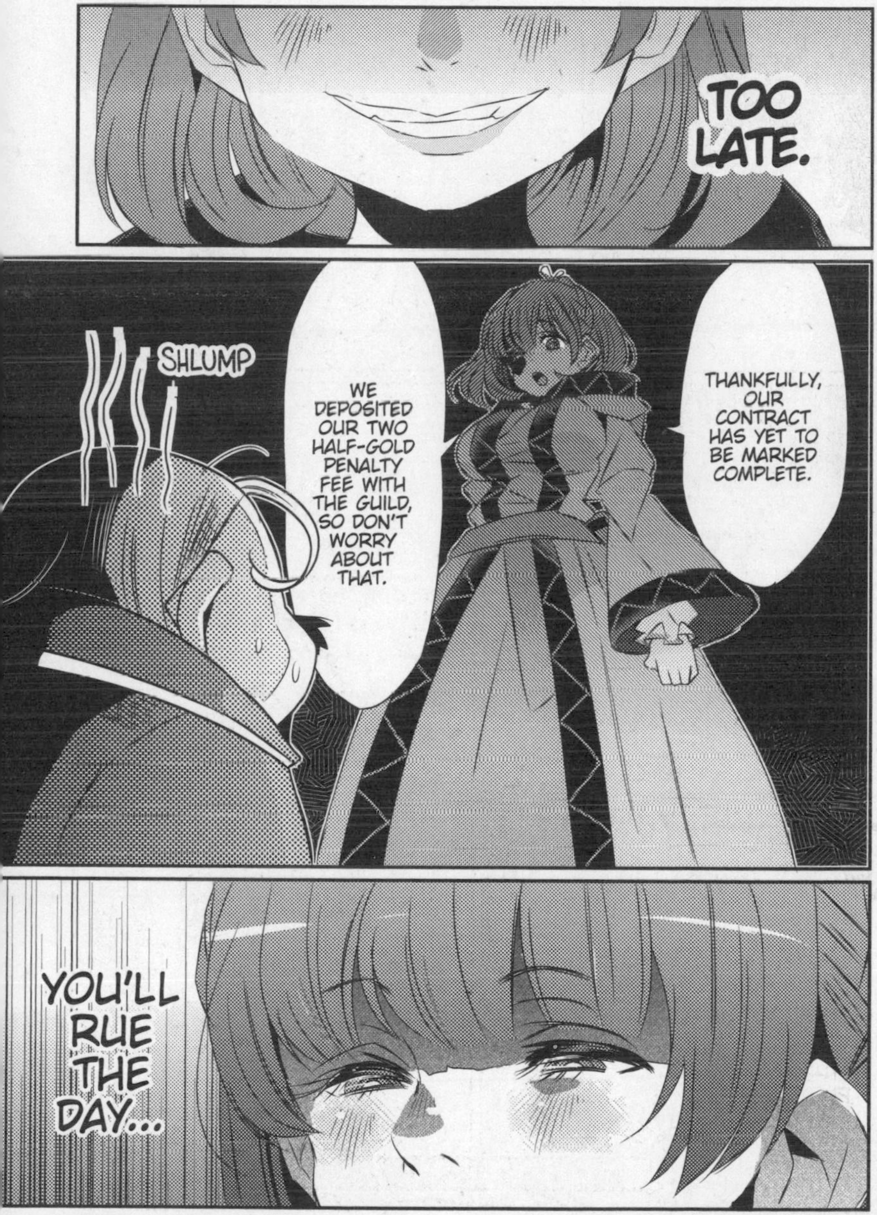
TOO LATE.
THANKFULLY, OUR CONTRACT HAS YET TO BE MARKED COMPLETE.
WE DEPOSITED OUR TWO HALF-GOLD PENALTY FEE WITH THE GUILD, SO DON'T WORRY ABOUT THAT.
SHLUMP
YOU'LL RUE THE DAY...

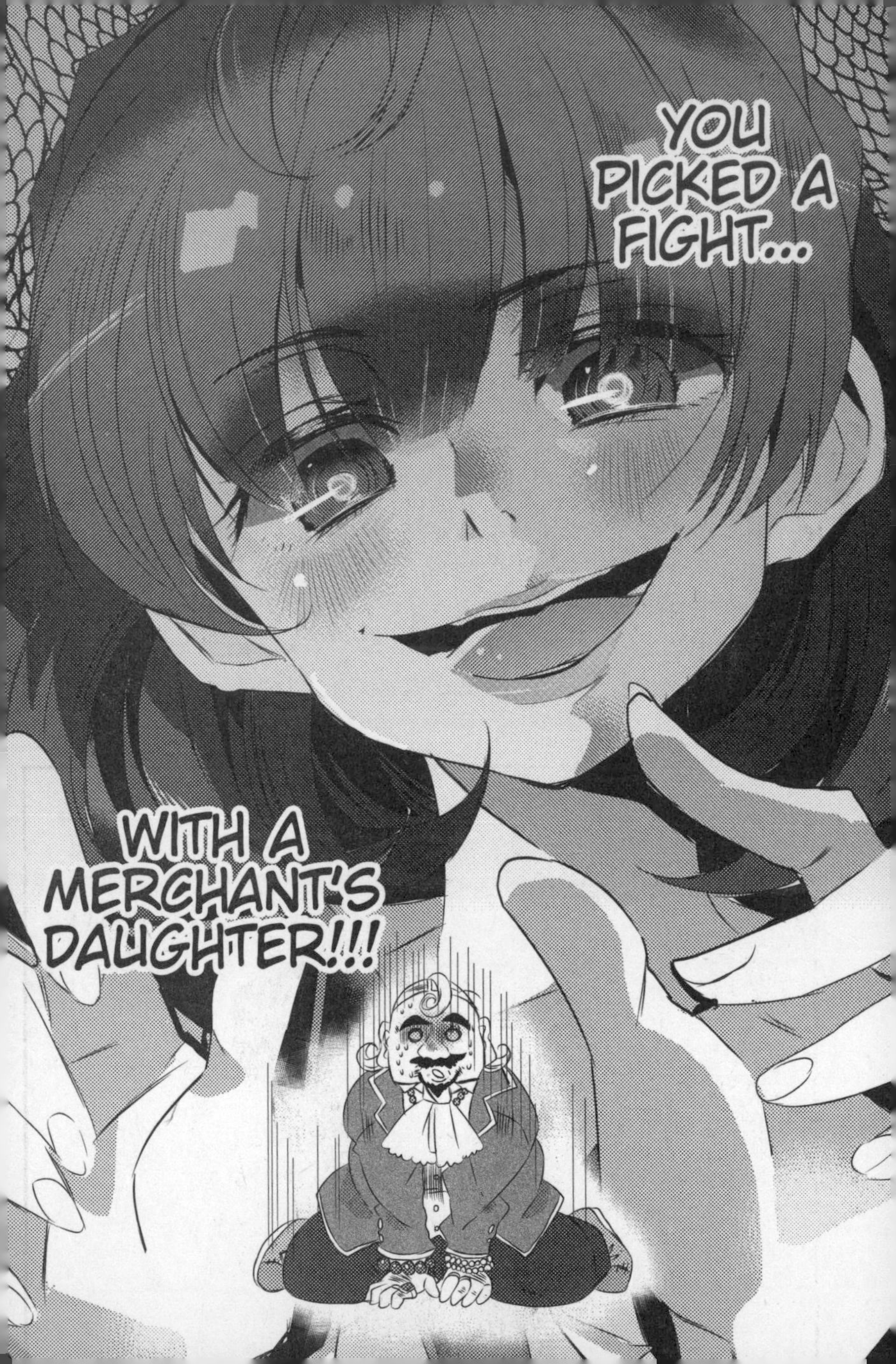
YOU PICKED A FIGHT...
WITH A MERCHANT'S DAUGHTER!!!

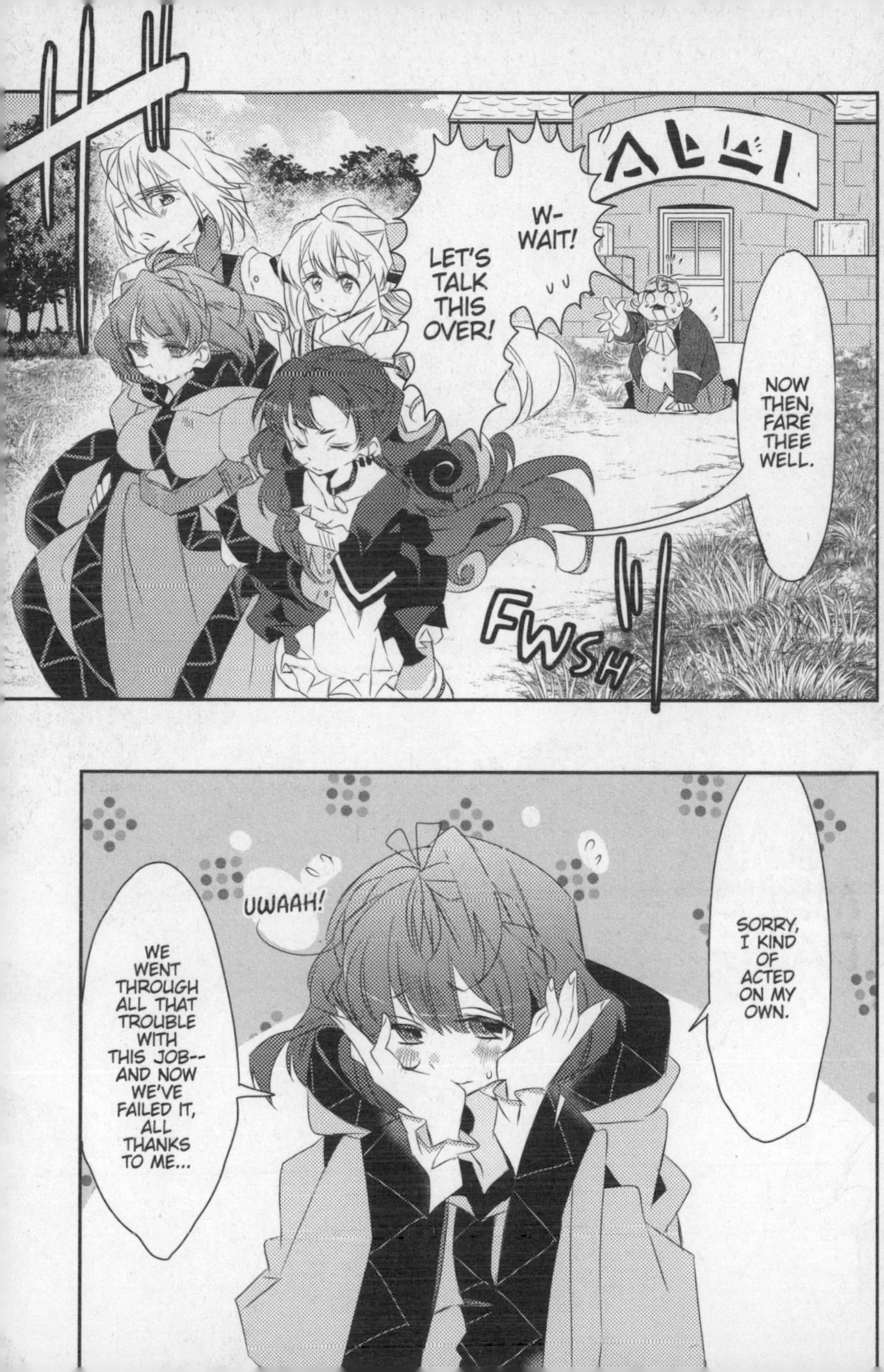
NOW THEN, FARE THEE WELL.
W-WAIT!
LET'S TALK THIS OVER!
FWSH
SORRY, I KIND OF ACTED ON MY OWN.
UWAAH!
WE WENT THROUGH ALL THAT TROUBLE WITH THIS JOB-- AND NOW WE'VE FAILED IT, ALL THANKS TO ME...

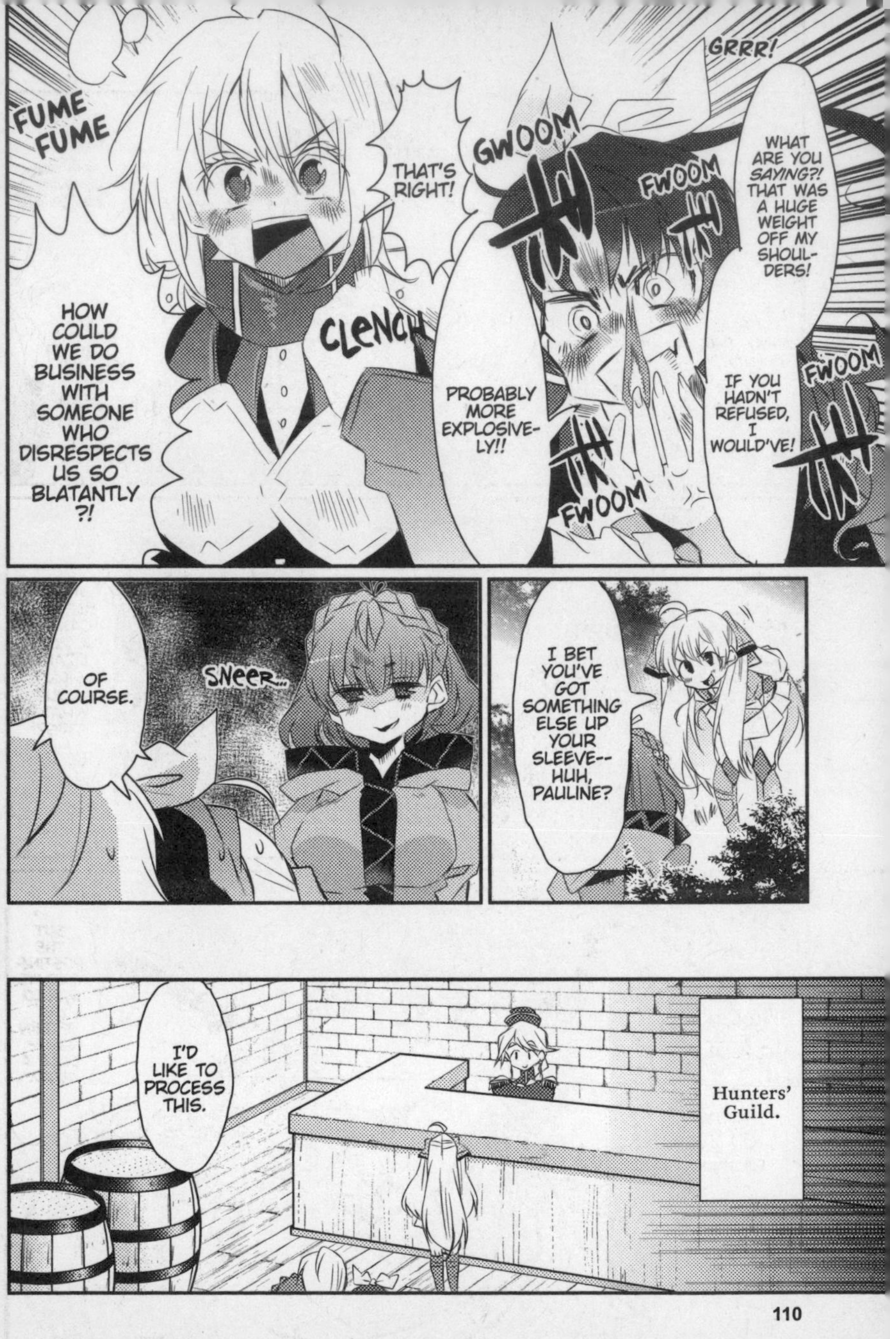
GRRR!
WHAT ARE YOU SAYING?! THAT WAS A HUGE WEIGHT OFF MY SHOUL-DERS!
GWOOM
FWOOM
FWOOM
IF YOU HADN'T REFUSED, I WOULD'VE!
PROBABLY MORE EXPLOSIVE-LY!!
FWOOM
THAT'S RIGHT!
FUME FUME
CLENCH
HOW COULD WE DO BUSINESS WITH SOMEONE WHO DISRESPECTS US SO BLATANTLY ?!
I BET YOU'VE GOT SOMETHING ELSE UP YOUR SLEEVE--HUH, PAULINE?
SNEER...
OF COURSE.
Hunters' Guild.
I'D LIKE TO PROCESS THIS.

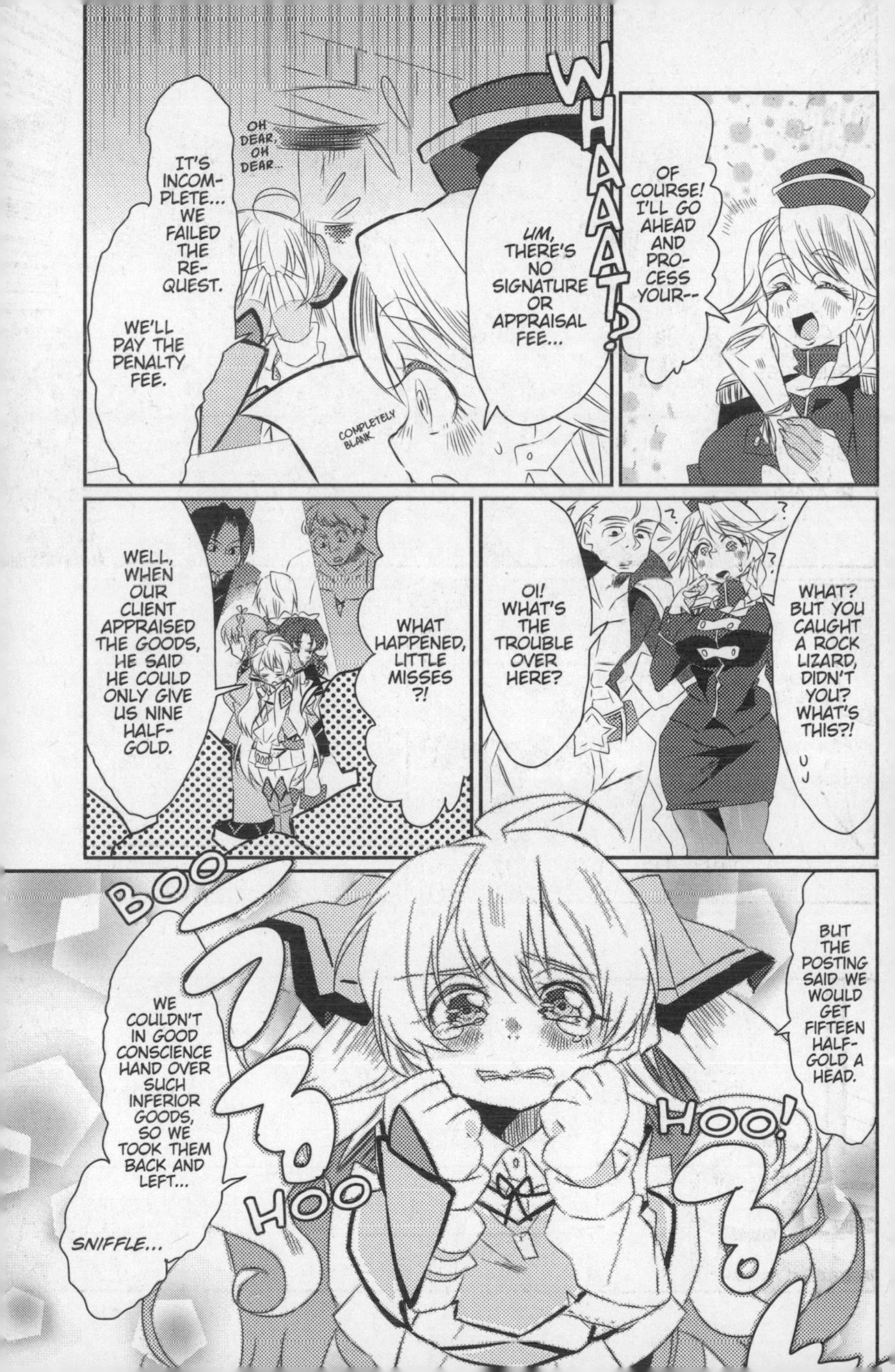

OF COURSE! I'LL GO AHEAD AND PROCESS YOUR--
WHAAAT?!
UM, THERE'S NO SIGNATURE OR APPRAISAL FEE...
COMPLETELY BLANK
OH DEAR, OH DEAR...
IT'S INCOMPLETE... WE FAILED THE REQUEST.
WE'LL PAY THE PENALTY FEE.
WHAT? BUT YOU CAUGHT A ROCK LIZARD, DIDN'T YOU? WHAT'S THIS?!
OI! WHAT'S THE TROUBLE OVER HERE?
WHAT HAPPENED, LITTLE MISSES?!
WELL, WHEN OUR CLIENT APPRAISED THE GOODS, HE SAID HE COULD ONLY GIVE US NINE HALF-GOLD.
BUT THE POSTING SAID WE WOULD GET FIFTEEN HALF-GOLD A HEAD.
HOO!
BOO
HOO
WE COULDN'T IN GOOD CONSCIENCE HAND OVER SUCH INFERIOR GOODS, SO WE TOOK THEM BACK AND LEFT...
SNIFFLE...

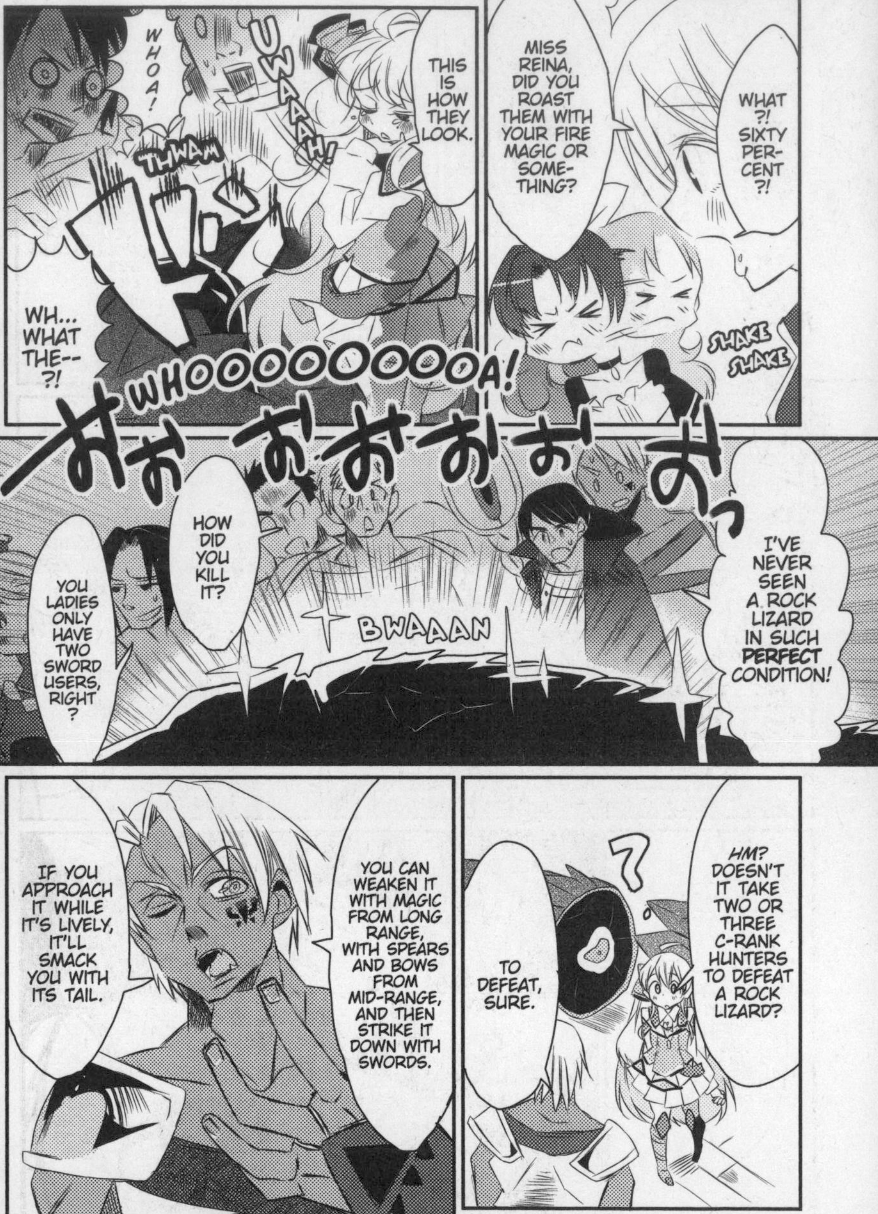
WHAT?! SIXTY PERCENT?!
SHAKE SHAKE
MISS REINA, DID YOU ROAST THEM WITH YOUR FIRE MAGIC OR SOMETHING?
THIS IS HOW THEY LOOK.
UWAAAAH!
WHOA!
THWAM
WH... WHAT THE--?!
WHOOOOOOOOOA!
おぉぉおおぉおっ
I'VE NEVER SEEN A ROCK LIZARD IN SUCH PERFECT CONDITION!
HOW DID YOU KILL IT?
BWAAAN
YOU LADIES ONLY HAVE TWO SWORD USERS, RIGHT?
HM? DOESN'T IT TAKE TWO OR THREE C-RANK HUNTERS TO DEFEAT A ROCK LIZARD?
?
TO DEFEAT, SURE.
YOU CAN WEAKEN IT WITH MAGIC FROM LONG RANGE, WITH SPEARS AND BOWS FROM MID-RANGE, AND THEN STRIKE IT DOWN WITH SWORDS.
IF YOU APPROACH IT WHILE IT'S LIVELY, IT'LL SMACK YOU WITH ITS TAIL.

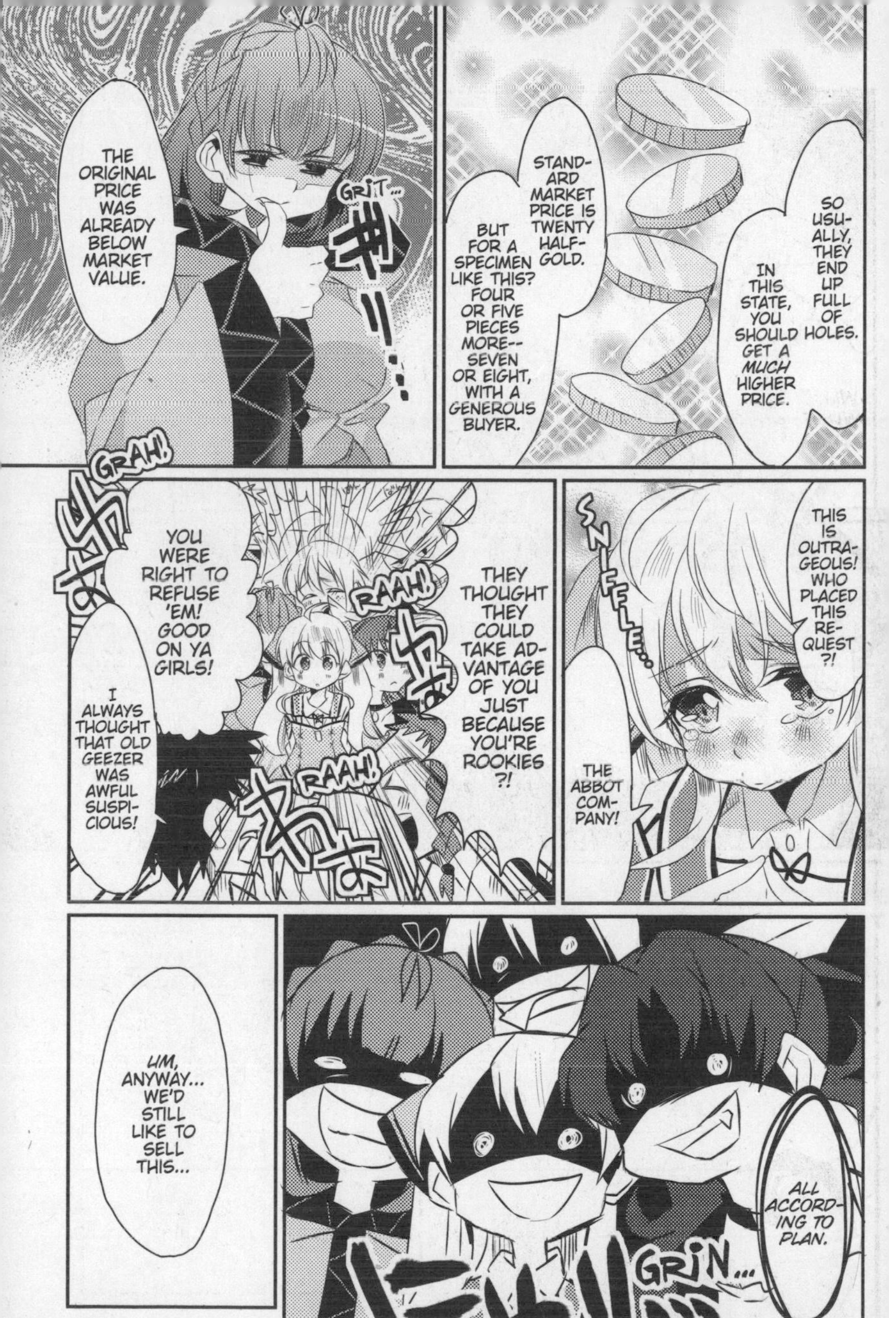
SO USUALLY, THEY END UP FULL OF HOLES.
IN THIS STATE, YOU SHOULD GET A *MUCH* HIGHER PRICE.
STANDARD MARKET PRICE IS TWENTY HALF-GOLD.
BUT FOR A SPECIMEN LIKE THIS? FOUR OR FIVE PIECES MORE--SEVEN OR EIGHT, WITH A GENEROUS BUYER.
GRIT...
THE ORIGINAL PRICE WAS ALREADY BELOW MARKET VALUE.
THIS IS OUTRAGEOUS! WHO PLACED THIS REQUEST?!
SNIFFLE...
THE ABBOT COMPANY!
THEY THOUGHT THEY COULD TAKE ADVANTAGE OF YOU JUST BECAUSE YOU'RE ROOKIES?!
RAAH!
YOU WERE RIGHT TO REFUSE 'EM! GOOD ON YA GIRLS!
GRAH!
I ALWAYS THOUGHT THAT OLD GEEZER WAS AWFUL SUSPICIOUS!
RAAH!
ALL ACCORDING TO PLAN.
GRIN...
UM, ANYWAY... WE'D STILL LIKE TO SELL THIS...

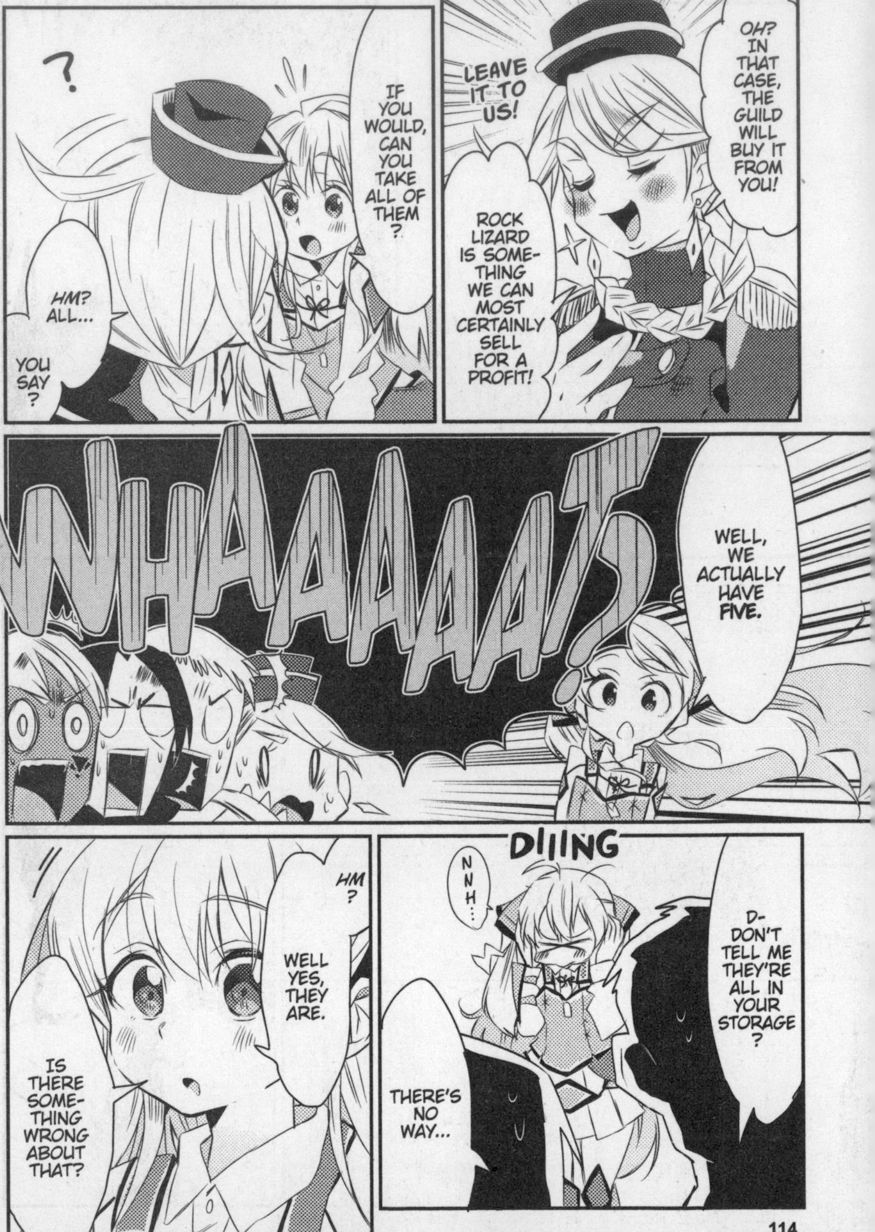
OH? IN THAT CASE, THE GUILD WILL BUY IT FROM YOU!
LEAVE IT TO US!
ROCK LIZARD IS SOME-THING WE CAN MOST CERTAINLY SELL FOR A PROFIT!
IF YOU WOULD, CAN YOU TAKE ALL OF THEM?
?
HM? ALL...
YOU SAY?
WELL, WE ACTUALLY HAVE FIVE.
WHAAAAAT?
DIIING
NNH...
D-DON'T TELL ME THEY'RE ALL IN YOUR STORAGE?
THERE'S NO WAY...
HM?
WELL YES, THEY ARE.
IS THERE SOME-THING WRONG ABOUT THAT?

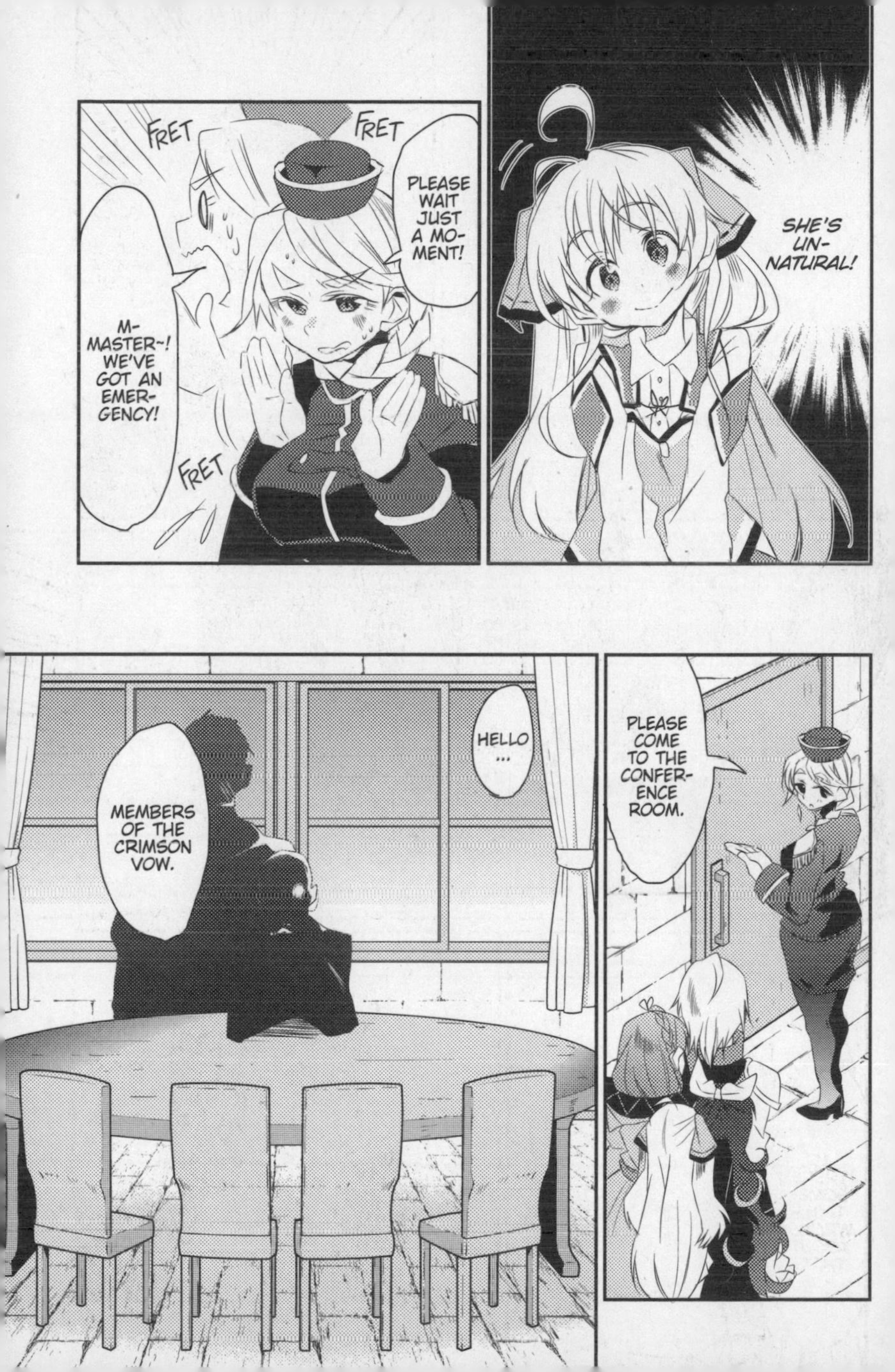
SHE'S UN-NATURAL!
FRET
PLEASE WAIT JUST A MO-MENT!
FRET
M-MASTER~! WE'VE GOT AN EMER-GENCY!
FRET
PLEASE COME TO THE CONFER-ENCE ROOM.
HELLO ...
MEMBERS OF THE CRIMSON VOW.

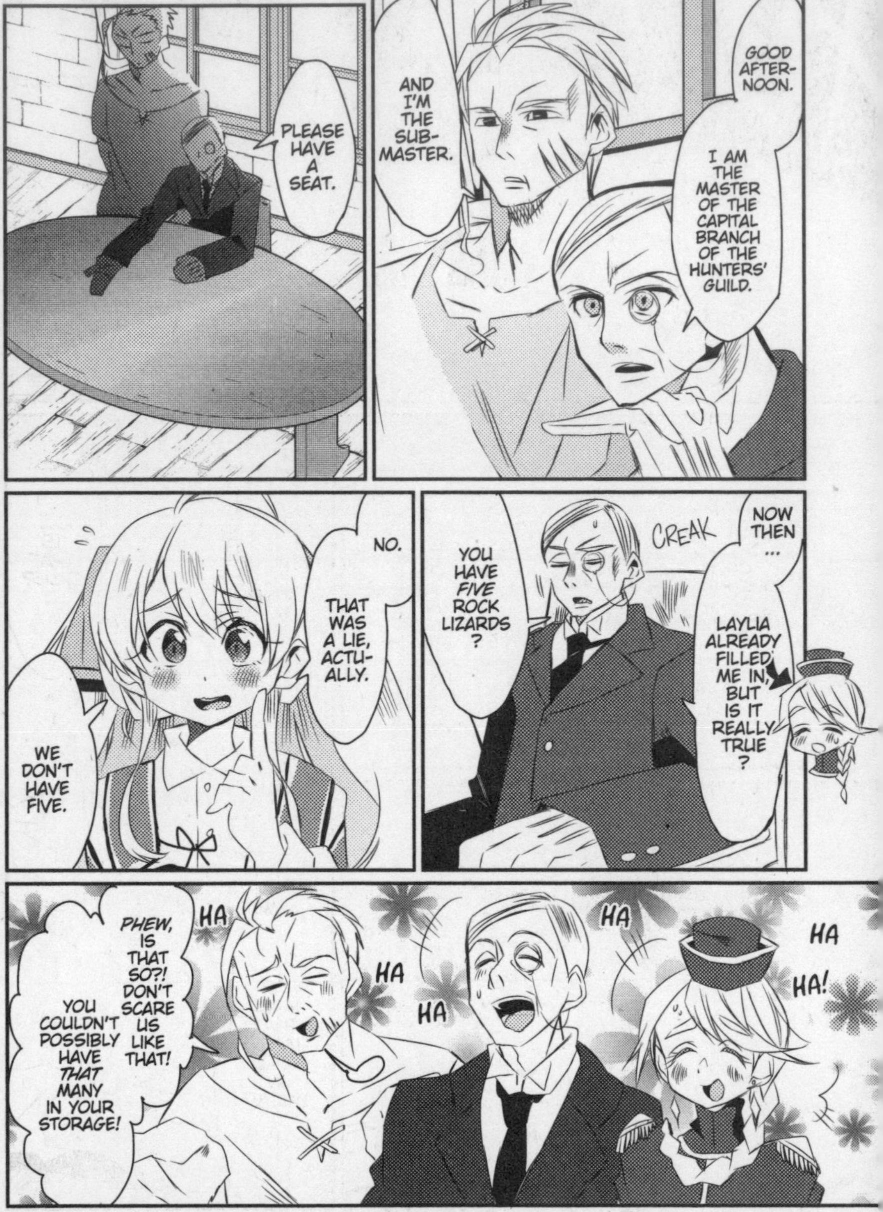
GOOD AFTER-NOON.
I AM THE MASTER OF THE CAPITAL BRANCH OF THE HUNTERS' GUILD.
AND I'M THE SUB-MASTER.
PLEASE HAVE A SEAT.
NOW THEN ...
LAYLIA ALREADY FILLED ME IN, BUT IS IT REALLY TRUE?
CREAK
YOU HAVE *FIVE* ROCK LIZARDS?
NO.
THAT WAS A LIE, ACTUALLY.
WE DON'T HAVE FIVE.
HA
HA!
HA
HA
HA
HA
PHEW, IS THAT SO?! DON'T SCARE US LIKE THAT!
YOU COULDN'T POSSIBLY HAVE *THAT* MANY IN YOUR STORAGE!

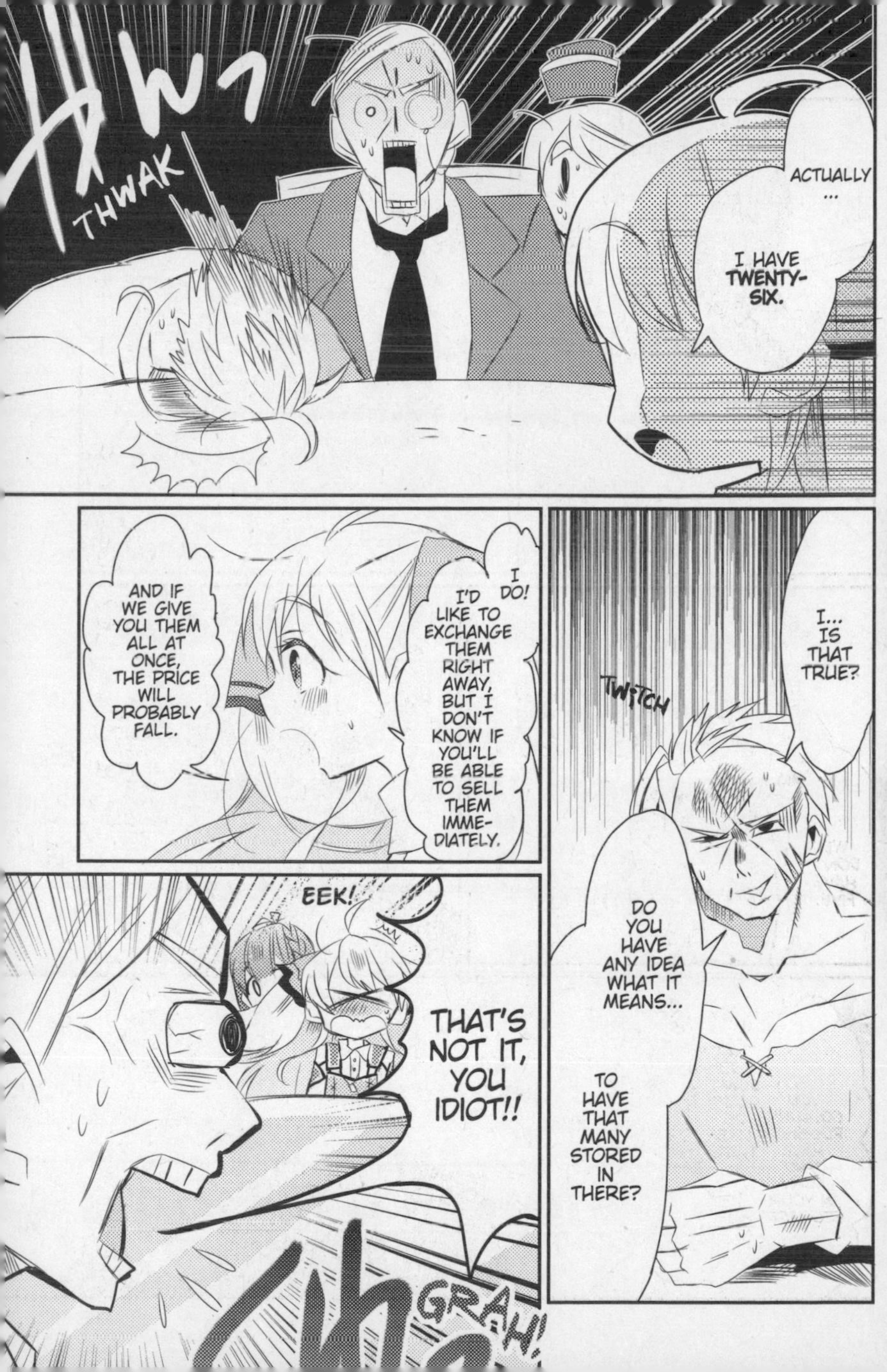
THWAK
ACTUALLY ...
I HAVE TWENTY-SIX.
I... IS THAT TRUE?
TWITCH
DO YOU HAVE ANY IDEA WHAT IT MEANS...
TO HAVE THAT MANY STORED IN THERE?
I DO!
I'D LIKE TO EXCHANGE THEM RIGHT AWAY, BUT I DON'T KNOW IF YOU'LL BE ABLE TO SELL THEM IMMEDIATELY.
AND IF WE GIVE YOU THEM ALL AT ONCE, THE PRICE WILL PROBABLY FALL.
EEK!
THAT'S NOT IT, YOU IDIOT!!
GRAH!

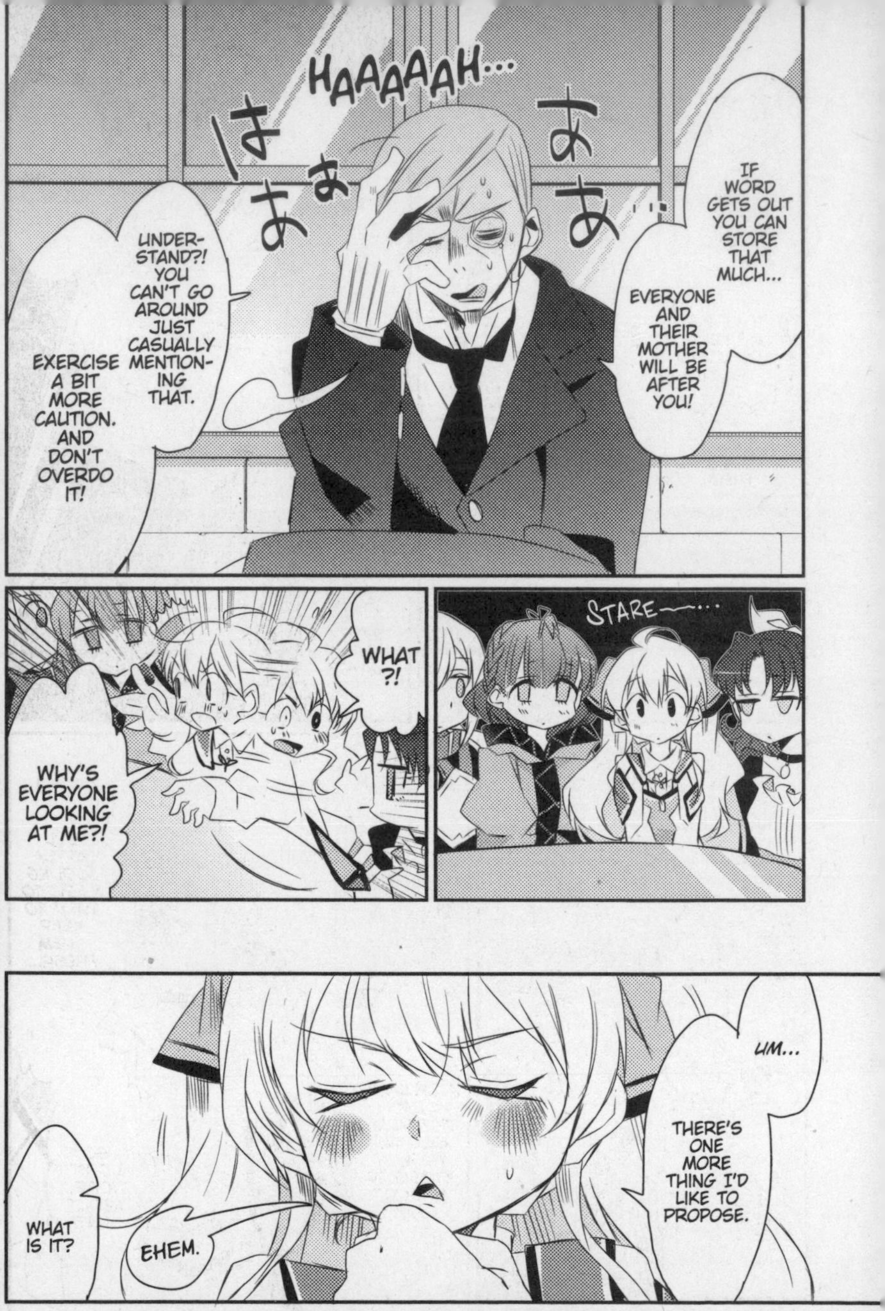
HAAAAAH...
はぁあああ...
IF WORD GETS OUT YOU CAN STORE THAT MUCH...
EVERYONE AND THEIR MOTHER WILL BE AFTER YOU!
UNDER-STAND?! YOU CAN'T GO AROUND JUST CASUALLY MENTION-ING THAT.
EXERCISE A BIT MORE CAUTION. AND DON'T OVERDO IT!
STARE---...
WHAT?!
WHY'S EVERYONE LOOKING AT ME?!
UM...
THERE'S ONE MORE THING I'D LIKE TO PROPOSE.
EHEM.
WHAT IS IT?

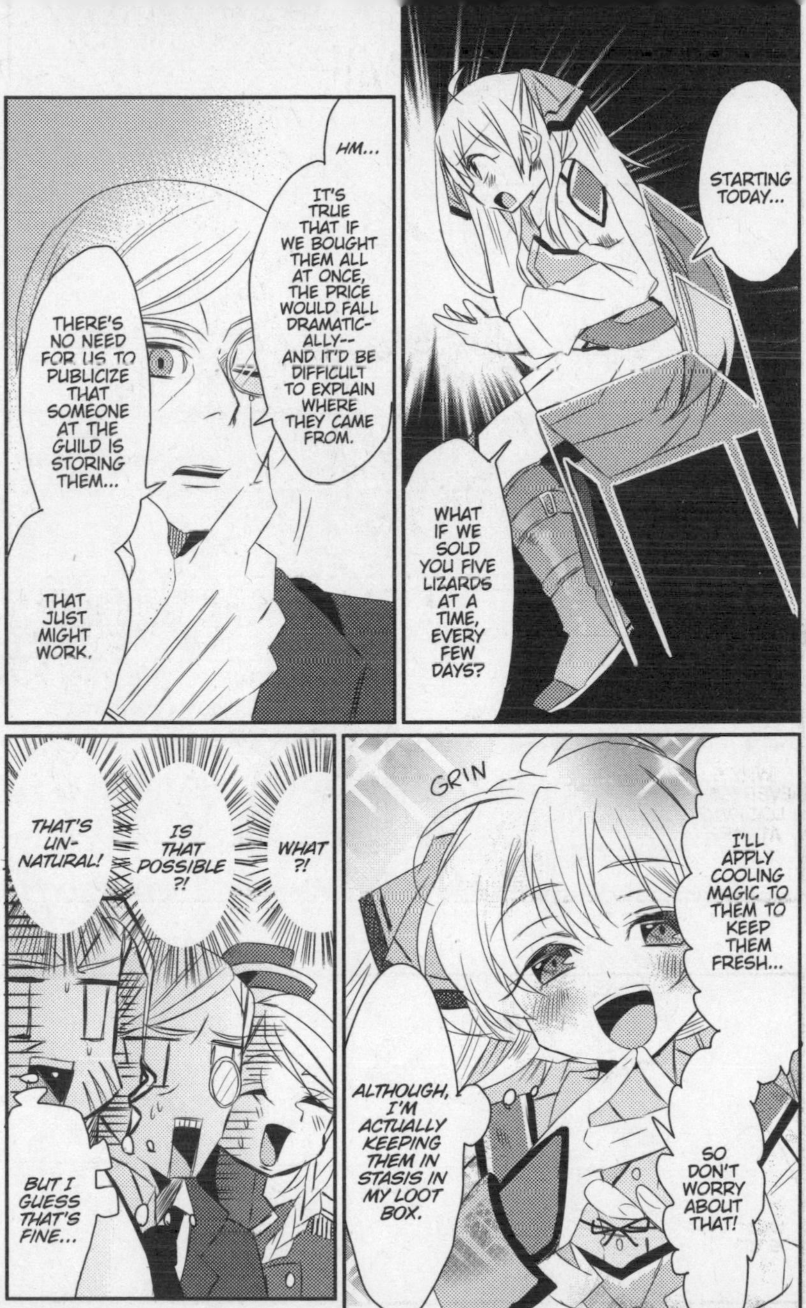
STARTING TODAY...
WHAT IF WE SOLD YOU FIVE LIZARDS AT A TIME, EVERY FEW DAYS?
HM...
IT'S TRUE THAT IF WE BOUGHT THEM ALL AT ONCE, THE PRICE WOULD FALL DRAMATIC-ALLY-- AND IT'D BE DIFFICULT TO EXPLAIN WHERE THEY CAME FROM.
THERE'S NO NEED FOR US TO PUBLICIZE THAT SOMEONE AT THE GUILD IS STORING THEM...
THAT JUST MIGHT WORK.
GRIN
I'LL APPLY COOLING MAGIC TO THEM TO KEEP THEM FRESH...
ALTHOUGH, I'M ACTUALLY KEEPING THEM IN STASIS IN MY LOOT BOX.
SO DON'T WORRY ABOUT THAT!
WHAT?!
IS THAT POSSIBLE?!
THAT'S UN-NATURAL!
BUT I GUESS THAT'S FINE...

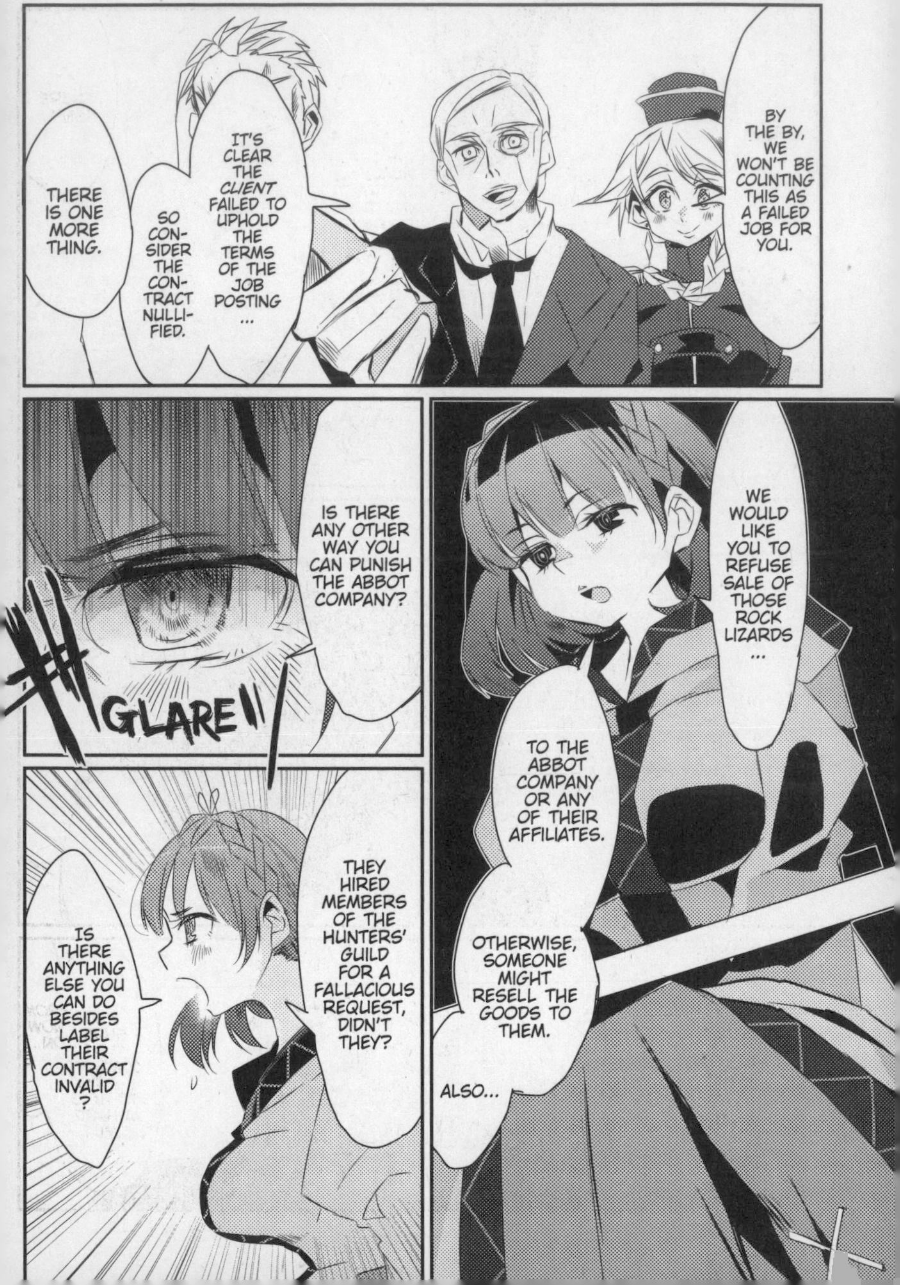
BY THE BY, WE WON'T BE COUNTING THIS AS A FAILED JOB FOR YOU.
IT'S CLEAR THE *CLIENT* FAILED TO UPHOLD THE TERMS OF THE JOB POSTING...
SO CON-SIDER THE CON-TRACT NULLI-FIED.
THERE IS ONE MORE THING.
WE WOULD LIKE YOU TO REFUSE SALE OF THOSE ROCK LIZARDS...
TO THE ABBOT COMPANY OR ANY OF THEIR AFFILIATES.
OTHERWISE, SOMEONE MIGHT RESELL THE GOODS TO THEM.
ALSO...
IS THERE ANY OTHER WAY YOU CAN PUNISH THE ABBOT COMPANY?
GLARE
THEY HIRED MEMBERS OF THE HUNTERS' GUILD FOR A FALLACIOUS REQUEST, DIDN'T THEY?
IS THERE ANYTHING ELSE YOU CAN DO BESIDES LABEL THEIR CONTRACT INVALID?

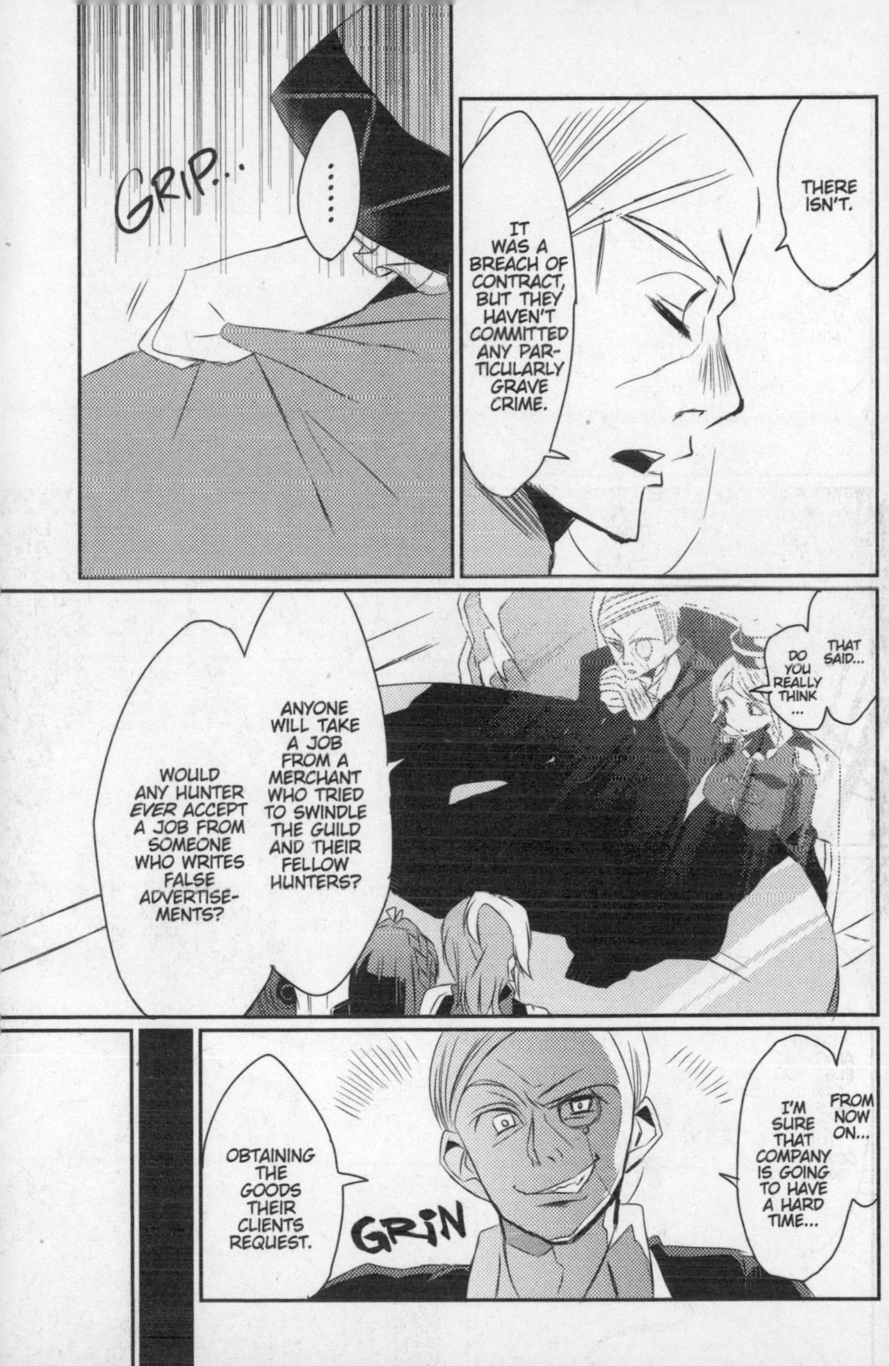

THERE ISN'T.
IT WAS A BREACH OF CONTRACT, BUT THEY HAVEN'T COMMITTED ANY PAR-TICULARLY GRAVE CRIME.
......
GRIP...
THAT SAID...
DO YOU REALLY THINK ...
ANYONE WILL TAKE A JOB FROM A MERCHANT WHO TRIED TO SWINDLE THE GUILD AND THEIR FELLOW HUNTERS?
WOULD ANY HUNTER *EVER* ACCEPT A JOB FROM SOMEONE WHO WRITES FALSE ADVERTISE-MENTS?
FROM NOW ON...
I'M SURE THAT COMPANY IS GOING TO HAVE A HARD TIME...
OBTAINING THE GOODS THEIR CLIENTS REQUEST.
GRIN

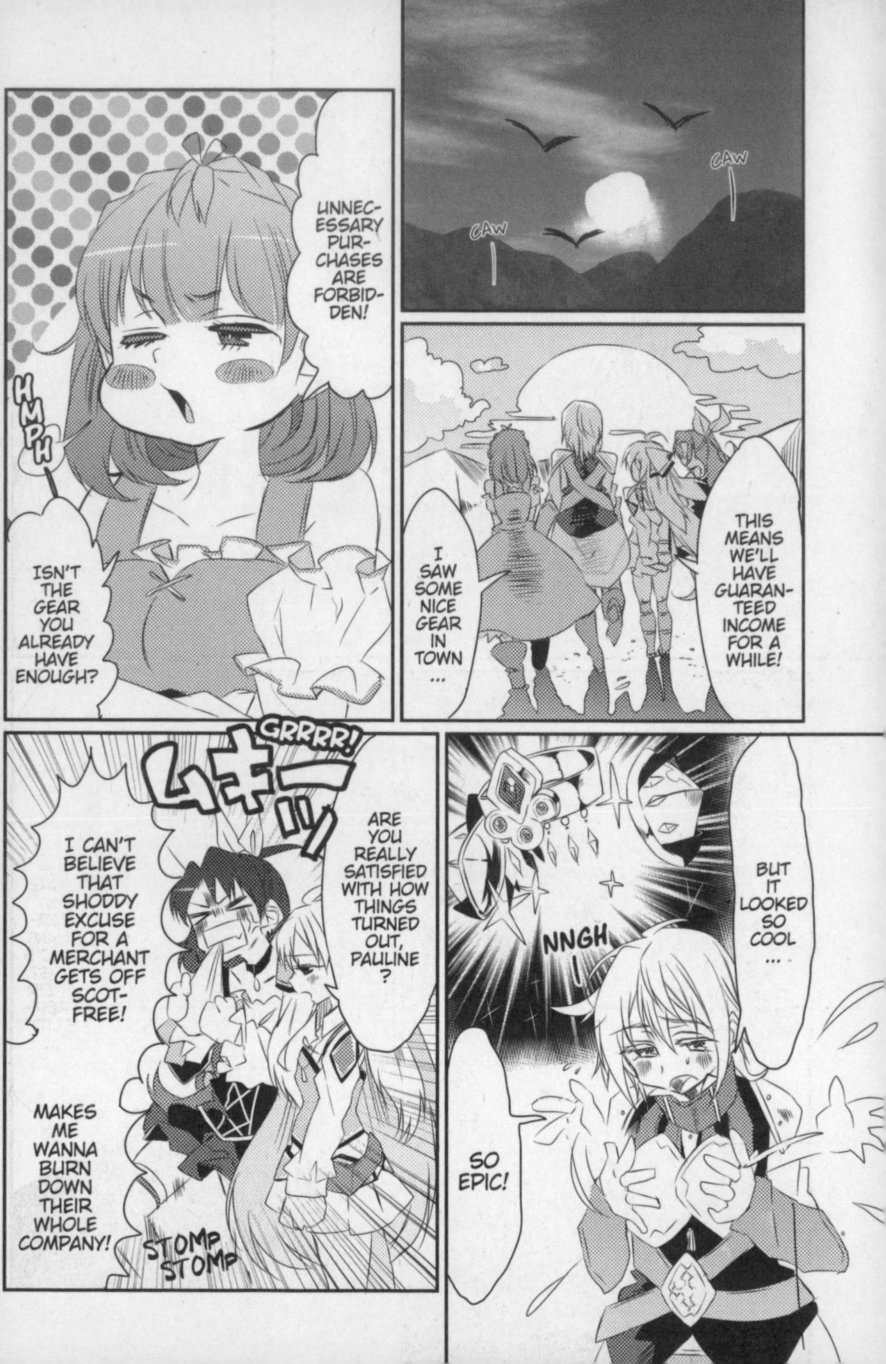
CAW
CAW
THIS MEANS WE'LL HAVE GUARAN-TEED INCOME FOR A WHILE!
I SAW SOME NICE GEAR IN TOWN ...
UNNEC-ESSARY PUR-CHASES ARE FORBID-DEN!
HMPH
ISN'T THE GEAR YOU ALREADY HAVE ENOUGH?
BUT IT LOOKED SO COOL ...
NNGH!
SO EPIC!
GRRRR!
ムキー!!
ARE YOU REALLY SATISFIED WITH HOW THINGS TURNED OUT, PAULINE?
I CAN'T BELIEVE THAT SHODDY EXCUSE FOR A MERCHANT GETS OFF SCOT-FREE!
MAKES ME WANNA BURN DOWN THEIR WHOLE COMPANY!
STOMP STOMP

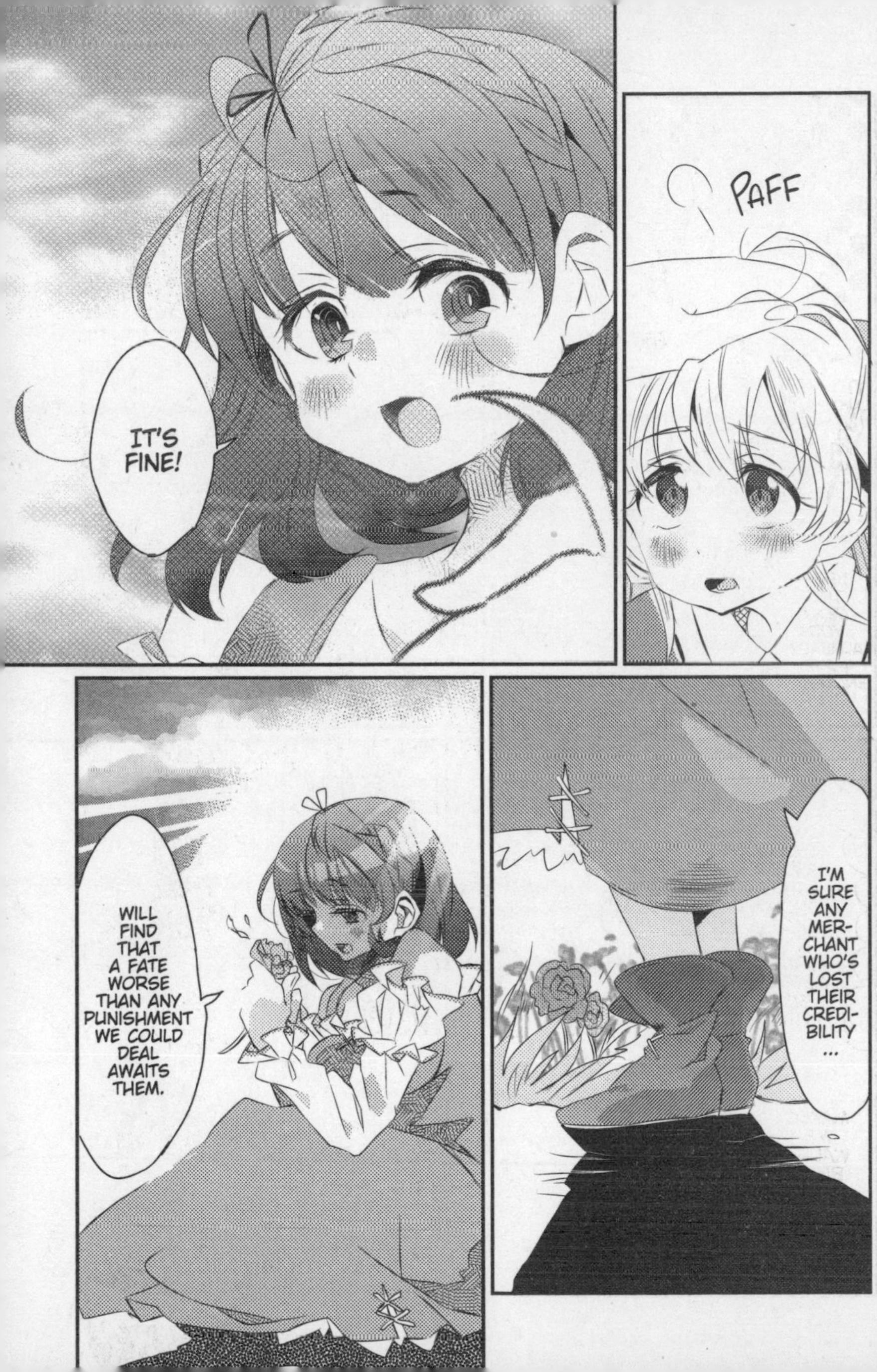
PAFF
IT'S FINE!
I'M SURE ANY MER-CHANT WHO'S LOST THEIR CREDI-BILITY ...
WILL FIND THAT A FATE WORSE THAN ANY PUNISHMENT WE COULD DEAL AWAITS THEM.

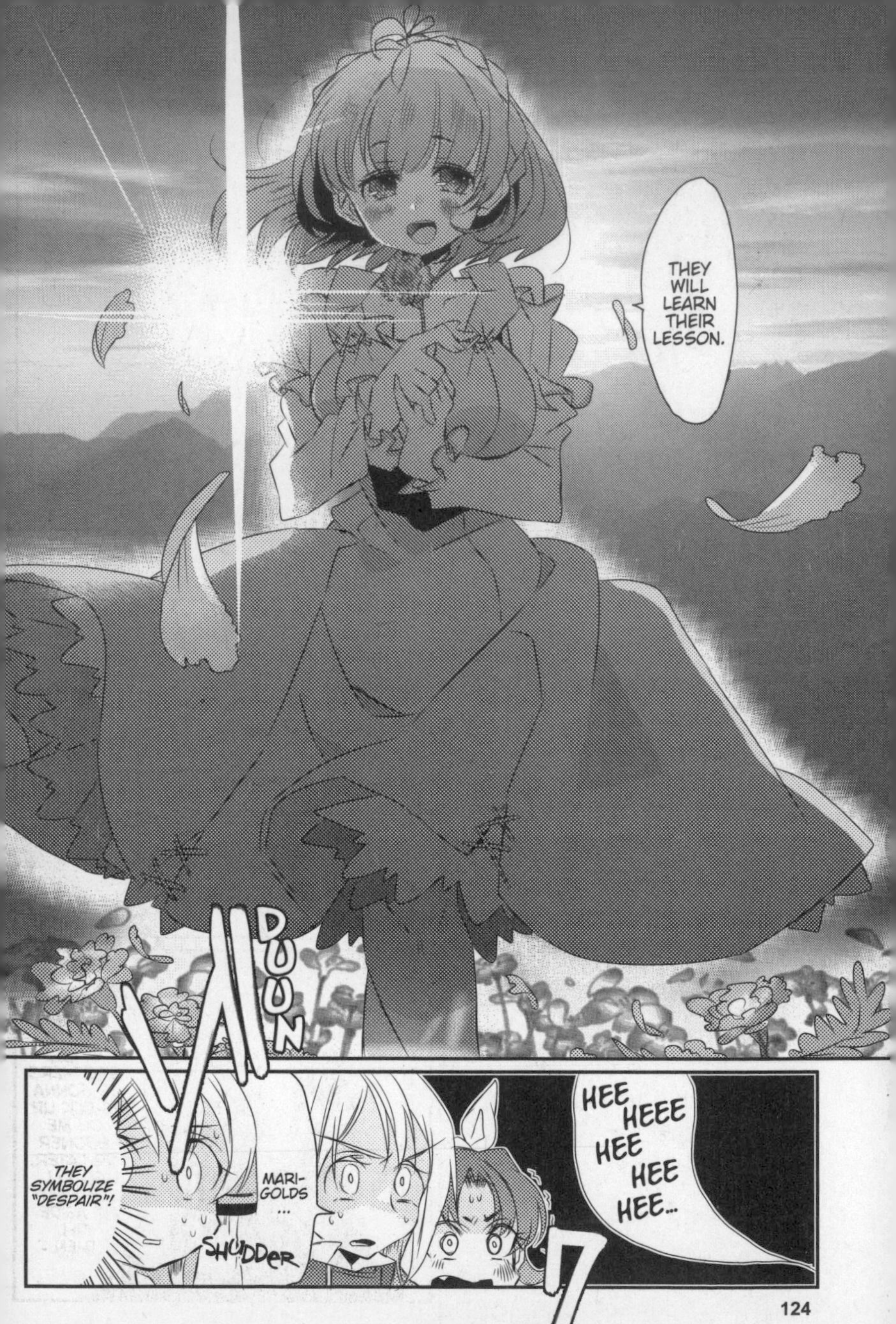
THEY WILL LEARN THEIR LESSON.
DUUN
HEE HEEE HEE HEE HEE...
MARI-GOLDS ...
THEY SYMBOLIZE "DESPAIR"!
SHUDDER

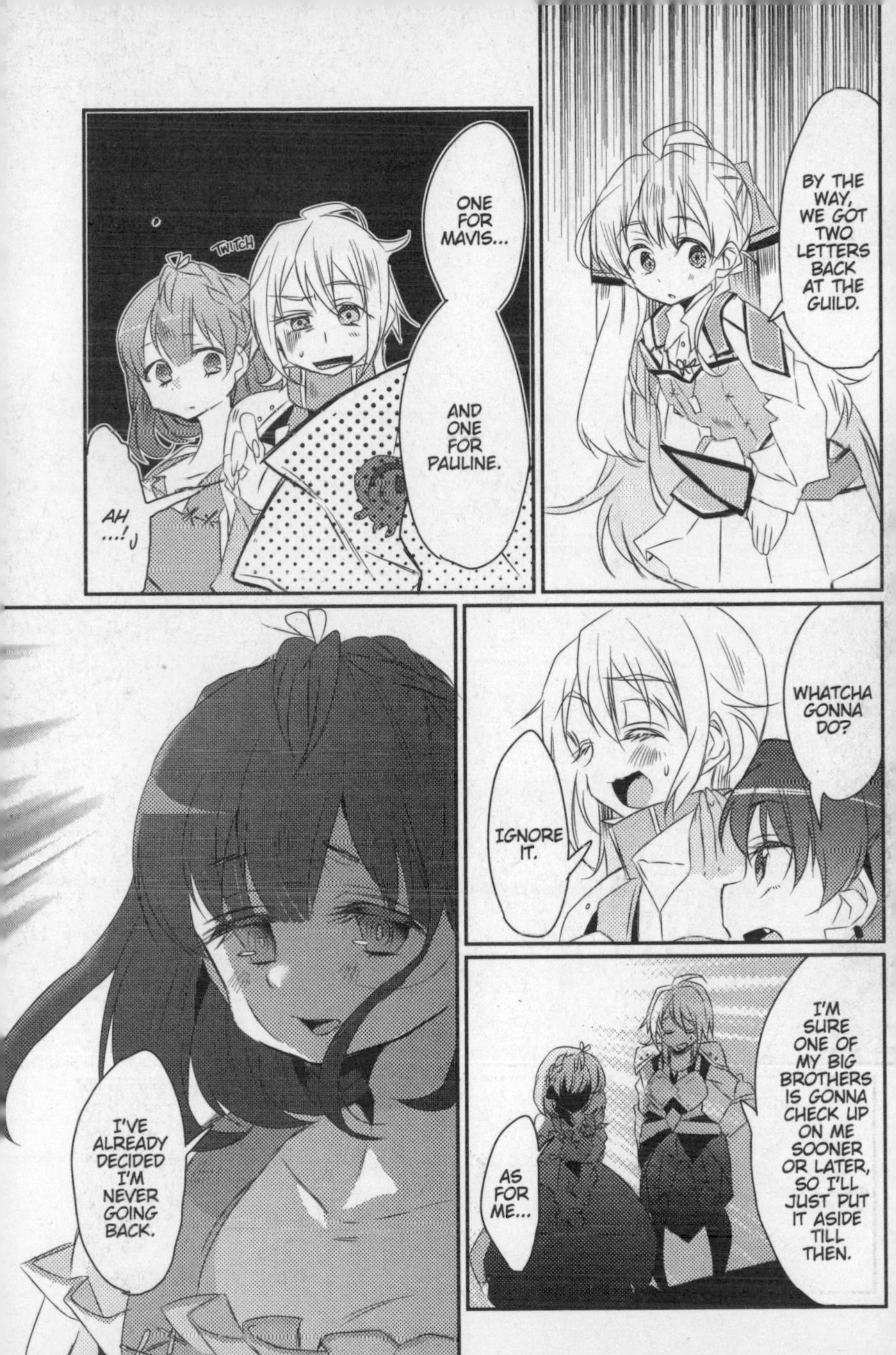
BY THE WAY, WE GOT TWO LETTERS BACK AT THE GUILD.
ONE FOR MAVIS...
AND ONE FOR PAULINE.
TWITCH
AH ...!
WHATCHA GONNA DO?
IGNORE IT.
I'M SURE ONE OF MY BIG BROTHERS IS GONNA CHECK UP ON ME SOONER OR LATER, SO I'LL JUST PUT IT ASIDE TILL THEN.
AS FOR ME...
I'VE ALREADY DECIDED I'M NEVER GOING BACK.

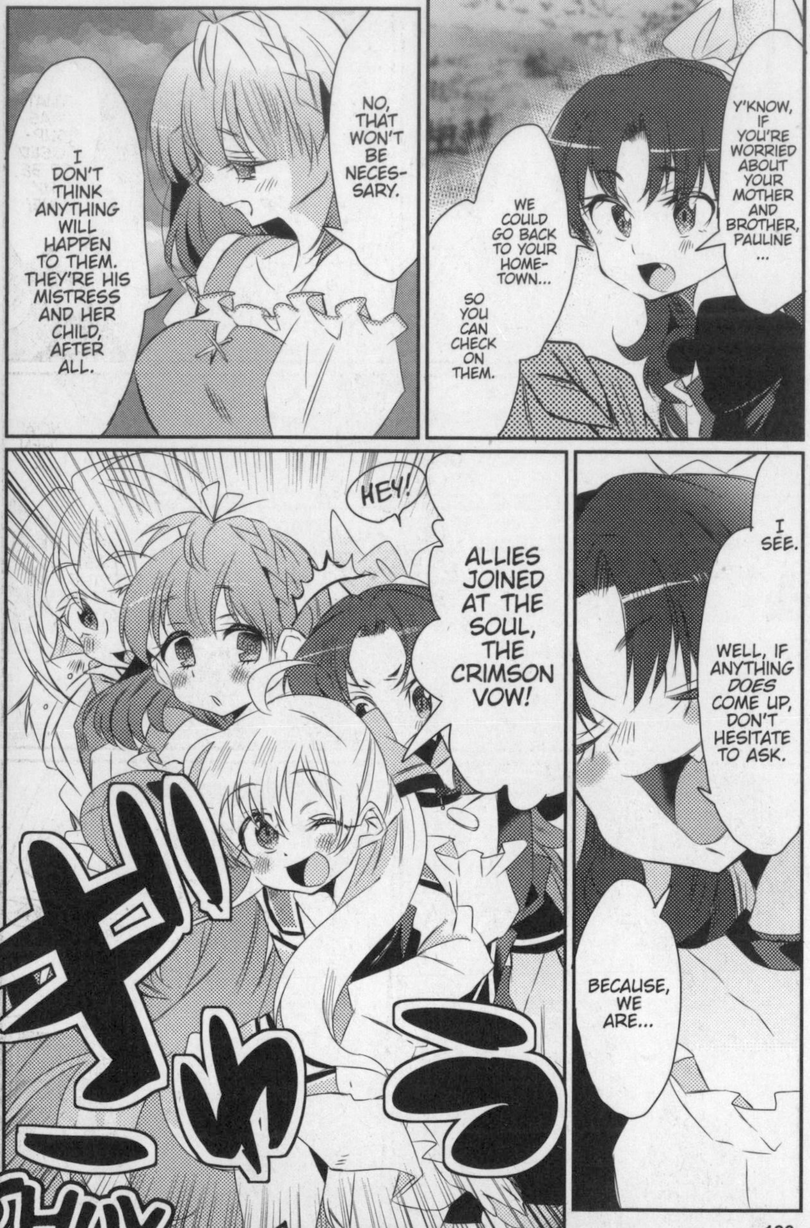
Y'KNOW, IF YOU'RE WORRIED ABOUT YOUR MOTHER AND BROTHER, PAULINE...
WE COULD GO BACK TO YOUR HOME-TOWN...
SO YOU CAN CHECK ON THEM.
NO, THAT WON'T BE NECES-SARY.
I DON'T THINK ANYTHING WILL HAPPEN TO THEM. THEY'RE HIS MISTRESS AND HER CHILD, AFTER ALL.
I SEE.
WELL, IF ANYTHING *DOES* COME UP, DON'T HESITATE TO ASK.
BECAUSE, WE ARE...
HEY!
ALLIES JOINED AT THE SOUL, THE CRIMSON VOW!

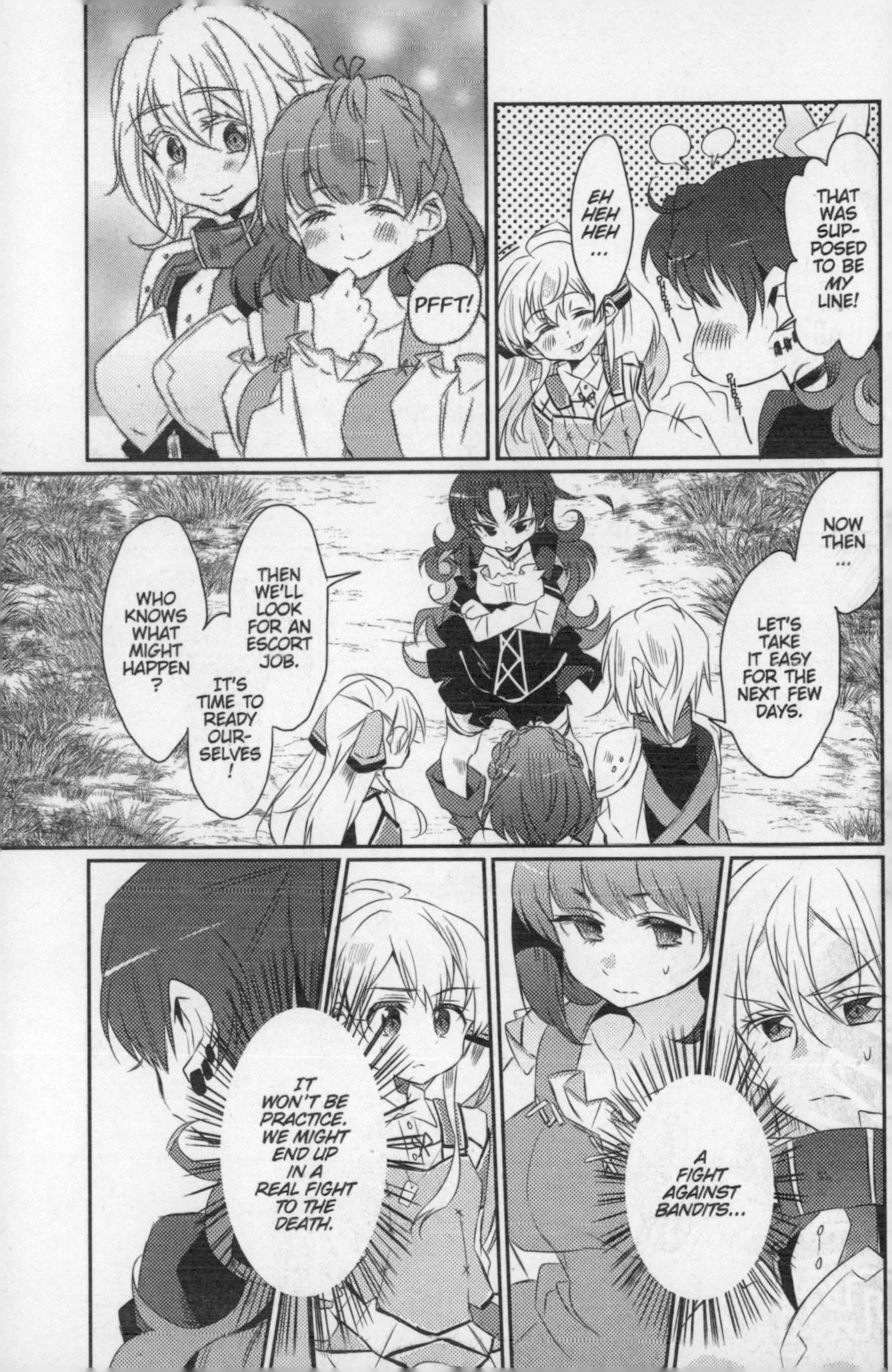
THAT WAS SUPPOSED TO BE MY LINE!
EH HEH HEH ...
PFFT!
NOW THEN ...
LET'S TAKE IT EASY FOR THE NEXT FEW DAYS.
THEN WE'LL LOOK FOR AN ESCORT JOB.
IT'S TIME TO READY OURSELVES!
WHO KNOWS WHAT MIGHT HAPPEN?
A FIGHT AGAINST BANDITS...
IT WON'T BE PRACTICE. WE MIGHT END UP IN A REAL FIGHT TO THE DEATH.

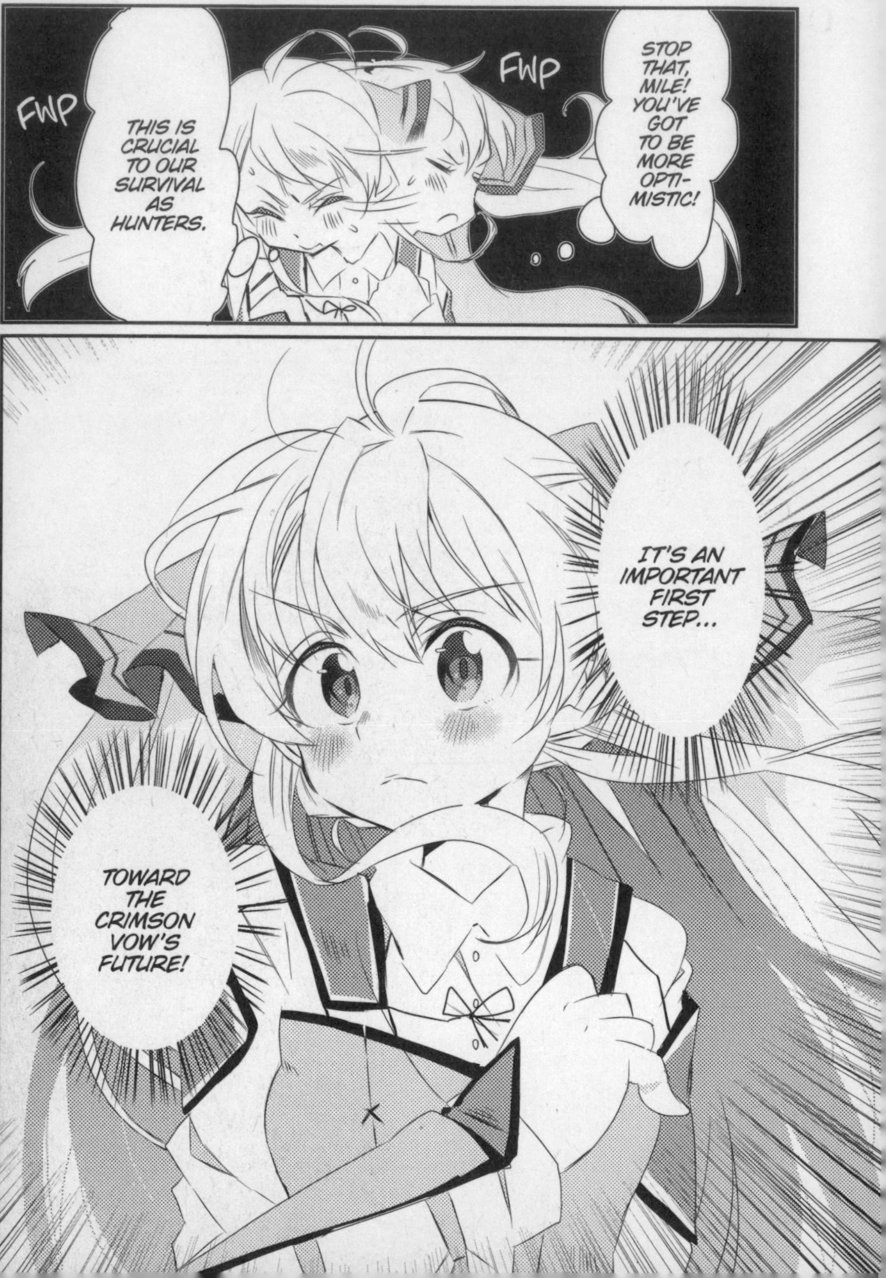
STOP THAT, MILE! YOU'VE GOT TO BE MORE OPTI-MISTIC!
FWP
THIS IS CRUCIAL TO OUR SURVIVAL AS HUNTERS.
FWP
IT'S AN IMPORTANT FIRST STEP...
TOWARD THE CRIMSON VOW'S FUTURE!

Chapter 16: Our First...

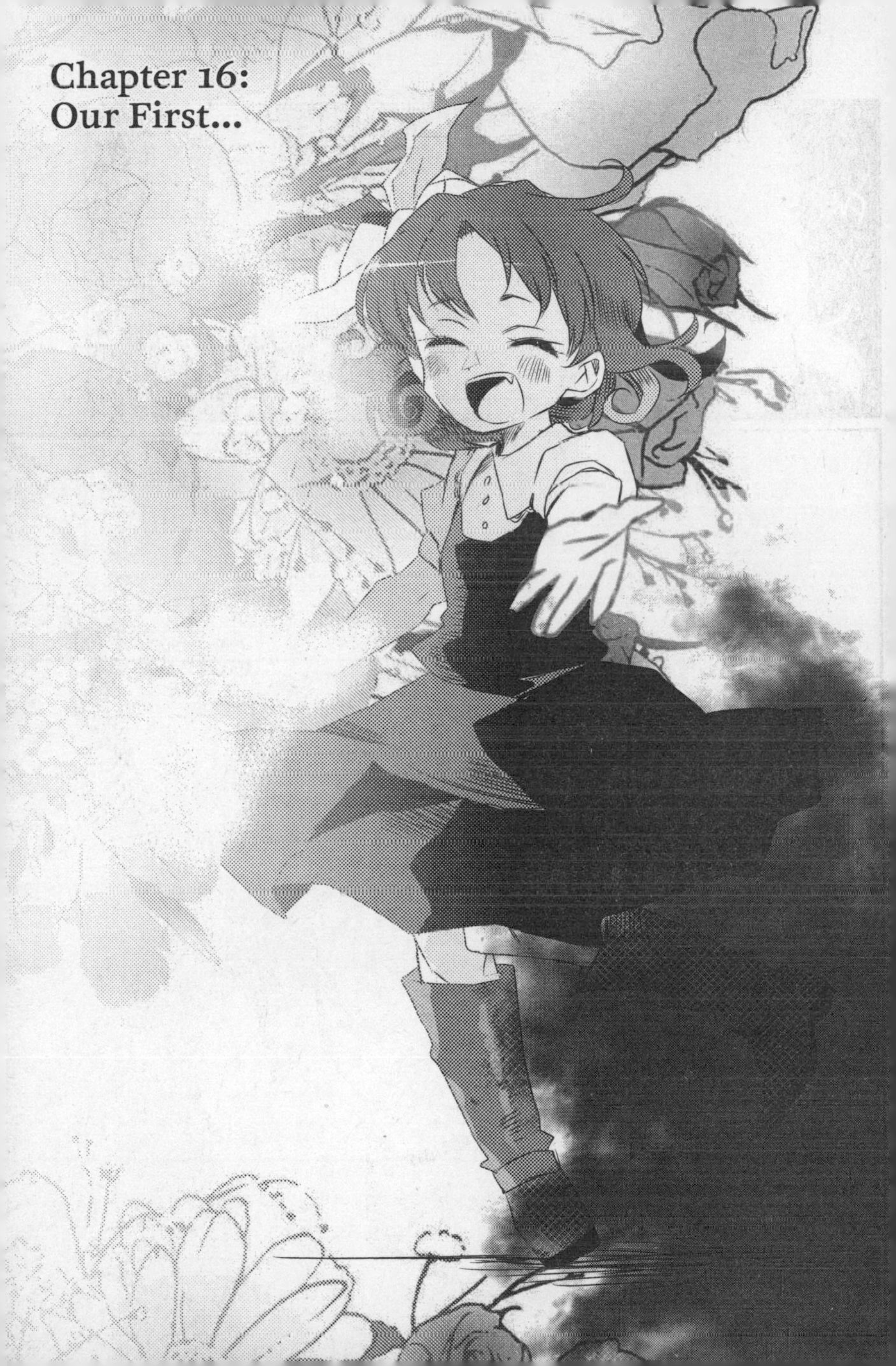

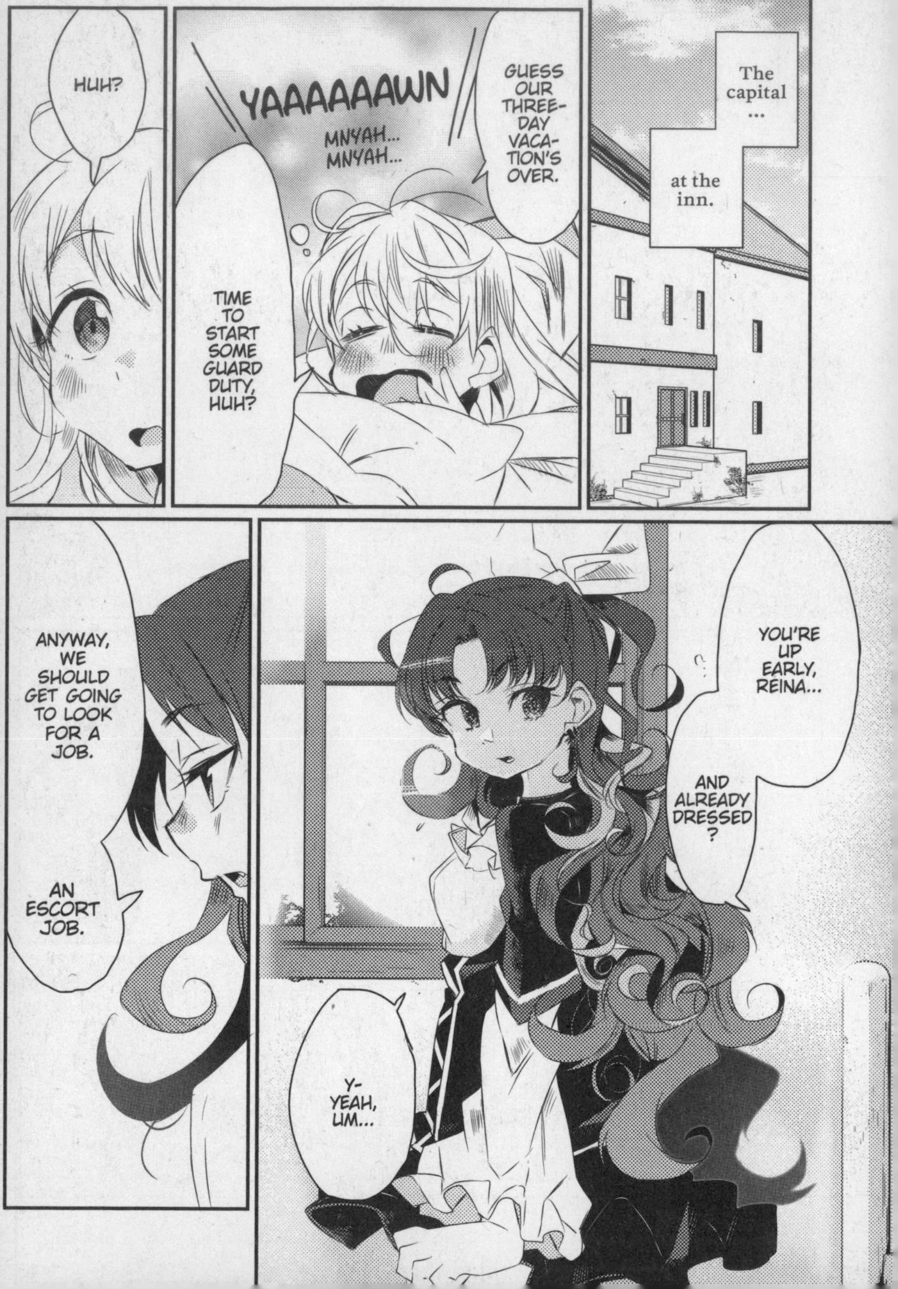
The capital ...
at the inn.
GUESS OUR THREE-DAY VACATION'S OVER.
YAAAAAAWN
MNYAH... MNYAH...
TIME TO START SOME GUARD DUTY, HUH?
HUH?
YOU'RE UP EARLY, REINA...
AND ALREADY DRESSED?
Y-YEAH, UM...
ANYWAY, WE SHOULD GET GOING TO LOOK FOR A JOB.
AN ESCORT JOB.

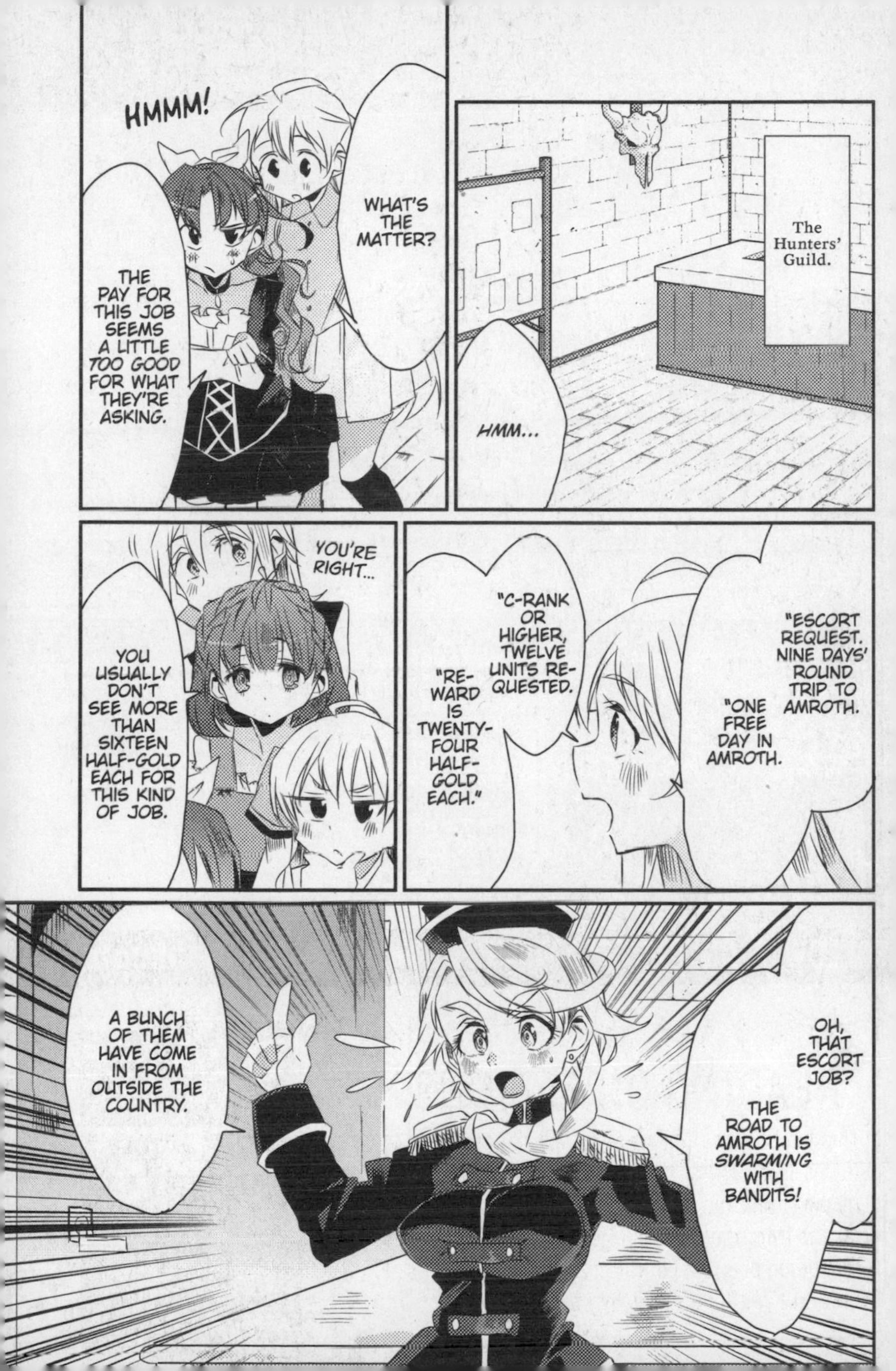
The Hunters' Guild.
HMM...
HMMM!
WHAT'S THE MATTER?
THE PAY FOR THIS JOB SEEMS A LITTLE *TOO GOOD* FOR WHAT THEY'RE ASKING.
"ESCORT REQUEST. NINE DAYS' ROUND TRIP TO AMROTH.
"ONE FREE DAY IN AMROTH.
"C-RANK OR HIGHER, TWELVE UNITS REQUESTED.
"RE-WARD IS TWENTY-FOUR HALF-GOLD EACH."
YOU'RE RIGHT...
YOU USUALLY DON'T SEE MORE THAN SIXTEEN HALF-GOLD EACH FOR THIS KIND OF JOB.
OH, THAT ESCORT JOB?
THE ROAD TO AMROTH IS *SWARMING* WITH BANDITS!
A BUNCH OF THEM HAVE COME IN FROM OUTSIDE THE COUNTRY.

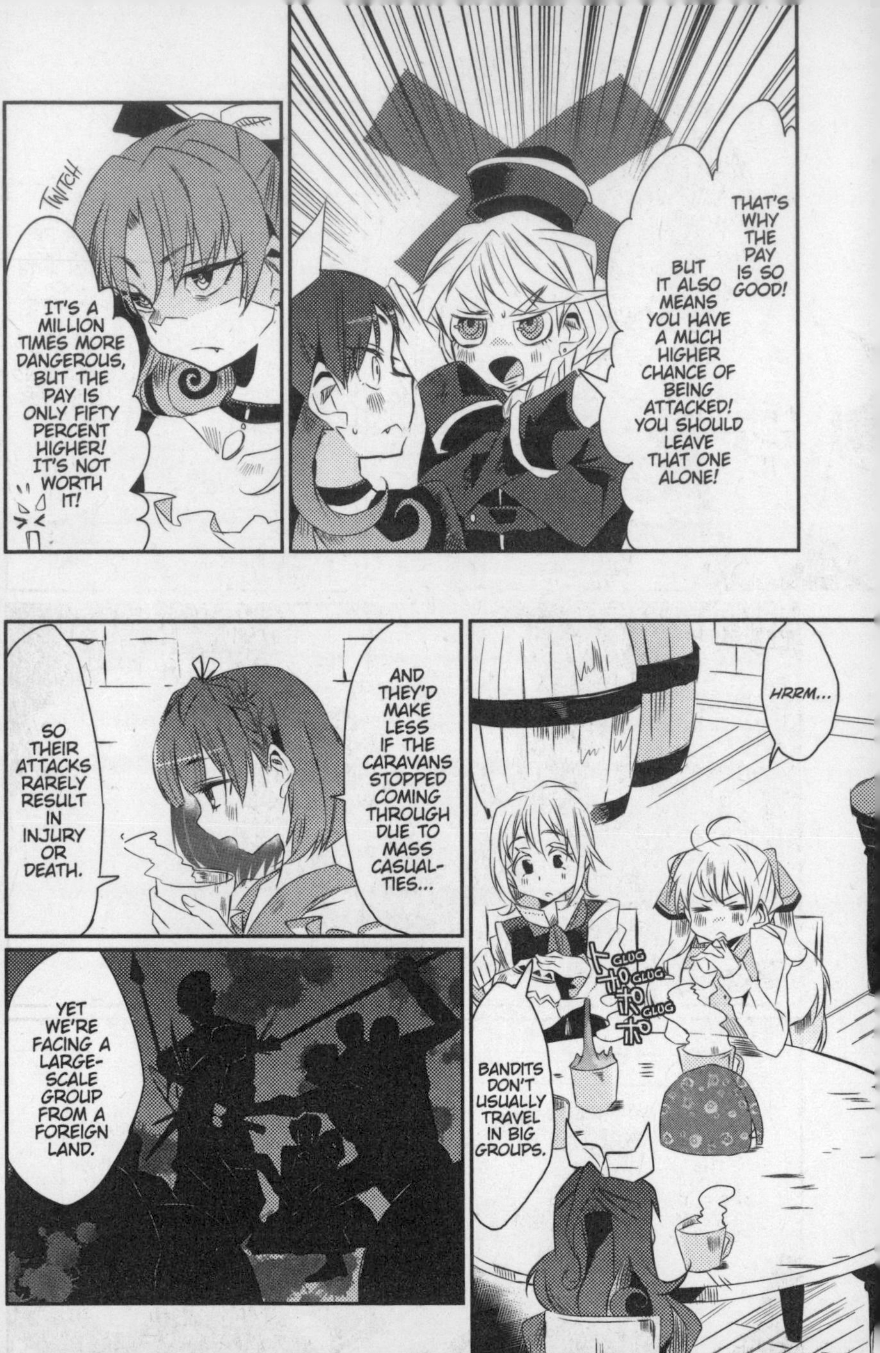
THAT'S WHY THE PAY IS SO GOOD!
BUT IT ALSO MEANS YOU HAVE A MUCH HIGHER CHANCE OF BEING ATTACKED! YOU SHOULD LEAVE THAT ONE ALONE!
TWITCH
IT'S A MILLION TIMES MORE DANGEROUS, BUT THE PAY IS ONLY FIFTY PERCENT HIGHER! IT'S NOT WORTH IT!
HRRM...
GLUG GLUG GLUG
BANDITS DON'T USUALLY TRAVEL IN BIG GROUPS.
AND THEY'D MAKE LESS IF THE CARAVANS STOPPED COMING THROUGH DUE TO MASS CASUAL-TIES...
SO THEIR ATTACKS RARELY RESULT IN INJURY OR DEATH.
YET WE'RE FACING A LARGE-SCALE GROUP FROM A FOREIGN LAND.

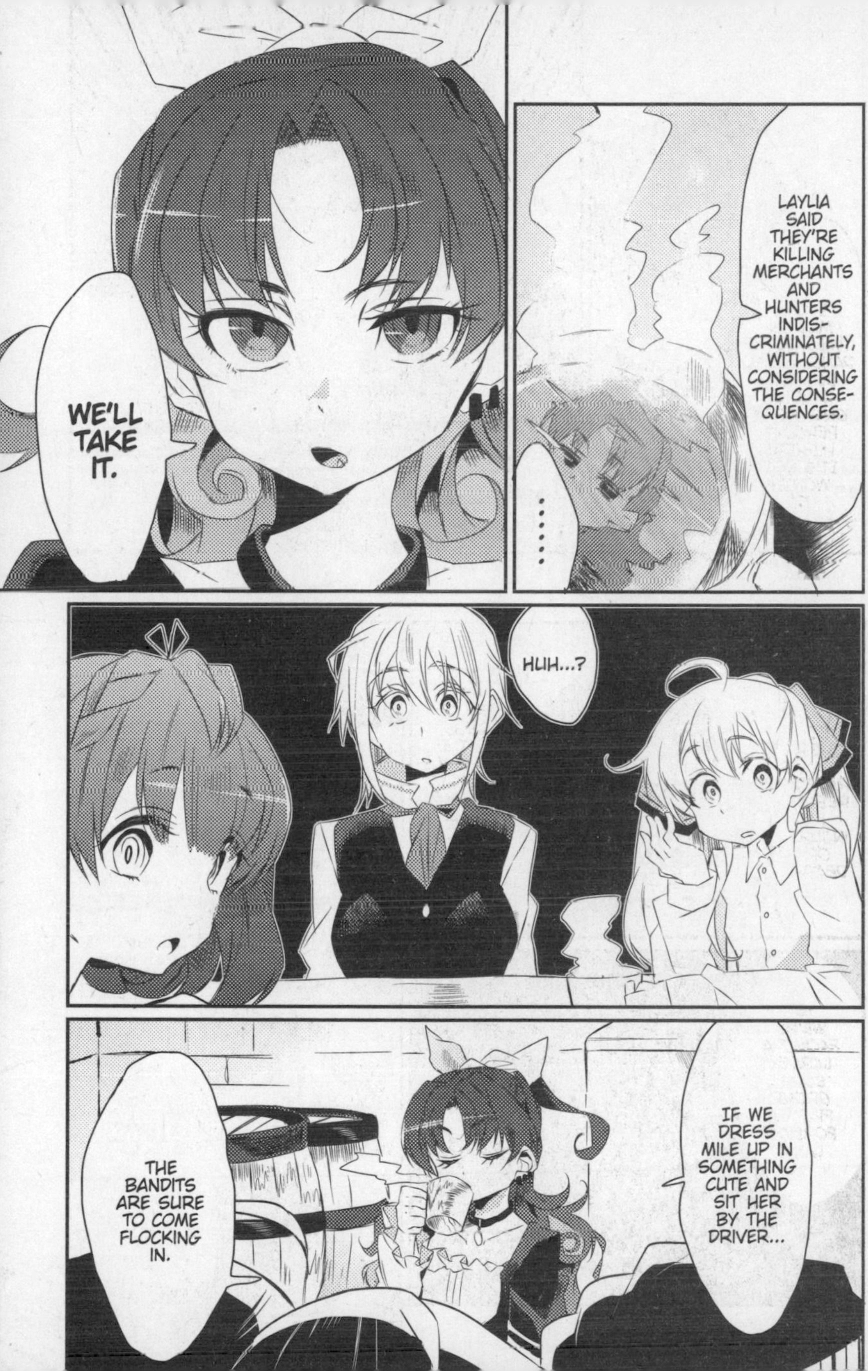
LAYLIA SAID THEY'RE KILLING MERCHANTS AND HUNTERS INDIS-CRIMINATELY, WITHOUT CONSIDERING THE CONSE-QUENCES.
......
WE'LL TAKE IT.
HUH...?
IF WE DRESS MILE UP IN SOMETHING CUTE AND SIT HER BY THE DRIVER...
THE BANDITS ARE SURE TO COME FLOCKING IN.

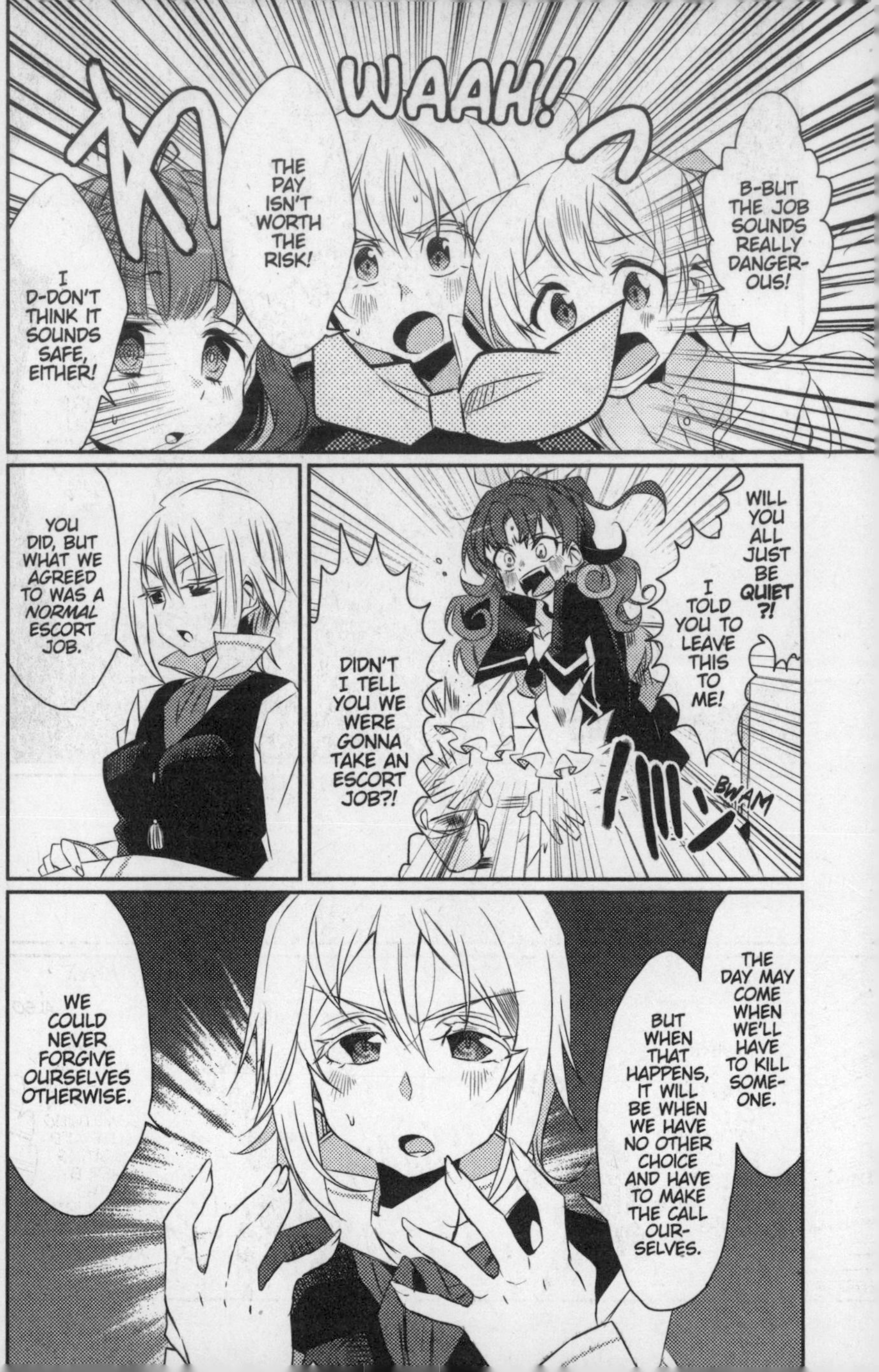
B-BUT THE JOB SOUNDS REALLY DANGER-OUS!
WAAH!
THE PAY ISN'T WORTH THE RISK!
I D-DON'T THINK IT SOUNDS SAFE, EITHER!
WILL YOU ALL JUST BE QUIET?!
I TOLD YOU TO LEAVE THIS TO ME!
BWAM
DIDN'T I TELL YOU WE WERE GONNA TAKE AN ESCORT JOB?!
YOU DID, BUT WHAT WE AGREED TO WAS A *NORMAL* ESCORT JOB.
THE DAY MAY COME WHEN WE'LL HAVE TO KILL SOME-ONE.
BUT WHEN THAT HAPPENS, IT WILL BE WHEN WE HAVE NO OTHER CHOICE AND HAVE TO MAKE THE CALL OUR-SELVES.
WE COULD NEVER FORGIVE OURSELVES OTHERWISE.

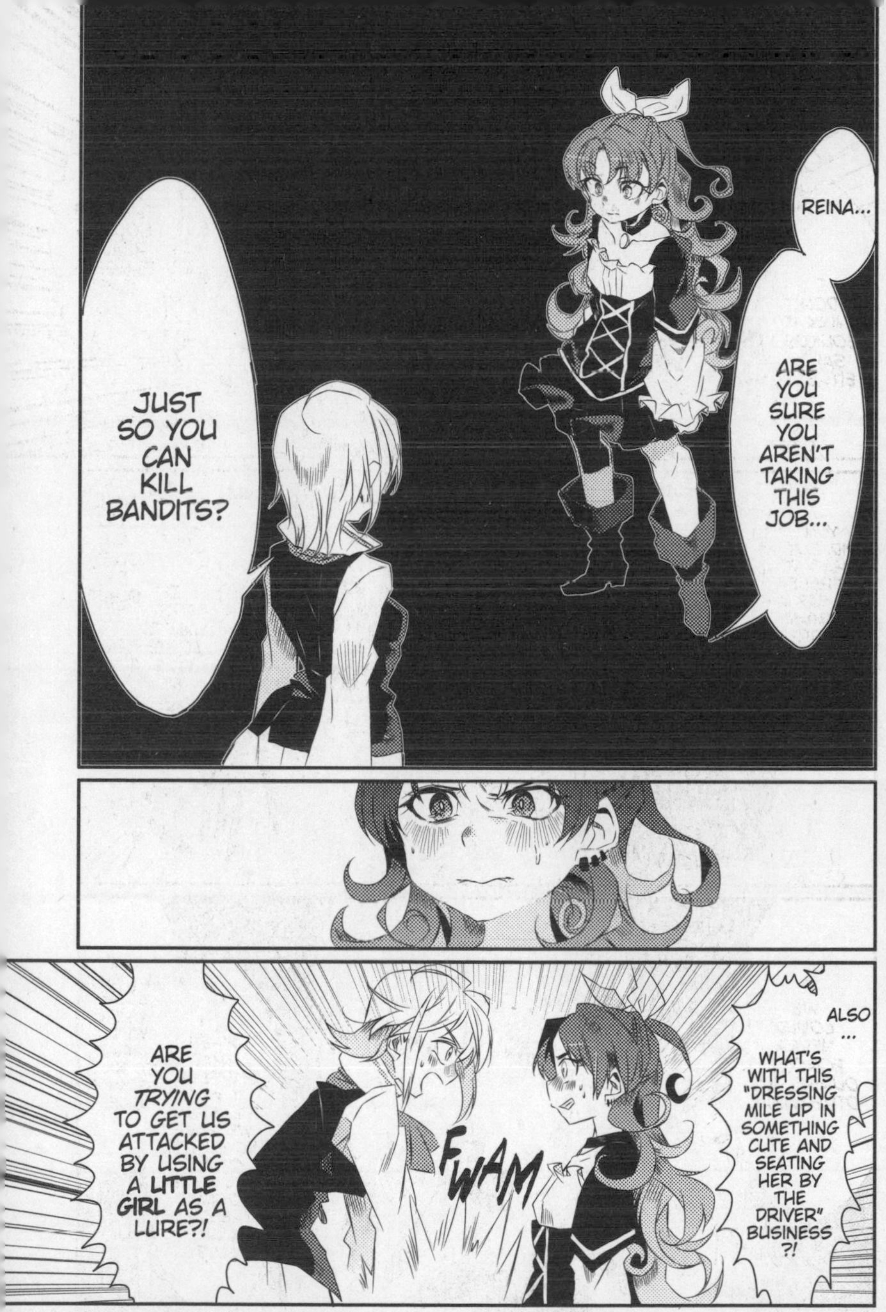
REINA...
ARE YOU SURE YOU AREN'T TAKING THIS JOB...
JUST SO YOU CAN KILL BANDITS?
ALSO ... WHAT'S WITH THIS "DRESSING MILE UP IN SOMETHING CUTE AND SEATING HER BY THE DRIVER" BUSINESS ?!
FWAM
ARE YOU *TRYING* TO GET US ATTACKED BY USING A **LITTLE GIRL** AS A LURE?!

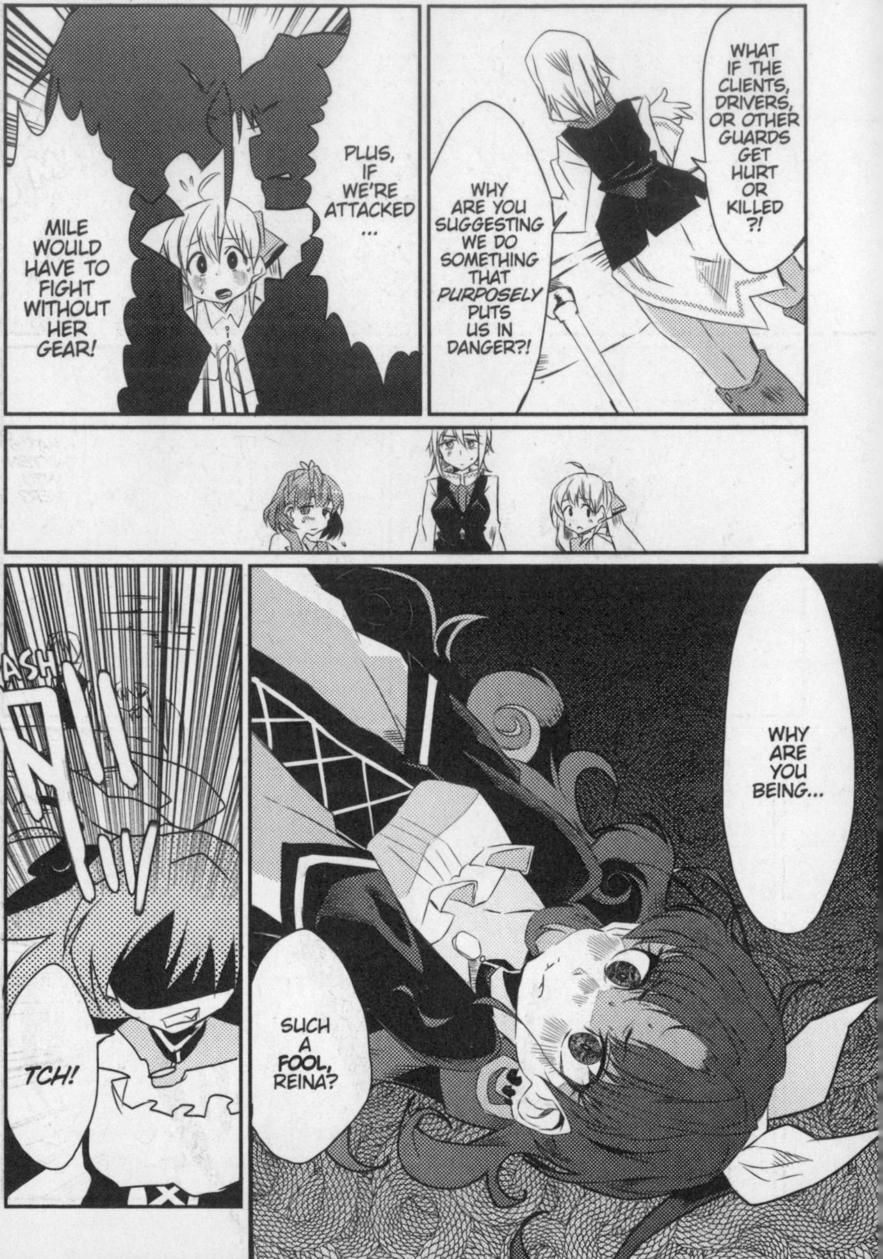
WHAT IF THE CLIENTS, DRIVERS, OR OTHER GUARDS GET HURT OR KILLED?!
WHY ARE YOU SUGGESTING WE DO SOMETHING THAT *PURPOSELY* PUTS US IN DANGER?!
PLUS, IF WE'RE ATTACKED...
MILE WOULD HAVE TO FIGHT WITHOUT HER GEAR!
WHY ARE YOU BEING...
SUCH A FOOL, REINA?
DASH
TCH!

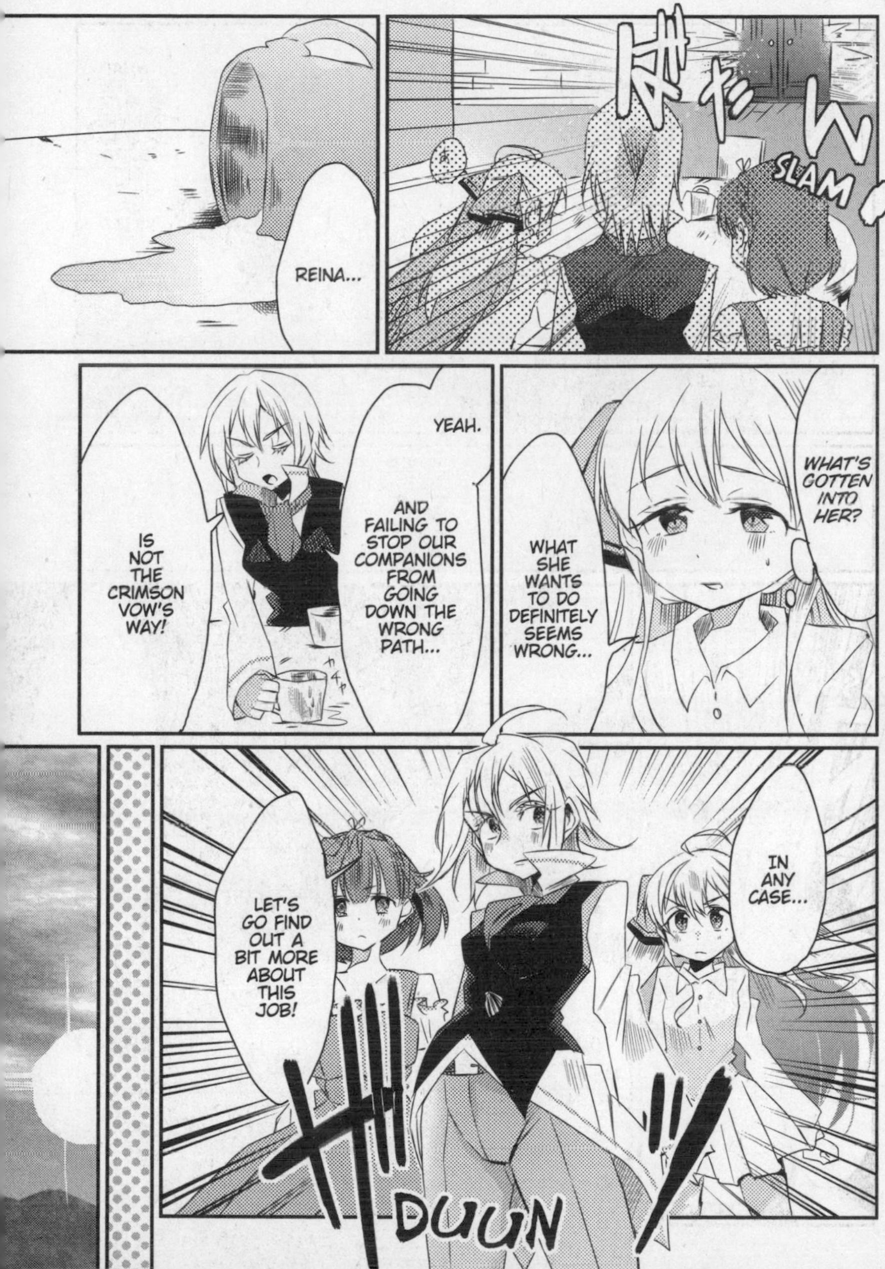
SLAM
REINA...
WHAT'S GOTTEN INTO HER?
WHAT SHE WANTS TO DO DEFINITELY SEEMS WRONG...
YEAH.
AND FAILING TO STOP OUR COMPANIONS FROM GOING DOWN THE WRONG PATH...
IS NOT THE CRIMSON VOW'S WAY!
IN ANY CASE...
LET'S GO FIND OUT A BIT MORE ABOUT THIS JOB!
DUUN

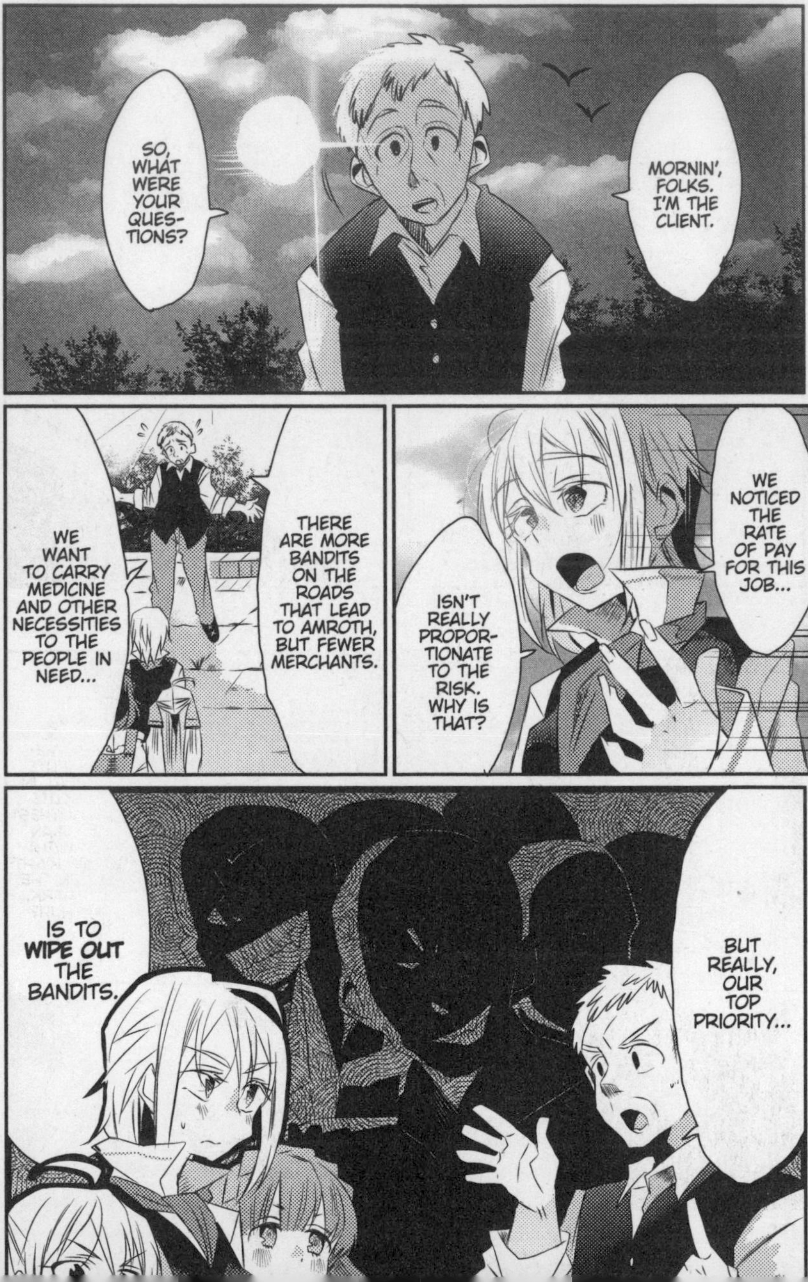
MORNIN', FOLKS. I'M THE CLIENT.
SO, WHAT WERE YOUR QUES-TIONS?
WE NOTICED THE RATE OF PAY FOR THIS JOB...
ISN'T REALLY PROPOR-TIONATE TO THE RISK. WHY IS THAT?
THERE ARE MORE BANDITS ON THE ROADS THAT LEAD TO AMROTH, BUT FEWER MERCHANTS.
WE WANT TO CARRY MEDICINE AND OTHER NECESSITIES TO THE PEOPLE IN NEED...
BUT REALLY, OUR TOP PRIORITY...
IS TO **WIPE OUT** THE BANDITS.

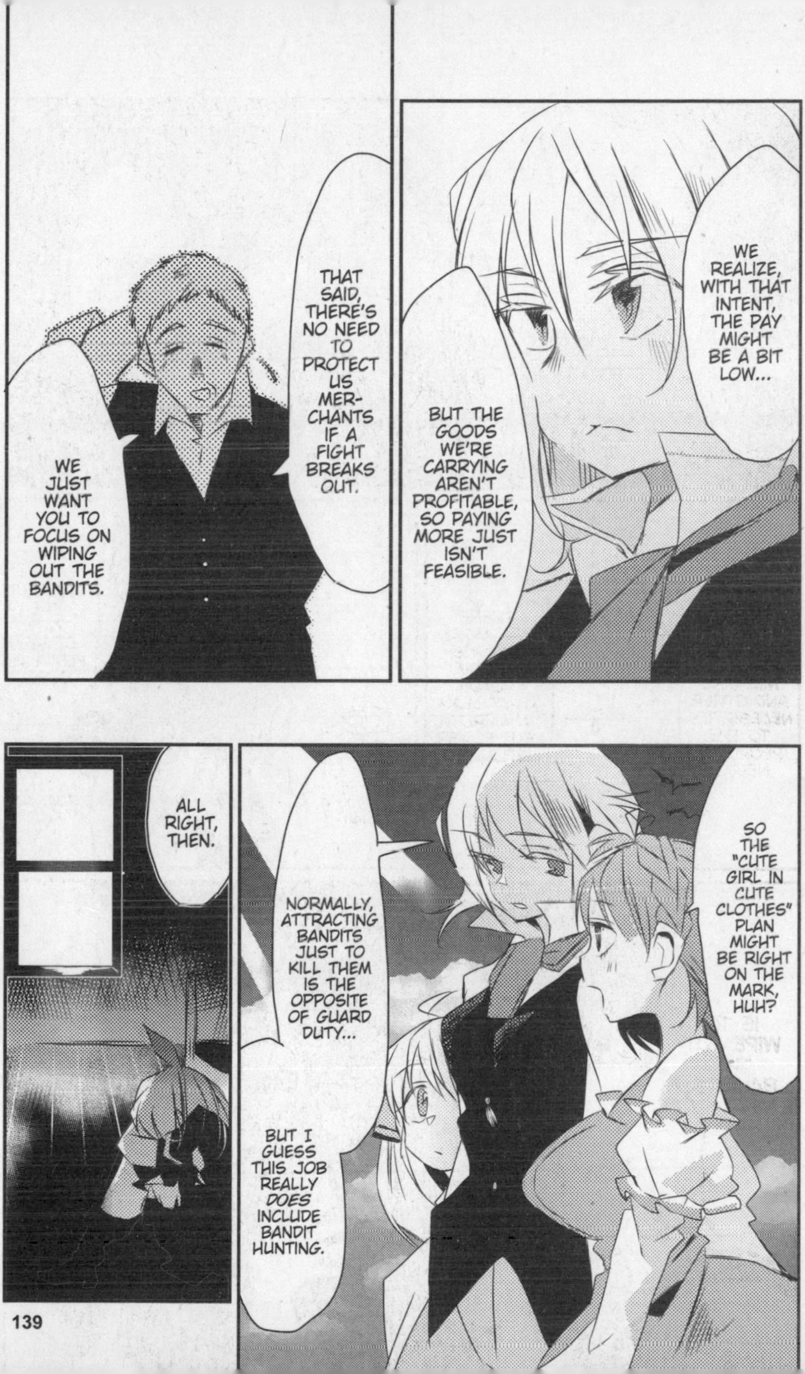
WE REALIZE, WITH THAT INTENT, THE PAY MIGHT BE A BIT LOW...
BUT THE GOODS WE'RE CARRYING AREN'T PROFITABLE, SO PAYING MORE JUST ISN'T FEASIBLE.
THAT SAID, THERE'S NO NEED TO PROTECT US MER-CHANTS IF A FIGHT BREAKS OUT.
WE JUST WANT YOU TO FOCUS ON WIPING OUT THE BANDITS.
SO THE "CUTE GIRL IN CUTE CLOTHES" PLAN MIGHT BE RIGHT ON THE MARK, HUH?
NORMALLY, ATTRACTING BANDITS JUST TO KILL THEM IS THE OPPOSITE OF GUARD DUTY...
BUT I GUESS THIS JOB REALLY *DOES* INCLUDE BANDIT HUNTING.
ALL RIGHT, THEN.

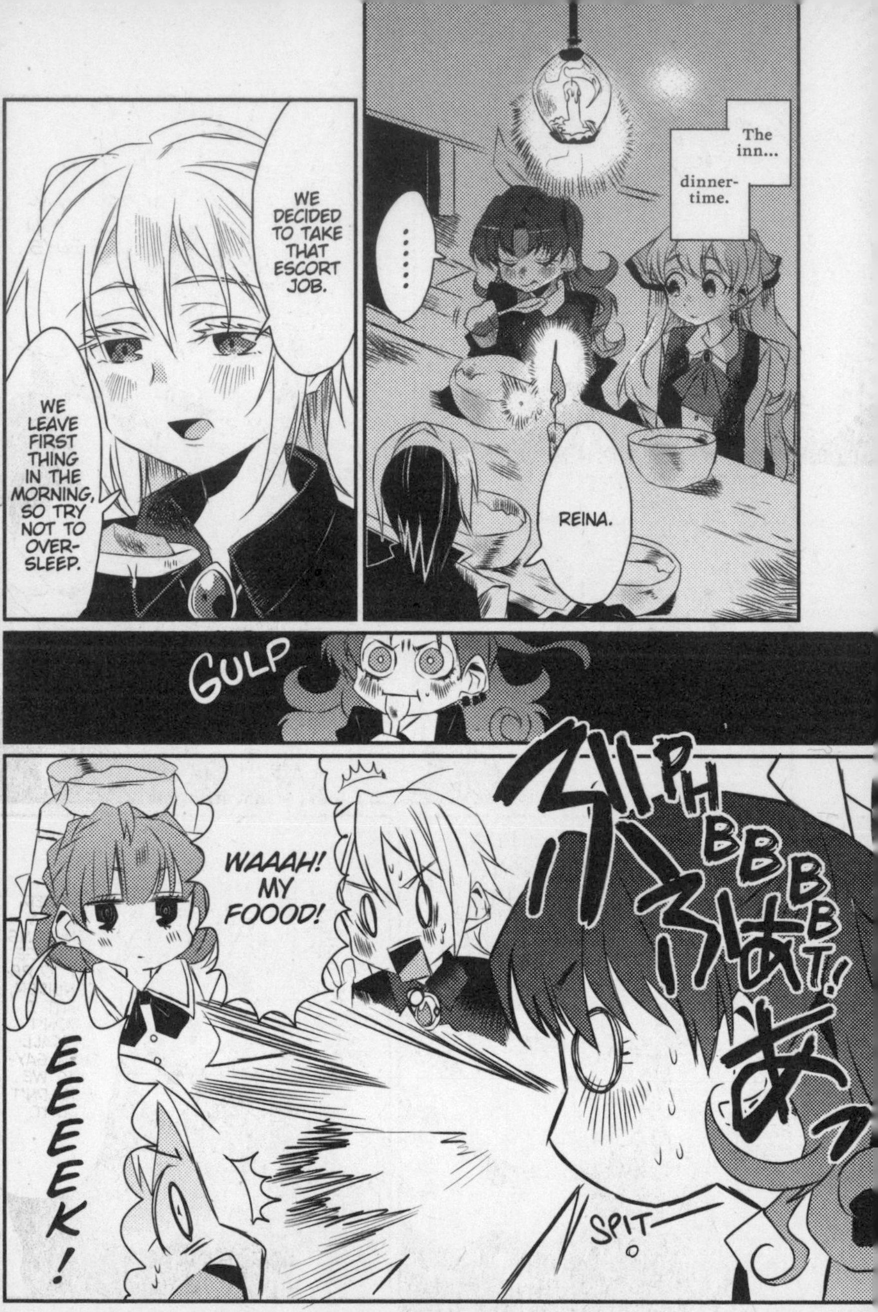
The inn...
dinner-time.
......
REINA.
WE DECIDED TO TAKE THAT ESCORT JOB.
WE LEAVE FIRST THING IN THE MORNING, SO TRY NOT TO OVER-SLEEP.
GULP
PHBBBBBT!
WAAAH! MY FOOOD!
SPIT
EEEEEK!

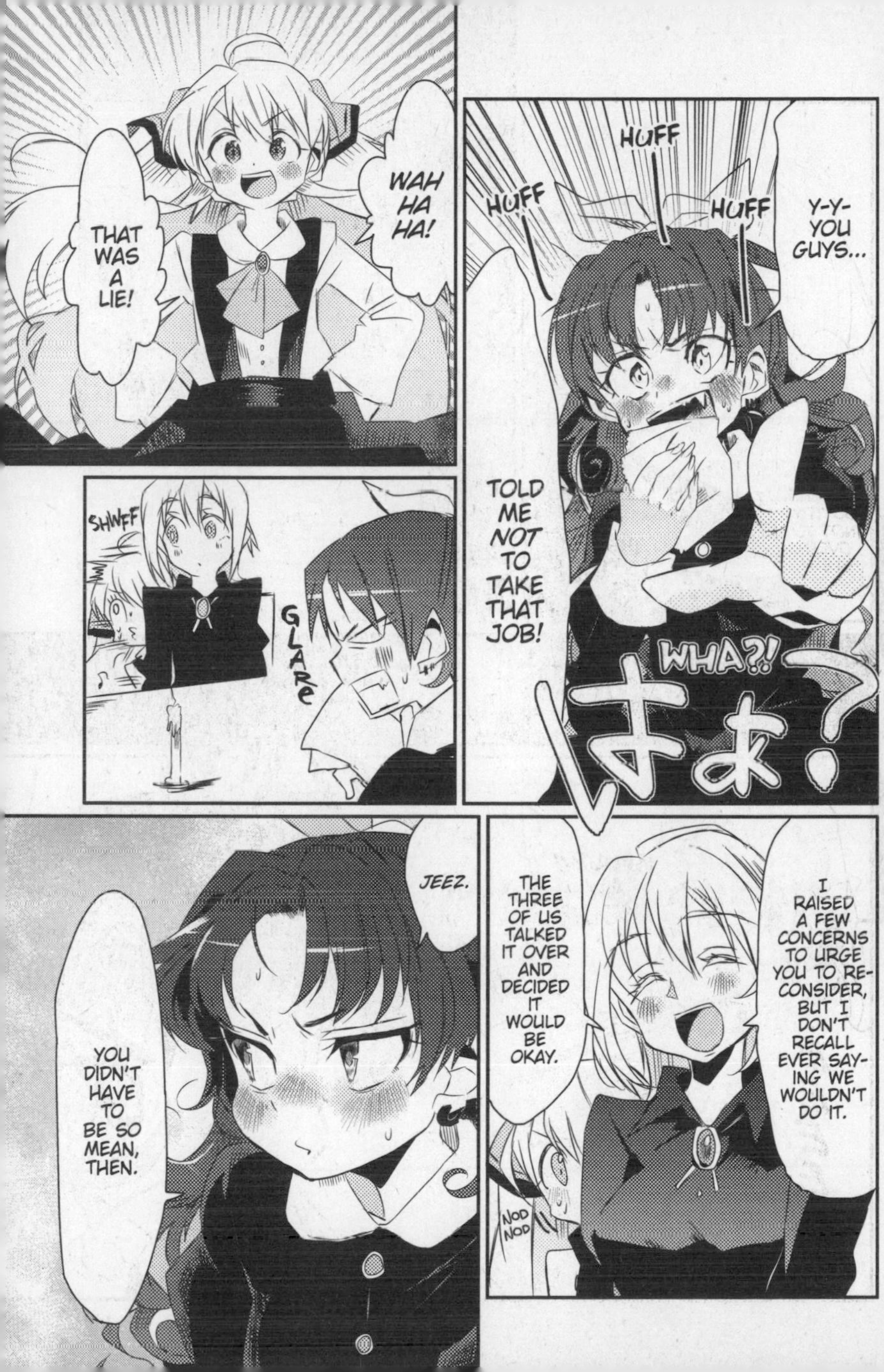
HUFF
HUFF
HUFF
Y-Y-YOU GUYS...
TOLD ME NOT TO TAKE THAT JOB!
WHA?!
はぁ?
WAH HA HA!
THAT WAS A LIE!
SHWFF
GLARE
I RAISED A FEW CONCERNS TO URGE YOU TO RE-CONSIDER, BUT I DON'T RECALL EVER SAY-ING WE WOULDN'T DO IT.
THE THREE OF US TALKED IT OVER AND DECIDED IT WOULD BE OKAY.
NOD NOD
JEEZ.
YOU DIDN'T HAVE TO BE SO MEAN, THEN.

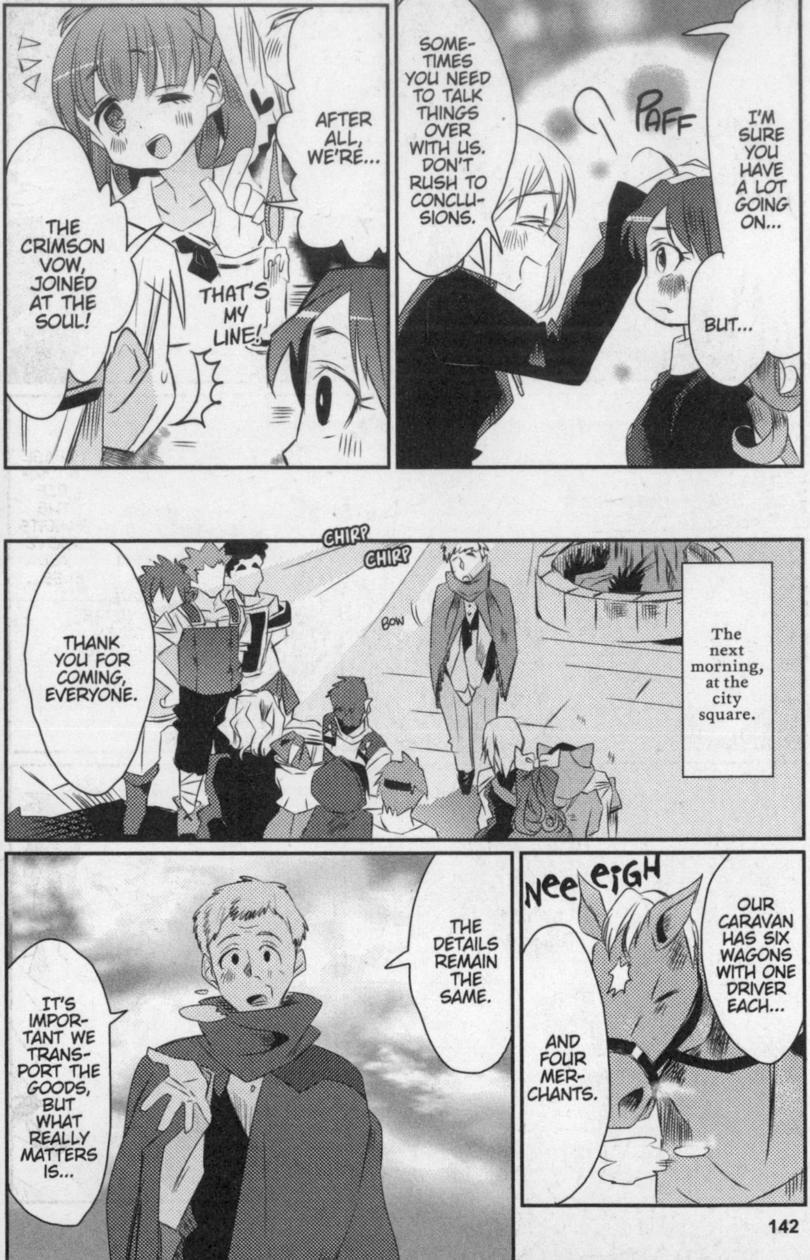
I'M SURE YOU HAVE A LOT GOING ON...
PAFF
BUT...
SOMETIMES YOU NEED TO TALK THINGS OVER WITH US. DON'T RUSH TO CONCLUSIONS.
AFTER ALL, WE'RE...
THE CRIMSON VOW, JOINED AT THE SOUL!
THAT'S MY LINE!
The next morning, at the city square.
CHIRP
CHIRP
BOW
THANK YOU FOR COMING, EVERYONE.
Nee eiGH
OUR CARAVAN HAS SIX WAGONS WITH ONE DRIVER EACH...
AND FOUR MERCHANTS.
THE DETAILS REMAIN THE SAME.
IT'S IMPORTANT WE TRANSPORT THE GOODS, BUT WHAT REALLY MATTERS IS...

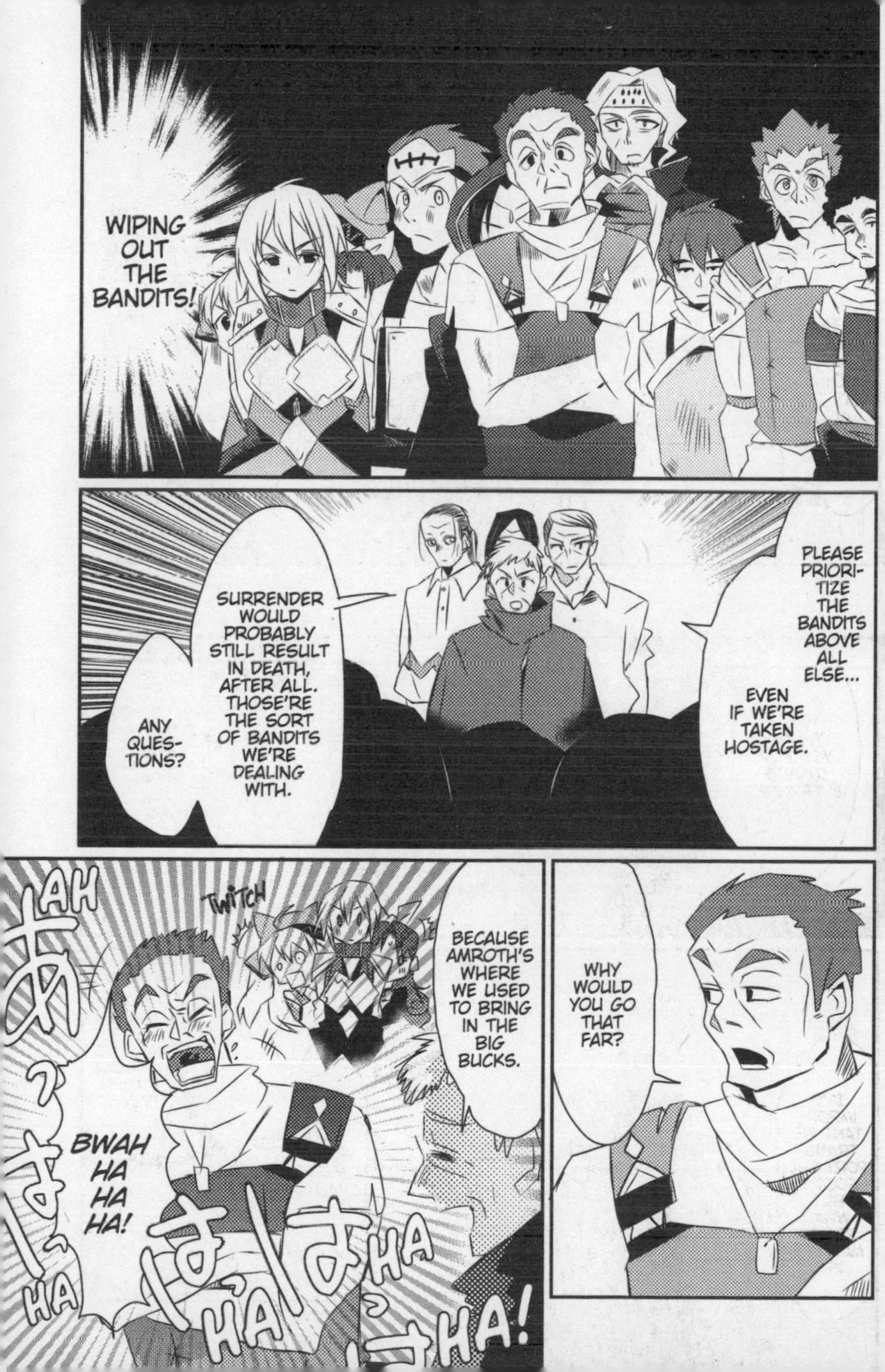
WIPING OUT THE BANDITS!
PLEASE PRIORI-TIZE THE BANDITS ABOVE ALL ELSE...
EVEN IF WE'RE TAKEN HOSTAGE.
SURRENDER WOULD PROBABLY STILL RESULT IN DEATH, AFTER ALL. THOSE'RE THE SORT OF BANDITS WE'RE DEALING WITH.
ANY QUES-TIONS?
WHY WOULD YOU GO THAT FAR?
BECAUSE AMROTH'S WHERE WE USED TO BRING IN THE BIG BUCKS.
TWITCH
あっはっはっはっ
AH HA HA HA HA!
BWAH HA HA HA!

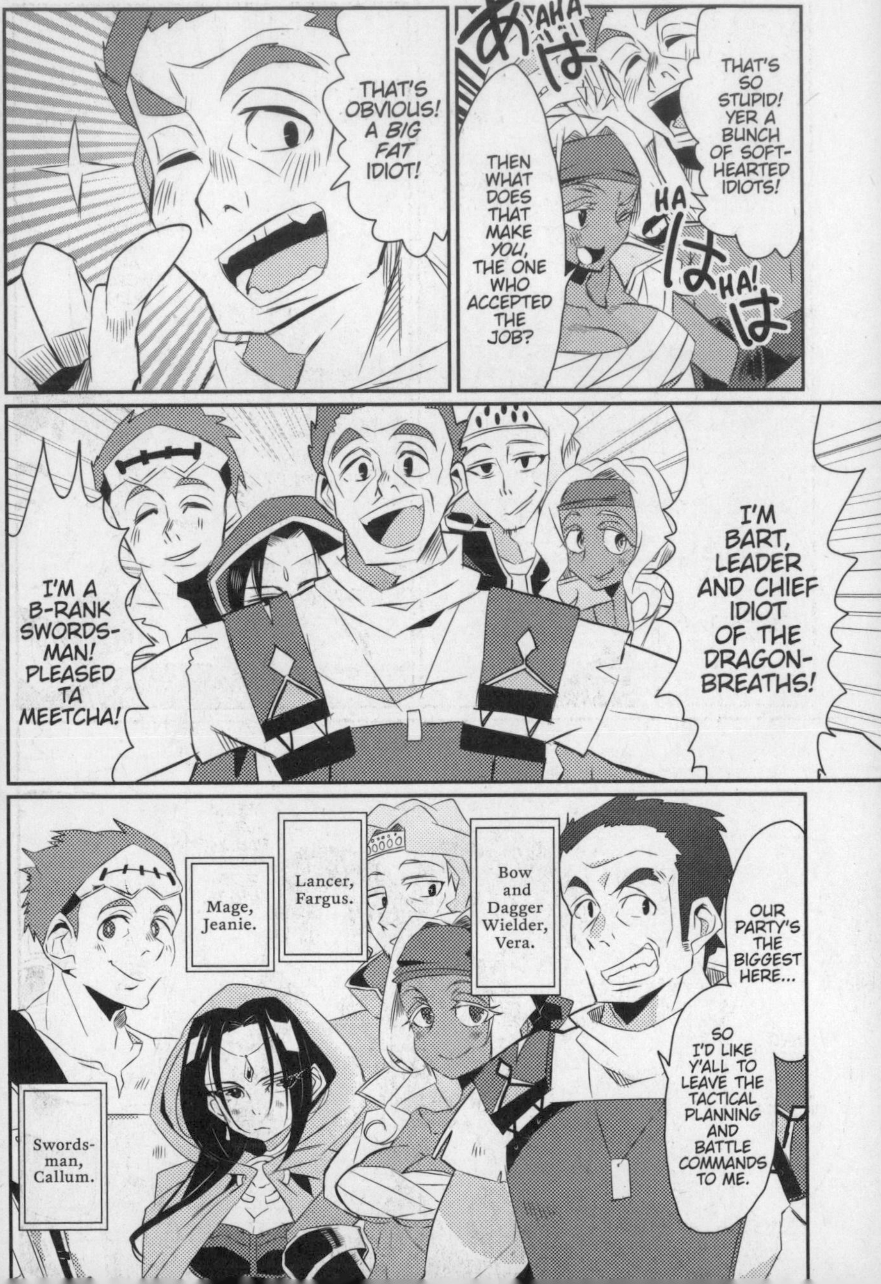
AHA あは
THAT'S SO STUPID! YER A BUNCH OF SOFT-HEARTED IDIOTS!
HA は HA! は
THEN WHAT DOES THAT MAKE *YOU*, THE ONE WHO ACCEPTED THE JOB?
THAT'S OBVIOUS! A *BIG FAT* IDIOT!
I'M BART, LEADER AND CHIEF IDIOT OF THE DRAGON-BREATHS!
I'M A B-RANK SWORDS-MAN! PLEASED TA MEETCHA!
OUR PARTY'S THE BIGGEST HERE...
SO I'D LIKE Y'ALL TO LEAVE THE TACTICAL PLANNING AND BATTLE COMMANDS TO ME.
Bow and Dagger Wielder, Vera.
Lancer, Fargus.
Mage, Jeanie.
Swords-man, Callum.

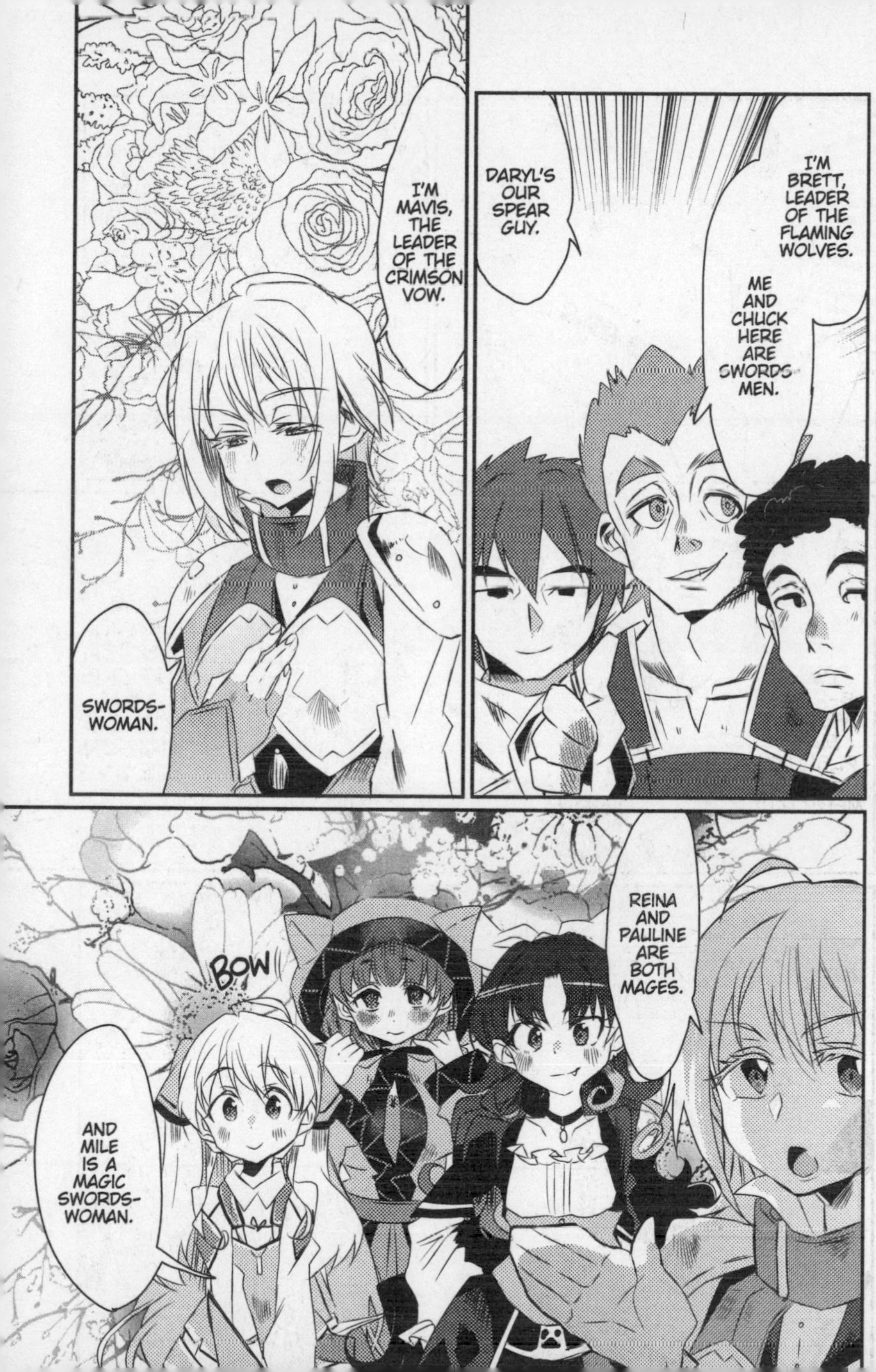
I'M BRETT, LEADER OF THE FLAMING WOLVES.
ME AND CHUCK HERE ARE SWORDSMEN.
DARYL'S OUR SPEAR GUY.
I'M MAVIS, THE LEADER OF THE CRIMSON VOW.
SWORDSWOMAN.
REINA AND PAULINE ARE BOTH MAGES.
BOW
AND MILE IS A MAGIC SWORDSWOMAN.

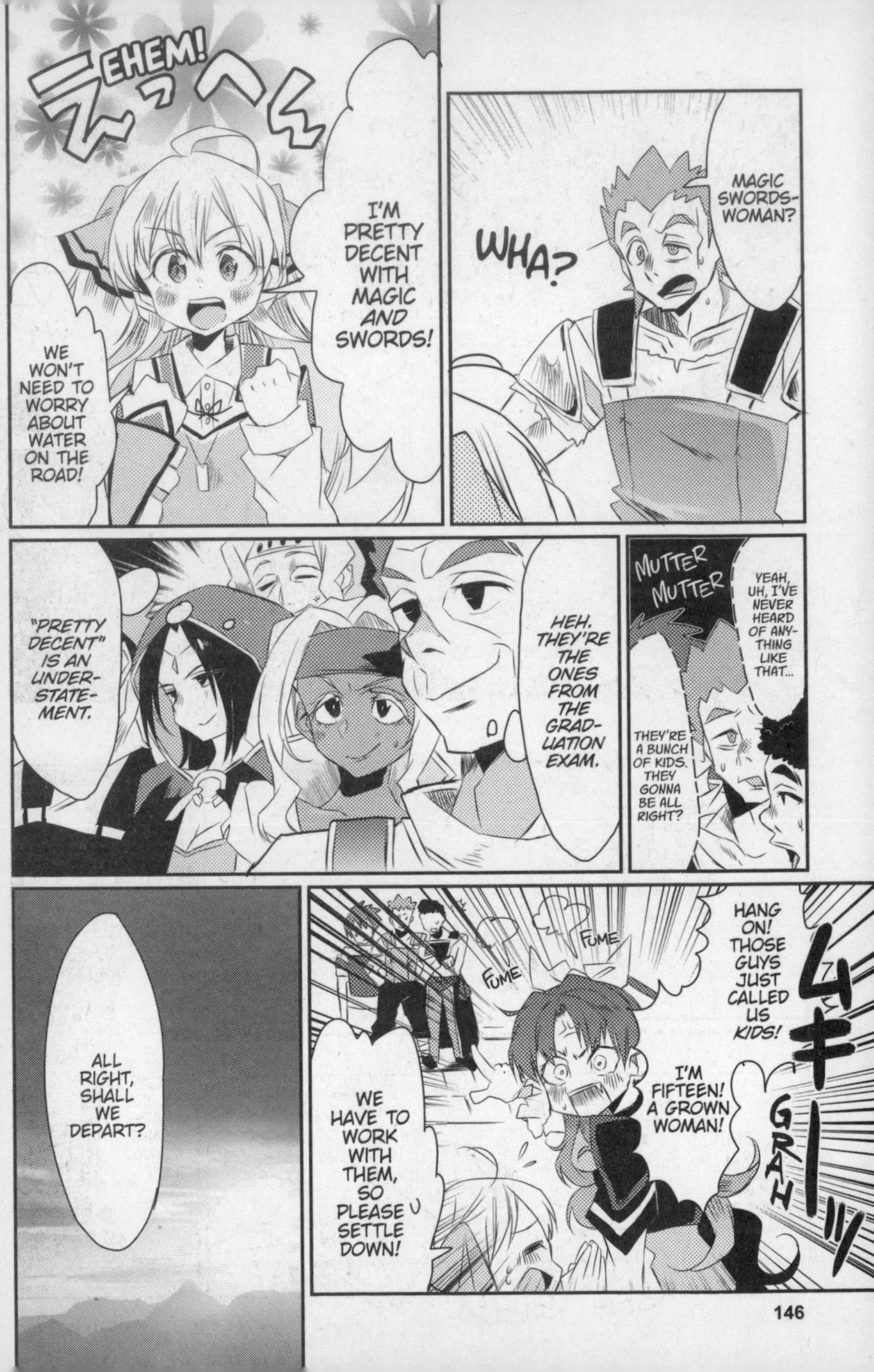

MAGIC SWORDS-WOMAN?
WHA?
EHEM!
えっへん
I'M PRETTY DECENT WITH MAGIC AND SWORDS!
WE WON'T NEED TO WORRY ABOUT WATER ON THE ROAD!
MUTTER MUTTER
YEAH, UH, I'VE NEVER HEARD OF ANY-THING LIKE THAT...
THEY'RE A BUNCH OF KIDS. THEY GONNA BE ALL RIGHT?
HEH. THEY'RE THE ONES FROM THE GRAD-UATION EXAM.
"PRETTY DECENT" IS AN UNDER-STATE-MENT.
HANG ON! THOSE GUYS JUST CALLED US KIDS!
ムキーッ
GRAH
I'M FIFTEEN! A GROWN WOMAN!
FUME
FUME
WE HAVE TO WORK WITH THEM, SO PLEASE SETTLE DOWN!
ALL RIGHT, SHALL WE DEPART?

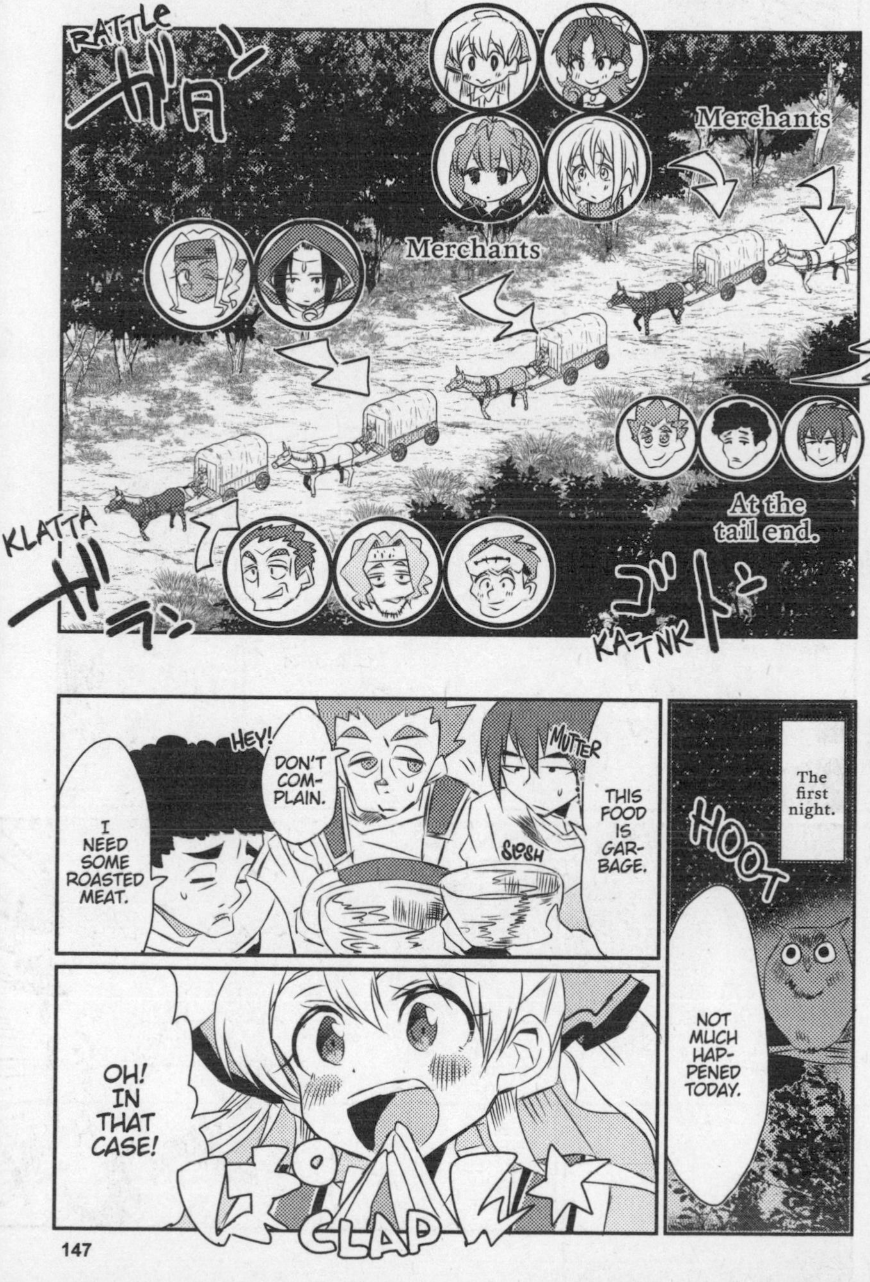
Merchants
RATTLE
Merchants
At the tail end.
KA-TNK
KLATTA
The first night.
HOOT
NOT MUCH HAP-PENED TODAY.
MUTTER
THIS FOOD IS GAR-BAGE.
HEY!
DON'T COM-PLAIN.
SLOSH
I NEED SOME ROASTED MEAT.
OH! IN THAT CASE!
CLAP

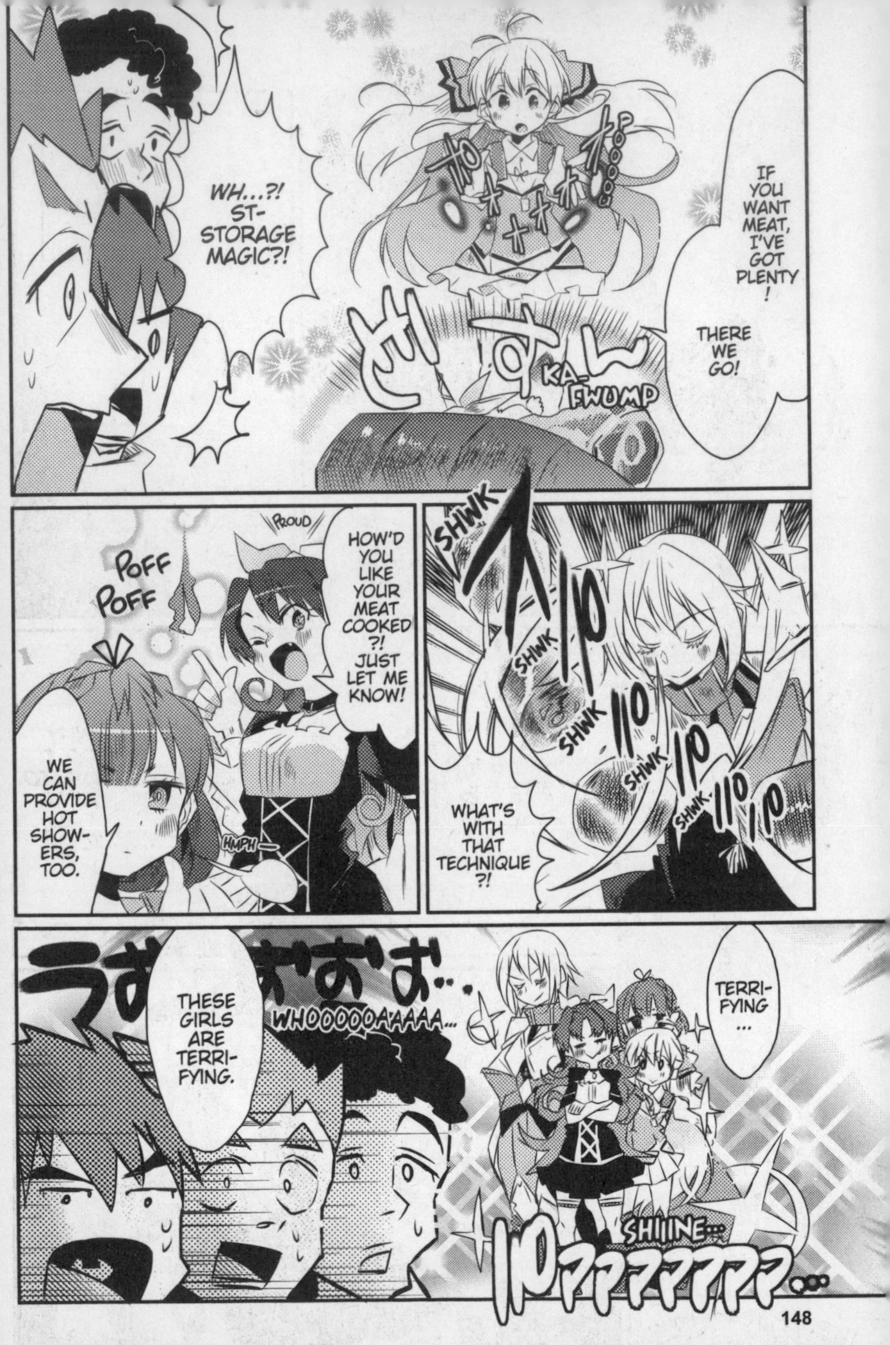
IF YOU WANT MEAT, I'VE GOT PLENTY!
THERE WE GO!
KA-FWUMP
WH...?! ST-STORAGE MAGIC?!
SHWK
SHWK
SHWK
SHWK
SHWK
WHAT'S WITH THAT TECHNIQUE?!
PROUD
HOW'D YOU LIKE YOUR MEAT COOKED?! JUST LET ME KNOW!
POFF POFF
HMPH—
WE CAN PROVIDE HOT SHOWERS, TOO.
TERRIFYING...
SHIIINE...
WHOOOOOAAAAA...
THESE GIRLS ARE TERRIFYING.

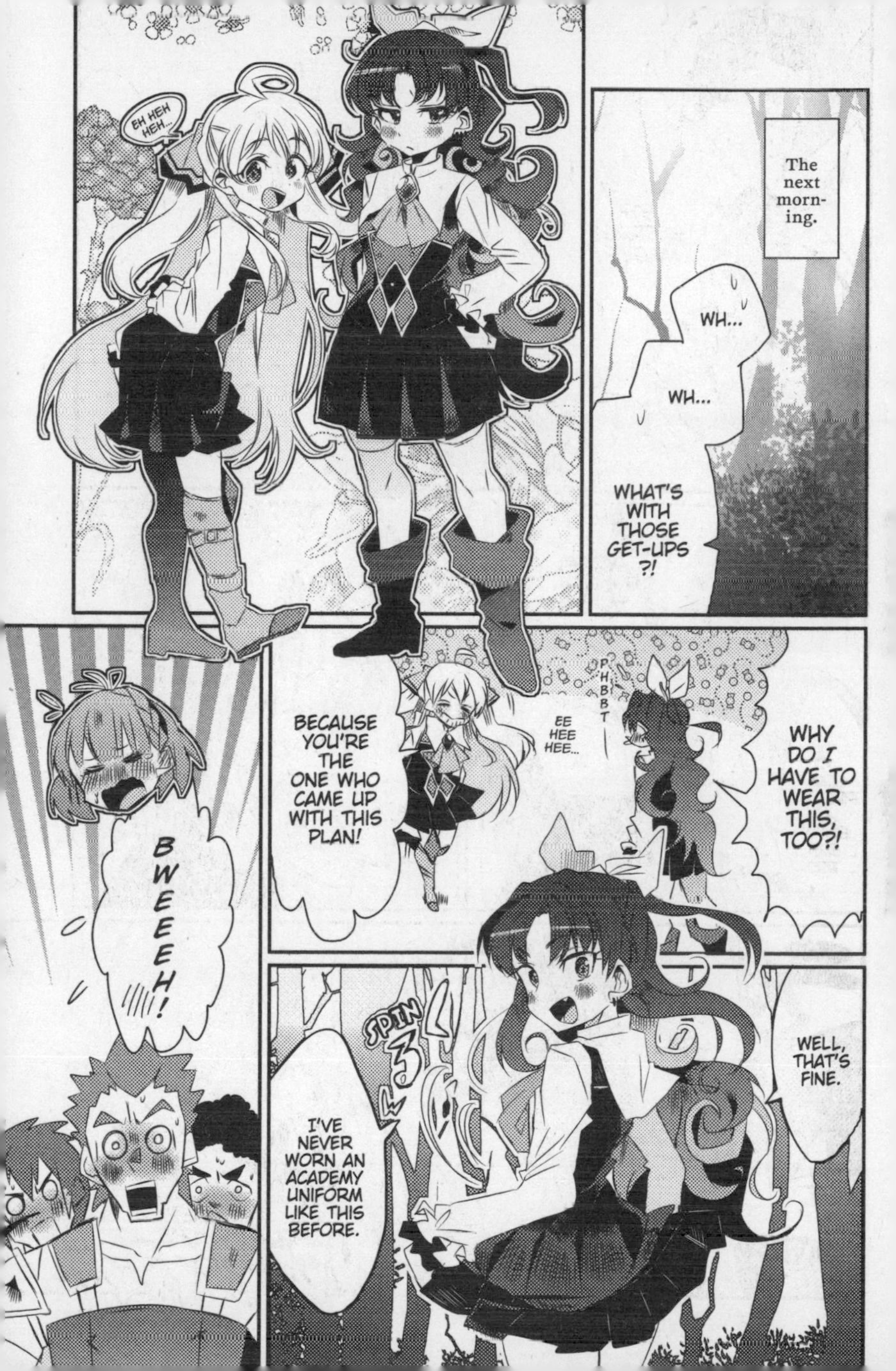
The next morning.
WH...
WH...
WHAT'S WITH THOSE GET-UPS?!
EH HEH HEH...
WHY DO I HAVE TO WEAR THIS, TOO?!
PHBBT
EE HEE HEE...
BECAUSE YOU'RE THE ONE WHO CAME UP WITH THIS PLAN!
WELL, THAT'S FINE.
SPIN
I'VE NEVER WORN AN ACADEMY UNIFORM LIKE THIS BEFORE.
BWEEEEH!

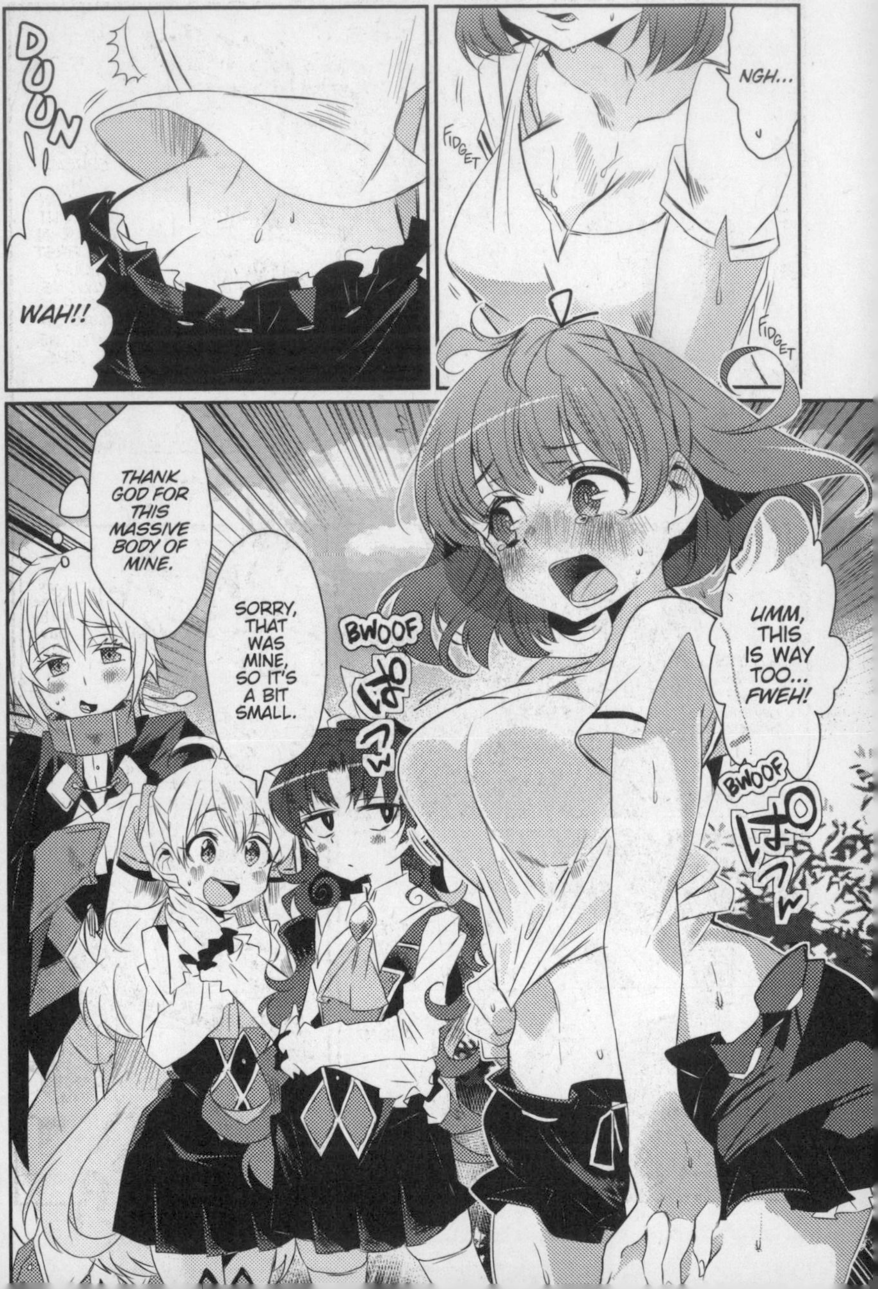
NGH...
FIDGET
FIDGET
DUUN
WAH!!
UMM, THIS IS WAY TOO... FWEH!
BWOOF
BWOOF
SORRY, THAT WAS MINE, SO IT'S A BIT SMALL.
THANK GOD FOR THIS MASSIVE BODY OF MINE.

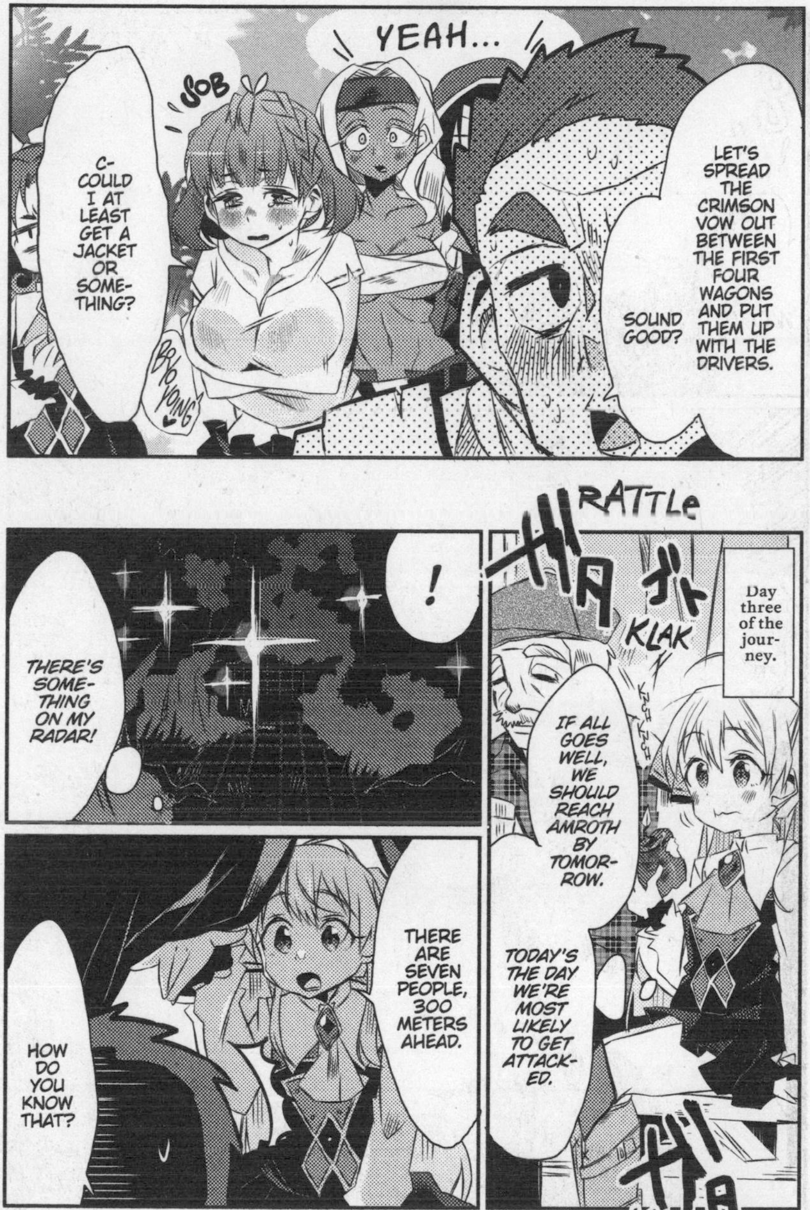
LET'S SPREAD THE CRIMSON VOW OUT BETWEEN THE FIRST FOUR WAGONS AND PUT THEM UP WITH THE DRIVERS.
SOUND GOOD?
YEAH...
SOB
C-COULD I AT LEAST GET A JACKET OR SOMETHING?
BOYOING
RATTLE
KLAK
Day three of the journey.
IF ALL GOES WELL, WE SHOULD REACH AMROTH BY TOMORROW.
TODAY'S THE DAY WE'RE MOST LIKELY TO GET ATTACKED.
KLAK
!
THERE'S SOMETHING ON MY RADAR!
THERE ARE SEVEN PEOPLE, 300 METERS AHEAD.
HOW DO YOU KNOW THAT?

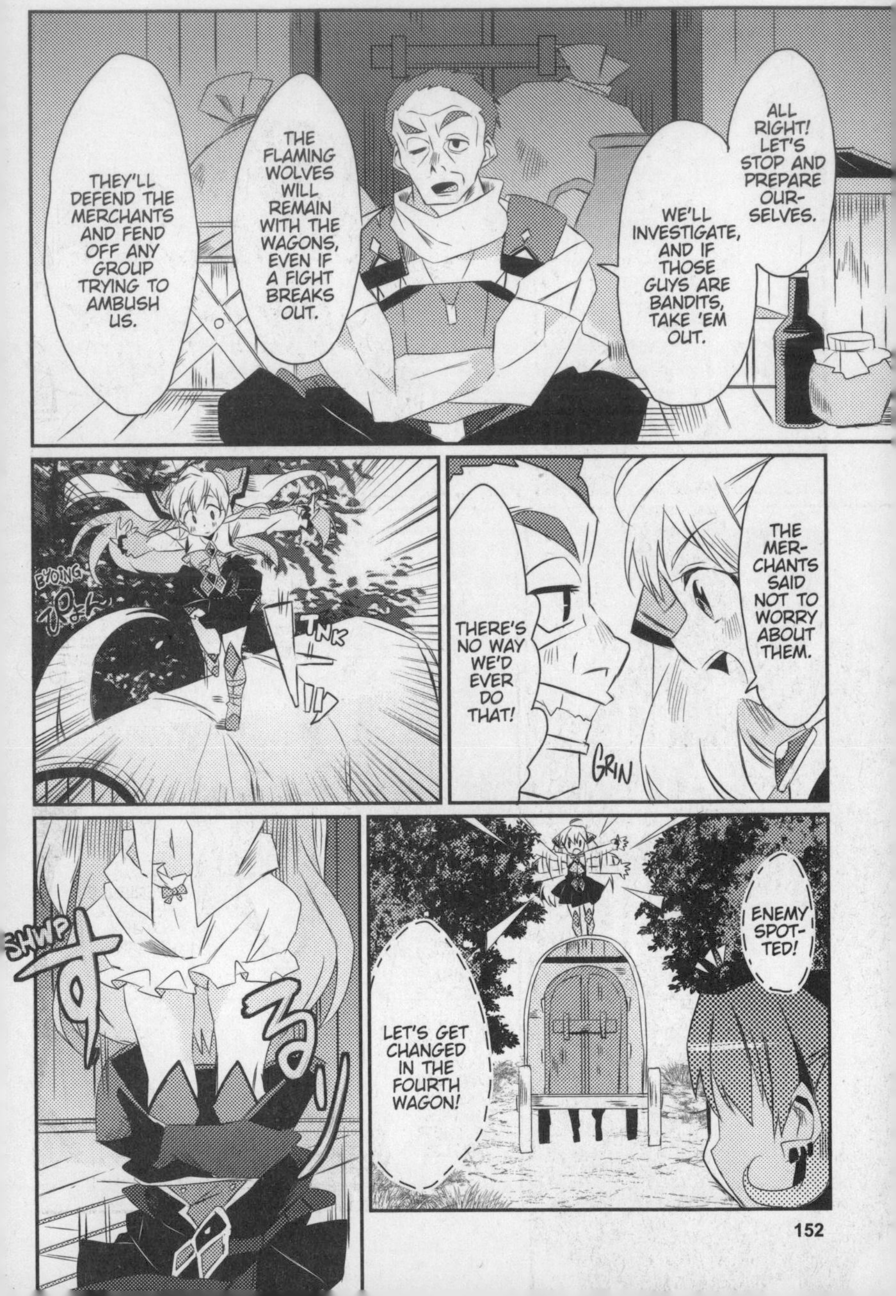
ALL RIGHT! LET'S STOP AND PREPARE OUR-SELVES.
WE'LL INVESTIGATE, AND IF THOSE GUYS ARE BANDITS, TAKE 'EM OUT.
THE FLAMING WOLVES WILL REMAIN WITH THE WAGONS, EVEN IF A FIGHT BREAKS OUT.
THEY'LL DEFEND THE MERCHANTS AND FEND OFF ANY GROUP TRYING TO AMBUSH US.
THE MER-CHANTS SAID NOT TO WORRY ABOUT THEM.
THERE'S NO WAY WE'D EVER DO THAT!
GRIN
TNK
BYOING
ENEMY SPOT-TED!
LET'S GET CHANGED IN THE FOURTH WAGON!
SHWP

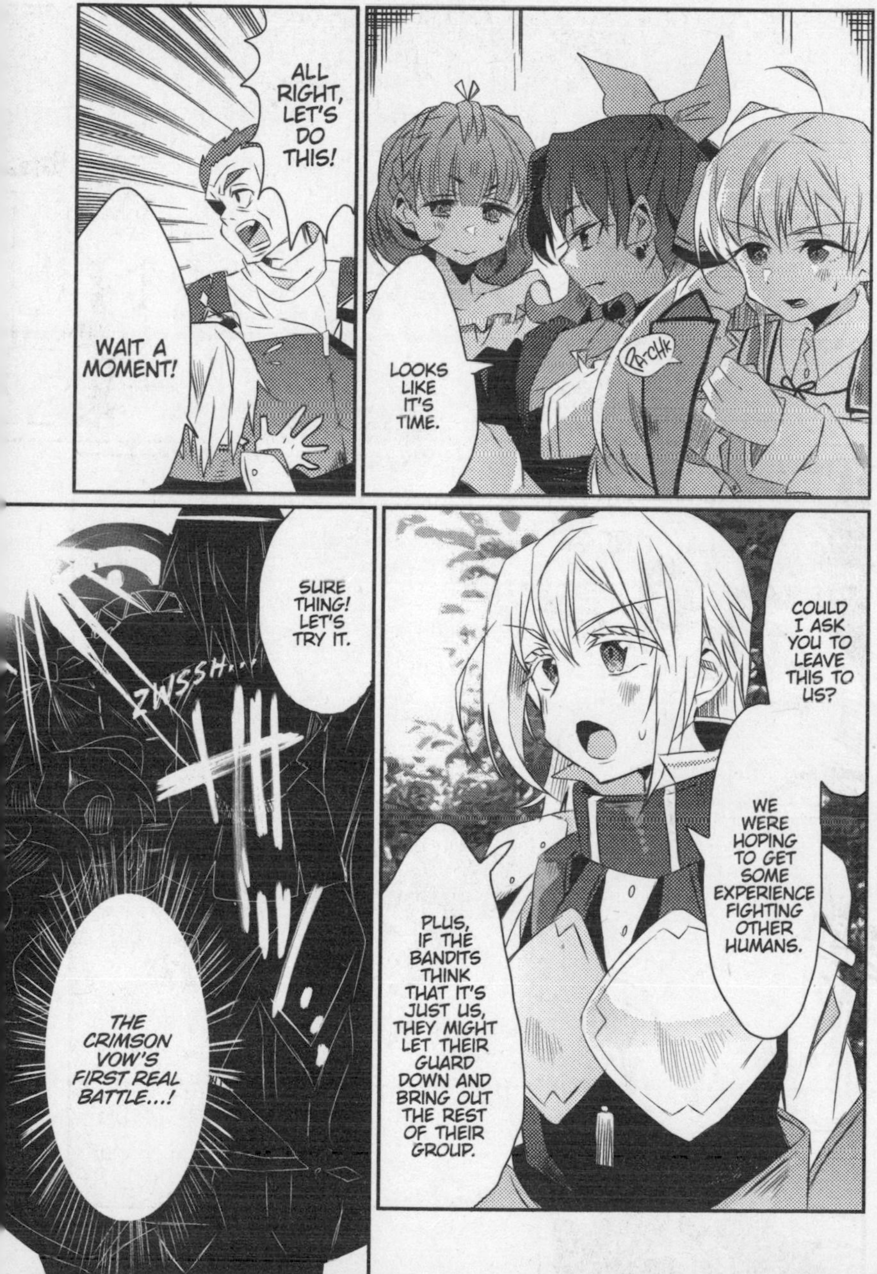
LOOKS LIKE IT'S TIME.
PA-CHK
ALL RIGHT, LET'S DO THIS!
WAIT A MOMENT!
COULD I ASK YOU TO LEAVE THIS TO US?
WE WERE HOPING TO GET SOME EXPERIENCE FIGHTING OTHER HUMANS.
PLUS, IF THE BANDITS THINK THAT IT'S JUST US, THEY MIGHT LET THEIR GUARD DOWN AND BRING OUT THE REST OF THEIR GROUP.
SURE THING! LET'S TRY IT.
ZWSSH...
THE CRIMSON VOW'S FIRST REAL BATTLE...!

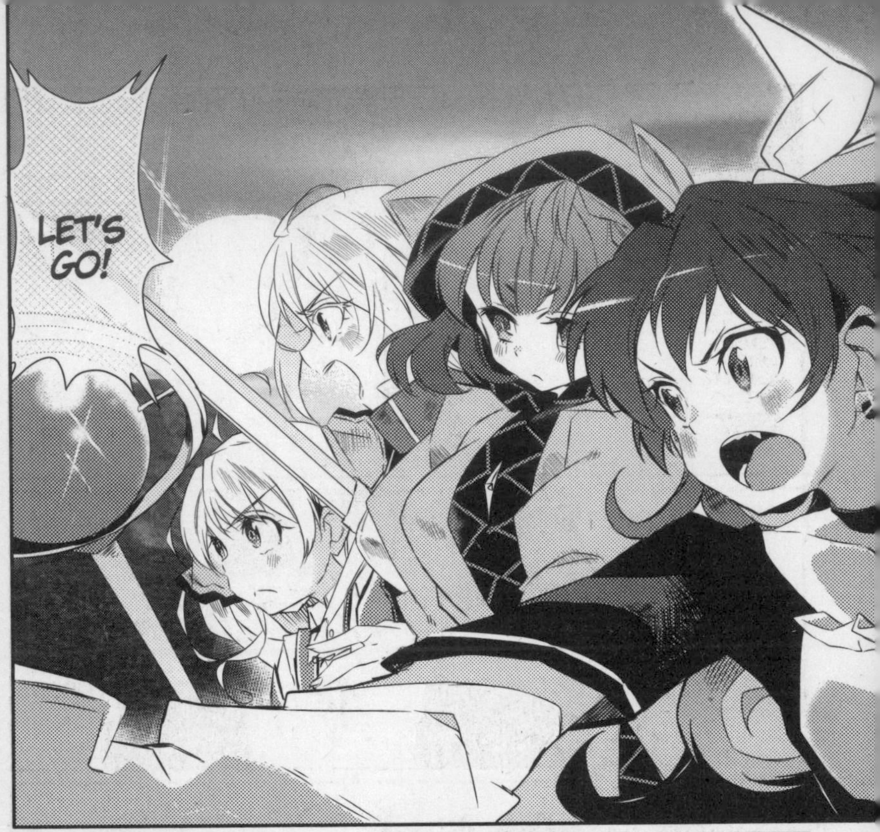
LET'S GO!

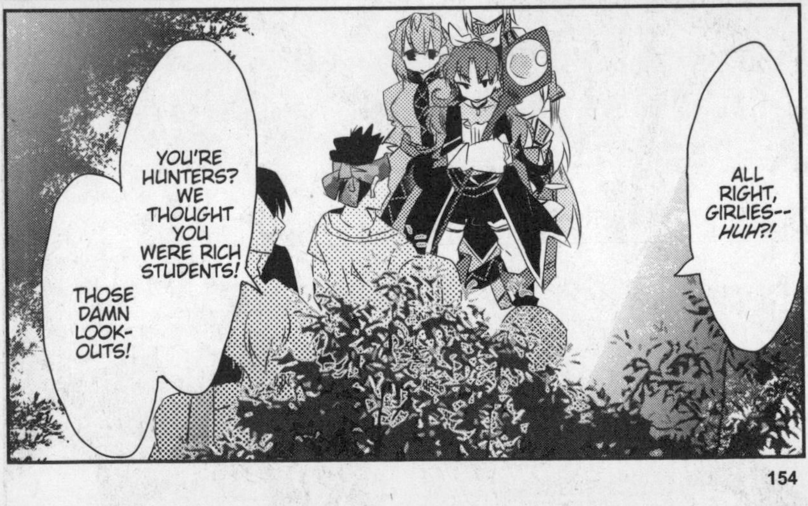
ALL RIGHT, GIRLIES-- *HUH?!*
YOU'RE HUNTERS? WE THOUGHT YOU WERE RICH STUDENTS!
THOSE DAMN LOOK-OUTS!

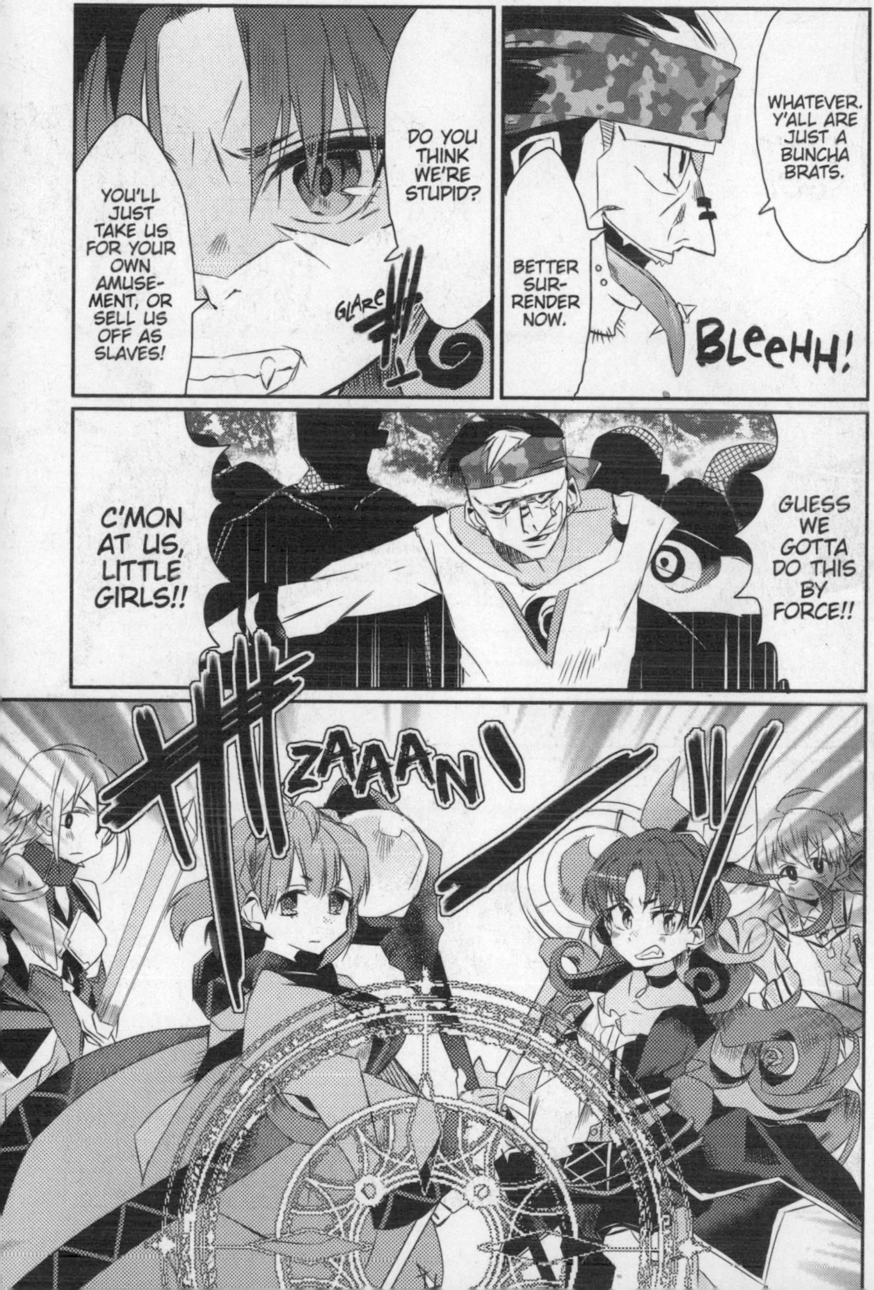
WHATEVER. Y'ALL ARE JUST A BUNCHA BRATS.
BETTER SUR-RENDER NOW.
BLEEHH!
DO YOU THINK WE'RE STUPID?
YOU'LL JUST TAKE US FOR YOUR OWN AMUSE-MENT, OR SELL US OFF AS SLAVES!
GLARE
GUESS WE GOTTA DO THIS BY FORCE!!
C'MON AT US, LITTLE GIRLS!!
ZAAAN!

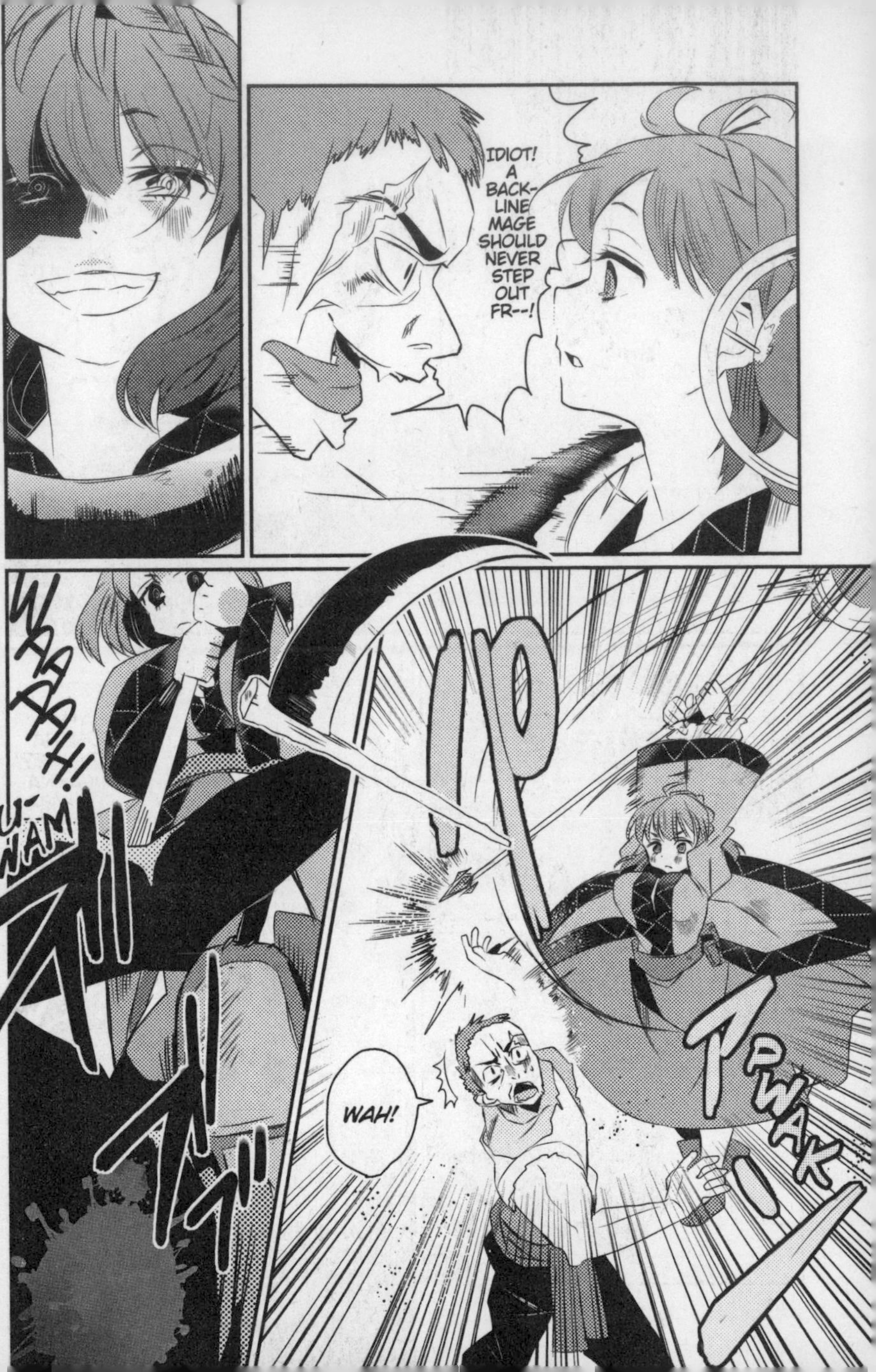
IDIOT! A BACK-LINE MAGE SHOULD NEVER STEP OUT FR--!
WAAAAH!
PWAK
GWAM
WAH!

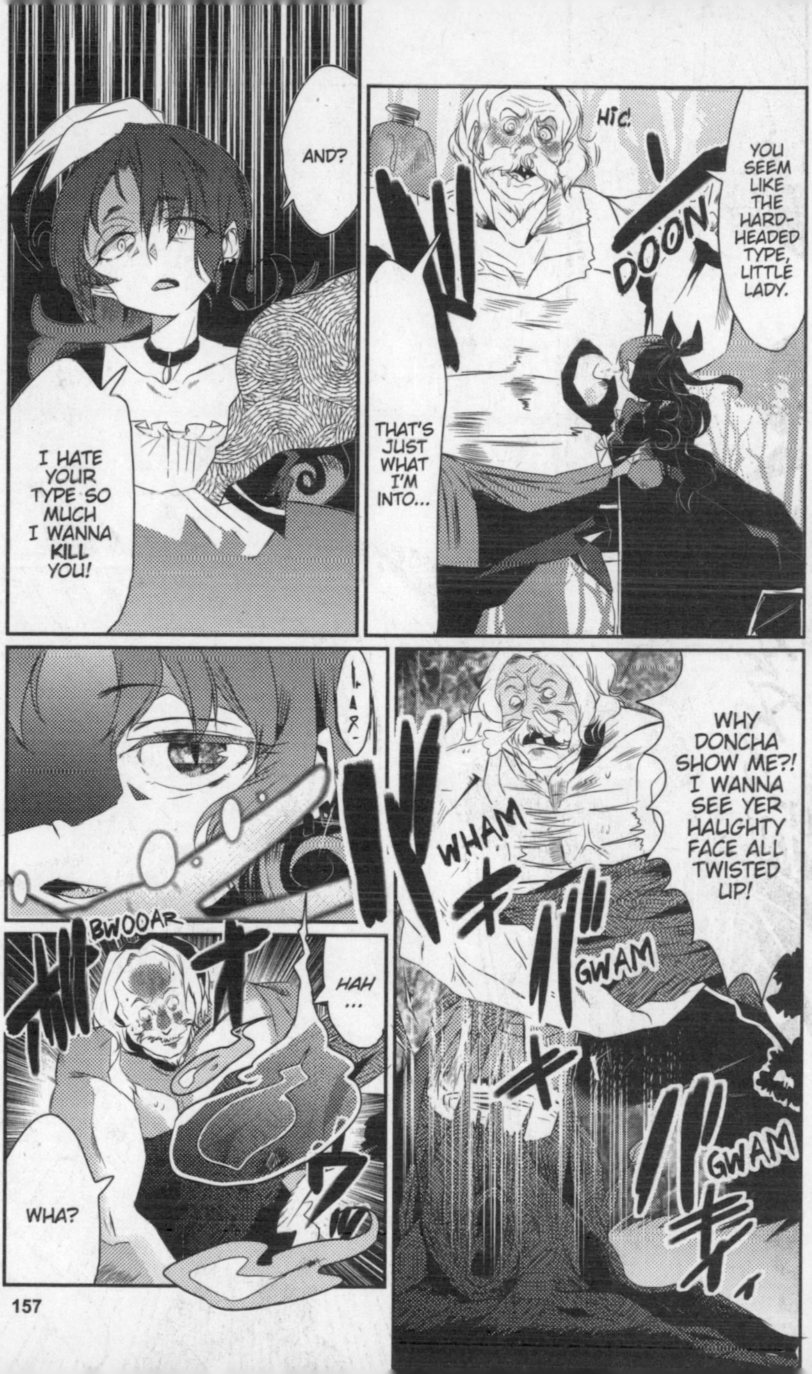

HIC!
YOU SEEM LIKE THE HARD-HEADED TYPE, LITTLE LADY.
DOON
THAT'S JUST WHAT I'M INTO...
AND?
I HATE YOUR TYPE SO MUCH I WANNA KILL YOU!
WHY DONCHA SHOW ME?! I WANNA SEE YER HAUGHTY FACE ALL TWISTED UP!
WHAM
GWAM
GWAM
BWOOAR
HAH...
WHA?

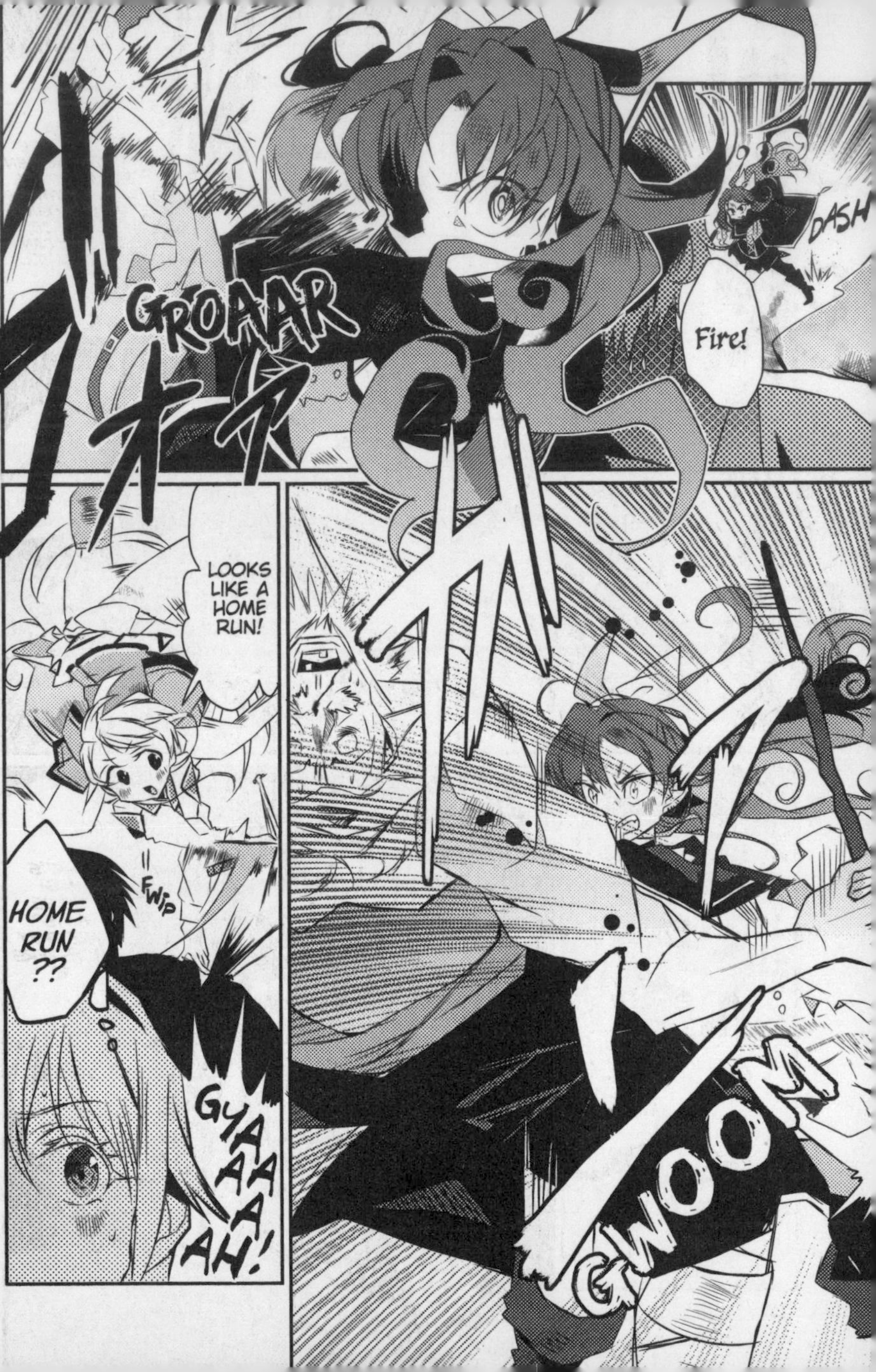
DASH
Fire!
GROAAR
GWOOM
LOOKS LIKE A HOME RUN!
FWIP
HOME RUN??
GYAAAAAH!

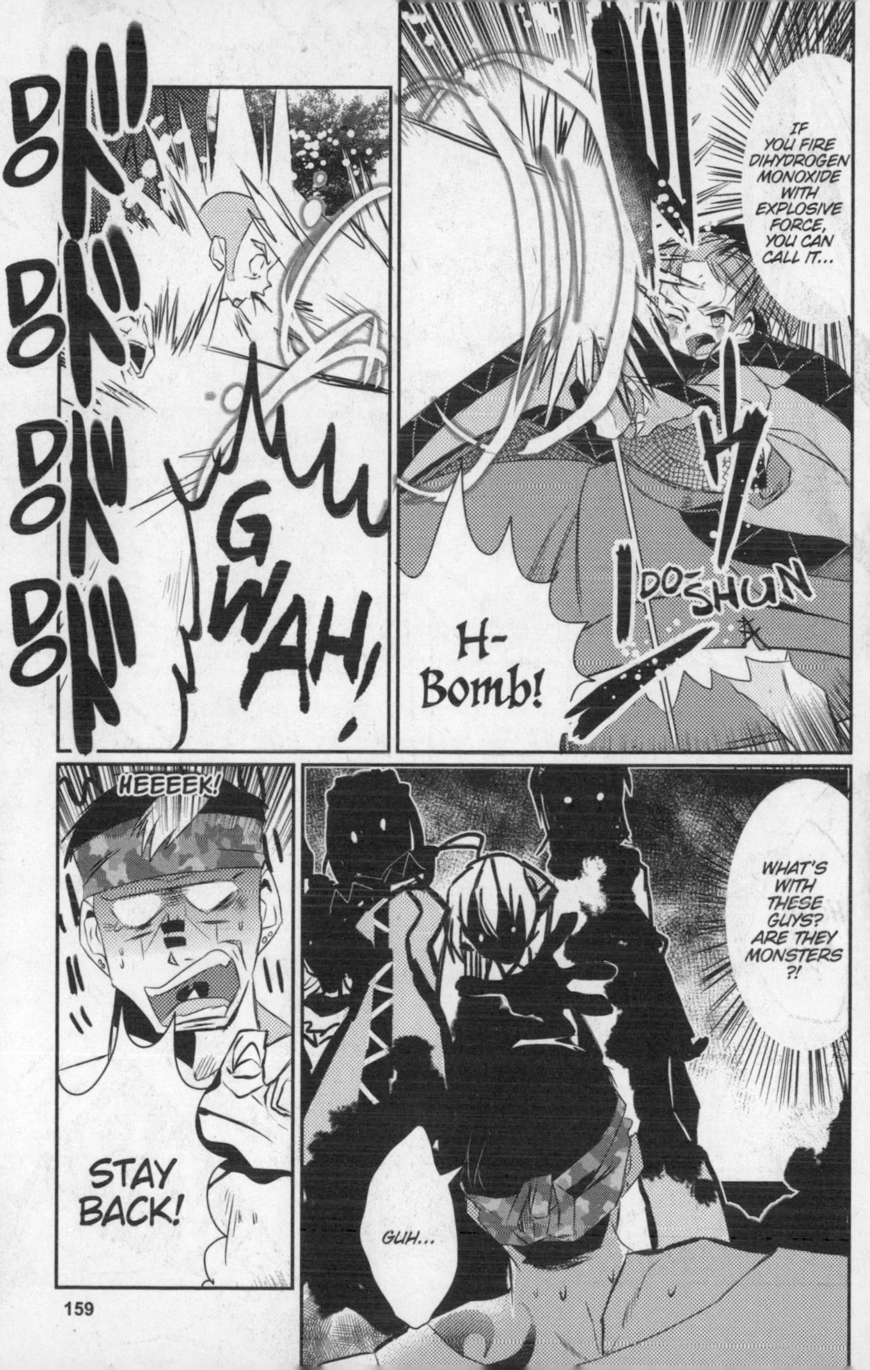
IF YOU FIRE DIHYDROGEN MONOXIDE WITH EXPLOSIVE FORCE, YOU CAN CALL IT...
DO-SHUN
H-Bomb!
DO DO DO DO
MUGWAH!
WHAT'S WITH THESE GUYS? ARE THEY MONSTERS?!
GUH...
HEEEEEK!
STAY BACK!

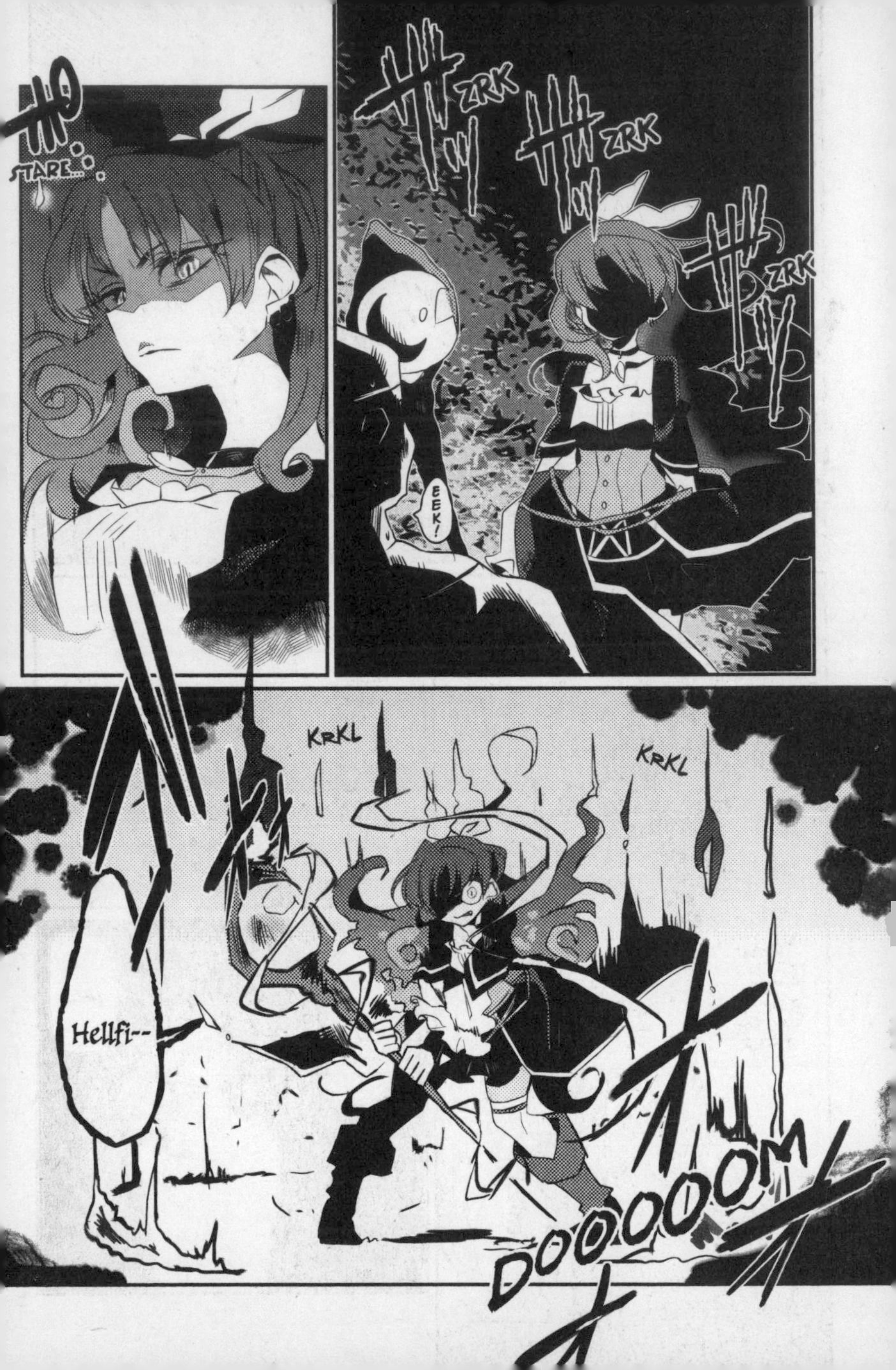
ZRK
ZRK
ZRK
EEK!
STARE...
KRKL
KRKL
Hellfi--
DOOOOOOM

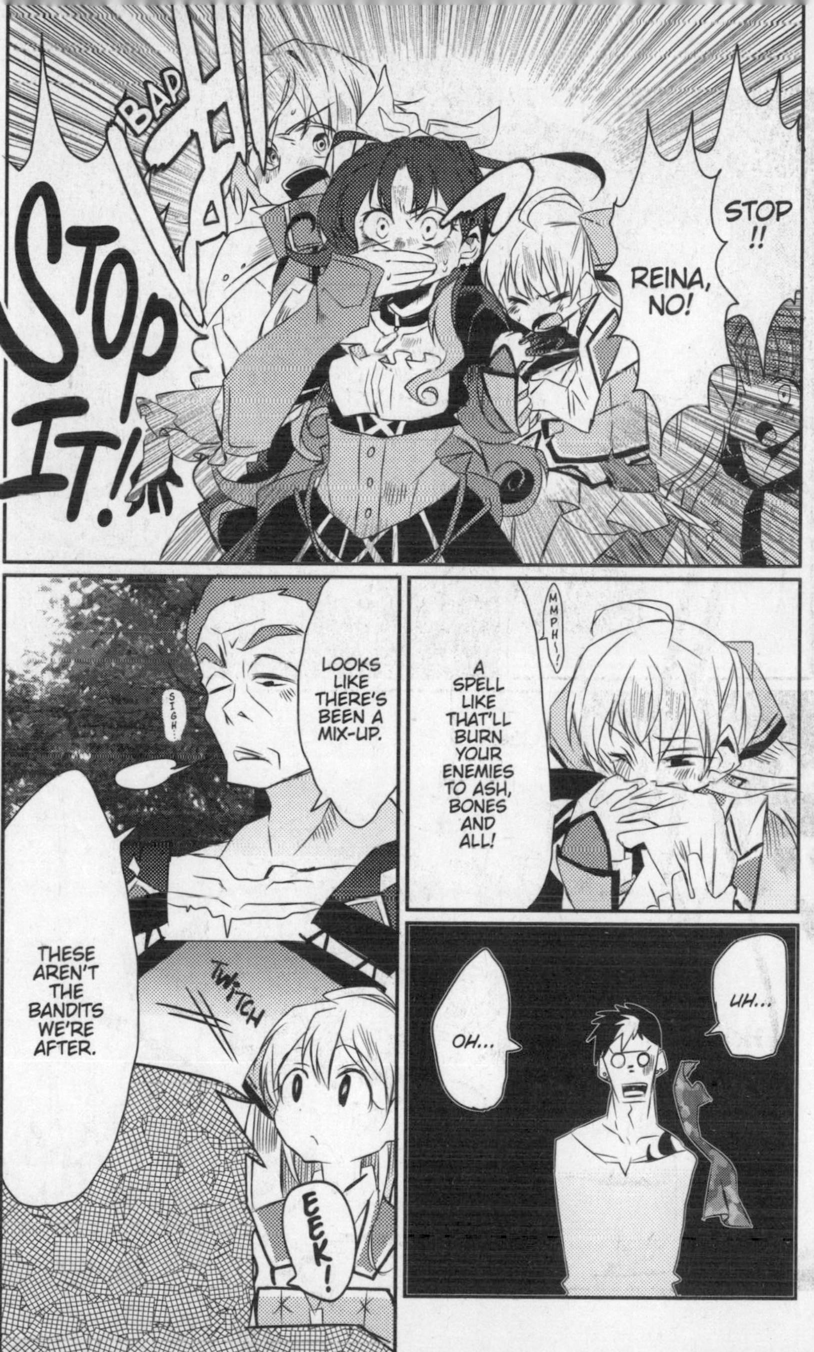
STOP !!
REINA, NO!
BAP
STOP IT!!
MMPH~!
A SPELL LIKE THAT'LL BURN YOUR ENEMIES TO ASH, BONES AND ALL!
LOOKS LIKE THERE'S BEEN A MIX-UP.
SIGH...
THESE AREN'T THE BANDITS WE'RE AFTER.
UH...
OH...
TWITCH
EEK!

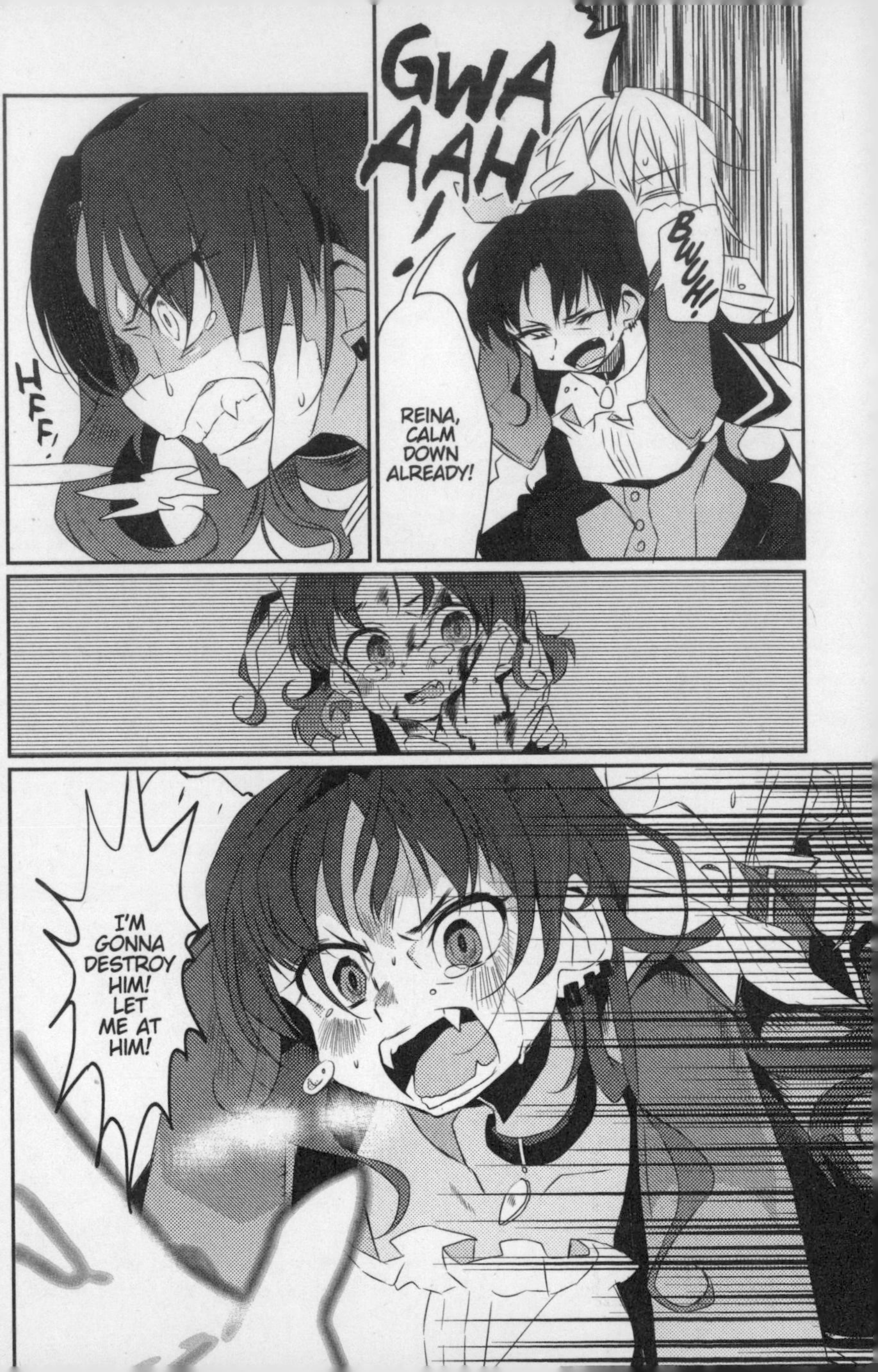
GWAAAH!
BWUH!
REINA, CALM DOWN ALREADY!
HFF!
I'M GONNA DESTROY HIM! LET ME AT HIM!

Didn't I Say to Make My Abilities Average in the Next Life?!

Didn't I Say to Make My Abilities Average in the Next Life?!

BONUS STORY
Didn't I Say to Make My Abilities Average in the Next Life?!

The Tale of Marcela,
the Wicked Maiden

"How very peculiar..."

"Whatever is the matter, Lady Marcela?" asked Miss Monika, whilst I sat deep in thought.

"Well," I replied, "lately I have been finding my handkerchief, penholder, and other small objects gone missing. I can understand my handkerchief, but the penholder isn't something I would be so likely to misplace."

I rarely ever moved my penholder from my desk, let alone took it from my room. I might have suspected burglary, but no one after valuables would be interested in such worthless things as my handkerchief and penholder. There were items far more valuable all around my room, after all.

Besides, this was the dormitory of a school for noble girls. It wasn't the sort of place outsiders could easily infiltrate. And within its halls, we were protected by the iron-clad defense of our matron.

"I suppose it is possible Cricket-Eater took them, mistaking them for toys."

There wasn't much point in pondering over it, and certainly no use in doubting one's fellow students...

Cricket-Eater, however, was the stray cat Adele used to care for, and who now frequented my room. The other students called him a number of names, such as Crooktail, Blackie, and Goldeneye.

My thoughts thus occupied by the cat, I soon forgot about all the little items I had lost.

"Miss Marcela, you will be attending Ardleigh Academy's anniversary celebration, ten days hence."

"Huh...?"

I had been called to the staff room, where a teacher delivered this stunning decree.

"Every year, we have the most promising student from Eckland Academy attend the anniversary, for the sake of healthy camaraderie and exchange between our schools."

This was the first I'd heard of it! It was a strange state of affairs, for surely students selected in the past would have gloated over the honor. Not to mention, the battle for such a coveted position would be intense—it was the sort of thing that should have been on every student's lips. A sense of unease began to overtake me.

"However, you are forbidden to speak of this to anyone."

Ah, so *that* was the reason.

According to the teacher, though it was described as a "healthy camaraderie and exchange between schools," in truth, it was more akin to headhunting. Indeed, Ardleigh Academy was hoping to snipe Eckland's most promising pupils.

Though Eckland Academy was considered somewhat inferior when compared to Ardleigh, that was only a matter of appearance. Eckland was an academy for lower nobles and commoners: third sons and beyond, and the daughters of higher nobles. Therefore, it was unsurprising that, every now and again, some exceptional student would join Eckland's ranks. Apparently, this was quite the inconvenience for Ardleigh.

Therefore, every year they invited Eckland's top student to visit them under false pretenses, hoping to lure and tempt them into transferring. If the student *did* have exceptional abilities, they would be allowed into Ardleigh, tuition-free. If they were found to be lacking, they were merely sent home.

Ardleigh was a school meant only for high-born nobles, royals, and the like. If the selected student happened to be a commoner, it was no matter; they would be adopted into a noble family, and that was that. There were plenty of noble families champing at the bit to volunteer, since it meant welcoming someone with prodigious talent into their lineage.

Considering this practice, and its careful regard for any student found lacking and sent home, it made sense to keep it a secret from all the other students. The discretion seemed only natural to me.

"Sometimes, Ardleigh leaves the appointment of the student to us," the teacher went on, "and sometimes they choose. In this case, Miss Marcela, *they* made the selection..."

Ah...

Naturally, I had no intention of transferring, but the invitation wasn't the sort one could refuse. At the very least, I had to attend the function. I would either fail to live up to their expectations and be sent away, or I would have the opportunity to give them a proper refusal myself. It wasn't as if the school would force a student against their will, after all. No institution of learning purporting its primary mission to be the guidance of youth would do such a thing.

Given their ages, it was likely their Highnesses, Prince Adalbert and Prince Vince, had already graduated, so that was one less thing for me to worry about. Indeed, from the moment her Highness, the third princess, had invited the three of us to the palace to make inquiries about Miss Adele and we were introduced, I had been receiving invitations and overtures from both of their Highnesses. It troubled me. However, this particular function had nothing to do with either of them, so I could rest at least a *bit* at ease—or so I thought.

Wait a second, why are they here?! Not only both princes, but their Majesties the King and Queen! And her Highness the Princess. All of them!!!

Now that I thought about it, Ardleigh *was* the most elite school in the country: the academy attended by their Highnesses, the extended royal family, and all the top nobles. As many of these students would likely seek work in relation to the Crown following graduation, it was only natural the royal family would attend their larger functions.

Well, I was but a normal guest of the affair—it wasn't as though I needed to do anything special. All matters concerning my "evaluation" would occur privately, just myself and the instructors, after the anniversary celebration was over. For now, all I had to do was sit quietly. I would be fine...

Except that my troubles began straight away, with a sudden loud voice from a girl roughly the same age as me.

"Well, if it isn't the little minx herself!"

"Eek!" I yelped in surprise. I wasn't fine at all!

"It is awfully brave of a lowly noble to try and lay a hand upon someone else's fiancé!"

"What...?" I had no idea what the girl was talking about.

"Don't play the fool! Did you think we wouldn't find out about how you've been toying with Prince Adalbert?!"

Huh? But that would mean...

"Are you, by chance, his Highness's fiancée?"

"That's correct! Anselda von Velanas, the eldest daughter of Margrave Velanas! The one you tried to lay your dirty hands upon is—"

"Congratulations on the engagement! I wish you both happiness, from the bottom of my heart!"

"Prince Adalbert, my—uh, what?"

Certainly, if the crown prince took the throne, he would end up with second and third wives, in addition to a slew of lovers. But now that he had become engaged to the woman who would be his first wife, he would no longer be able to look for other lovers publicly. In other words, he could no longer make solicitations of me!

At any rate, there was no way the third daughter of an impoverished baron could be a true match to a member of the royal family. While I was aware I was only kept around for the sake of luring in Miss Adele, I wasn't about to let such a thing adversely affect *my* life!

"Congratulations! You have my deepest and truest congratulations!"

Overwhelmed with joy, I grabbed the girl by her hands and shook them vigorously.

"J-just a moment! St-stop that!"

I couldn't help myself. I was so suddenly, thoroughly overjoyed.

"A-anyway! You can't deceive me with your kind words! I shall expose your wicked deeds to all!"

Wicked deeds? What in the world was she on about?

Suddenly, I realized the hall was silent. Everyone was focused on us. Of course—the ceremonies were about to start, and the attendees had all taken their seats...

Aaaaaaaah!! I made a spectacle of myself! The two of us were a complete spectacle!!

"Look closely!" said Lady Anselda as she pulled a single

handkerchief from her breast pocket.

"What is that, exactly?" I asked.

"Proof of your foul deeds! This is *your* handkerchief, which I found at the scene of the crime! When I was shoved down the stairs! And *this*..." She pulled another item from her breast pocket: a penholder. She had quite a lot of things stored in there. "I found this left behind when I was shoved before a carriage!"

Oh! This felt just like one of those Japanese folktales Miss Adele told us, "The Tale of the Wicked Maiden's Foiled Engagement." Except that was the story of a prince smitten with the daughter of a lesser noble, and his young, high-born fiancée was attempting to ruin the other girl. This was the opposite! In the story, the lower-born girl was the one being ruined. The positions were switched! I'd been beaten to the punch!

Wait, but that wasn't right at all. I had no interest in taking someone else's betrothed away. I certainly never thought of laying hands on the crown prince.

It was true the handkerchief and penholder were items I had lost. However...

"Um, begging your pardon, Lady Anselda, but I don't believe I ever made your acquaintance before today. Furthermore, I am a student of Eckland Academy, not Ardleigh, so the chances of us having been in proximity before now are..."

"It was on a holiday! Last week, and the week before last, when I was in town doing some shopping." Lady Anselda looked a bit nervous as she explained this.

"On those days, I was with others while attending to business, from dawn until dusk—the entire time any shops would have been open," I said. "Ah, are Lady Satya of the house of Count Cavelius and Lady Mefilicia of the house of

Margrave Gotholtz here presently?"

The two young women quickly stood from their seats.

"I-It's true," said Lady Mefilicia. "The week before last, Lady Marcela was with me the whole time. As part of the guards we requested, the Wonder—"

"There you have it!"

That was close! I wasn't about to let our carefully-guarded secret—that we three had registered with the Hunters' Guild and served as bodyguards exclusively for noble girls—slip in front of such a large assembly! There was no telling who might pass that news along to my father.

"Yes, and last week, she was with me," Lady Satya continued, blessedly curt.

"Furthermore," I said, "while I can understand the handkerchief, if I were intending to attack someone, why would I bring my penholder with me? How would I drop such a thing without noticing?"

"Er..." Lady Anselda began to look a bit pale, but what was said had to be said.

"Also, though we may be proud, my house is an impoverished one. We haven't the money for handkerchiefs to be embroidered, nor penholders stamped, with our family crest. Both of those items are stock goods we purchased from the shops. So, how did you know those items belong to me— someone you had not yet met?"

"Uh..."

"If I might?"

Just as things were beginning to fall apart, his Highness, Prince Adalbert himself, called out to us.

"I have to say, this is the first *I've* ever heard of my engagement to Lady Anselda. Am I to believe this is fact?" he asked, turning to his and her Majesties, the King and Queen. The two shook their heads emphatically. Which meant...

"I suppose the Lord and Lady Velanas must have filled your head with such talk," he said to Lady Anselda. "Something like, 'You're going to marry the crown prince someday,' yes? They thought they could motivate their daughter into giving her all to studies and refinement, for the sake of their own dreams. But of course, that engagement was never announced, was it?"

"Uh..."

"Well, I suppose it is true such a thing is possible for the daughter of a margrave, Lady Anselda."

"Wh-why are you speaking as though you already know this?!" Lady Anselda appeared flabbergasted by Prince Adalbert's assertion.

Though there were a number of guests in attendance, that didn't necessarily mean the students' parents were among them. It would be impossible to confirm the truth of the matter with Lady Anselda's parents, but the shock on her face suggested the Prince had hit the mark.

Which meant... *M-my peace and quiet! My life unbothered by his Highness's overtures!*

But that was beside the point! What was worse was the position Lady Anselda had put herself in by causing such a fuss. If I didn't do something, this whole affair was going to sour, and fast!

I quickly stood from my seat, declaring, "T-truly, it was nothing! Lady Anselda was mistaken, but it appears I caught her too sharply with my joke! *Oh ho ho,* what a serious girl you are, Lady Anselda! Where is your sense of humor? *Oh ho ho ho ho!*"

I-It hurt! It hurt so bad!!!

"Now Marcela, dear, you shouldn't laugh at other people's missteps," Prince Vince said. "Don't you think dear Anselda has been hurt enough?"

"Mm, y-yes, you're right," I said, shocked he could read the room so well.

When Prince Adalbert caught me looking at Prince Vince with admiration, he suddenly became flustered, quickly agreeing with his younger brother. I was surprised to see such a thing from the typically expressionless Prince Adalbert. I wondered why that might be.

However, things weren't settled yet. I needed one more push.

"I am certain the proud pupils of Ardleigh Academy would never accuse anyone, let alone one of their dear classmates, of such a trivial slip-up, or speak to others of it, yes? And most certainly, the staff and honored guests would never dream of it."

Though the words of someone like me carried no weight of their own, there was still power here, within the grasp of even *my* fingertips. It was the power of both their Highnesses, and their parents, their Majesties the King and Queen. It was the focal point of one of the sayings Miss Adele used to toss around: "Make the best of whatever you've got lying around."

And of course, since no noble would ever wish to kick up a needless fuss, everyone nodded, quietly.

* * *

"So, what did you all think of her?" the principal asked the teachers, who answered in turn.

"She's a top pupil, a combat magic user, skilled in repartee, popular with most everyone—including commoners—has admirable grace even for a noble, and quick critical judgment. She shows compassion even to those who oppose her, and has the courage to go toe-to-toe not only with higher-ranking nobles, but the royal family themselves."

"And judging by the way they looked at her, their Highnesses and their Majesties are completely taken with her."

"I wouldn't be shocked to see her as the main wife of a well-ranked noble, or even a future queen, herself."

"There's no need to even test her."

Their judgments appeared to be unanimous.

"So then, in the matter of inviting Lady Marcela to enroll in Ardleigh Academy...?"

The group answered as one: "We have no objections!"

Yet when the principal went to extend to Marcela an invitation to Ardleigh Academy, her reply was swift. "I must refuse."

"Huh? Wh-why?!" the principal asked.

"There would never be any reconciling the position of the third daughter of a poor baron amongst the children of higher nobles and royals," she replied. "Also..."

"Also?"

"I have so many friends at Eckland! And I need to be here, waiting, for the day a very dear friend of mine returns home."

* * *

"Wh-what is this all about...?"

Recently, Marcela had been inundated with countless invitations: invitations to parties, from various nobles; personal invitations from the princes and the King and Queen; an invitation to dinner from Lady Anselda von Velanas, eldest daughter of Margrave Velanas; as well as impudent letters of invitation to enroll from the staff of Ardleigh Academy.

"Why is this happening...?"

In sync as always, Monika and Aureana replied, "Lady Marcela, have you ever heard the saying, 'You reap what you sow'?"

Thank you for your purchase!

Volume 3 featured a lot of meaningful expressions from Reina--

and evil ones from Pauline.

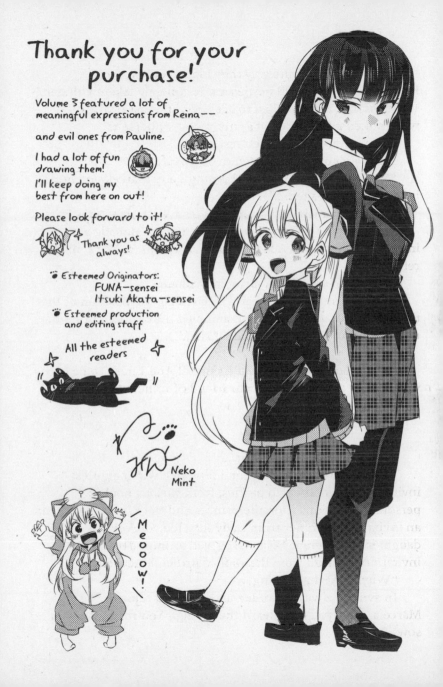

I had a lot of fun drawing them!

I'll keep doing my best from here on out!

Please look forward to it!

Thank you as always!

- Esteemed Originators:
  FUNA-sensei
  Itsuki Akata-sensei
- Esteemed production and editing staff

All the esteemed readers

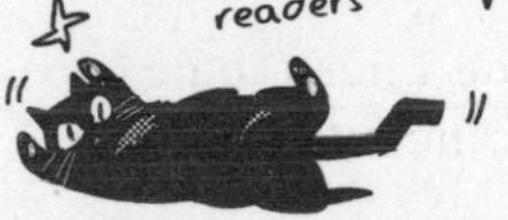

Neko Mint

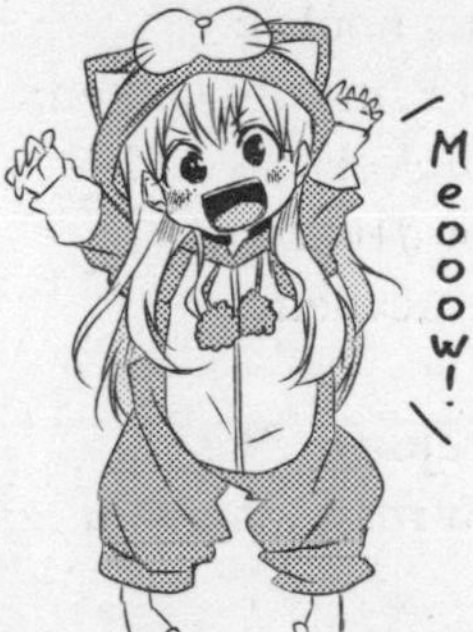
Meooow!

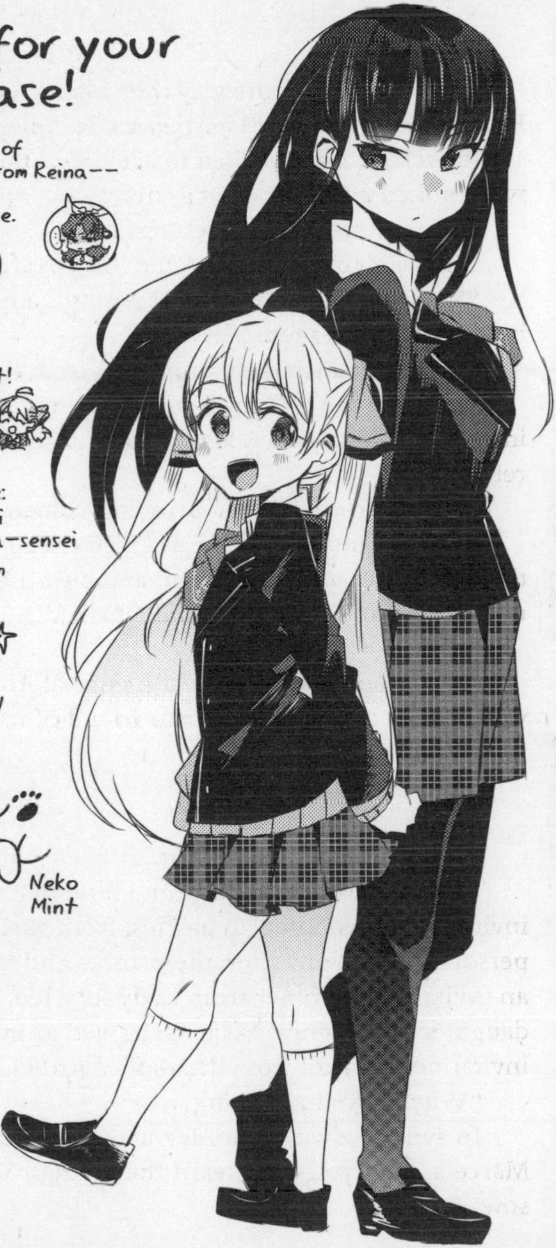

Didn't I Say to Make My Abilities Average in the Next Life?!

SEVEN SEAS ENTERTAINMENT PRESENTS

Didn't I Say to Make My Abilities *Average* in the Next Life?! vol.3

story by FUNA & ITSUKI AKATA   art by NEKOMINT

TRANSLATION
Diana Taylor

ADAPTATION
Michelle Danner-Groves

LETTERING
Simone Harrison

COVER DESIGN
Nicky Lim

PROOFREADER
Stephanie Cohen
Cae Hawksmoor

EDITOR
Jenn Grunigen

PRODUCTION MANAGER
Lissa Pattillo

MANAGING EDITOR
Julie Davis

EDITOR-IN-CHIEF
Adam Arnold

PUBLISHER
Jason DeAngelis

WATASHI, NOURYOKU WA HEIKINCHI DE TTE ITTA YO NE! VOL. 3
© FUNA / Itsuki Akata 2016
© Nekomint 2018
Originally published in Japan in 2018 by EARTH STAR Entertainment, Tokyo.
English translation rights arranged with EARTH STAR Entertainment, Tokyo,
through TOHAN CORPORATION, Tokyo.

Seven Seas press and purchase enquiries can be sent to Marketing Manager
Lianne Sentar at press@gomanga.com. Information regarding the distribution
and purchase of digital editions is available from Digital Manager CK Russell
at digital@gomanga.com.

Seven Seas and the Seven Seas logo are trademarks of
Seven Seas Entertainment. All rights reserved.

ISBN: 978-1-64275-084-3

Printed in Canada

First Printing: May 2019

10 9 8 7 6 5 4 3 2 1

FOLLOW US ONLINE: www.sevenseasentertainment.com

READING DIRECTIONS

This book reads from ***right to left***, Japanese style.
If this is your first time reading manga, you start
reading from the top right panel on each page and
take it from there. If you get lost, just follow the
numbered diagram here. It may seem backwards at
first, but you'll get the hang of it! Have fun!!

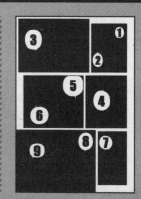